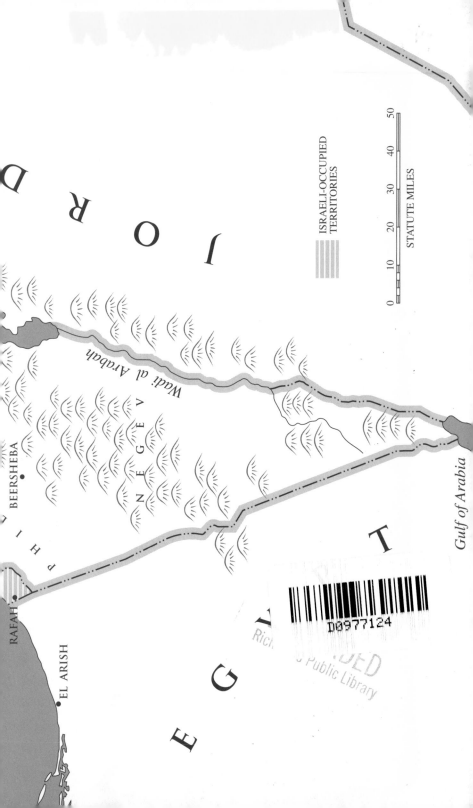

JORD

Wadi al Arabah

BEERSHEBA

N E G E V

PHI

RAFAH

EL ARISH

E G Y

T

Gulf of Arabia

THE NEW PALESTINIANS

THE EMERGING GENERATION
OF LEADERS

THE NEW PALESTINIANS

THE EMERGING GENERATION OF LEADERS

John Wallach and Janet Wallach

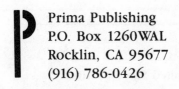

Prima Publishing
P.O. Box 1260WAL
Rocklin, CA 95677
(916) 786-0426

Production by Carol Dondrea, Bookman Productions
Copyediting by Elliot Simon
Interior design by Detta Penna
Cover design by Kirschner-Caroff Design
Composition by AeroType, Inc.

Library of Congress Cataloging-in-Publication Data

Wallach, John.
    The new Palestinians : the emerging generation of leaders   John Wallach and Janet Wallach
        p.   cm.
    Includes index.
    ISBN 1-55958-215-4 :
    1. Palestinian Arabs—Biography.   I. Title
    DS126.6.A2W3 1992
    920'.00929274—dc20
    [B]   92-24551
                                             CIP

92 93 94 RRD 10 9 8 7 6 5 4 3 2 1

Printed in the United States of America

Contents

Preface   vii
Hanan Mikhail Ashrawi   1
Faisal Husseini   41
Sari Nusseibeh   82
Zahira Kamal   101
Ziad Abu Zayyad   121
Sami Kilani   140
Mamdouh Aker   164
Sameh Kanaan   185
Abdul Aziz Rantisi   200
Riad Maliki   225
Ghassan Khatib   246
Radwan Abu Ayash   269
Conclusion   293
Glossary   311
Documents   315
Index   337

Preface

When we wrote *Still Small Voices* in 1988, the voices of the Palestinians in the West Bank and Gaza Strip were indeed small, having been stilled by both Israelis and Arabs. All that was heard was the noisy din of extremism and the screeching of ambulance sirens wailing for the victims of the *intifada*, the Palestinian uprising against Israeli occupation. The Palestine Liberation Organization (PLO) had not yet recognized Israel's right to exist, nor had the PLO renounced the use of terrorism as a weapon against the Jewish state. Despite the fact that it was the "insiders" who were fighting and dying in the rebellion against Israeli rule, few of the indigenous Palestinians had emerged as political leaders. A right-wing government in Israel also was deaf to their suffering and to their passionate cries to be heard. The outside world seemed equally preoccupied, consumed by the momentous fall of communism and the breakup of the Soviet Union and its empire in Eastern Europe.

Much has changed since the spring of 1988, but the people we wrote about, the Palestinian "insiders" who were voicing their demands for recognition of Palestinians as a people, have remained largely the same: a generation of highly educated, mostly secular leaders fully prepared to accept the existence of the Jewish state, provided the Palestinians are given the opportunity to achieve their own independence and statehood. But until the Madrid peace conference in October 1991, the world was not paying much attention to these Palestinians. The gruff image of the guerrilla, face covered in a checkered *kaffeyah* and fist menacingly clutching a hand grenade, obscured the reality of an emerging generation of more moderate, pragmatic, even pro-Western Palestinians in the West Bank and Gaza. The television viewer saw mainly the common, often daily, confrontations between Palestinian adolescents and often equally youthful but far better armed Israeli soldiers.

Madrid was a turning point, as the *Washington Post* noted: instead of wearing camouflage fatigues and packing pistols, the Palestinians the world saw wore business suits and packed portable computers; instead of speaking in the staccato tones of terrorists, they spoke with British accents, in the reassuring tones learned at Exeter and Eton as well as at their own universities on the West Bank and Gaza Strip. Although these voices had been around for more than a decade, they were heard for the first time at Madrid speaking for themselves, loudly, intelligently, and eloquently. They were no longer still, small voices. Palestinian "insiders" such as Faisal Husseini, Haidar Abdul Shafi, and Hanan Ashrawi evocatively projected an image of their people that was compassionate and also impossible for the world to ignore.

In *The New Palestinians* we take a closer look at this generation of leaders, one that, like the Israelis, has much that makes them unique. Indeed, they are a generation that has reached political maturity under Israeli occupation. Like the Jews before them, they are the outcasts, the resented, even the persecuted in much of the Arab world. One need only think of the forced exile of several hundred thousand Palestinians from Kuwait after the Persian Gulf War; they were the architects, the engineers, and the construction workers who, like the Jews, transformed a primitive desert into a blooming oasis of modern society.

In June 1992 the Palestinians of the West Bank and Gaza Strip marked the end of an era, a quarter century of life under Israeli rule. As adults they have known no other occupier: no Turkish, no British, no Jordanian taskmasters. Instead, they have witnessed frequent Israeli beatings, even killings, of their neighbors, the bulldozing of their homes, and the increasing loss of their lands to Israeli settlers. But they have also seen a democratic system inside Israel that aspires to equality and human rights. With more than 100,000 Palestinians crossing the "green line" every day to work in Israel, they have had a rare view of a society that attempts to respect the rights of its minorities, including the 900,000 Arabs living in Israel. This has given the Palestinians a new perspective on their own lives and on the surrounding Arab regimes, which have historically oppressed them as well. The emerging generation of Palestinians profiled in this book has lived on the border between two countries, in a spiritual no-man's-land where the actualities of their daily existence have been determined by their living inside Israel and Israeli-occupied territory, but where their pride and their identity and their consciousness have been determined by their allegiance to a yet-unborn entity, the new nation of Palestine.

The following profiles of twelve Palestinians are intended to bring the observer one step closer toward *feeling* life in the occupied territories, toward *sharing* some of the disappointments as well as the simple victories, toward *understanding* the conviction that comes when the struggle is intensely personal. These twelve individuals have all spent their adult life under Israeli military rule. They differ from their parents, who remember life before the establishment of the state of Israel in 1948; they differ from their children, who have known no other reality than Israeli occupation. Some—such as Faisal Husseini, Zahira Kamal, Sari Nusseibeh, Riad Maliki, and Hanan Ashrawi—are from the triangular area of Jerusalem-Ramallah-Bethlehem; others—such as Sami Kilani, Mamdouh Aker, Sameh Kanaan, and Ghassan Khatib—are from Nablus and the northern region of the West Bank; Abdul Aziz Rantisi is from the Gaza Strip.

The twelve also come from different locales on the political map. Each is inclined toward a certain political faction, whether it be the mainstream group, *Fatah*; the leftist faction of the Democratic Front for the Liberation of Palestine (DFLP), headed by Yasser Abed Rabbo; the Popular Front for the Liberation of Palestine (PFLP); or the People's Party (formerly the Communist Party of Palestine). Still others support the Islamic Resistance Movement, known as *Hamas*. As such, some support the peace process and are members of the Palestinian delegation and negotiating teams; others protest the conditions under which the Palestinians entered the negotiations at Madrid and prefer that the process be aborted altogether.

But the twelve also have much in common. Most of them are in their mid-forties; three are still in their thirties; one is in his early fifties. Most were born after World War II, and all share the experience of the postwar events that have shaped their lives: the Cold War between the United States and the Soviet Union; five Arab-Israeli wars; the Camp David Accords and the signing of a peace treaty between Egypt and Israel; the Israeli invasion of Lebanon; and the Iraqi invasion of Kuwait. They have suffered at least partly because their future, and the fate of the Palestinian people as a whole, has never been divorced from the broader Arab-Israeli conflict; consequently, whether involuntarily or not, they have often been at the mercy of other Arab leaders.

The *intifada* ended this period of *summud*, or passive resistance; it marked an awakening, a protest against their alleged powerlessness to determine their own future. The Palestinian uprising that began in December 1987 is the most important event in their lives. The Palestinian "insiders" proved to the world they could resist with their own resources and moral courage. It was a message to the outside world that they would no longer tolerate the denial of their aspirations for self-determination and, indeed, were willing to die for them. The *intifada* was self-empowerment. It was the assertion of Palestinians living under occupation and inside the territories that they would no longer wait for anyone— the superpowers, the United Nations, other Arab leaders, even their own PLO leadership—to deliver them from Israeli oppression.

That is why we have chosen to write about Palestinians who are from inside the territories. They are the generation, the men and women, who will determine how and when the Palestinians will finally achieve their true independence and statehood. The twelve Palestinians here are among those who have already emerged as the new leadership. They are part of the generation that has now been given the main responsibility for turning yesterday's sacrifices in the guerrilla struggle, and in the *intifada*, into tomorrow's victories at the negotiating table. They still have to navigate a treacherous road between their Israeli adversaries and opponents both inside and outside the territories. Therefore, it is essential for them to maintain their links to the outside leadership. It is from that leadership, from the PLO, that they derive their legitimacy. They secure their credibility from being on the inside. They are, in short, among those who have already emerged as probable leaders of a new Palestinian entity or state.

We wrote this sequel to *Still Small Voices* and to *Arafat: In the Eyes of the Beholder* because we believe these twelve people need to be heard and understood. They represent all factions of the Palestinian people in the West Bank and Gaza Strip. And although they are not totally innocent of past involvement with terrorism, most of them are now willing to foreswear the armed struggle against Israel if the Jewish state recognizes that its birthright also applies to the Palestinian people. In our view, there is no other choice if Israel is to survive as a civil society, indeed as a Jewish state. Continuing occupation will only sap Israel's own strength as a democracy; furthermore, with the rise of Muslim fundamentalism, the consequences of continued delay will be far worse than the risks of empowering the current generation of Palestinian leaders with real authority and responsibility. We believe the current Israeli government headed by Prime Minister Yitzhak Rabin understands this historical imperative.

Israel is fortunate that a generation of Palestinians has emerged from a quarter century of domination prepared to accept the political and territorial prerequisites that will safeguard Israeli security. The sooner this group of Palestinians is given a genuine mandate from its own people, through democratic general elections in the West Bank and Gaza, the sooner Israel will find an ally against the fanaticism sweeping much of the rest of the Middle East.

When we wrote *Still Small Voices*, the *intifada* itself was only a few months old; television pictures of a steady stream of violence were dehumanizing the conflict, reducing its victims to abstractions and caricatures of the causes for which they were fighting. Hatred had replaced reason; emotion obscured any clear picture of the moderate forces that existed on both sides of the conflict. The *intifada* may not be over, but it has achieved its primary goal: it has shown the world that the Palestinian "insiders" are willing to die rather than to continue living under Israeli occupation. A new generation has emerged from the *intifada*, one we believe is prepared to lead the Palestinians into a lasting peace with Israel. We have tried in *The New Palestinians* to tell their story in order to foster a better understanding of the human issues that undergird this struggle and to obtain a closer view of the people who will be among the Palestinian leaders of the future.

Acknowledgments

In making this project a reality, we were fortunate to have the help of Mona Ghali, an Arab, and Ori Nir, an Israeli. Mona Ghali, a graduate of the Johns Hopkins School of Advanced International Studies (SAIS), was with us from the beginning, serving as a sounding board for our ideas, joining us for many interviews, and conducting many of them herself, both in Washington, D.C., and in the West Bank and Gaza Strip. Mona never hesitated, in her understated gentle way, to tell us when we were wrong or to suggest that there might be deeper meanings hidden behind the commonplace occurrence. Her dedication to the people we have profiled is manifested by her personal decision to return to the West Bank to work as a journalist. She will be a valuable addition to the staff of any newspaper or magazine.

Over the past decade we have spent many months in the Middle East, at work on *Still Small Voices*, our first book about the Palestinians of the West Bank and Gaza Strip, and *Arafat: In the Eyes of the Beholder*, an effort to look at that controversial figure through the eyes of both those who admire and those who abhor him. If there was one Israeli journalist who inspired us throughout, it is Danny Rubinstein. Danny spent countless hours with us explaining the intricacies of Palestinian life. No Israeli has a deeper understanding of, or greater sympathy for, the Palestinians' plight.

But there is another Israeli, Ori Nir, the Washington correspondent for *Ha'aretz*, whose sensitivity and wisdom rivals that of his older colleague. Ori spent four years as a correspondent in the territories; with his fluent Arabic he quickly developed friendships and a rare knowledge of the inner workings of Palestinian society. We could not have completed this book without his guidance; he patiently answered queries from us, at all hours of the day and night, and carefully reviewed all of the drafts of each profile, providing valuable insights and intriguing anecdotes that had eluded us in our reporting. We could not have asked for a more thoughtful editor.

We also were helped by Hillel Kuttler, a talented journalist who transcribed much of the material from the hundreds of hours of interviews and contributed drafts for four of the profiles. The wonderful photographs are the work of Rula Halawani, a Palestinian who was always ready, often on short notice, to travel to Gaza or remote areas of the West Bank to complete this assignment. Mubarak Awad provided valuable background material for us, and we are grateful to the many other Palestinians who also gave generously of their time: Nabil Shaath, Haidar Abdul Shafi, Raja Shehadeh, Saeb Erakat, Zakaria Agha, Hassan Abu Libbeh, Freih Abu Meiden, Nazmi Jubeh, and Akram Hanieh. Lawrence Jurdem, a graduate student at the University of Louisville, also helped us with the research for this book. Lawrence's sincere interest in the Middle East and his wise counsel and keen sense of humor made an invaluable contribution to this book.

Finally, we would like to thank the Middle East Institute and the Washington Institute for Near East Policy for making their extensive libraries available to us. Leila Ansari, a very talented writer and a student at Sarah Lawrence College, read many of the profiles and suggested stylistic changes that we hope have made them more readable. Jennifer Basye, our editor at Prima Publishing, and Elliot Simon, our copyeditor, were a delight to work with. Throughout, our sons, Michael and David, both wonderful writers, encouraged us to persevere.

Hanan Mikhail Ashrawi

Out of the group of three Palestinians seated on one side of the
fence at ABC-TV's April 1988 "Nightline" Town Meeting, the
sharply featured face of Hanan Ashrawi appeared a refreshing
image on the television screen. With millions of Americans
watching her for the first time, the dark-haired, fashionably
dressed Arab woman spoke crisply and concisely, in easily digested
sound bites. "This is not a tribute to Israeli democracy," she
announced, even though this was clearly the first time such an
important group of Palestinian leaders from the West Bank and
Gaza Strip were publicly debating high-ranking Israeli officials on
worldwide television. The fence on the TV set had been erected
at the insistence of Hanan, a reminder that although the two sides
were cramped together on the small stage of a Jerusalem theater,
there still existed between them a wide chasm, a political,
psychological, and emotional divide.

"We decided to come here not to have dialogue with the
Israelis, because the correct address as I said is the PLO," she
declared, "but rather to express our opinions clearly. For years
we have relied on the justice of our cause in order to make our
points clear. But it is obvious that the Americans and the rest of
the public opinion has to know that justice is not sufficient to
give us our rights. So we are here to address you directly, to tell
you that we need our own basic rights, to be recognized. We need
to be recognized as people."

In these opening remarks in front of an audience of several
hundred Israelis in the Israeli part of Jerusalem, the western sector,
Hanan was doing what local Palestinian leaders had long urged

PLO leader Yasser Arafat to do—take their case directly to the Israeli people. To the Americans, 6000 miles away, the intelligence and eloquence of Hanan's arguments came as both a shock and a pleasant surprise. Here was a woman who looked more like their suburban neighbors than the khaki-clad, pistol-toting guerrillas they had come to associate with the Palestinians. Here was a voice of moderation and subdued eloquence that contrasted sharply with the staccato rhetoric of terrorists.

To one Palestinian sitting alone in an Israeli prison—Faisal Husseini—Hanan's face looked vaguely familiar. He knew who she was, of course, from her reputation, but something about her stuck in his mind. He listened carefully as the husky-voiced woman held firmly to her position, resisting the taunts of Israeli hardliner Eliahu Ben-Elissar to "Say it, say it," to abandon the PLO hardline, and to recognize the existence of Israel. "She is great! She is great!" Faisal cheered from his prison cell. The more he watched her, the more her aggressiveness jarred his memory. In his mind she was transformed from the well-tailored Birzeit professor into the young miniskirted student at the American University of Beirut (AUB) who was supposed to join his guerrilla training group more than two decades earlier.

After Egypt, Jordan, and Syria sent troops to attack Israel in 1967, Faisal was in charge of recruiting a Palestinian army to help fight the new war. He set up the Lebanese training camp at the estate of Ahmed Shukeiry, then the leader of the PLO, near Kaifoun in the foothills of the Shouf Mountains. It was the first camp to recruit both men and women; 1200 Palestinians volunteered. Hanan Ashrawi was supposed to be among them. "We were thinking of training Palestinians for one month every year for a standing army," says Faisal. "I was waiting for them. Hanan was in AUB. The other girl was Leila Shahid," says Faisal, speaking proudly about his cousin, the PLO's current ambassador to the Netherlands. In the Palestinian training camp, at dawn each morning, as he assembled the recruits "according to their height and not their sex," he read out the names of those assigned to his unit. Each morning, as he looked at his list, he would ask himself, "Where is Hanan Mikhail? Where is Hanan Mikhail?"

Several weeks after the "Nightline" broadcast, when Faisal finally confronted her, Hanan acknowledged that she never showed up for his *Fatah* guerrilla training. But, she says, she was not shirking her military duty: "I went to Syria instead." Across the Syrian border, Palestinian fedayeen had set up staging areas to continue the assault on the Golan Heights. When they had their long-delayed reunion, Hanan recalls, Faisal could not resist a good-natured tease: "You know, our meeting has been delayed for quite a while. You were supposed to show up at my camp. After twenty-two years you show up!"

. She has been showing up ever since, on TV screens across the globe, at news conferences and peace rallies from Stockholm and Moscow to Cairo and Washington, as the chief spokesperson for the fourteen members of the Palestinian delegation negotiating with Israel. She and Faisal have become a close-knit team: the shy Muslim man who has assumed the Palestinian leadership on the West Bank and the Western-educated Christian Arab woman able to articulate the pain of her people for foreign television consumption. He has become her godfather, her protector against the vociferous critics at home who contend that this urbane, smartly attired, and seductive woman, a member of one of the earliest sects of Christianity, has no business representing the Palestinians. Their friendship began during meetings with American government representatives: "We started talking in our meetings at the [Jerusalem] consulates," he explains, and it developed when they protested the massacre of seven Gaza workers by Ami Popper, a young Israeli from Rishon LeZion, a new town south of Tel Aviv, in June 1989. "We spent twelve or thirteen days under a Red Cross tent during the hunger strike. There, also, she proved herself," says Faisal. "She was tough, strong, ready to go on with the hunger strike for another ten days!" He relies on Hanan for many things outside her role as official spokesperson. Whenever the two of them met with American Secretary of State James A. Baker III, it was Hanan who often found the phrases for Faisal, since his English is not good enough to cope with diplomatic nuances and legal niceties. Baker felt he could communicate easily with her. Says an admiring American official, "Faisal struggles for a word, she picks it up and they are off and running!"

As she nervously takes a few puffs on her ever-handy Salem Lights cigarette, flicking the ashes as she slouches on the sofa in her suite at the Grand Hotel, Hanan Ashrawi resists talking about herself. "That's the worst interview. I hate talking about myself. It drives me nuts. Everybody now wants to do profiles!" she protests. "It's very boring for me to do it." A few seconds later, however, she seems to have reconciled herself. "Well, okay, I'll tell you, I had a very—ah, wait," she says, catching a glimpse of herself on CNN.

The newscast is reporting that the first round of bilateral Arab-Israeli talks, scheduled to begin that December day, are deadlocked because of a procedural dispute. The Palestinians are insisting they be treated as a separate group and not subsumed in the Jordanian delegation. Binyamin "Bebe" Netanyahu, Israel's former deputy foreign minister, with whom she is often compared, stridently condemns the latest Palestinian curve ball. She seems to relish the comparison with Netanyahu, former special forces commando, brother of the national hero who perished in the daring Entebbe hostage raid and ex-Israeli ambassador to the United Nations. For a fleeting moment, Netanyahu has lost his fabled ability to depict Israel as the victim surrounded by hostile Arab neighbors; as he lashes out at the Palestinians for demanding separate status, the underdog has turned into a bulldog. Quips Hanan, with the special sarcasm she reserves for the Israelis, "They cannot reverse it. We had a high profile in Madrid. Now they want a low profile. They discovered there are Palestinians!"

Slowly, methodically and with calculating precision, she begins to unwind, but she is clearly uncomfortable talking about her childhood. "It goes against the grain, frankly speaking. I've always been a very private person. I view this as part of my responsibilities to work in this capacity, to interpret, to present, to articulate the Palestinian position. I would much rather have stayed in a backstage role, but, unfortunately, there was a need and I have to do it."

As she talks, she seems to have nothing in common with the guerrillas waging the urban battles against Israeli occupation. And yet as she begins to sketch in the details of her upbringing, it becomes clearer and clearer that Hanan Mikhail Ashrawi is not merely the more articulate and attractive face of Palestinian nationalism. She is tough, a Chaucer-quoting street fighter who is feisty with language, a born politician who can rant and resonate with rhetoric. While she may not look the role, this professor of comparative literature also is a protege of the PLO school of self-sacrifice. Says Hanan, "Those who know, know I have deep-rooted ties to the Palestinian national struggle." A true believer who has served an apprenticeship in the refugee camps, Hanan sees herself as a sharp-tongued victim of Israeli oppression who has turned her back on a legacy of family wealth and privilege.

She is asked about Faisal Husseini's claim that he discovered her on "Nightline." "I don't want to keep stressing 'Nightline.' 'Nightline' is not the landmark," Hanan says, obviously annoyed by the implication that her telegenic talents—and not her earlier activities as an activist—led him to ask her to be on the Palestinian delegation. "It's not a question of recruiting," she says, insisting she was involved in key decision making long before Faisal found her. "We set up the coordination committee when Faisal was in jail, so when he came out [of jail] it was already in motion," says Hanan.

The committee, membership in which was outlawed by the Israelis and punishable by a ten-year jail term, was led by Birzeit professor Sari Nusseibeh, Nablus surgeon Mamdouh Aker, Ghassan Khatib, Zahira Kamal, and Riad Maliki. They comprised a small group of *Fatah*, DFLP, PFLP, and Communist Party supporters. It was this group, she says, that took the bold step of deciding to debate Israelis on their own turf on "Nightline." "The committee decided we would do this as a breakthrough. Primarily the discussions were inside [the territories]," she says. Thus the real landmark was not the airing of the ABC-TV program in front of an audience of millions of Americans; it was the fact that the decision to appear on the show, when the *intifada* was less than four months old, was made by the new Palestinian leadership that had been forged inside the West Bank and Gaza—and only afterwards urged on the PLO leadership in Tunis.

Hanan was born on October 8, 1946, in Nablus, heir to the hatreds that divided the British from the Arabs and Arabs from Jews, a child of the partition of Palestine that led to the creation of the Jewish state. Hanan is the youngest of five children, all girls. Her family moved every two years, and the girls were born in different parts of Palestine: Nadia, like Hanan, was born in Nablus; Ablah and Muna in Jerusalem; and Huda, now a sculptor, in Hebron.

In the early 1940s, before Hanan was born, their father, Daoud

Mikhail, a physician, frequently socialized with his Jewish colleagues. Nevertheless, he would often become upset over the raids by the Irgun, the Stern gang, and other underground Zionist militias. "But he tried to remain neutral because he had so many Jewish friends who also were doctors," says Huda. Daoud had graduated from the medical school at AUB and would often return to Beirut, a drive that took less than two hours, for a weekend of shopping and relaxation. In those days, the Mikhail family lived in a square house high on a hill in Tiberias that had a magnificent view of the lake. The girls loved to squeeze the dry root nuts from the giant carab tree in front of their house and extract the molasses from them. Their friends also included Jews, the children of immigrants who had come to Tiberias in the 1920s and 1930s fleeing pogroms in Russia, the Ukraine, and Poland. "We had a lot of friends who were Jews. We opened our homes and our hearts to them. They were neighbors," says Huda.

But shortly after Hanan was born, political passions became heated, and Daoud Mikhail, who had enlisted as a doctor in the British army, became involved in clandestine activities, getting food to the *thuwwar*, the Arab resistance, in the mountains. When the British hastily withdrew in 1948 and a Jewish state was proclaimed, the family was forced to leave Tiberias. "Somehow my father got us all out," says Huda. He sent his wife and their five children to Amman, but "he stayed behind because he was still in the army." Later Daoud joined his family in Amman, where he went to work as a health inspector for the government of Transjordan.

As the youngest of the five Mikhail girls, the infant Hanan was pampered and precocious. By the time she was three years old, she could read and write. But, says Huda, she did not get the same amount of attention the older girls received from their parents "as far as actually being there with her and for her all the time. It was impossible because we kept shuttling from one uncle's place to another uncle's place."

The children spent most of their time in the home of Wadi Assad, an officer in the Palestinian fedayeen force, which fought in the 1948 war but was disarmed by the Arab armies. Assad had two girls of his own. The crowded house was at the edge of the train station, a noisy place made even more so by the screams and squeals of seven active children who were seldom allowed to go outside because Amman was in rubble. To make matters worse, the girls were under strict orders not to misbehave. Her mother's words still ring in the children's ears: "It is not your house. It is your uncle's house. So behave!" With so much upheaval in their lives, and no place to really call home, Hanan "was left a little bit in the background," says Huda. "She became a bit of a loner."

In 1950, having decided the situation was not going to improve, Daoud made up his mind to start a new life. He took his family back to Ramallah, where he had practiced medicine for a brief period before fleeing to Jordan, and within months resigned from his government post. The Mikhail house was in the heart of town, six miles north of Jerusalem, on the main thoroughfare and across the street from the Zabani family grocery. There was a separate entrance to the clinic at the rear of the house where Daoud set up his practice. In those early years, when Hanan was only four, it was their grandmother, who lived with them, who had a profound influence on the family. She had been a missionary; her husband was an Anglican priest.

Gathering all five girls around her bedside, the elderly woman would prop a pillow behind her back, sit up and tell the children stories from the Bible. After the storytelling, she would explain the religious meaning to them. Since these bedside sessions often preceded church, they were not uniformly popular. "I would sneak out of the room when my grandmother was preaching and then an hour later I would try to sneak back in, crawl in, and pretend I never left the room," recalls Huda. "But Hanan and Ablah would stay. Each of them was probably thinking about something entirely different but they stayed."

In those childhood days, Hanan was not interested in politics. "Hanan was just a cute little doll who wanted to dress pretty and look pretty," says Huda. They would walk together to the Friends Girls Academy, a private elementary school in Ramallah, and her older sister would raise the issues their father had discussed at dinner the night before.

During school Huda went out alone on demonstrations against the British and against "Glubb Pasha" (the nickname for the British chief-of-staff of the Arab Legion). "Hanan had no idea what was going on politically. Just give her a book and a bag of nuts and she would lock herself in her room and read forever," says her older sister. "The kid would read a book a day, and I'm talking English short stories, paperbacks, absolute trash, and pure literature. Anything that was printed, she would read it!" Hanan's love of learning came from her parents, both of whom had university educations. The healing arts were at the center of their marriage; Hanan's father was a physician, her mother, Wad'ia, was a nurse in a hospital ophthalmology department. Wad'ia, too, was a voracious reader.

But her parents also had their differences: Wad'ia was a practicing Christian and insisted the girls go to Sunday school (and take piano lessons), Daoud was an atheist. Wad'ia was a disciplinarian, Daoud was not. Finally, Wad'ia was completely apolitical, except, says Hanan, "on the human level, she kept worrying about what politics would do to people: politics was a very dangerous field."

Today her eighty-five-year-old mother still worries about Hanan. "Every time I talk to her, she says 'God protect that girl. I hope she is all right,'" says Huda. "I tell her, 'Mother, if anyone is going to protect that girl it's God,' because she's wise and she's unlike the rest of us!" Hanan says, "My mother's main fear was always, 'I just hope she won't be arrested. I hope she never gets arrested because she gets very cold.' Lately, she's been saying 'Maybe it's a good idea that she get arrested. I hope they arrest her because she'll be safer in prison.' That means she's really worried, because for her prison was the worst thing."

Hanan remembers her father as a nonbeliever who was never very strict with his children; he was an intellectual and an idealist who tried to imbue in them respect for all creeds and religions, and he was an activist. "He's always been a very special person for me, progressive, way ahead of his time. He was always politically very active but also very modest, very mild, very soft-spoken and low key," says Hanan. More than anything else, he respected the role of the woman in society. His own mother had died when Daoud was very young, and his sisters brought him up. So when he matured he had respect and admiration for the woman. Hanan has many of her father's traits, especially his power of persuasion, Huda believes. "He was powerful but very, very soft-hearted. He never ordered us around. He would say something and it's just like Hanan: you didn't question it because he was so convincing."

As a doctor, Daoud reached out to victims wherever they were. Once, she says, when he was involved with a Palestinian resistance group in the Nablus area years later, her father witnessed an Arab ambush of several Israeli soldiers. Daoud was with his driver. "He went down and took all the wounded Jews in his car and treated them in the house and sent them to the hospital and had the driver go and take them to their homes. He would do the same thing for any wounded or hurt person, regardless of their ethnic background or religious group."

But Daoud Mikhail also believed that each Palestinian had to make a personal commitment to the cause. He became involved in the nationalist struggle as soon as he returned in 1950 from Amman to Ramallah, when almost any involvement in politics was seen as a threat by King Abdullah. From the early days of his ascension to the Hashemite throne in 1921, Abdullah saw himself as the leader of all the Arabs in Palestine, not only those in the area he dubbed eastern Palestine or Transjordan. With Amman as his family base, Abdullah envisioned a kingdom of Greater Syria for the Hashemite clan, with himself as king of Palestine.

Throughout his rule Abdullah sought help from the Arabs in Palestine in running his government and encouraged them to come to the East Bank. Although Ottoman rulers had used the natural border of the Jordan River and established the district of Palestine and the district of Jordan, people traveled easily back and forth between the two banks, the eastern and western sides, of the river. The officials Abdullah chose as his prime ministers included West Bankers like Tawfik Abdul Huda from Acre, Samir Rifai from Safed, and Ibrahim Hashim from Nablus. Without the political acumen and training of these and others such as Daoud Mikhail, who had served in the Ottoman and British civil service, Abdullah would have had almost no one capable of organizing an administration. These Arabs from Palestine, in turn, considered themselves true citizens of Transjordan. But a large faction of Palestinian Arabs, under the strong leadership of Haj Amin Husseini, had no interest in following Abdullah. Their aim was to expel the British and then to establish their own sovereign Arab state on all of Palestine.

When Abdullah agreed to a ceasefire in 1948 in exchange for a promise from new Israeli minister Golda Meir that the Hashemite king could keep the West Bank, Haj Amin accused him of having sold out Palestine to the Jews. The former *mufti* of Jerusalem immediately set up an independent Palestinian government in Gaza. Called the All-Palestine government, it claimed authority over all of Palestine. Of course, it was bitterly opposed by Abdullah because it conflicted with his plans to annex the West Bank. The Hashemite ruler reacted by acclaiming himself "King of Palestine and Jordan," banning the use of the term "Palestine," and demanding that the territory west of the Jordan River be known as the West Bank. In April 1950 he formally annexed it to Jordan. Fifteen months later, on July 21, 1951, as he was entering Jerusalem's Al-Aqsa Mosque to pray, Abdullah was assassinated by followers of Haj Amin.

In Ramallah, Daoud Mikhail began writing pamphlets espousing the virtues of the National Socialist Party, and by the mid-1950s had become one of the party's key leaders on the West Bank. The left-wing, nationalist party was formed by Suleiman Nabulsi, a Palestinian lawyer, to protest the increasingly pro-Western, anti-Palestinian tilt of Jordanian policy.

As part of his effort to unify the country following the death of his grandfather, the young new ruler, King Hussein bin-Talal, insisted that all citizens of his country call themselves Jordanians. References to Palestinians were frowned upon and even the name was dropped from books. But among the Palestinians who were moving from the West Bank to the East Bank were many who had contempt for the young king and his ties to the British and who belittled the primitive ways of most East Bankers. West Bankers, although not allowed to call themselves Palestinians, always made reference to where they had come from and identified themselves as from Nablus or Jerusalem or Ramallah. While the King suffered their vocal criticism, the more militant Palestinians ran raids across the river into Israel, trying to antagonize the Jewish farmers whose fields lined the border.

Jordan became the victim of massive Israeli retaliation; although the Palestinian fedayeen attacked individual Israeli farms, the Israeli army went after entire Jordanian villages, destroying Kibya and others. King Hussein, badly in need of arms to protect his country, sought help from the Turkish and the British. They suggested that Jordan join an anti-Soviet defense group formed in February 1955 when Iraq, Turkey, and Britain signed the

Baghdad Pact. In return, Jordan would receive British help.

Hussein was agreeable, but the Palestinians (who made up a majority of his country's population), particularly those who favored the Egyptian leader Gamal Abdel Nasser, were vehemently opposed. To them Britain represented weak Arabs under colonial repression while the socialist Nasser, preaching nonalignment toward the West, was the symbol of Arab strength. The Egyptian president, they believed, would lead the way to a Palestinian homeland by uniting the Arab world, and his military prowess came from the Soviets. When four West Bank ministers resigned in protest in December 1955, Hussein understood there would be an uprising if he joined the Baghdad Pact. As the mood of the country turned more and more anti-British, Hussein felt compelled to keep the Palestinians calm and to untangle himself from the web of relationships he and his grandfather had built with the British.

In March 1956 Hussein demanded the resignation of the British commander of the Arab Legion, Lt. General Glubb ("Glubb Pasha"), who was regarded by most Palestinians as the symbol of British imperialist domination. But even this move failed to satisfy the Palestinian community. The king, who claimed to be their protector, was accused of defaulting on his duties when the Israelis attacked the West Bank. To Hussein it seemed the Palestinians wanted things both ways: they insisted they had the right to rule themselves in what they considered to be part of Palestine, and yet, living in Jordan as full citizens, they wanted the king to defend them. They challenged Hussein's authority at the same time that they demanded his protection.

In October 1956, with his citizens in an uproar over another major Israeli reprisal against the West Bank town of Kalkilya, Hussein tried a different tack. This time he held the first real elections in his constitutional monarchy. Unfortunately for the king, the winners in the voting were the left-wing West Bankers, including Daoud Mikhail, who were led by Suleiman Nabulsi and his National Socialist Party. Nabulsi's pro-Soviet positions were in direct conflict with Hussein's pro-Western and Islamic beliefs. The new Palestinian prime minister was more inclined to take his orders from Nasser or Haj Amin in Cairo than from Hussein.

The Israeli raids had brought the mood in Jordan to a fever pitch; demands for war against the Jewish state were encouraged by similar cries from Egypt and Syria. To maintain calm, Hussein signed a pact with Syria and Egypt, justifying it as a move toward pan-Arab unity. The pact was short-lived.

When the British, the French, and the Israelis attacked the Suez Canal on October 29, 1956, Hussein offered to send in troops to help Nasser. But the Egyptian leader refused the offer, expressing his preference for a political solution over a military battle he knew he could not win. Nevertheless, Hussein, after expelling the British from Jordan, invited Syrian, Iraqi, and Saudi troops into his country. Nabulsi objected, seeing this as a test of his power. The clash was bitter, and made even more so when, a few days later, the Palestinian prime minister opened diplomatic relations with the Soviet Union and the People's Republic of China. At the same time the United States government, under President Eisenhower, issued a doctrine declaring they would send their troops anywhere in the Middle East to stop communist aggression.

Hussein was distraught. Not only were the Palestinian leftists such as Nabulsi and Daoud Mikhail a threat to Jordan, but, as Hussein became aware, they were a danger to his throne. They plotted with Egyptian and Syrian leaders, had direct meetings with Soviet military officials, infiltrated the Jordanian intelligence agency, which was primarily Hashemite, bribed army officers, and lured the head of the army, General Ali Abu Nowar, a longtime friend of the king's, to their side. Hussein pleaded with Nabulsi, but his pleas went unheeded, and by April 1957 the feud between the king and Nabulsi exploded into an open fight. Mass riots in support of Nabulsi in the Palestinian refugee camps combined with a mutiny in the army, now under the control of, Ali Abu Nowar, and led to a bitter showdown. Hussein announced that he had discovered a Syrian-Egyptian plot against him and dismissed the elected Nabulsi cabinet.

This led to more riots in the refugee camps, and all political parties were suppressed. General Ali Abu Nowar was dismissed and fled the country. Hussein's ouster of the Nabulsi government was seen by the United States as a friendly move in support of the Eisenhower Doctrine. The United States returned the favor by sending the Sixth Fleet to the eastern Mediterranean to protect him, and it began supplying economic and military aid to Jordan. But one of those trapped in the turbulence of Nabulsi's rapid rise to power and equally swift ouster was Daoud Mikhail. The National Socialist Party was now outlawed. As one of its main organizers on the West Bank, Hanan's father was arrested and sentenced to a term of six years in prison.

His crime was "advocating a Palestinian state and claiming that the West Bank is Palestine—not Jordan," says Huda. Daoud was jailed across the street from the Mikhail family home in a prison named for Colonel Taggart, an officer in the British army. The Jordanians had discovered several books in Daoud's clinic, among them one that contained the names of people who had registered for the National Socialist Party. Shortly after Daoud began his term, his health started to deteriorate. But what made his imprisonment so unbearable for Hanan and her sisters was that they were regularly visited by the one individual who had the power to commute his sentence or to set him free. "We had connections, for crying out loud: the king, we knew him: the king came personally and stayed at our sister Muna's house," recalls Huda.

In 1957 King Hussein began building a summer home in Ramallah, a town famous for its temperate climate and wide boulevards lined with palm trees. It was a popular resort for many wealthy Arabs. While construction was under way, the king would come and stay at a villa that belonged to Muna, the oldest of Hanan's sisters, who had married a brilliant and well-to-do Palestinian eye surgeon from Jaffa. "It was the only place the king could come by helicopter," says Huda.

But Hussein, who was twenty-two years old, already knew the Mikhail children. Wad'i Assad, their mother's brother, "owned half of Aqaba port," explains Huda; his holdings included a small hotel, the only one in the Red Sea harbor town, and the Aqaba fishery. In addition, he had a speed boat, a tempting lure for the sportive king. Hussein brought his new wife, Princess Dina Abdul Hamid, whom he had married a year earlier, to stay with the family and even to go water skiing with them.

"We would be sitting, having an early supper at my uncle's house, and all of a sudden we would hear a couple of cars. 'Knock, knock, what are you having for dinner?' Cheese and cucumbers and whatever, and he comes and sits with us," recalls Huda. Four years later, in 1961, Hussein divorced Dina and married Antoinette Gardiner, the daughter of a British army officer who had converted to Islam and changed her name to Muna Hussein. They also brought their two sons and two daughters to relax at the Mikhail home in Aqaba. "I used to have stacks of pictures of his little boys, Abdullah and Faisal, and Toni Gardiner running around the beach with their horse." Then, "On the other hand," Huda suddenly recalls, "there is my father sitting in jail."

The family did not blame Hussein for his imprisonment. "I don't think he knew until after the fact," she says. His confinement, they were convinced, was the work of the Jordanian *Mukhabarat*, the intelligence services. The family tried to persuade the Hashemite ruler to commute Daoud's sentence. Their uncle Wad'i would tell Hussein, "Come on, he just talks. He's not dangerous. He's not talking about bringing down the Jordanian government!" A few weeks later, Hussein relented and, citing his failing health, transferred Daoud Mikhail to a hospital, where he was put under round-the-clock guard. A month later, he was released.

Hussein did not take much notice of Hanan, who was only twelve, during those summers. But when he saw her again in the fall of 1991 with the Palestinian delegation that traveled to Amman, Hussein immediately remembered her father and complimented Hanan on her mastery of the media. "If I had one person, a woman like you, in Jordan," he told Hanan, "I would make her a prime minister!"

In 1961 Daoud built a new, much larger home for his family, on a promontory in Ramallah. It was his dream, a modern stone-and-marble house with etched glass windows in the front, constructed on four levels, with a wide circular staircase draped with plants leading to the bedrooms and living rooms on the upper floors. At the very top a protected roof garden provided an expansive view of Ramallah. "Nadia and I convinced our father that we wanted to have the top floor. He built me a studio there," says the sculptor Huda. An emergency medical clinic was established on the ground floor, which they nicknamed the "gardener's level" after the live-in caretaker. The house was shelled during the 1967 war, forcing the family to replace the etched glass windows on the ground floor with concrete slabs. Later, when it became difficult for their elderly mother to climb the stairs to get to the bedrooms, the first floor was transformed into two separate suites and the existing kitchenette was enlarged. Hanan today lives on the second floor of the house, still one of the most imposing in Ramallah.

Even though Daoud Mikhail had realized one ambition, his magnificent new family home, he kept working for his real dream, a Palestinian state. Indeed, Hanan's coming of age at eighteen as an activist in the Palestinian struggle coincided with her father's involvement in another development. In 1964, the same year that the teenage Hanan began her undergraduate studies at the American University of Beirut, a renowned Protestant center of learning that produced the elite of the Arab world's leadership, Daoud Mikhail helped to form a new group in Cairo. "He was one of the people who worked for the establishment of the PLO," says Hanan. Adds Huda, "He was with Ahmed Shukeiry, the first [PLO] organizer in Egypt. That was when he realized that nothing could be achieved unless we had some kind of organization to speak for the Palestinians, to try to convince the Arab countries that we have to do it politically; he believed we could liberate the country by logic."

The PLO was initially created as much to contain the continuing fedayeen raids against Israel as to launch a major guerrilla struggle to destroy the Jewish state. The Arab world did not want to be provoked into a new war with Israel by the hot-blooded Palestinians; if war was inevitable, Egypt wanted to pick the time and the place. In January 1964 President Gamal Abdel Nasser invited thirteen Arab leaders to the first Arab summit in Cairo. Using the excuse that Israel was diverting water from the Sea of Galilee to the Negev desert and could, therefore, afford a sizable increase in its population, Nasser declared there should be an official Palestinian group to fight the Israelis. Its political arm would be the PLO; its military side, which would not be a separate army but battalions under the control of Arab governments, would be named the Palestine Liberation Army. The words of the new charter, unanimously adopted when the PLO held its founding conference in Jerusalem in May 1964, were as vitriolic as Ahmed Shukeiry's bombastic rhetoric, but they were both part of an attempt by Nasser to create an organization that would speak for the Palestinians but be under Arab control.

While Daoud Mikhail helped Shukeiry set up the new group, Hanan was experiencing her own political conversion. She began undergraduate classes at AUB. She recalls, "There was a rude awakening in 1964 when I went to Lebanon. We had led a very sheltered life and I hadn't seen such squalor and pain and suffering and so much yearning." Like hundreds of her classmates, Hanan joined the General Union of Palestinian Students (GUPS).

Their role models, however, were not Shukeiry and his colleagues but rather the leaders of a new group that had been formed in reaction to Shukeiry's PLO: *Fatah*. This name was derived from reversing the Arab letters of the acronym *HATAF*, which stood for "Palestine National Liberation Movement." *Hataf*, forebodingly, spells "death"; *Fatah* means "opening," in the sense of liberating territory from control of the infidels; the first conquests of Mohammed's army are called *Futuh* (plural of *Fatah*) *al-Islam*. Taken from the Koran, where *Fatah* means "opening the gates for glory," it also can mean "conquests in study, in commerce, in marriage, or in military activities."

Fatah's strength would be its military threat. If *Fatah* stood for anything, it was independence from the Arab states. Its leaders had contempt for the new Egyptian-dependent PLO, which drove them to plan their first military action against Israel, the sabotaging of an Israeli water installation in 1965, and quickly made them heroes of a new generation of Palestinian students.

In the late 1960s Palestinians in the refugee camps of Beirut began to revolt against the Lebanese, who since 1948 had clamped nightly curfews on them and had run the camps under very strict secret police control. "They simply threw off all the shackles of the Lebanese police, stopped obeying orders, and overnight built stone-and-concrete homes over their tents and tin barracks," recalls Nabil Shaath, who was a professor of business administration at AUB and today is a key political adviser to PLO Chairman Yasser Arafat. The sudden building of permanent structures, says Shaath, "was not a sign that we were going to live there forever but somehow that we were asserting our identity." The revolt forced the new national leadership of the PLO to take responsibility for running the camps, he adds. "It also brought Palestinian culture into vogue," says Shaath, as playwrights and poets and artists suddenly discovered their Palestinian heritage. With the liberation of the camps came new responsibilities, and all the student members of GUPS were expected to register with the *Fatah* office in Beirut for volunteer duty among the refugees. The tasks they were assigned included handicraft training, teaching in the nurseries and schools, educating women to their new rights and responsibilities, and escorting foreign television crews through the newly liberated camps.

Hanan worked as a volunteer at Bourj al-Barajneh and at Tel Zatar, the largest refugee camp in Beirut. She taught classes in "what we called consciousness raising and political awareness" and also was assigned to accompany journalists through the camps. She was "the typical upper-middle-class girl with money to spend, living in the dorms and enjoying university life," says Shaath. Like so many other AUB students, "she gradually started getting conscious of her Palestinian identity," he adds. Barrie Dunsmore, ABC-TV's U.S. State Department correspondent, remembers that Hanan was assigned to help the network film "Palestine: A New State of Mind," a program he cohosted with Peter Jennings, the current anchor of "The ABC Nightly News." The hour-long documentary was the first on American television to take a sympathetic look at Palestinians, going beyond the prevailing image as refugees and terrorists. Nabil Shaath, son of an Egyptian banker, was featured as one of three Palestinians on the program. Dunsmore recalls Hanan: "Her role in the show was to help us meet important Palestinians, to take us into some of the refugee camps and basically to act as a liaison with us in the community."

He also remembers her being "quite glamorous and well turned-out" in her miniskirts and short, dark hair. "Beirut was the Paris of the Orient in those days, and they all wore the most glamorous fashions," says Dunsmore. There have been rumors that Hanan was romanced by Peter Jennings during the ABC filming. "We did go out but so what? That's my private life," says Hanan. Jennings says they were friends and still are close. "She was incredibly smart then, and we all went out with her. I went to the movies with her. She was very attractive and very fashionable." Beirut, says Jennings, was "where all the smart Palestinians lived; Amman was regarded as an altogether too banal place to live." Hanan agrees; despite the squalor and starvation, Beirut, with the romance of its seaport on the Mediterranean and the splendor of its shops, became a magnet that would not free her. Even after she received her B.A. degree in 1968, "I couldn't go home. I felt the work had to be done. I simply didn't know how much Palestine meant until I saw the people who were deprived of everything. I felt the Palestinian problem was no longer an abstraction or part of my parents' past. It became my own. I took it very personally."

In the fall of 1969 Hanan attended the first GUPS convention in Amman. "I remember there were two to three hundred young men, and I was the only woman among them." The men reacted predictably, whispering behind her back, "Aha, trust the Palestinians from Lebanon to bring a woman with them!" Being a woman—and the spokesperson for the Lebanese chapter of GUPS—put an additional burden on her. "I had to prove I was serious. I was elected to all sorts of serious committees, constantly trying to show them it's not frivolous to have a woman," she recalls. It was at the GUPS convention in Amman that Hanan first met Yasser Arafat, the new leader of *Fatah*. She was photographed with Arafat in the Lebanese newspaper *Al Nahar*. "Then we sat down and talked. First of all, there was the whole issue of armed struggle."

These were heady days for the PLO. On March 21, 1968, it had won its most important victory, and against seemingly insurmountable odds. Using the full force of their armor, infantry, and artillery, the Israeli army and air force attacked a Jordanian border village, Karameh, which was being used as a staging area for fedayeen raids against the Jewish state. Although the Israelis destroyed the village, they encountered a much larger Palestinian force in the Jordan valley, many more of them under the cover of the regular Jordanian army, than they had expected. When they finally withdrew, the battlefield was littered with the carcasses of Israeli tanks and young soldiers: their own count listed 28 dead and some 100 wounded; the Jordanian army said 207 Jordanian soldiers and 97 Palestinian fedayeen were killed. Despite the lopsided death toll, the battle was seen as a great victory for the Palestinians, and it was transformed into an even bigger media triumph when Yasser Arafat arranged a public funeral in Amman for the dead fedayeen. Tens of thousands of Palestinians lined the streets, venting their rage almost as much at King Hussein as at the Israelis.

Within a few months it was clear the Palestinians inside Jordan were becoming an almost uncontrollable force. When Jordanian troops, on November 4, 1968, attacked Jabal Ashrafiyeh and Jabal Hussein—two training camps of the Popular Front for the Liberation of Palestine (PFLP) near Amman—that was all the proof that was needed that their real enemy was Jordan, not Israel. Even though that battle had been fought between the PFLP and the army, it was Arafat who was seen as the major player in the resistance effort. His position had become so strong that *Fatah* had enough votes to take control of the movement, and in February 1969 Arafat was named chairman of the Palestine Liberation Organization. The PLO had changed from a dull instrument of the Arab states to a lethal weapon of the guerrillas.

"The focus was on this. In a sense," says Hanan recalling her earlier radicalism, "I was very altruistic and idealistic." Like thousands of other young Palestinians, Hanan believed her duty was to recover all of Palestine. At twenty-two she was as impressionable as any of her militant male counterparts. At the GUPS convention, she recalls, two leaders made an even bigger impact on her than Arafat, because they vowed to destroy Israel. "The people who struck me the most were Abu Iyad [Salah Khalaf] and Abu Jihad [Khalil Wazir]. Abu Amar [Arafat] had this sort of halo above him as the symbol." Hanan admits she was a member of *Fatah*, but today she is uncomfortable when the issue of her membership is raised, hardly mentioning the word *Fatah*. "I was and I left," she says pointedly. "I decided to work as an independent. But I was for a long time."

When Hanan returned to Beirut that fall, something happened that brought the guerrilla struggle home to her in a far more personal and soul-wrenching way. Perhaps it led to her later disenchantment with *Fatah* and to a change in her attitude toward the use of guns. She is not a pacifist, however. "Even if somehow you feel you have to go through a phase," she says, "I don't like weapons. I have a personal abhorrence of them. I don't like to see them. I don't like to handle them."

Hanan had seen her share of suffering in the refugee camps. But no one could predict the impact that the disappearance of a cousin would have on her. His name was Hanah Mikhail. Next to her father, he was her role model, a Palestinian similarly consumed by the twin passions of education and politics and the constant painful struggle to choose between them. He was the only son of her father's sister, and was six years older than Hanan. Physically, he was short and thin, with a receding hair line, and he wore glasses. He left Ramallah in 1955, when he was sixteen, to study in the United States, where he was known as John Hanah, and quickly rose to the top of his class. His career was a paradigm of the Palestinian success story: he earned his Ph.D. at Harvard University, where he met and married an American; he graduated summa cum laude and was offered a teaching position at Princeton.

Hume Horan, an American diplomat, was a friend of Hanah's when they both were graduate students, and the Palestinian was a teaching assistant at Harvard's Middle East Center. "He was a very winning kind of person; he was cheerful and honest and there was a directness, a vitality to him," recalls Horan. Unlike other Arab intellectuals, who were radicalized by events in the 1958-to-1960 period, including the revolution that toppled the Iraqi monarchy, Horan recalls, Hanah "wasn't that political a guy, there was no baring of the teeth, and he didn't have a personality problem the way some Arabs had on the campuses."

At Princeton Hanah Mikhail taught courses in political science and international relations that were among the most popular at the university, and he was soon asked to appear as a guest panelist on "The Advocates," a Public Broadcasting System (PBS) program that televised national debates on global issues, including the Middle East conflict. He quickly established credentials as an effective spokesperson for the Palestinians. "He was like Hanan, or Hanan is like him," says Huda. "He just had his facts, and he was very good at presenting the issues on television at a time when no one would allow a Palestinian to say anything."

In the late 1960s Hanah Mikhail began traveling regularly to Beirut, where it became more and more difficult for him to maintain the intellectual detachment of a Princeton don. Nabil Shaath, a leading member of the Palestine National Council, was a professor at AUB at the time. He recalls that the mood in Beirut in the late 1960s was one of euphoria: "These [1968 and 1969] were two years of romance for the Palestinians coming immediately after the Arab defeat in 1967. Palestinians felt a resurgence, a reemergence, a rebirth. They felt like they were responsible for liberating the whole Arab world, not only Palestine. They felt Palestine was at the center of things, at the heart of things, they were proud again of being Palestinians."

Hanah decided his calling was there, with his people in the ravaged refugee camps, not with his more refined and scholarly Ivy League colleagues. "He was quite well known in academic circles, but he chucked it all and went to Lebanon. He wanted to serve the cause and be with the cause," says Huda. In Beirut, Hanah Mikhail was the model of self-sacrifice. He owned only two garments, both of them khaki safari suits, and lived in a small single room near a refugee camp. He divorced his blonde American wife and married "a girl from the movement," recalls Shaath. "We all helped with little pieces of furniture" for the tiny apartment. Hanah went to work in the Planning Center of the Political Department of the PLO, which Shaath headed, but he spent almost all of his time in the refugee camps, where he helped organize and teach the fedayeen.

Within weeks of assuming his new role, Hanah became one of the key advisers to PLO Chairman Yasser Arafat, taking on the twin responsibilities of press spokesperson and policy planning chief, and like so many others, disguising his true identity. Hanah Mikhail called himself Abu Omar. "He was almost an absolute model of purity and dedication," says Shaath. "To that extent, he was not unique but a foremost model of the upper-middle-class, American-educated Palestinian who gives up everything to come back home to work for the people. Nobody knew from the way he looked and talked that he was John Hanah Mikhail from Princeton." Shaath stresses that his allegiance was total: "He never compromised, he never bought a car, and until he got married, he never got a salary, just an allowance whenever he needed one." Explains Huda, "He felt if you want to fight and work for the cause, you have to live like them to understand what is happening to them. He had ten piasters (ten cents) a day as his pocket money, that's all." Hanan Ashrawi recalls that her cousin was "hungry most of the time because he refused to take any money from the revolution. As a student, I had better food and a better apartment so I used to find every pretext to bring him over to feed him at my apartment on Bliss Street."

Hume Horan had not seen his old friend from Harvard Yard for a decade or more when the American diplomat returned to Jordan. "I had heard he had been caught up in the Palestinian revolution," he recalls, but did not know where he was. Meanwhile, Horan had been appointed as the political officer at the U.S. Embassy in Amman, with the assignment of tracking the Palestinians. "Those were very heady days for them before the September 1970 confrontation between the army and the guerrillas," says Horan, speaking about a series of battles that almost cost King Hussein his throne and that came to be known in Palestinian folklore as "Black September." Even though his task was to maintain quiet contact with "people on the fringes of the PLO," the American says he deliberately made no effort to find Hanah Mikhail. "The last thing I wanted to do was to look up somebody like that, because I figured that would really screw him with his bosses. He was shouldering enough of a burden with a former American wife and being a Christian and having gone to two leading American schools," says Horan.

But after the first big spate of fighting in Amman, Egyptian president Gamal Abdul Nasser was able to arrange a ceasefire, and the new Jordanian prime minister, Wasfi Tel, wanted to be sure he had the cooperation of the PLO. So in early October the Jordanian asked Munib Masri, a loyal Jordanian from Nablus who also was a close friend of Arafat, to arrange a meeting between them. Since it was a public affair, Horan drove out with an aide to report back on the Arafat-Tel meeting. It was held in a villa on the outskirts of Amman, "no big fancy place at all, kind of a no-man's-land with lots of security on both sides," he recalls. Waving his U.S. diplomatic passport, Horan was able to get into the villa to attend the press conference that accompanied the signing of "one of their many ceasefire and desist agreements."

As soon as Arafat and the Jordanian official sat down, recalls Horan, "I looked up and there was Hanah Mikhail." Their eyes locked and they recognized each other, but neither said anything. "I thought I better play it cool. I thought to myself, 'These are people's lives that are involved.' I thought, 'Jeez' and almost regretted going." As the PLO party left the room to get back into the motorcade, however, Hanah Mikhail stopped right in front of Horan. "Almost impulsively, he shook my hand and said, 'Let me wish you the best of luck, Hume, in your personal capacities.' I was really touched. To shake hands with an American, a political officer in the embassy, publicly, takes a lot of guts. I said, 'Hanah, let me wish you as a friend, in your personal capacities, the very best of luck and happiness.'"

The two friends never saw each other again. Several weeks later Horan was asked to report to the State Department on his old school chum. "It was suggested, why don't we take a look at Hanah Mikhail? I just thought there are other contacts, these [PLO] guys are coming out of the walls, I didn't really want to compromise him. I said, 'Leave it alone.'"

No one in the Mikhail family knows exactly what happened to Hanah Mikhail. "He just disappeared. They say maybe he was killed by the Lebanese, maybe by the Syrians or by the Israelis," says Huda. Shaath says the last time he saw him, in 1976, was during the early months of the Lebanese civil war. He was on a mission to Tripoli, the Muslim capital of northern Lebanon, to help the Palestinians organize themselves to withstand an expected siege by the Syrians. "He would always go to a refugee camp that was in trouble," recalls Shaath. He had to travel by boat from Beirut because the Phalangists, the paramilitary arm of the Maronite Christians, had blocked the road to Tripoli. None of the twelve Palestinians on the boat ever came back. His Palestinian wife, Jihan Helou, however, never gave up hope. "She nurtured the dream that he was captured by the Phalangists and handed over to the Syrians. She even remained celibate for ten years," says Shaath. "But we never received his body." Says the diplomat Horan, who later became U.S. ambassador to Saudi Arabia and Sudan, "One person who does know, a Quaker friend, told me he was caught and tortured to death." The two cousins, Hanan Mikhail and John Hanah Mikhail, grew very close during those years in Beirut. She never forgot the example he set for the Palestinians or the work he had done as spokesperson for Arafat.

Hanan was barred from returning to the West Bank, so she left Beirut in 1970 to begin her postgraduate work in America. She could not go home, because Israel prohibited any Palestinians who were outside the country in June 1967, when the West Bank was lost to Israel, from returning. "They were made to leave," says Hanan, "because they didn't have what Israel calls Israeli I.D. cards to live in the occupied territories. This is what we called the invisible deportation . . . the silent transfer."

Hanan had already earned her master's degree in textual

criticism of Renaissance literature and was accepted in the Ph.D. program in medieval studies at the University of Virginia. By the time she went home to Ramallah in 1973, after a new Israeli census and the passage of the Family Reunification Act, she was completely transformed. "She stopped caring about how she looked. She was wearing the humblest clothes, corduroy pants, and plain shoes," says Huda. The glamorous girl had become a serious scholar and a dedicated activist.

In the three years she spent in America, Hanan studied the great works of medieval English literature: Chaucer's *The Canterbury Tales* and the oldest English epic, *Beowulf*. By her bedside she kept her private passions: the poetry of Yeats and Auden and works by Marxist scholars. The early 1970s in America were years of student rebellion against the Vietnam War, and Hanan was a part of it. She was active in the Black Students Alliance, often joining protest marches and speaking out against the colonial oppression of her own people as well as of the Vietnamese. She also became an outspoken advocate of feminism and started writing her own poetry. "At first I was worried she wouldn't do well because of all her outside interests, but then I discovered she was tutoring the bottom third of the class in her spare time," Hoyt N. Duggan, her thesis adviser, told *People* magazine.

"She was also very feminine, very attractive to a lot of men," Martin King, a friend of hers at the time, told the *Washington Post*. She would drive friends to Washington, D.C., in her "beat-up old car," he recalls, and sit debating with them for hours at the Crystal City sidewalk cafe on Connecticut Avenue. "She was intellectually provocative, and would challenge anyone to a good political argument, which she usually won by her powers of persuasion, or by being tactful, or by being incredibly charming," says King. She still had time to enjoy herself, and would take friends on shopping expeditions for clothes and antique jewelry. In her spare time she also loved to play Scrabble.

When in 1973 the Israeli government adopted a new law permitting family reunification, Hanan was able to return for the first time in six years. Back in Ramallah, the twenty-five-year-old doctoral candidate took the post of head of the English Department at Birzeit University, where she eventually became dean of the Faculty of Arts. She immediately "felt the pressure of the occupation," says Peter Jennings, "because when she would come home at night, the Israelis in the prison across the road would follow her into the house with a spotlight and shine it on her room." In October a new war began when Egyptian forces launched a surprise attack on the eve of the holiest Jewish holiday, Yom Kippur. The mood in Israel was one of reprisal and anger at the Palestinians, who cheered the initial victories of the Egyptian armies. For Hanan, however, the new conflict reinforced the dovish beliefs she had nurtured abroad. "I remember starting to talk to Israelis in the 1970s. I remember starting to think then about a two-state solution," she says. "If you want a future for Palestine, you have to accept the existence of Israel."

Her early work revolved around raising the consciousness of women to their dual challenge: throwing off the yoke of Israeli oppression as well as the suppression of the Arab woman by the Arab world. Liberation and self-determination were not merely manifestations of Palestinian nationalism; they had a personal meaning for thousands of women whose role had been almost entirely determined by overly dominating male forces.

Many of the girls Hanan grew up with had typical Muslim lives: they received almost no education, married by the age of eighteen, and bore as many as a dozen children. Their world centered around the home; and while their husbands went off to earn a living or to fight a war, they stayed inside, prayed, and wept, able to do little else. Hanan preached a new message of coexistence with Israel and personal liberation. It was not one that the Islamic fundamentalists wanted to hear. "We used to have these *nadwas*, where groups of friends and I would go to Gaza, Jenin, Nablus, and other places to give public talks. In Gaza, when we talked about women's rights, we were viciously attacked by the sheikh from the mosque, who declared these people are advocating immorality."

Hanan's commitment to women's liberation came from a heritage of devotion to liberal causes espoused by her father. "He became more liberal after he started begetting, one after another, girls," says Huda, explaining that "not having a son he just treated us as if we were [sons]." Peter Jennings also remembers spending a lot of time with Daoud Mikhail when he visited Hanan. "I used to go and call on her father a lot because he was a very important doctor in Ramallah. He was utterly charming," recalls Jennings. "I got sick once when I was there and he took wonderful care of me in his clinic." When Daoud died in 1988, Hanan and her sisters found his high school diary and suggested that their bishop read from it in his eulogy at the December memorial service. Among the entries was one that said: "There should be no passports and no borders and no different nationalities because we all have the passport of humanity." Another entry said: "Women have the right to be equal by natural right. It is not a gift that men bestow upon women and if men will not recognize this fact, women everywhere will have to rise up and struggle to win their equality. Once they do that," Daoud warned, "men beware the injustice of somebody who has been oppressed too long, especially when she takes over power!" Says Hanan, "He was the first advocate of women's rights that I know of."

Within weeks of her return to Ramallah, Hanan was introduced by her sister Nadia, an actress, to Emile Ashrawi, a drummer in a rock band called The Blooms. "We played rock music with Arabic lyrics. We did not really know how to play Arab music," explained Emile, who also played the guitar. He later became a film maker and an actor and today earns his livelihood as a photographer for a United Nations refugee relief group in Jerusalem. Emile was four years younger than Hanan, but they were instantly attracted to each other. "I was touched by his looks," Hanan told *People* magazine, particularly his strikingly handsome face, neatly cropped beard, and long hair. "He was obviously living his art," she says. "We went dancing and have stayed together ever since." Two years later, in 1975, they were married.

By then, Hanan had become accustomed to being detained by the Israeli authorities and interrogated in the prison across the street from their home. "Sometimes they would come and pick me up in an army vehicle and sometimes they would send a summons. Once we were herded off in a truck. They used to call these 'preventive measures': on special occasions for Palestinians, like the Fifth of June or the Second of November, they would go around picking up Palestinians and detaining them to prevent any activities. I used to go around carrying a book and cigarettes and chocolates in my handbag because we made a point of not eating anything that they gave us and always having something to read," explains Hanan.

With the start of the *intifada*, the Palestinian uprising against Israeli occupation, in December 1987, she organized underground classes for students at Birzeit University, sessions the Israelis accused her of using to teach the tactics of resistance. "Hanan Ashrawi doesn't have contact in the field. She doesn't have hit squads like Faisal. She didn't have a direct connection to the organizers of the violent riots," says a senior Israeli authority on the West Bank. "Her importance was much more in the strategy of the war of images: how to organize the new gimmicks to sell to the mass media." The extent of her direct involvement in the uprising, however, mattered little.

Under the Israeli military law that governs the occupied territories, any Palestinian can be arrested and put under administrative detention for as long as one year without being charged and without a trial. However, charges were usually brought against Hanan on such varied allegations as disturbing the public peace, breaking the terms of her family reunion, inciting to demonstrate, and even threatening the security of the state. "I felt I was very dangerous," she jibes. Hanan knew, however, that if she was not transferred by midnight from the Taggart compound across the street from her home to another prison, she would be freed, because Taggart was for men; women could not be incarcerated there overnight. But the most humiliating experience occurred on the morning after her wedding. "They sent the summons to my father's home, and my father came to me at seven in the morning and said, 'In half an hour, you have a summons.'" On another occasion, her trial was set for the twenty-fifth of December. "We were having Christmas lunch and I had to leave to swear in before the judge." The Israeli magistrate asked Hanan where she came from, and when she said Ramallah, a largely Christian town, he gave her a Bible, the New Testament, to swear her oath on. "He said, 'What are they doing scheduling your hearing on Christmas Day?' Then he gave me six months or a fine. The teachers at Birzeit, about thirteen of them, chipped in to pay the fine."

Even though she has spent far less time in prison than many

other activists, the experience was no less intimidating. "One day that was the worst for me was when nobody would talk to me. I was put in a room with nothing. I just sat there for the whole day from 7:30 in the morning until 12:00 at night, totally incommunicado. The interrogator would stop at the door and look at me and not say a word, just shake his head at me. It was freezing cold. I didn't have a book. That's why we always say now, whenever there's anything dangerous, prepare a list of books you want to have with you." Hanan has a small attaché case ready to go. Inside she keeps several feminist novels in which the woman is depicted as strong and assertive; a work by the American philosopher Herbert Marcuse, whose theories combine Marxist and Freudian psychology, and a work by her favorite writer, the Nobel Prize-winning Colombian novelist Gabriel García Márquez.

She does not claim to have shared the pain and suffering of many Palestinians who have spent years in desert prison camps, but Hanan insists she has paid her dues. She has ducked bullets on the Birzeit campus and seen four of her students gunned down by Israeli army troops. "I'll tell you what's so bad about this," she says. "It's the relentless, day-in, day-out, not just suffering and pain but provocation, irritation, lack of freedom, lack of any sense of security, lack of rights. Any day, in everything, you cannot make plans, you cannot take anything for granted, you wake up not knowing if you are under curfew or not, if your children are going to school or not, if you are going to be detained or arrested or not, or who is going to be killed today."

Despite the rash of murders of Palestinians by other Palestinians, and the increasing verbal attacks on her in PFLP, DFLP (Democratic Front for the Liberation of Palestine), and *Hamas* broadsides, Hanan says she feels "very comfortable, very safe" among her own people. The most frightening experience for her, she admits, took place in November 1991 when she and Faisal Husseini were being questioned about an "illegal" rendezvous they allegedly had with Yasser Arafat in Algiers the month before. The interrogation took place at the Central Police Headquarters in Petah Tikvah, a maximum-security facility near the main bus station on the outskirts of Tel Aviv. When they arrived, demonstrators from three militant Israeli factions were waiting for them: Rehavam Zeevi's Moledet, which advocates transfer of all the Palestinians from the West Bank and Gaza; the Tsomet, which supports Israeli annexation of the territories; and the late Meir Kahane's Kach, the blatantly anti-Arab, racist group that believes Arabs should not be allowed to live anywhere in the Jewish state.

As Hanan and Faisal were answering questions, they suddenly saw several Israelis, civilians with machine guns strapped over their shoulders, march menacingly into the room. Hanan jumped up and demanded to know who had let them in. She was told they also were being summoned for interrogation. "With their weapons?" she asked incredulously. "Then it dawned on me. I recognized them. I had seen them on television: they are the Kach people, the thugs of Kach." She says she got up out of her chair and "out of the line of fire," again demanding to know how they had entered the very room where she and Faisal were being questioned. "Nobody could just walk into that Division for Serious Crimes, through cordons of police and army and border guards, through two floors of electric and electronically controlled doors, and down corridors all the way up to the second floor." Finally, the police escorted the intruders out.

An Israeli official says of the incident: "He didn't shoot. He only came to take pictures to boast that he threatened Faisal Husseini!" But Hanan says, "I got the message. It was a deliberate message. The real threat was, they were able to walk in, heavily armed with their own automatic guns and weapons. The irony was my husband and lawyer couldn't walk in with me but they could, the Kach people, with their weapons." As she and Faisal left the police station, they were subjected to another display of Kach displeasure. "They started pounding on the car and spitting at the windows," recalls Hanan. The incident prompted American president George Bush to volunteer to a group of Arab Americans the short, but memorable, comment, "Hanan is on my mind." Coming on the eve of Israeli Prime Minister Yitzhak Shamir's departure for the White House, it helped insulate Hanan from further official harassment for allegedly meeting Arafat.

Despite the harsh encounter, Hanan met with Arafat again, this next time as a member of the Palestinian delegation visiting Jordan. This was an especially sensitive time, on the eve of the June 1992 elections in Israel, several weeks before the new Rabin government would change the law to permit meetings with PLO officials. Hanan allowed herself to be photographed with her head nestled on Arafat's shoulder. For most of the members of the delegation, publicizing the meeting in Amman was important in order to embarrass the Shamir Government. At least it was interpreted that way in Israel. But for Hanan and Arafat, there was an additional personal significance to their meeting, in light of their waning popularity in the Palestinian arena. Both were struggling against accusations of immodest and immoral conduct. The radical Islamic movement *Hamas* had issued a leaflet in the West Bank and Gaza charging Hanan with being a "loose" woman. Meanwhile, Arafat was being accused both by *Hamas* and privately by some of his own supporters of being irresponsible and thoughtless in marrying a twenty-eight-year-old, blonde-haired Christian woman, Suha Tawil, the daughter of another attractive Palestinian woman, Raymonda Tawil, herself a frequent target of the Muslim fundamentalists. To many in the occupied territories, the marriage seemed a betrayal of Arafat's vow that he would never take a wife because he was married to the Palestinian revolution.

In her Grand Hotel suite, with one eye on the television but with the sound muted, Hanan is doing what she does best, verbalizing the pain of suffering, creating the well-hewn script for the perfect sound bites, the sculptor of language giving sense and form to the Palestinian nightmare. "Psychologically you cannot dream," she says, "you cannot plan freely. What bothers me the most is that you cannot even take sunshine and fresh air for granted. It's amazing," she adds, becoming introspective. "The liberties we allow to intrude into our own lives, into the most intimate details of our lives. This is what drives me crazy, in a sense it's like you have no mental, emotional, personal privacy, no space: right there the occupation intrudes, makes itself felt at every level, in every way. That's why I said we need to end this fatal proximity. We need to disengage from this imbalanced situation in order to reengage freely as equals. But this situation of intrusion, coercion, manipulation, of twisting the knife constantly, this is not healthy for either side."

Hanan has made a personal effort to engage with Israeli women who make up the bulk of support for the peace movement in the Jewish state. "I have seen how people with principle

stand up for their principles and struggle side by side with you
even though they have nothing to gain and everything to lose.
They take tremendous risks and," she adds, "many of them are
given the Palestinian treatment."

Among her closest Israeli friends is Leah Tsemel, a lawyer who
has frequently represented Hanan in the courtroom across the
street from her Ramallah home. Leah is virtually a member of the
Ashrawi family, says Hanan, who has left "standing instructions"
for the Israeli woman to eat or sleep with them whenever she
comes to Ramallah. In 1982, when Leah gave birth to her first
child, Wad'ia gave her one of the Mikhail family rings. When Leah
was called away to defend some of Hanan's students, the Palestinian breast-fed her Israeli friend's infant. "So her daughter is my
daughter's 'milk sister,'" says Hanan. "There is so much love in
that woman; she is so warm and human and genuine," she adds.
She wrote the following poem for Leah in October 1989 because,
explains Hanan, her Israeli friend "feels that the only way Israel
can be liberated is by liberating the Palestinian people." The poem
is called "Women and Things."

Women make things grow.
Sometimes like the crocus,
Surprised by rain,
Emerging fully grown from the belly of the earth.
Others, like the palm tree,
With its promise postponed,
Rising, in a slow, deliberate spiral to the sky.

Women make things light, afloat,
Like the breathless flight of soap bubbles
Shimmering in the eyes of a lone child
In a forbidden schoolyard,
And heavy, like the scent of an overripe fruit
Exploding at the knowledge of summer-hardened soil
On days of siege.

Women make things smooth to the touch,
Like the kneading of leavened bread
At the dawn of hunger,

And coarse, like the brush of a homespun coat
On careworn shoulders and bare arms
Barely touching on the night of deportation.

Women makes things cold, sharp, and hard,
Like a legal argument
Thrust before the threat of search and detention,
Or warm and gentle,
Like justice in a poem,
Like the suggestion of the image of freedom
As a warm bath and a long soak
In an undemolished home.

Women make things—

And as we, in separate worlds,
Braid our daughters' hair in the morning,
You and I, each humming to herself,
Suddenly stops and hears
The tune of the other.

After Faisal Husseini was released from a ten-month jail term in June 1988, he asked Hanan to join the handful of Palestinians who were preparing position papers for conferences abroad and holding talks with Western envoys. In April 1991 they became the core group that represented the West Bank and Gaza in eight subsequent months of talks with American Secretary of State Baker, and they were the main channel for Baker's unofficial dialogue with the PLO.

It was Hanan, the scribe, who introduced a novel practice at these talks. She suggested that precise notes be taken so that a verbatim record would exist of what Baker and the other State Department officials had said. Some Palestinians believe this was her way of making sure she would be included in all the meetings with Baker and other senior American officials. "She was the only one who could take good notes," says one such critic. He concedes that the idea of keeping the minutes of their meetings was an innovation in Palestinian politics. It was not a surprise, however, to Hanan's sister. "A professor is used to telling her students to take notes and I'll quiz you later," explains Huda. "But the Arabs always sit around in a 'majlis'; they are used to shaking hands and agreeing verbally." Hanan insisted they "get the facts on paper and compare notes afterwards." In a technical sense, she says, "this is what started the peace process, because you have to have guidelines to deal with."

Although Hanan was not a member of the Palestinian delegation to the Arab-Israeli peace conference in the fall of 1991—she was ineligible, as the holder of a blue ID card identifying her as a Jerusalem resident—her presence on the seven-member "advisory" team in Madrid almost overshadowed Israeli Prime Minister Yitzhak Shamir and President Bush. She captivated the international press corps with her cogent arguments, repeatedly transforming tired propaganda into pragmatic appeals for sympathy. Overnight, the Palestinians, dehumanized for decades and depicted as terrorists, acquired a warm, human face; whenever Hanan walked into the room, she was surrounded by a phalanx of camerapeople and reporters waiting on her every word. She gave nonstop interviews to ABC, CBS, NBC, CNN, BBC, and PBS, appearing on "Good Morning America," "Nightline," "The Today Show," "The McNeil-Lehrer NewsHour," and endless network special reports. Only Peter Jennings, her old friend, resolved not to use her so there could be no appearance of conflict of interest. "I've never booked her on 'Nightline,' nor do I use her on this broadcast ['ABC Nightly News']. We photograph her if she is part of the story but I've never used her as a specialist," he says.

Hanan says she never got more than four hours' sleep during the three days of the early November conference. According to Rashid Khalidi, director of the Center for Middle Eastern Studies at the University of Chicago, Hanan played "a major role" in drafting the keynote speech that was delivered by Haidar Abdul Shafi, the chief Palestinian delegate. It was a collaborative effort, says Khalidi. The political rhetoric in it was written by others, including Mamdouh Aker and Nabil Shaath. "But the turns of phrase people remember, she wrote," he explains.

Steeped in reality and compassionate toward the Jews, the speech was hailed as a breakthrough for the Palestinians. It equated their suffering with the anguish of Israeli mothers and fathers "with whom we have had a prolonged exchange of pain. Your security and ours are mutually dependent, as entwined as the fears and nightmares of our children." The message was a simple and eloquent one: the Palestinian experience mirrored that of the Jews. "We have seen you look back in deepest sorrow at the tragedy of your past, and look on in horror at the disfigurement of the victim turned oppressor. Not for this have you nurtured your hopes, dreams and your offspring," were the words uttered by Abdul Shafi to the hushed statesmen at the conference.

The humanity of his appeal dwarfed politics; to a television audience of millions, the Palestinians appeared instantly to be victims. Thus, when Haidar said, "It is time for us to narrate our own story, to stand witness as advocates of a truth which has long lain buried in the consciousness and conscience of the world," his words, penned by Hanan, had a special resonance. No longer could any Israelis contend "there are no Palestinians" with whom to talk. Here they were, in living color, their reality magnified by the revolutionary power of television, meeting with kings, prime ministers, and presidents: their existence could no longer be denied. In the eyes of most of the world, their transformation from terrorist to tactician was complete. "We proved," explains Palestinian journalist Radwan Abu Ayash, "that we have representatives who can appear in a dignified manner in front of the whole world."

Even Shamir unwittingly contributed to the Palestinian success at Madrid. "The issue is not territory but our existence," he pleaded, equating the need for recognition of both people: the Israelis and the Palestinians. By sitting across from Abdul Shafi at the peace conference and bowing to American pressure to allow him to deliver a separate speech, Shamir conveyed recognition and respect on his Palestinian rival. And when Elyakim Rubinstein, one of Shamir's closest aides, approved a communique calling for future talks on two separate tracks, an Israeli-Palestinian one and an Israeli-Jordanian one, the Jewish state was finally and formally elevating the Palestinians to equal status with all the other parties to the conflict. "We surprised ourselves in Madrid," admits Faisal Husseini. "After that there can be no surprises."

The Palestinian delegation returned as heroes to the West Bank and Gaza. Despite the added Israeli security, and checkpoints where their bus had to stop as it made its way across the Allenby Bridge and through Jericho, thousands of Palestinians defied army orders and mobbed their newly elevated envoys to the world. Small boys thrust olive branches onto the metal grilles of Israeli jeeps and police cars. An elderly man held a white dove over his head. When the bus stopped briefly at a checkpoint, Hanan's nine-year-old daughter, Zeinah, clutching a teddy bear, pushed past photographers and jumped into her waiting mother's arms. "I'm overwhelmed, absolutely overwhelmed. It's a grand homecoming," Hanan told reporters. Tears streamed down her face. For several generations, the celebration was more than merely a Palestinian homecoming. After more than two decades of occupation, they believed they were going home to Palestine.

That, of course, was the threat Israel feared most: that Palestinian dreams of a separate state were so engendered by their success in Madrid they would settle for nothing less. "Where was Yasser Arafat when we needed him most?" moaned an aide to Shamir. It was not long before the Israeli counterattack began, and one of its central targets was the woman who had proved a more potent Palestinian weapon than Arafat: Hanan Ashrawi. To discredit her, Israeli spokespersons seized on her gender, her family's wealth, her religion, her alleged pacifism, even her husband's preoccupation with doing the dishes. "Have you noticed the big change in her?" asked Yossi Olmert. "She's acquiring an almost royalistic demeanor, going around with this young girl who is her secretary. She's like the Israeli ministers," he quipped, "with boys around them, like 'Bebe' Netanyahu." He noted that "Faisal works closely with her because he understands the advantages in her and can make good use of her. But everybody else is gossiping about her: [saying] she's ugly, she's nasty, she's a Christian, she's a woman; she's appeared too much." Snipes the former Israeli spokesman: "She's not influential at all. She's only a spokesperson, she's nothing."

To be sure, Hanan has enemies among both Israeli and Palestinian opponents of the peace process. When Moustafa Akkawi, a Popular Front prisoner, died recently from what the Palestinian faction charged was Israeli torture, the PFLP let Hanan know she would not be welcome at the funeral. Faisal Husseini attended; she did not. Women's groups in the Hawatmeh-led faction of the Democratic Front also have attacked her, charging Hanan was born with a golden spoon in her mouth and never paid her dues in blood and sweat. At a press conference in January 1992 to protest the deportation of eleven Palestinians, Khalida Jarrar, the wife of one of the deportees cried out angrily, "You do not represent us, the families of the deportees!" Says Hanan, "I had set up a press conference. Ghassan Jarrar was a former student of mine. He did not appreciate the attack and sent me an apology from prison." It is hard to know how much her high profile has made Hanan a natural target for the Palestinian underground and how much is fueled by Israeli disinformation.

Hanan does not mince words about the Israelis, however, calling Israel itself an apartheid state. Even after it was repealed, she did not try very hard to disguise her support for the United Nations resolution condemning Zionism as a form of racism. "They have transformed Judaism into a national identity in Israel," she told *Mirabella* magazine. "Any Jew can automatically become a citizen. So I don't know whether this is racist or not. What do you think? I think Israel is an apartheid state and the way Palestinians have been treated under occupation is very clearly racist."

Several months later, when the Israeli delegation first proposed municipal elections as a test to determine whether the Palestinians were capable of organizing a peaceful poll, Hanan also charged the Jewish state was using "patronizing, I would say even a racist approach." She vowed: "We will not be placed on probation or under scrutiny to find out whether we are worthy or not!" When a reporter later challenged her use of "patronizing racist terminology," she shot back, accusing the Israelis of terming her people extremist and violent and therefore unsuitable to manage their own wider national elections. "No people can be described as violent and extremist," Hanan said, using the exchange to drive home one of her favorite themes. "This is a good example," she said, "of why we need a period away from intimidation and coercion."

Occasionally, Hanan also loses her patience with a reporter, as she did when she reprimanded a correspondent in Madrid representing the American Christian Broadcasting Network. He asked Hanan how she could demand that Israel "exchange land for peace" to create a homeland for the Palestinians because "when Judea and Samaria were in the hands of the Arab world, Israel was attacked three times." "First of all, I find your reference to 'Judea and Samaria' a statement of extreme bias, and rather offensive," Hanan replied, referring to the ancient biblical names for the West Bank used by Israel to justify its claim to the territories. "I am a Palestinian Christian, and I know what Christianity is. I am a descendant of the first Christians in the world, and Jesus Christ was born in my country, in my land. Bethlehem is a Palestinian town. So I will not accept this one-upmanship on Christianity. Nobody has this monopoly."

Huda concedes that Hanan is "articulately dangerous—or dangerously articulate." The Birzeit professor can understand people being uninformed, but she cannot tolerate willful ignorance. "She feels like she has said this over and over again, and how come some reporter comes and asks her the same dumb question?"

Hanan's impetuousness has also needlessly exposed her. When Yasser Arafat's plane disappeared in April 1992 and this father of Palestinian nationalism was presumed dead, Hanan told "Nightline" that his death would not mark the end of the PLO, because it has its own democratic institutions to choose a successor. She repeatedly parried Ted Koppel's efforts to prod her into assuming Arafat was dead, but her remarks nonetheless touched off a firestorm of criticism. It was fueled by an Israeli Radio bulletin in Arabic reporting what she had said about the need for new PLO elections. "The people of the Occupied Territories resented her statements," retorted the Arab Media Center, a Jerusalem-based Palestinian news agency headed by Radwan Abu Ayash.

Other Palestinians called for her to step down after it became clear that Arafat had indeed miraculously survived the crash in the Libyan desert. "She was attacked in the West Bank as really having buried the man too soon," concedes Nabil Shaath, "because she said what she said before we knew he was alive. But what she said really was taken out of context." He explains that "she said two things: that the PLO will not die if he dies, because there are ways and processes to succeed him. At the same time she said he [Arafat] is the father and leader and it would be a great loss to lose him. They took the first sentence, which really was meant to say 'No, we shall not all fold up our tent, we shall continue'; rather than saying 'good riddance.' She never really meant it in that sense, but having been quoted out of context before people knew he was alive, it looked like she was burying him too soon."

Hanan herself seems unperturbed, charging the whole thing was a "deliberate provocative distortion" by the government-run Arabic service of Radio Israel to sow discord and undermine her effectiveness among her people. She says the handful of Palestinians who played into Israeli hands by publicly criticizing her have been reprimanded. The important thing, she adds, is that Faisal Husseini immediately came to her defense, and the PLO issued a statement the next day clearing her of any malicious intent. "There was no criticism of what I said from the PLO itself," says Hanan.

But many Israelis believe that the incident, even though it caused no permanent damage to her reputation, indicates how precarious Hanan's position remains within the local leadership. The insightful Yael Dayan, daughter of the late war hero Moshe Dayan and a recently elected Labor Party Knesset member who supports Palestinian rights, wrote that Hanan's advocating Western-style democracy reminded many people of the qualities that make her atypical among the local Palestinian leadership. Her high intelligence does not take account of the power of Oriental sentiment, Dayan wrote in *Al Hamishmar.* "If she had an adviser interested in her welfare, he would have given her a kilo of sliced onions, she would have appeared weeping and wailing, saying—in Arabic, not Oxford English—that emotion and hope had so upset her she was unable to express herself. And she would have called for a prayer for the well-being of the chairman. In the mosques. . . . Except that she is a Christian, urban, European in concept and attitude, American in her sense of timing. The call from the territories to depose her, when she tackled the issue of electing an heir to Arafat, was also to have been expected."

In fact, one senior Israeli official suggests the reason her remarks proved so provocative is that her call for democratic elections was not merely the predictable Western response but ran counter to decisions that already were being made secretly in the salons of Palestinian leaders in Tunis and Jerusalem. Before the plane crash, "it was not allowed to ask, even behind closed doors, who was going to come after Arafat. Simply raising such a question was national treason! His disappearance for the first time legitimized open discussion about whether or not they should or should not have a number two, a 'declared' second-in-command," the official explained.

As the sixth round of Arab-Israeli talks began in Washington in late August 1992, the mood was transformed. The new Israeli government led by Yitzhak Rabin announced a series of confidence-building measures: offering elections to the Palestinians, ending the deportations and the demolishing of Palestinian houses, and releasing 800 Palestinian political prisoners. "The fact that he (Rabin) chose the opening of this round to carry out some symbolic gestures indicates he is responding; he is listening," says Hanan. Nevertheless, she is skeptical. "The most important yardstick continues to be the settlement activity. There is a real schizophrenia, a real discrepancy between what they say and what is happening. The Palestinian cannot be satisfied with declarations of intent when they see their own lands being confiscated. There has to be a clear commitment to the cessation of settlements," she insists.

There is a different climate for the talks, however. For the first time, it seems everyone wants them to succeed. The Palestinian stake in the talks was underscored by a phone call Hanan received in the middle of our final interview in her suite at the Grand Hotel. An aide wanted guidance on how to respond to the press should the United States begin shooting down Iraqi planes in southern Iraq. The PLO had already issued a statement supporting Iraq. What did the Palestinian delegation think? "The Palestinian delegation does not make statements like this. The delegation should not be brought into matters of high policy right now," Hanan told the caller. After she hung up the phone, we asked whether she was taking pains to avoid the same mistake the Palestinians made during the Gulf war, when they supported Arafat's embrace of Saddam Hussein. She implied that the talks had become more important than rhetorical flourishes: "The talks should not be held hostage to any external developments unless they are directly connected to the negotiations." The Palestinians of the West Bank and Gaza were speaking for themselves.

Despite her admiration for Yasser Arafat, Hanan does not hesitate to talk of her mentor, Faisal Husseini, as a future Palestinian statesman, perhaps even prime minister or president of a Palestinian state. "I think he is a leader already," she says. "I can see a very decisive role for Faisal. He is a man of principles and integrity and he is honest. That's why I respect him. Our relationship is based on mutual respect. We have sort of complementary roles," says Hanan. What she likes most about him, she adds, is that "Faisal has no personal agenda. He doesn't play factional politics. He doesn't do anything for his own personal aggrandizement. He has a deep commitment to the Palestinian cause, which is what I have. I do not have a personal agenda either. I want to work for the Palestinian people."

If Faisal Husseini assumes a new leadership role, it is likely Hanan Ashrawi will be at his side. Just as Faisal, a Jerusalemite, personifies the ties between Palestinians living under occupation and the diaspora abroad, Hanan seems a natural bridge to the West, a Palestinian who thinks and speaks in concepts that are easily understood on the borderless airwaves that are the new medium of diplomacy. Hanan will always have her critics. Says one obviously jealous colleague, "She started as a translator for Faisal. Then she became the spokeswoman of the delegation. Now she's the spokeswoman of all the Palestinian people!" But for millions of Palestinians she is just what was needed to communicate their hopes and aspirations to the outside world. With the politics of the Palestinian struggle switching from war and violence to the equally hard-fought battle for public opinion, Hanan Ashrawi is a potent new weapon in the Palestinian arsenal.

Faisal Husseini

━━━━━━━━━

When the Soviet-built turboprop carrying Yasser Arafat crash-landed near the Libyan desert town of al-Khufrah, most of the world began writing his obituary. When more than nine hours after the crash there was no word from the plane or its occupants, those obituaries seemed set in stone. But one Palestinian did not believe the death notice. Faisal Husseini, the most prominent supporter of the pro-Arafat *Fatah* faction in the territories, told Israeli Radio that Arafat had miraculously survived.

Faisal's tone was confident but his heart was pounding. He desperately wanted to believe what the American consul in Jerusalem had told him: that the scruffy, sixty-two-year-old guerrilla leader was still alive, that he had walked away from the desert crash and had defied the fates once more. Yasser Arafat has always seemed larger than life; he often compares himself to the mythical phoenix that rises from its own ashes, the bird created by the Egyptians as a symbol of indestructibility. For Palestinians like Husseini, Arafat is the modern embodiment of their unbreakable dream—their phoenix, their hope, their claim that will not disappear.

When it was verified that their charismatic leader had indeed survived, the Palestinians were jubilant. At the National Palace Hotel in East Jerusalem, musicians dressed in black trousers, white shirts, red bow ties, and green cummerbunds—the colors of the Palestinian flag—played rousing Arab melodies while a young man furtively removed a Palestinian flag from beneath his shirt and waved it for a brief, exhilarating moment. Others in the street threw candy, and women undulated "in celebration for the safe return of Abu Amar."

Yet, in those tense early April hours when Arafat appeared to be dead, another reality set in: a sense of his mortality, a feeling that this small, bald, and bearded revolutionary, who for decades had seemed like a colossus on the world's stage, was suddenly reduced to size; that he had made his contribution to history and now appeared human; that even though he survived the crash, a myth was ending; that mixed with the jubilation was a pervasive sense of the passing of an era. One Israeli official even suggested that a new triumvirate had been secretly chosen to succeed the legendary Abu Amar (Yasser Arafat): in this supposed PLO troika were Farouk Kaddoumi (Abu Lutuf), Mahmoud Abbas (Abu Mazzen), and Faisal Husseini.

However, when Faisal received the news that Arafat had survived, he showed only relief. He told cheering Palestinians crowded into the spacious living room of his Wadi Joz home, "Ours is a great people capable of overcoming all problems. A people that can produce an Abu Amar can produce another. Still, thank God that he has spared us that test." Faisal did not have to draw comparisons between himself and the PLO leader; they were obvious. Arafat is theatrical and boastful, his voice often loud and abrasive; Faisal is soft-spoken and understated, with the modest style of a teacher, not that of a preacher. Arafat is the outcast, the perpetual refugee neatly clad in the drab olive fatigues of the fighter, the personification of the enduring Palestinian dream of one day being able to go home again to Palestine. Faisal Husseini is the embodiment of relinquishing the dream, the reminder of the daily truth that confronts the Palestinian people—that they may never be able to go back to their homes in Jaffa, Tel Aiv, and Haifa; that they will have to build a new home alongside the Jewish state of Israel.

If Arafat fits the Palestinian mold of the folk hero, Faisal is the antihero. He conveys quiet charisma and an authoritative air, often dressing casually in a sweatsuit or an open shirt to meet guests at his home or office. For years, while Arafat was flying in Gulfstream jets borrowed from Libyan leader Muammar Qaddafi or Saudi King Fahd, Faisal drove a used Fiat, an Autobianca, a car so small it reminded many of a golf cart. It seemed fitting therefore that Arafat, who spends much of his time in the air because he has no home, would escape death by plane crash. The irascible pride of Arafat's past suddenly contrasted with the humbling present of Faisal Husseini's: Faisal is a Palestinian rooted to East Jerusalem, a captive of the drudgery of a quarter century of Israeli occupation, whereas Arafat is a man who can travel freely, who has a house but no home, the earthbound descendant of a rich heritage, with his feet stuck in the ground of a Palestinian generation that, like the Jews, will never forget history.

For many Palestinians, particularly those who have grown up under occupation and now are in their late twenties or thirties, Faisal Husseini exemplifies their past, their pain, and their future. Despite their differences, the clean-shaven Faisal, who is so soft-spoken he sometimes speaks almost in a whisper, shares much of the same history with the brash, outspoken Arafat. Indeed, like Arafat, the Husseini family has been at the center of the modern struggle for Palestinian identity. Faisal Husseini—descendant of the Prophet Mohammed, son of the greatest Arab hero of the 1948 Arab-Israeli War, nephew of the grand *mufti* of Jerusalem whose zealous prosecution of the Arab cause made him a legend even among those who despised him—Faisal Husseini is the successor generation. Ask almost any Palestinian on the West Bank and you will be told Faisal is a nationalist, a pragmatist, and an aristocrat. Tall and broad-shouldered, his quiet bearing belies his stature, but his roots lie deep in the legend, lore, and religion of Palestine, stretching back to the beginning of the seventeenth century, when the post of *mufti* (the highest Muslim authority on religious law) of Jerusalem was held by Abdel Kader ibn Karim al-Din Husseini. Even though Abdel Kader died without a male heir, the Husseinis held other key religious posts, including *Naqib al-Ashraf* (Chief of the Prophet's Descendants) and *Sheikh al-Haramayn* (Keeper of the two Jerusalem mosques, al-Aqsa and Dome of the Rock), until the end of the eighteenth century. Then the family recaptured the post of *mufti*, which they held almost uninterruptedly into the twentieth century.

Since the end of the nineteenth century, the Husseini family has also had wealth. It owns property in the fashionable East Jerusalem neighborhood of Wadi Joz. The American Colony Hotel, once the fabulous home of a Turkish pasha and his three wives, sits on property owned by Faisal's grandfather. The New Orient

House, close by, was built by the Husseini family a few decades ago and is now home to his Arab Studies Society. And nearby is the small cemetery that protects the graves of Husseini family members. Faisal's lineage also reaches back to the founder of his faith. Unlike most Palestinians who trace their origin to the biblical Canaanite period but who were only Arabized after the Arab invasion of Palestine in 638 A.D., the Husseinis claim their descent directly from the Prophet Mohammed. Indeed, the two Palestinians who are most famous for fighting the Zionist threat in the mid-twentieth century are both Husseinis—Haj Amin Husseini and Abdel Kader Husseini—while a third, whose nickname has become synonymous with the more recent guerrilla struggle against Israel, also is a distant counsin. He is Mohammed Abder Rauf Arafat Kudwa Husseini, nicknamed Yasser (meaning "easygoing") Arafat.

Faisal remembers his cousin was one of the youngest recruits in his father's fedayeen army and would sometimes visit them at their home in the overcrowded Cairo suburb of Shubra. There, in his father's kitchen, the youthful Palestinians learned to make bombs and to defuse them; on different occasions Yasser and other students were secretly trained to be commandos by a German officer who had traveled with his great uncle Haj Amin to Egypt. "We started to understand what was going on in Palestine. We started seeing our father leaving, traveling, coming back," recalls Faisal. He was seven; he looked up to Yasser, his cousin, who was seventeen.

Sometimes his father would allow Faisal to join the older boys in cleaning the rust off the rifles and other weapons. Just like their father and his friends, the boys rubbed the grime off the tommy gun and the Sten gun and the British Bren until the submachine guns were as shiny as their father's glossy boots. "It was exciting to see that we were doing something that was supposed to be done by the older boys," recalls Faisal. Their favorite game was to clean carefully the old guns and then to pretend to shoot them, "without any bullets, of course, so there was no danger in this." The year was 1947 and his father Abdel Kader was still spending much of his time at home. He would leave for Palestine, where he led his fedayeen forces in strikes against the Jews, but would come back to Cairo, where he trained the young volunteers. His presence in

Egypt was important because the Palestinians needed guns almost as much as they needed guerrillas. The organized Arab legion of the neighboring Arab states wasn't sharing arms with the irregular fedayeen forces, and although both the Allied and the Axis troops had left behind vast quantities of vintage World War II weapons, procuring the arms was even more difficult than training the men. Buying arms was illegal, and the price often exorbitant. There were secret missions, meeting agents arriving from Palestine, their pockets stuffed with cash, to rendezvous with underground arms dealers in Cairo and Alexandria. From Cairo the weapons were smuggled out on airplanes owned by the Imam of Yemen to an old British airstrip in Jericho. There, after midnight, the arms would be loaded onto trucks by Abdel Kader's men.

Faisal's father often told his sons about their exploits and their victories, about the mystery and the adventure. However, the stories about the skirmishes against the Jews soon ceased to be fun for Faisal. His father started spending much more time in Palestine, and before long, relatives began congregating at the Husseini home. They seemed apprehensive. "One of my mother's cousins was killed during the war, and so we started to understand the meaning of war, the price of war not from far away but from near: a relative, the cousin of my mother and also someone we knew very well," recalls Faisal.

Indeed, by the fall of 1947 the fighting between the Arabs and the Jews had become so intense and widespread that it was clear to the British they would have to give up control of Palestine. In November the British announced they were withdrawing their administration from the mandate and asked the United Nations to take over. On November 29, 1947, with help from Swedish judiciary expert Emil Sandstrum, the U.N. General Assembly, meeting at Lake Success, New York, voted to end formally the British mandate and to partition Palestine into Arab and Jewish states. After much heated debate, the Jews accepted the plan. But the Arabs, infuriated that they should have to give up any of their land, rejected it flatly. Both sides prepared to escalate the struggle; they prepared for open warfare.

Under the direction of Abdel Kader, who headed the central command headquartered at Bir Zeit, north of Jerusalem, and Hassan Salameh in Ramle, the Arab fedayeen fortified their positions. In addition to smuggling weapons out of Egypt, they purchased arms from Transjordan, Iraq, Syria, and Lebanon. As the fighting intensified they gained important strategic territory. By the middle of March 1948 the Jews had suffered two setbacks that were as serious as any battlefield defeat. The British announced they had agreed to supply arms to Transjordan for the next twenty years. Then, on March 19, the United States proposed to the United Nations that, in view of the increasingly fierce fighting in Palestine, the partition plan be abandoned and a trusteeship be established for the entire country. The U.S. move was precipitated by the growing belief that the Jews could not successfully resist the Arabs and would not be able to maintain themselves as a state when the British left.

Especially vulnerable was Jerusalem, where the Jews were fighting desperately. The Arabs had many more arms and supplies; they had plenty of water, had control of the electricity, and, in effect, controlled the city. By the beginning of April 1948 Abdel Kader and his men were in control of the main highway linking Tel Aviv with Jerusalem. The British inspected the road and believed the Jews would not be able to get their convoys past the Arab roadblocks. The meaning was clear: Jerusalem was isolated.

Aware that the war could be lost if Jerusalem were suffocated, the Jews went on the offensive. They had received two large shipments of arms—several hundred light machine guns and thousands of rifles—sent secretly from Czechoslovakia. No more time could be lost. At the beginning of April they launched Operation Nachshon aimed at conquering the Arab villages that were serving as springboards for attacks on the relief convoys. On the eastern side their Haganah fighters blew up the Ramle headquarters of Hassan Salameh, the *mufti*'s commander in the area, killing some of his most important men. Then, two days later, on April 3, an Arab from the village of Abu Ghosh brought news that the women and children at Kastel were being evacuated and that only a small group of fighters remained. Kastel, an Arab village on the site of an old Roman fortress high up in the hills five miles west of Jerusalem, was vital because it controlled the approach to the city. The Jews had tried to take it once, but had failed when a Haganah commander slipped on a stone, his gun discharged, and the Arabs were forewarned of the impending attack.

Seeking to exploit their temporary weakness, the *palmach* (paramilitary Jewish force that was part of the British army) at Kiryat Anavim were ordered to attack Kastel that very night. They surprised the handful of fighters and forced them to retreat from the village. But the next morning the Arabs began a savage counterattack that continued throughout the day and well into the night. The Arabs were sure of victory and watched with joy as the Jews retreated. The next morning, April 5, in the dim light of early dawn, Meir, one of the Jewish commanders, took advantage of a lull in the fighting and went with two of his men to inspect the command post in the center of the enclave. He was wearing a British camouflage coat. Three men suddenly started to approach from behind enemy lines. They wore helmets, were dressed in khaki uniforms, and were armed. Believing they were part of the Haganah reenforcements he expected, Meir called out to them in a mixture of Hebrew and slang Arabic, "Come on, yah *jama'cah.*"

"Hello, Tommy," one of the Arabs called back in English, mistaking Meir for a British soldier. Sensing something was wrong, Meir raised his Sten submachine gun and shouted, "Put up your hands!" The men did not obey. They kept coming and Meir began shooting. One of them fell immediately; the other two escaped. Some of Meir's men went out to retrieve the body of the fallen Arab. He had been hit in the face by one of Meir's bullets. His features were barely distinguishable. But this was no ordinary fighter. He was armed with an American pistol, a British rifle, and an American submachine gun. In one of his pockets Meir found a leather wallet containing his identity cards. The dead man was Abdel Kader Husseini, nephew of the grand *mufti* and the military commander of the Palestinians. He had boasted that he would halt the convoys to Jerusalem and that he would hold Kastel, "the knife at the throat of the Jews."

Meir knew the Arabs would come for the body of their leader. He called for reinforcements, setting up a defense to hold the village. None came, but for the next day and night the Arabs came, in wave after wave, to recapture Kastel. In the fighting, Meir was killed. Finally, on April 9, Abdel Kader's body was recovered and at orders of the Haganah, the *palmach* again attacked Kastel. This time, there was little resistance. The Jews believed there had been a fight among the Arabs over who would succeed Abdel Kader and that their armies had dispersed in anger, taking their troops with them. In truth, they had quit Kastel to attend the solemn funeral of their greatest hero, in the Old City of Jerusalem. On the same day, seventy members of the extremist Jewish group the Stern Gang entered the Arab village of Deir Yassin, a few miles southwest of Jerusalem. The Jews believed the Arabs there harbored arms, guerrillas, and agents of the *mufti*. On this day most of them were attending Abdel Kader's funeral. The Sternists shot everyone they found in the village: 254 people were killed, many of them women and children. The massacre became a symbol of brutality; the fear that it could be repeated prompted 250,000 Arabs to take flight from their homes. They became the first Palestinian refugees.

Abdel Kader Husseini was immortalized in Palestinian lore for his courageous stand against the Jews, being accorded the Palestinian nickname of "the first *shahid* [martyr] of Palestine." But Faisal remembers when he first understood the meaning of his father's death. "I was at home and my elder brother, Moussa, came to me with the Egyptian newspaper," recalls Faisal Husseini. "Read the headline," the ten-year-old Moussa told him. When he did, his older brother asked him, "Do you understand what it says?" Faisal told him, "Yes I understand. It's about the Kastel battle." Then go and tell your younger brother, Moussa said, and the eight-year-old Faisal went off to tell his little brother, Reza, that their father was dead. He remembers that their mother, Wajiha, didn't cry, "at least not in front of us, so we didn't cry." But about three days later, when someone showed Faisal another newspaper story that the Egyptian government would take care of his family and provide them with free schooling, the little boy started to cry. "In the very moment, I felt the first real thing—that I really lost something, not that my father was killed in the war, that he is a national figure, or that he is a hero, but that I lost my father."

On the same day the news arrived of their father's death, ten-year-old Moussa moved to take his place at the head of the table. "He started to act as though he was responsible. For example, the rent for the house—he didn't allow anyone else to go and pay it but him," recalls Faisal. Thrust into his new role, Moussa no longer played games with his brothers, "but in this way he saved our childhoods; he gave us the opportunity to go on being children."

On May 15, 1948, when the British withdrew from Palestine and the Jews declared their state of Israel, Arab forces from Egypt, Iraq, Syria, Lebanon, and Transjordan attacked. The war was relatively short lived; the Arab armies disarmed the irregular Palestinian forces when they discovered they could not control them, and King Abdullah of Transjordan cut his own deal with the embryonic state, agreeing to a ceasefire inside Jewish territory when Golda Meir, a minister in the new Israeli government, promised the Hashemite leader a part of Palestine. Although a formal agreement was never reached, the talks played a significant role in easing hostility between the Hashemites and Israel, but only at the expense of the Arab nationalists—the Husseinis and Haj Amin, who were supported by the Egyptians. During the war, 700,000 Palestinians fled their homes, some going north to Lebanon and Syria, others south to Gaza, and yet others across the river into Transjordan. Ten months later, in February 1949, the United Nations concluded an armistice agreement between Israel and its bordering Arab neighbors—Egypt, Lebanon, Jordan, and Syria. The Palestinians had already dispersed throughout the area. They were homeless, stateless people wanting only to return to Palestine. They would never allow their Arab brothers, who had betrayed them, to forget their plight; they would never allow their enemy, Israel, to live in peace.

The Husseinis moved from Shubra to the slightly more affluent district of Zeitoun, but their Cairo home remained a magnet for the embittered nationalists. Haj Amin came regularly to look after the Husseini family, and with him, the youthful Arafat, who had just been elected to head the General Union of Palestinian Students (GUPS) at Cairo University. The teenage Yasser had worked diligently for Faisal's father, organizing students and, after he left school, training under his command in Cairo. Faisal was only nine, but he remembers Arafat coming to their house to coach him on how to speak to the crowds of Palestinians who would travel long distances to commemorate the anniversary of his father's death. Faisal read them a song his father had written. Composed as a conversation between a child and his mother, the lyrics said, "Talk to me about the land; is it right that the Zionists got our land? Give me my sword, Mother, and I will go and fight for our land."

For the next six years, until he was fifteen, Faisal traveled throughout Egypt, standing before gatherings of Egyptian notables and hundreds of Palestinian refugees, leading them in singing his father's words. "When I was nine years old," he says today with a laugh, "I was more courageous than when I was thirty or forty years old!" By the time he was fifteen Faisal was writing his own poetry, beginning to discover an identity apart from simply being the son of Abdel Kader. "I decided I am big enough now. I don't need to just read what my father wrote," he recalls. "Usually after this event, the next day in Cairo, a lot of people would come and spend the evening with us, including Yasser Arafat and Haj Amin Husseini," he says. He recalls that Arafat was working closely with the Muslim Brotherhood in Cairo, "although I don't think he was a member of them."

Arafat, he says, was particularly sympathetic to Haj Amin's plight, having tried in 1948, when the Jews declared their independence, to also set up an independent Palestinian government in Gaza. Called the All-Palestine Government, it claimed authority over all of Palestine. Haj Amin presided over an eighty-six member parliament, but the nascent entity was never given real power by the Egyptians, who governed Gaza, and was bitterly opposed by King Abdullah because it conflicted with his plans to annex the West Bank. Fearing the government-in-exile in Gaza contained the seeds for a Husseini-dominated state on the West Bank, Abdullah had himself acclaimed "King of Palestine and Jordan," appointing a longtime rival of the Husseini family, Raghib Nashashibi, as military governor of the West Bank. Abdullah also banned the use of the term *Palestine* and instead demanded that the 2200-square-mile territory be known as *the West Bank*. In April 1950 he formally annexed it to Jordan. Faisal regrets that his uncle Haj Amin failed, because, he says, "had he succeeded, we would have witnessed from the beginning the formation of two states, a Palestinian state and an Israeli state. Maybe then we would have stopped fighting each other and history would have been different." He adds, with a sigh, "There would not have been all these problems about who would represent the Palestinians." Fifteen months later, on July 20, 1951, a group of Palestinians, under the guidance of Haj Amin, assassinated King Abdullah while he was entering Al-Aqsa to pray. Among those tried and executed for the murder was a prominent member of the Husseini clan.

Faisal Husseini is familiar with the legacy of family squabbles and the fights between rival clans in this part of the world. His is one of only a handful of families—the Husseinis, the Nashashibis, the Dajanis, and the Khalidis—accorded the nomenclature of "notables," families that for centuries have been in ruling positions within both the political and the religious hierarchies of Jerusalem, the third-holiest city in Islam. Throughout the period of Turkish Ottoman and later British rule, these families were torn between the need to cooperate with their colonial masters and their battle to achieve independence from both their Arab and their European rulers.

The British and the Arabs, fighting together, ended 400 years of Turkish rule over Palestine. But Britain's subsequent bow to Zionist pressure, permitting the number of Jewish immigrants to Palestine to jump from a mere 4075 in 1931 to almost 62,000 in 1935, set the stage for a new, more violent struggle pitting the Palestinian Arab against both the British and the Jews. In 1882 there were only 25,000 Jews among the Muslim and Christian populations of Palestine; they represented only 5 percent of the 500,000 inhabitants. When the British first arrived in 1917, the Jews still comprised less than 20 percent of the population of Palestine. But by 1936 the Jewish presence had increased substantially: they represented almost a third of all the people living in Palestine and were a majority in Jerusalem, with 400,000 Jews living amidst 1 million Arabs.

From 1921 to 1937 Haj Amin Husseini was the *mufti* of Jerusalem, the founder of the Arab Higher Committee, and president of the Supreme Moslem Council. As the most widely recognized Palestinian nationalist of his era (he died in July 1974), he had a profound influence on Faisal, not only because of the untimely death of the younger man's father but also because of Haj Amin's prolonged involvement in militant activities against the Jews. That militancy reached its zenith during the three-year Arab Revolt, the series of disturbances that began when a general strike was declared by the Arab Higher Committee on April 19, 1936, following a train of events similar to the series of attacks and counterattacks that would ignite the Palestinian uprising, the *intifada*, in December 1987.

As chairman of the Arab Higher Committee, and bowing to pressure from a new Arab National Committee, which had called a strike in Nablus, Haj Amin ordered a general strike. The goals of the strike, clearly aimed at the British, were to halt Jewish immigration, to stop land transfers to the Jews, and to establish a national government with parliamentary representation. The *mufti*'s son, Muheideen Husseini, recalls: "Every Palestinian knew it was revolution. Every small child thought we were fighting the Zionists and the British, and we have to hurt them in any way we can." Like other youngsters in the Maghreb neighborhood of Jerusalem, Yasser Arafat, then only seven years old, put nails in the roads, slashed the tires of the British cars, and threw rocks.

The strike lasted six months but its impact lasted much longer. In October 1936 the leaders of Saudi Arabia, Iraq, Transjordan, and Yemen, at the behest of the British, asked that Haj Amin and his organizers end their rebellion. The following summer the British responded with a recommendation by an investigative committee headed by Lord Peel. The Peel Commission advocated partition of Palestine into three areas: a Jewish state, an Arab state that would be united with Transjordan, and a separate British-controlled zone that would include Jerusalem and Bethlehem. Although there was division between the Zionists and the non-Zionists in the Jewish Agency, Jewish leaders eventually accepted the plan on condition that they receive a sufficiently large area. The Arabs, however, rejected the concept of a divided land; they responded with increased violence and brutality.

Arabs attacked Jewish settlements, cut telephone wires, blew up bridges, derailed trains, and attacked police stations. An effective boycott of Jewish products cut considerably the income of Jewish merchants. Weapons were stolen from police stations, while more attacks were carried out by nationalist guerrillas against towns and government buildings. The revolution became widespread and well organized and even received financial and moral support from Syria, Lebanon, Transjordan, Saudi Arabia, Egypt, Iraq, and Yemen. To show their allegiance to the revolution's leaders, who wore the traditional Arab headdress, all Palestinians took to wearing the *kaffeyah*, which later became the trademark of Yasser Arafat. In an effort to contain the violence, the British assisted in training and arming the Jewish defense forces, disbanded the Supreme Muslim Council, and outlawed the Arab Higher Committee, arresting and imprisoning a number of strike leaders and deporting others. Fearful for his life, Haj Amin and his close followers fled from Palestine during the early days of September 1937, first to Lebanon and Syria, where he continued to direct the Palestinian uprising, and then, in 1939, to Iraq. It was here, a year later, that Faisal Husseini was born.

But even in Iraq, Haj Amin and Abdel Kader could not resist political activity against the British, and both were soon forced to flee again. Haj Amin went to Iran, where Reza Shah granted him political asylum. Abdel Kader was not as fortunate. The Iranians would only permit him to enter alone. He refused to accept asylum without the right to bring his small militia group with him. When the Iranians turned him down, he returned with them to Baghdad, where he was promptly arrested and imprisoned. In 1944, when Faisal Husseini was four years old, his father was released and the family—his wife, three sons, and a daughter—fled across the border to Saudi Arabia. "That was the only time that I remember seeing much of our father. It was when we were in Saudi Arabia," Faisal recalls. The Saudi regime of King Ibn Saud, anxious to maintain its neutrality in World War II, had refused to support the anti-British revolt in neighboring Iraq. Faisal, five at the time, recalls that neither his two older brothers, Haifa and Moussa, nor his younger brother, Reza, were allowed to attend Saudi schools, so their father, Abdel Kader, "was teaching us reading and writing and arithmetic at home." Finally, on January 1, 1946, King Farouk granted the family entry into Egypt.

It was in Cairo that they would be reunited with Haj Amin. The *mufti* had taken a different route. After a brief stay in Iran, he had moved to Italy, forming a friendship with Benito Mussolini. The *mufti* promised the Axis powers he would supply them with fighters; his recruits, mostly Muslims living in Yugoslavia, not only would fight in battle, but could perform vital military sabotage, disrupting British communications and cutting off the British supply of oil. Mussolini embraced the *mufti* and, in 1941, responded to his pleas by declaring "If the Jews want [a state] they should establish Tel Aviv in America." By April 1942 the *mufti* convinced both Hitler and Mussolini to support him and to agree to a secret document. In a letter addressed to Haj Amin and signed by German Foreign Minister Joachim von Ribbentrop and Italian Foreign Minister Count Galeazzo Ciano, the Axis powers promised to help the Arab countries with "every possible aid in their fight for liberation . . . as well as to the abolition of the Jewish National Homeland in Palestine."

In May 1942, only a few weeks after he received the confidential memorandum, the *mufti* and his associates settled in Germany and went to work helping the Nazis. On a radio program broadcast in Berlin and transmitted to the Arab world, Haj Amin called for his Muslim brothers' help: "Oh, Arabs, use and avenge your martyrs. Avenge your honor. Fight for your independence. I, *mufti* of Palestine, declare this war a holy war against the British yoke of injustice, indecency, and tyranny."

Haj Amin was also determined to stop the transport of German Jews to Palestine. The Nazis, concerned about the safety of German citizens living in Palestine, had struck a deal to exchange German and East European Jews for their own citizens. But in a letter to the German foreign minister, the *mufti* begged the Germans not to send 4000 Jewish children and 500 Jewish adults to Palestine; similar letters were sent to Romania, where 1800 Jewish children and 200 Jewish adults were about to be transported, and to Hungary, where 900 Jewish children and 100 Jewish adults were to be transferred.

By 1945, when the war ended with the Nazis' defeat, Haj Amin's efforts had come to naught. But he escaped formal charges by the Soviets and the Yugoslavs as well as attempts of Jewish groups to bring him to trial at Nuremburg and, after a search for safety, fled in disguise to Egypt. Ensconced so close to Palestine, and reunited again with Abdel Kader and his family, Haj Amin set to work once more to establish an independent Palestinian state. The Palestinians, like many Egyptians living under British rule, saw the English as an oppressive colonial power and the corrupt, pro-British monarchy of King Farouk as foisting a travesty on the Arabs. But their energies were now directed at the most immediate threat, the plan to partition Palestine into an Arab and a Jewish state.

From their Egyptian base, the members of the Arab Higher Committee began a new drive to oust the British from the mandate awarded to them by the League of Nations. Their immediate aim was to build a military force to counter the Jewish underground groups, which had been able to acquire arms for their own effort to drive the British out of Palestine. Zionists such as David Ben-Gurion, had organized the widespread Haganah; others, such as Menachem Begin, helped form the more radical Irgun; still others, such as Yitzhak Shamir, started the similarly extremist Lehi. In the years right after World War II, when tens of thousands of Jewish immigrants had come to Palestine illegally, the *mufti* and his colleagues appealed to Islamic interests to repel the Zionists. They not only recruited young Palestinians living in Cairo but roused the support of religious fundamentalists in Egypt who belonged to the underground Muslim Brotherhood.

As a teenager, Faisal Husseini supported the pan-Arab cause espoused by Gamal Abdel Nasser, believing it was the best vehicle for advancing the Palestinian cause. He opposed the more radical Islamic philosophy of the Muslim Brotherhood, which had sent several squads of volunteers to fight with the Arabs from Palestine in 1948 and had used violence and political assassination against the pro-British regime of King Farouk. But in 1961, after Syria seceded from the United Arab Republic, Faisal admits, he no longer held the same illusions about the willingness of Arab states to further the Palestinian cause. "I started to think like the way of Arafat" because "all of a sudden I discovered that all our work towards Arab unity, which we thought would lead us towards Palestine, just collapsed. I was working for the Egyptians within an Egyptian structure, and for the Syrians within a Syrian structure; but we, the Palestinians, where were we?" Nowadays he says Arafat was right in the 1950s to support the Muslim Brotherhood. "Arafat understood Haj Amin. Arafat was the new generation, and Haj Amin the old generation."

Faisal continued to travel back and forth to Jerusalem, spending the summers there, "sometimes with my mother, sometimes alone," and was anxious to return for good so he could administer the properties his family owned there. He finished high school in 1958, the same year the abortive union was formed between Egypt and Syria and the same year another organization began to take shape, the Palestine Liberation Movement (whose acronym in reverse is *Fatah*). "I went to Iraq, to the University of Baghdad, to study geology," recalls Faisal. His real intention, however, was to enroll in the Iraqi military academy, his father's alma mater. But nine months later, when a revolution erupted to overthrow the Iraqi monarchy, he was forced to return to Cairo and to resume his efforts to raise consciousness among Palestinian students "about our homeland, our hopes, and our history."

No longer able to ignore the demands of the refugees, and concerned that the terror tactics of *Fatah* and other guerrilla groups would lead them into an unwanted war with Israel, the Arab League, a loose confederation of fourteen Arab countries, including Egypt, Jordan, Syria, Iraq, and Lebanon, created a new body they hoped would channel Palestinian aspirations into political, not military, action. The new body was called the Palestine Liberation Organization—the PLO.

The PLO's founding conference took place in May 1964 in Jordanian-annexed East Jerusalem; its charter called for destruction of the Zionist state and for the establishment of a Palestinian entity. Egypt and Jordan insisted on the use of the word "entity"; both Arab nations feared an independent Palestinian state might threaten their own existence. Although he did not attend the first conference, Faisal Husseini immediately opened offices for the PLO at the Ambassador Hotel and then at the United Nations Relief Work Agency (UNRWA) building nearby.

Two years later, however, Faisal became frustrated with the fiery rhetoric of Ahmed Shukeiry, the PLO chairman. Shukeiry delivered impassioned speeches calling for the extermination of the Jewish state but did not appear to be achieving very much. Faisal decided to complete his military training. He left for Syria, where he was enrolled in the officers' school and soon was commanding a small squadron of thirty soldiers. It was, he says, "my father's will, my father's way."

When the war broke out against Israel in June 1967, the Syrians sent Faisal to Lebanon to recruit soldiers for the Palestine Liberation Army, the official fighting arm of the PLO, and, he acknowledges, "to try to start something there," presumably the opening of another front against Israel. Shukeiry gave Faisal the use of his estate above Beirut, in the Druze-controlled mountains near Kaifoun, to set up a guerrilla training camp. There he enlisted and trained more than 1200 men. But the Israelis' swift victory, routing the Arab armies in six days, once again doused the Arabs' hopes. Once more Faisal was forced to choose between the life of a guerrilla chieftain and the urgent task of helping to create an indigenous Palestinian leadership inside the territory Jordan had lost to Israel, the West Bank. "If I stayed outside, maybe I could reach some high position in the Syrian army, but I felt that I missed Jerusalem, so I decided to come back." A month after arriving in Lebanon he was on his way back to his homeland.

With his Jordanian passport, Faisal had no problem traveling to the Hashemite Kingdom. But with all of Jerusalem, even the Arab quarters of the Old City, now in the hands of the Israelis, there was only one way to return and that was to infiltrate illegally. He began his journey by car. But when he got to the east bank of the Jordan River, he got out, lifted his trouser legs, and tried to wade across the shallowest part of the narrow waterway, more a stream than a river. He walked about a hundred feet and then looked up, startled at the soldier in his path. "Halt!" the voice rang out in Hebrew. It was the first Israeli Faisal had met since he'd begun his guerrilla training. "I tried to have a conversation with him." But the border guard had his orders, so when Faisal kept advancing, he started shooting between Faisal's legs. "The next one will be through your eyes," the soldier said. Retreating, Faisal waited for several hours and then tried his luck again at a different site along the river. Again he was chased back. Finally, after two more attempts, he crossed into the West Bank and, on the fifth day after he'd left, reached Jerusalem.

By late July of 1967 Yasser Arafat also had infiltrated into the West Bank. Omar Khatib, a *Fatah* representative in Amman, recalls that in those days Arafat was not very well known and had not adopted the olive green uniform, checkered headdress, and pistol in his open holster that became the guerrilla's trademark. "He wore a white *kaffeyah* and regular pants and a shirt. He was without the beard," says Khatib. For several months Arafat skulked around the West Bank, sometimes dressed as a shepherd, other times as a physician, using aliases such as "Abu Mohammed" and Dr. Fawzi Arafat or simply "the Doctor." Arafat's job, says Khatib, was "organizing the infrastructure of *Fatah*. He organized the military missions. He was moving around from one house to another, meeting up with people and telling them what to do."

It was on one of these missions, in August 1967, that Arafat encountered the pupil he had coached in Cairo. "He saw me, he was in the car, and he saw me so he stopped and asked me to join him in his car. He asked me what I am doing here, and asked, 'Who sent you?' I said, 'Nobody sent me. I'm here because I want to be here. This is my land, my property is here, and my family is here,'" Faisal told him. Arafat brought Husseini to the Ramallah house where he was hiding. They started talking about the Israeli occupation. Arafat, who had his headquarters in a deserted building in the Casbah of Nablus, spoke of his duty to resume the guerrilla struggle because for the first time the Palestinians themselves were directly "facing the Jewish people." He told Faisal, "You have just finished your military training, so you can start training our people here right away." The idea wasn't exactly what the twenty-seven-year-old Husseini had in mind. He suggested his talents could be put to better use developing a political strategy against the occupation. Faisal was certain that Arafat was thinking "Was I talking this way because I believed in political activities or because I was afraid of military activities?" After more cross-examination, the two men reached a compromise. Its broad outlines, says Faisal, were that "if we found there were problems using political activities, then we decided we could start with military activities." Adds Faisal, "I tried to tell him that I wasn't afraid of weapons."

When he heard that, Arafat suggested Faisal could carry out a mission for him, one that would test his courage but not expose him to real danger. He asked Faisal to conceal a few weapons for him in his home in Wadi Joz near the Jerusalem broadcasting station. Faisal agreed. "He gave me two machine guns: a Russian Kalashnikov and a Czechoslovak Samosar." He brought the weapons home; slowly, carefully, took them apart; and stored the guns in a place where he thought they would not be found, secretly hoping he would never have to use them.

By mid-October of 1967 the pace of guerrilla activity on the West Bank had escalated sharply. *Fatah* had carried out more than sixty separate operations against civilian Israeli targets, bombing factories, homes, movie theaters, and bus terminals. Faisal tried to contact Arafat, wanting to know if he had abadoned their secret pact or needed the weapons he was storing. When he arrived at the Ramallah villa where he had met Arafat, Faisal discovered that the Israeli army had already been there and that the *Fatah* leader had fled the country for Jordan. "I started feeling that I am under someone's eyes, that someone is watching me," recalls Faisal. Two days later, as he strolled near his Jerusalem home, the police apprehended him. When they searched the house, they found the dismantled machine guns. Faisal was booked at Moscobiya Jail, the old Russian compound near the green line that divides East and West Jerusalem. Then the Israelis demanded Faisal take them back to the house in Ramallah where Arafat had been hiding. He will never forget the jeep ride.

With his hands tied behind his back, the scion of the famous Husseini clan says, he got a taste of frontier justice. He was beaten in the stomach, then in the chest, then once more in the stomach and then slapped again and again. "I tried to run away," he remembers. "I was handcuffed to two soldiers, and I jumped from the jeep, taking the two soldiers with me. I even tried to put my leg on the wheels so that they would run over me. It was more like suicide than running away." On his first two days in prison, the Israelis tried to force Faisal to identify other *Fatah* guerrillas and to confess that he was their ringleader. "They beat me and they made me hobble," he recalls. Suddenly it all stopped. "An officer came to me and told me that the government decided that it was forbidden for anyone to beat me or attack me and that I should complain if anyone dared to do such a thing." Earlier that morning, on his third day in prison, the Israeli government had discovered the identity of their new prisoner.

It was big news. The public had no idea that the disciple of such a notorious guerrilla hero was even living in their midst. "Jail for Son of Abdel Kader Husseini," screamed the headlines in Hebrew and in English. Another headline amused Faisal: "Israeli Police Capture Colonel." The news stories reported that he had been caught red-handed in his headquarters, that he held one of the highest ranks in the Syrian army, that several of his guerrilla lieutenants had also been apprehended, and that a huge cache of weapons had been seized. "I became a colonel," Faisal recalls in astonishment, "Colonel Faisal Husseini, the right hand of Ahmed Shukeiry, the new commander of *Fatah* in the area." In reality, he says, "I was an officer, but I was just finishing school and only had one star, the lowest rank in Syria. I was not the right-hand man of Shukeiry. I was not the leader of *Fatah* in the area. There was no cell; I operated alone, and the only thing they found were two old weapons. And they were in pieces."

He was sentenced six months later, on March 17, 1968, to a year in prison and two years of probation for "illegally possessing arms and ammunition." His lawyer, Shmuel Tamir, who later became an Israeli minister of justice, used the newspaper headlines to help persuade the military tribunal that Faisal had been arrested not for what he had done but as revenge against his father. Faisal told the court that he kept the weapons in his Wadi Joz home so that he wouldn't lose contact with other members of *Fatah*. Faisal read a statement in which he said the only means of achieving peace was through nonviolence. The prosecutor said that in light of both Faisal's lineage and his apparent commitment to peaceful political pursuits, he would drop the additional charge of "membership in an illegal organization." He noted that such a statement, "coming from a member of a highly respected Arab family, must carry considerable weight and should be encouraged."

Indeed, barely one week after he started to serve his sentence, Faisal told Amnon Rubinstein, a reporter for the Israeli newspaper *Ha'aretz*, of his willingness to recognize that the Jewish people had rights to a homeland in Palestine—provided they recognized that Palestinians had similar rights. It was an extraordinary statement, considering that less than four months later, in July 1968, the Palestine National Council would adopt its now-famous charter. That document declared the 1947 partition of Palestine and the establishment of the state of Israel "entirely illegal." It vowed to eliminate Zionism, which it described as "racist and fanatic in its nature, aggressive, expansionist, and colonial in its aims, and fascist in its methods." To achieve that purpose, the charter called on Palestinians to use "all possible means," including "armed struggle."

In the March 22, 1968, interview, Faisal already had formulated a view that was contrary to Article 6, the core principle of the Palestine National Charter: that only "the Jews who had normally resided in Palestine until the beginning of the Zionist invasion" had a right to remain "and will be considered Palestinians." He told the interviewer: "It's nonsense to separate, to make a distinction between the Jews who were born here and those who came here from overseas. Jews sit here naturally. They were born here, or they view this country as their natural home."

Here are other excerpts from this revealing interview that took place less than a year after the crushing Arab defeat in the June 1967 war and the reunification of Jerusalem:

Q. What was your reaction when you saw Jerusalem?

A. I was outraged when I saw my city, al-Quds [Arabic name for Jerusalem, meaning "the sacred"] under foreign rule, Israeli rule. A considerable part of it was taken in the past. Now everything was taken, and it's being named differently: "Urshalim" [the way Jews in Israel officially refer to Jerusalem in Arabic so as to avoid using the Arab name of al-Quds]. They are also changing the Arabic names of streets. They are forcing a foreign rule upon us. They are a forcing a foreign lifestyle upon us.

Q. Who will represent you?

A. We can't allow a group of notables to represent us, even if they want the best for Palestine. Even if it's a good group, they will fail in their mission, a dangerous precedent will be created, and then a group of opportunists and defeatists will emerge that will speak on our behalf. That's why we have to block the formation of such a group.

Q. Had we met a year ago, would you say the same things you are saying today?

A. No. We change all the time, and times are changing. In 1948 it was a war of a people in its country against foreign immigrants, Zionists. They came here knowing that we were here. Today, twenty years later, the situation has changed. Jews sit here naturally. They were born here, or they view this

country as their natural home. They are not
Zionists who came here against another
people. Today we do not have a war that has
to end with "throwing the Jews into the
ocean." And it's nonsense to separate, to make
a distinction between the Jews who were born
here and those who came here from overseas.
You see, I'm giving up my militant nationalism,
and I expect a similar gesture from you. We
both have rights over this land. History dictates
a war between us, but reality compels peaceful
coexistence.

In fact, even in 1968, a quarter of a century ago, Faisal Husseini
was contemplating forming his own political body inside the territories to represent the Palestinians there, an entity that would
be loyal to *Fatah* but would by its nature implicitly challenge the
PLO claim to speak on behalf of all Palestinians. He told Rubinstein: "We, the Arabs of Gaza, Nazareth, and all the territories that
are under Israeli rule, lack an organization that will lead us and
help us to avoid accepting the defeat, and accepting the fait
accompli that followed it. This organization must convince the
Jews that giving rights to the Palestinians does not mean a clash
with the Jews. Forming such an organization will create the chance
to solve the conflict through peaceful ways. It's important that
we have an organization of our own." Since he already had served
several months awaiting trial, Faisal Husseini was released exactly
one year after his arrest. He still remembers the date, October 24,
1968.

For the next eight years the Israelis devised another method
of keeping track of Faisal Husseini, less penal than the prison cell
but almost as efficient. They simply refused to issue him an identity card. With one, he was a person, listed by the census takers,
able to obtain yellow Israeli license plates that would allow him
to travel with less hassle at military checkpoints. With one, he
could vote in municipal elections, collect Social Security, organize
conferences, and conduct political activities without obtaining
a license from the military government. Under Israeli law, which
governs Jerusalem, he would be entitled to almost the same

judicial process as an Israeli; he could not be deported; his house could not be demolished; and he could, had he wanted to, even become a citizen of the Jewish state. Without an identity card, Faisal knew, he could not leave the country; he could not even walk freely in the streets, afraid that if he was stopped and asked to produce it, he would be arrested and sent back to Moscobiya. There he would explain who he was and why he did not have a card and eventually the authorities "would say yes, we know about you, okay, go home." But it wasn't easy. "Whenever I would see a soldier or a policeman or a checkpoint, I would start counting, thinking, "Will they stop me or won't they? Will they know my story or won't they? Will they arrest me or won't they?" He was arrested at least half a dozen times and even though he was treated better than most other prisoners, he often was forced to spend the night being interrogated at the police compound.

The 1970s were difficult years for Faisal. He had not completed his university degree, and without an identity card it was almost impossible to find work. Of course, his family earned a comfortable income from the real estate revenues and rents they received, but Faisal did not want to be dependent on them. At first he became a merchant, selling homemade marmalade. Then he tried to open a dealership selling tractors to the Palestinian farmers in Gaza. But he needed to raise a lot of capital and he couldn't. By 1973 "I was broke," he insists, and had to turn to his family. For the next five years he worked as an x-ray technician at a Jerusalem clinic owned by one of his relatives. His son, whom he named Abdel Kader, was born in 1976. Since then, Faisal has carried the nickname of *Abul Abed*, the shortened Arabic version for "father of Abdel Kader." A year later, in 1977, he finally obtained the small I.D. card with the official imprimatur of the Israeli authorities stamped over his likeness. This photo, he thought, was a fitting reminder of the occupation. But, at least in official Israeli eyes, he finally existed and could begin a new life.

Becoming a full-fledged Jerusalem resident, however, did not ease the pain of occupation. When his mother died in 1984, Faisal asked Rafi Levy, the administrator of the Jerusalem district for the Israeli Interior Ministry, for permission to bring her body back from London for burial. Levy granted it. "But a few hours later he called back and said, 'Your mother was the wife of Abdel Kader Husseini.

State security forbids her being buried here.' So I said to him, 'If the body of a dead woman endangers the security of Israel, then tell me, what are your security demands from the Arab world?' "

Despite Faisal's bitterness, some Israeli leaders began to regard him as a useful counterweight to Yasser Arafat, particularly after the collapse in 1982 of Israeli-Egyptian talks on Palestinian autonomy. The peace process appeared deadlocked. A new national-unity government was formed in Israel in 1984 that installed Shimon Peres as prime minister for the first two years and his Likud rival, Yitzhak Shamir, for the final twenty-four months of the term. In the spring of 1985 and in Paris in October, Peres had secretly held talks with Jordan's King Hussein that were part of an effort to persuade him to reincorporate parts of the occupied territories into his Hashemite kingdom. When the talks culminated in an agreement between Peres and Hussein, signed in London in April 1987, to convene an international conference on the Middle East conflict, it became a challenge to Prime Minister Shamir—whose party had an ideological claim to Judea and Samaria and feared that an international conference would force Israel to abandon the West Bank—to develop an alternative strategy.

Faisal Husseini was also becoming exasperated at the Israeli courtship with Jordan and the PLO's failure to do anything about it. In an interview with noted Israeli correspondent Ehud Ya'aari, the West Bank leader expressed some of his frustrations toward both the Jordanians and the PLO. "Until lately, Palestinians here said to themselves, there is a PLO. There is Arafat. There are those who are deciding what to do and how to do it. But in the last year people feel everything is over. The PLO isn't there. The Palestinian state has been taken off the agenda. King Hussein's officers will come back together with [Meir] Kahane's thugs! Suddenly people understand that our situation is going to get much worse and that all their dreams have been shattered. People hear and see the hatred raining down on them from TV screens and it makes them jump." Then, in an allusion to Shimon Peres, whose Labor Party had at least been committed to a territorial compromise, Faisal warned: "This can happen even at a time when you are being treated with a gentle hand and in a liberal manner. Louis XVI was better to his people than his predecessors, but he was the one who went to the guillotine!"

Faisal's words were prophetic. At an Arab summit in Amman in the spring of 1987, the Palestinian issue was hardly mentioned (King Hussein even snubbed Arafat at the airport). And when U.S. President Ronald Reagan and Soviet leader Mikhail Gorbachev met in June, the Middle East also got short shrift. Events thus conspired to make Faisal attractive to the Likud coalition (Shamir saw in him the possibility of outflanking Peres in his efforts to court Jordan) at the same time that the Likud became attractive as a possible partner to Faisal. He knew the coalition of right-wing parties, headed by Likud, had an irredentist biblical claim to the West Bank and therefore supported the expansion of settlements throughout what it called *Eretz Israel*, or "Greater Israel." But Faisal also had seen Shamir's mentor, Menachem Begin, abandon both strategic airfields and civilian settlements in returning the Sinai to Egypt. He had seen how skillfully Begin, the ideologue, had won the support of even hardline elements of his constituency for sacrificing territory and forcing Jewish settlers to abandon their settlements. He had seen Begin sign the 1978 Camp David accords and make peace with Egypt.

So when Faisal received a phone call inviting him to join a new effort to negotiate peace with the Likud, he cautiously welcomed the initiative. The call, in July 1987, came from Sari Nusseibeh, a Palestinian political analyst and Birzeit professor. It came less than twenty-four hours after Faisal was released from another term of administrative detention. When Nusseibeh informed him he had held preliminary talks with Moshe Amirav, a member of the Likud central committee, Faisal immediately welcomed the initiative. Perhaps, he thought, the Likud could be coaxed into opening its own channel with the PLO. It was inconceivable that Amirav could have made such an approach without Shamir's knowledge. And regardless of the outcome, the prospect of peace talks with the Likud seemed far preferable to being coerced back under the vehemently anti-Arafat tutelege of King Hussein.

When Amirav arrived a few days later at Nusseibeh's home for the first of more than a dozen meetings that summer, Faisal recalls, they shook hands and were escorted outside to a large, shaded veranda where the three of them were introduced to two others, an Arab and an Israeli, who had helped arrange the meeting. They were peace activitist David Ish-Shalom and Salah

Zuhaika, editor of the pro-PLO newspaper *As-Sha'ab* ("The People"). "I shook hands with everyone, and he [Amirav] said, 'Faisal Husseini?' I said, 'Yes.' He said, 'Moshe Amirav.' We started talking in Hebrew, but the others didn't know Hebrew," recalls Faisal. "So we talked English." The first meeting was a discussion of the basics. At their next meeting Amirav provided them with a copy of a proposed document for expanded Palestinian self-rule in the West Bank and Gaza Strip, a formula that skirted the explosive issue of statehood but would, the Israeli argued, put the Palestinians on the road to self-determination. The plan for a three-year period of autonomy included several features that had been omitted from the Camp David model, notably the creation of a demilitarized Palestinian "entity" that would have its "administrative" capital in East Jerusalem and many of the trappings of nationhood: a flag, an anthem, its own currency, a broadcasting station, and its own identity cards. At the end of the interim period, Israeli-Palestinian talks would commence on the "final status" of the territories, as outlined in the earlier Camp David accords.

Amirav explained that their negotiations were aimed at creating a basis for an eventual meeting between Shamir and Arafat and that the memorandum they would draft would be based on the following principles:

- There could be no peace without the Likud and the PLO.

- The Israelis and the Palestinians had been fighting each other for dozens of years, and two items were nonnegotiable: that Israel was entitled to live within secure and defensible borders in the state it formed in 1948, and that the Palestinians could not be asked to abandon their claims to some part of the territory they inhabited in 1948.

- Any solution that did not recognize the right of Israel to exist, or the right of the Palestinian people to eventually exercise their self-determination, would be worthless.

In the course of the next several weeks both sides agreed

that, during the three-year interim, practical measures would be implemented to reduce tension: Israeli troops would withdraw from populated towns and villages to specific security zones; Palestinians would refrain from acts of violence provided Israel agreed both to cease building new settlements and to admonish its settlers to refrain from attacks on Palestinians; finally, direct peace talks would get under way between Israel and the PLO immediately after the two sides exchanged pledges of mutual recognition. The final step was crucial. "We told them, 'No Jordan.' We told them that there is no way, if you really want to make peace, to do it with Jordan," recalls Faisal. As the talks dragged on into their second month, however, he began to harbor serious doubts about whether they really had Shamir's backing. "Amirav told us this piece of paper has been seen by Prime Minister Shamir," says Faisal, "that Shamir was the head of a certain new stream inside the Likud, and that he wanted to end his political career with something dramatic. Just as Begin had made peace with the Egyptians, he said, Shamir wanted to make peace with the Palestinians."

The extent to which Shamir actually encouraged Amirav still is a mystery. Amirav reported regularly on his contacts to Ehud Olmert and Dan Meridor, two Knesset members who were proteges of Shamir. They presumably briefed the prime minister. Olmert also met with Nusseibeh for several hours of talks but later denied that they had discussed the secret peace plan. Meanwhile the talks themselves were floundering. Amirav would not agree to include the trappings of statehood during the initial three years in which the Palestinian self-governing authority would rule the territories. "He told me," says Faisal, "that with coins and flags, with a foreign office and economic offices outside, all the people will understand that this already is a state."

By August 24 the two sides were nearing completion on the memorandum. Faisal suggested they refer their remaining disagreements to Arafat, who was scheduled to be in Geneva in early September attending a United Nations conference. Amirav, however, suggested Faisal get permission from Arafat for a delegation of local Palestinian leaders to meet first with Shamir. "They started asking me if I would like to create the delegation and to go and meet with Shamir. They even started asking if I could give them the names of the delegation," says Faisal. "I told them that before I would do such a thing, I would have to get the complete blessing of the PLO, not just a green light, and I told them that I hope you, Moshe Amirav, like me, believe your leadership is strong enough, and has enough courage, to meet with me and Arafat in order to ratify this agreement." Neither meeting ever took place.

On August 26, 1987, Faisal Husseini was imprisoned. As his hands were tied behind him, he snapped at the Israeli policemen who had come to arrest him: "You're sabotaging a political initiative you know nothing about!" In fact, the *Shin Bet* (Israeli FBI) had checked with Shamir before ordering his arrest and had received no orders to cease or desist. The initial orders were to lock up Husseini for ten days, long enough for him to miss the planned Geneva rendezvous. Nusseibeh was left as the only member of the Palestinian team that showed up in Geneva. Amirav also canceled his trip there, leaving David Ish-Shalom as the lone Israeli to meet Arafat. Faisal remains convinced to this day that even though Shamir may not have been "informed of all the details," he knew about the initiative and cynically exploited it so that he could fend off both internal Labor Party pressures for an international conference and external pressures to deal directly with the PLO.

In fact, when a few days after Faisal's initial detention Shamir traveled to Bucharest, he produced the Amirav document—entitled "A Framework for Peace in Greater Israel"—for Romanian president Nicolae Ceausescu. "Don't push us to establish relations with the PLO," Shamir told him. "As you can see, we have relations with the [West Bank] Palestinians." Ceausescu shot back that he had already seen the memorandum. "He told him Arafat was here some days ago and showed him the same paper," says Faisal. Arafat had picked up a copy of it while on an official visit to India. "This was the end. He didn't dream Arafat was involved. I was arrested immediately afterwards." Shamir subsequently denied any complicity in or knowledge of the entire affair. His statement said: "Messrs. Husseini and Nusseibeh, who are known to be PLO men, exploited Amirav's naivety, but this has nothing to do with the Likud, which is united in its negative attitude towards the PLO." Within days, Amirav was expelled from the Herut Party and the Likud-led coalition. For his role in organizing the initiative,

Nusseibeh's arm was broken by Birzeit militants, and Faisal Husseini languished in jail much longer than he had expected. He was sentenced to two consecutive terms of administrative detention. When he was finally released in June 1988, he had served ten months in prison, regaining his freedom seven months after the start of the *intifada*.

The Amirav affair taught Faisal several lessons, among them that he would have to act unilaterally if he wanted to advance the goal of Palestinian statehood. But it also served as a kind of political baptism with the Likud. It reinforced his conviction that the right-wing coalition would respond to overtures that tended to promote the indigenous Palestinian leadership of the West Bank and Gaza Strip at the expense of Yasser Arafat and his PLO cadres in faraway Tunis. When he was released in the early summer, Faisal went to work at once on a new document that would achieve both objectives: to help insulate the Palestinian cause from Israeli politics, and to promote the political power of Palestinians inside the territories.

The result was a plan for the proclamation of Palestinian independence with a provisional government that, while headed by Yasser Arafat, would derive the bulk of its authority from a legislature made up of—and solely elected by—Palestinians living under occupation. This "Plan for Making a Declaration of Independence," which subsequently became known simply as the "Husseini document," was a natural outgrowth of the street revolt against Israeli rule. It was, in fact, a very deliberate effort to channel that popular uprising into a political structure that would help vent the anger of Palestinians while advancing their cause through less violent means.

Such a unilateral step, however, was more than the Israeli body politic could stomach. In Israeli eyes, any move toward Palestinian self-government that did not emanate from a negotiated accord with the Jewish state threatened both the legitimacy of the Israeli presence and the ability of the Israeli military and civil administrations to govern. Israel would never permit a Palestinian state to be created as a de facto reality; to do so would expose the Israelis to their greatest fear, that they could no longer unilaterally dictate the terms for safeguarding their own security.

On July 31, 1988, less than two months after he had been

released from prison and only an hour after King Hussein dramatically announced he was renouncing Jordan's claim to sovereignty over the West Bank, Faisal Husseini was arrested. Only seventy-two hours earlier he had traveled to Tel Aviv to appear with three Israeli politicians in the latest of several personal efforts to persuade the Israeli public of his moderate stance. His arrest, however, came as no surprise to the Palestinian leader. "I've been expecting you," Faisal told the policemen who forced their way into his home. A small suitcase filled with the things he needed to take with him was already packed.

The practical impact of the unilateral Jordanian disengagement was minimal. It meant that 16,000 Arab employees of the civil administration would no longer receive stipends from the Hashemite kingdom and that Palestinians appointed to represent the territories would be dismissed from the Jordanian parliament. But it was a crushing blow to the Labor Party's long-held view that the only road to resolving the Palestinian dispute ran through Amman, that a joint Israeli-Jordanian condominium eventually could be created to control Palestinian aspirations. Faisal knew he was being arrested for another reason: King Hussein's cutting of ties to the West Bank forced the PLO to take over the political and administrative responsibility for Palestinian institutions, from universities to *waqfs*—the Muslim charitable institutions—and that he, Faisal Husseini, was the PLO's most important surrogate in the territories. He knew his arrest was intended to send a message to the PLO that Israel would not tolerate any more unilateral moves. But he also knew that the cadres of street fighters had won their most important victory since the *intifada* began. Regardless of what the Israelis did to enforce their authority, the West Bank and Gaza now were, in the minds of their most important constituency, the people living there, independent of foreign rule. It remained for them to formulate a plan to govern themselves and, of course, to get rid of the Israeli occupiers.

The confiscation that July night of the "Husseini document" in the offices of the Arab Studies Society, and Faisal's sentence to another six-month term of administrative detention, put the kabash on plans to convene an assembly on the *Haram a-Sherif* ("Noble Sanctuary") to declare Palestinian independence. But neither move would be able to suffocate the growing awareness among Palestinians that the fulfillment of their aspirations for statehood was now in their own hands and not in those of self-serving Arab leaders. In November 1988, with Husseini back in jail, the Palestine National Council, meeting in Algiers, proclaimed an independent Palestinian state. A month later, in Geneva, Arafat announced PLO recognition of Israel and renounced terrorism. Nusseibeh contended the Palestinians of the West Bank and Gaza should move without delay to build the infrastructure and institutions that would accompany statehood.

Faisal Husseini takes a few steps away from the guests assembled on white jacquard sofas and overstuffed arm chairs in the stylish salon of his Wadi Joz home and, signaling his intent to maintain the confidentiality of his conversation, walks into the adjoining hallway, a portable cellular phone held tightly to his ear as he listens intently to the grievance of the caller. The living room is filled with people, some there to urge his intercession in family disputes, others to ask him to visit their village to help assuage a parent demanding revenge for the assassination of a son, alleged to have been an Israeli collaborator, or to settle some other feud. Outside, in the reception area, a diplomatic emissary awaits the signal that Faisal is ready to receive the envoy who has been instructed to deliver his message directly to the West Bank leader. Although the territories are highly politicized, what still bonds people together are family ties, the loyalty to a clan rather than to any political entity.

As he listens to the caller, Faisal knows how little has changed from the Ottoman era, when the *qadi* (an authority in Islamic law) would adjudicate family quarrels. His parlor has become a kind of family court. But he also has become the instrument of change, the politician who has to persuade his people to put their national interests above their sectarian ones, who has to meld a constituency for the peace process in a climate where hate, revenge, and murder—not ballots—still dominate the political landscape. He does not recoil from the task; it is part and parcel of the mission he inherited from his father, the war hero, from his great uncle, the grand *mufti*, and from the succession of Husseinis who were mayors of Jerusalem or held other high municipal posts during the mandate period.

Yet the task often seems daunting, certain to make him as many enemies as supporters. He found that out in the fall of 1991 when he had to mold a single delegation of Palestinians for the Madrid peace talks and was forced to steer a course that met the demands of three parties that do not agree with, much less talk to, each other: the United States, the PLO, and Israel. At the time, the price of such accommodation seemed high: for a Palestinian admission ticket to Madrid, there could be no PLO officials, no Palestinians from outside the occupied territories, and no Palestinians from Jerusalem. Faisal knew he was exposing himself to charges of breaking the umbilical cord with Tunis, of kowtowing to the Israeli catechism that Jerusalem is not a part of the West Bank, and of implicitly conniving in an arrangement that would divide the diaspora of 4 million Palestinians living outside the territories from the 1.7 million Palestinians in the West Bank and Gaza Strip.

Nevertheless, the potential rewards seemed to outweigh the risks. The Palestinians needed to convert their victories on the *intifada* battlefields into a process that would advance their nationalist goals; they needed to recover from the public relations disaster caused by their widely perceived support of Iraqi dictator Saddam Hussein; above all, they needed to stop Israeli settlement activity that threatened to change the demographics of their homeland, robbing them of what could be their last chance to prevent the incorporation of the West Bank and Gaza Strip into the state of Israel. For all these reasons, and to win the backing of the United States (the only remaining superpower and the only country that, in Palestinian eyes, could help "deliver" Israel), Faisal knew he really had no other choice. But comprehending the reality of their plight and successfully merchandising it among a disparate and divided populace were two different things. The latter proved harder than Faisal thought.

He intended to build broad popular support for the Palestinian delegation to Madrid by blending intellectuals with freed prisoners. Among them would be veterans of the 1985 swap engineered by Ahmed Jabril, the Damascus-based leader of the Popular Front for the Liberation of Palestine-General Command (PFLP-GC), in which Israel released some 1000 security inmates for six Israeli soldiers captured during the 1982 war in Lebanon.

Ha'aretz columnist Danny Rubinstein writes that Faisal wanted to combine the wisdom and learning of graduates of Birzeit University, the Harvard of the territories, with the experience and common sense of Palestinians who had suffered at the hands of the Israelis, "graduates of the university of the occupation." When anyone asked who was responsible for coordinating political activity during the uprising, one often heard the joke "The head is the head of Birzeit and the hands are the hands of Jibril's released prisoners." The delegation would, Faisal hoped, reflect the *intifada* itself.

Once a consensus was reached with Faisal's advisers inside the territories, he cleared the list with the PLO. To win its support, Faisal used two of the most prominent deportees as middlemen with Arafat: Akram Hanieh, a personal aide to the chairman, and Jabril Rajoub. Both men had impeccable credentials inside the territories. Both had been deported by the Israelis for allegedly helping to plant the seeds for the intifada. Hanieh had been editor of *As-Sha'ab*. Rajoub was freed in the Jabril exchange. Both also were members of *Fatah*, the mainstream faction to which Faisal owed his allegiance. There were, to be sure, squabbles with Tunis; at first the PLO demanded that Elias Freij be included in the delegation because of his international standing as the mayor of Bethlehem and his close ties to Jordan. Freij was a part of the original group; he was later dropped, a sign of the growing independence of Husseini and Sari Nusseibeh, his second-in-command, then reinstated at the urging of the PLO.

Faisal Husseini was aware of opposition to the talks with Israel. On October 22, 1991, the PFLP and Nayef Hawatmeh's wing of the Democratic Front for the Liberation of Palestine (DFLP) declared their "strong oppposition to those who have bowed down to the Israeli and American conditions." The two groups had joined with *Hamas*, the Islamic fundamentalists, in distributing a leaflet that ordered a general strike for the next day. Their joint aim was to protest the peace conference. Many did not heed the order, however, and schools, businesses, and bus and taxi companies continued to operate. But Faisal was concerned. He told a crowd of 300 people that day that "what is important is to limit our differences to the walls of the Palestinian house and to manipulate them in a democratic way. We have to prepare ourselves for a state where there is more than one thought."

Only hours before he announced the names of the Palestinian delegates who would be traveling to Madrid, Faisal also granted an interview to the *Jerusalem Post*, an English-language daily that often reflected the views of Israel's ruling Likud government. For years Faisal had understood the need to allay the fears of the Jews, to speak to them directly about his own hopes and fears, as he often did when he appeared before audiences in Israel and addressed them in Hebrew. *Post* reporter Joel Greenberg asked Faisal if he felt Palestinian participation would change "your relationship to the Israelis, who will now be dealing with you diplomatically, as an opposite number." Faisal immediately grasped the importance of the question. "It certainly is a new era," he replied. "We will be talking with Israelis to create a relationship of mutuality." He added: "Palestinians and Israelis will be sitting as equals to talk business."

Winning Israeli recognition as a separate but equal delegation would be a Palestinian goal at Madrid. Israeli Prime Minister Yitzhak Shamir and the foreign ministers of Egypt, Syria, Jordan, Lebanon, and the United States, and the Soviet Union would be addressing the conference. And so would the representative of Palestine. Faisal had won a pledge from the U.S. and Soviet cosponsors that even though the Palestinians would attend as part of the Jordanian delegation, their chairman, Haidar Abed el Shafi, would be allowed equal time to deliver his own speech.

"Isn't the PLO participating in the process by remote control?" Greenberg wanted to know. "Aren't you his nominee?" "Call it what you want," Faisal shot back. "There are realities that can't be obscured by wearing glasses of a different color. You can change glasses, but you can't change the real world." What, then, had changed that persuaded the Palestinians to pick up an offer they had spurned since Camp David, namely, to negotiate with Israel for an interim period of self-rule and autonomy? Faisal's answer is revealing. It demonstrates his ability to make the same reality fit his new purpose, to advance the cause of the "insiders" even if it means alienating Tunis: "I was stranded in the desert. Someone brought me a lifeboat and told me to use it, but I rejected the ridiculous offer. Then came a big flood, and I found that I could use the boat that had once been an absurdity. Maybe I don't like everything about the boat, but I could utilize it to move elsewhere, toward my goal. I was right to reject the boat then, and I'm right to accept it now. Many things that seemed impractical in those days are now useful."

In this brief interview, Faisal had summed up a dramatic shift in Palestinian politics. In 1978 it was "impractical" for any West Bank leader to challenge Arafat's grip on the PLO. But the *intifada* and the Gulf War changed that. Since the start of the uprising in December 1987, more than 1000 Palestinians, including many young men and women, had been killed; the Palestinians had proved to the outside world, and to themselves, that they were prepared to pay a heavy price for their freedom. By early spring of 1991, with the *intifada* entering its fifth year, it was evident that Tunis could no longer veto decisions of the local leadership.

The first sign that the balance of power had shifted decisively toward the insiders occurred in March 1991, only weeks after the end of the Gulf War, when a Husseini-led group defied long-standing PLO policy and met with U.S. Secretary of State James Baker in East Jerusalem. The PLO now had to decide: either support the pivotal meeting or be left outside the new consensus. The *intifada* created the constituency, but it was the Gulf War that permitted the local leadership to mobilize Palestinians behind a peace process. The PLO had tied its mast to Saddam Hussein; his humiliating defeat meant that Yasser Arafat no longer could count on the support of Saudi Arabia and other wealthy Arab benefactors among the oil-rich sheikhdoms of the Persian Gulf. These nations were now beholden to the United States for liberating Kuwait and defending them against Iraqi aggression. Consequently they were prepared to support a new U.S. initiative to resolve the Arab-Israeli conflict and the Palestinian problem at its heart.

As he prepared to leave for Madrid, Faisal told the crowded news conference: "I am not in the need of tanks to achieve victory. Rather, I need to prove to Israel that it cannot be the sole ruler on the ground at a time when there will be negotiations. The aim of all Palestinians is to get rid of the Israeli occupation as a way to establish the independent Palestinian state." At age fifty-one, Faisal Husseini had a chance to fulfill the legacy he had inherited from his family. Like that childhood moment when he stopped chanting the words of his father and composed his own song, he was ready to emerge from the shadows of his past and to help write the script for Palestinian success on the world stage.

On Sunday, November 10, 1991, the hope sparked at Madrid was felt in the streets as two buses of Palestinians, carrying the four-teen negotiators and the two advisory teams, crossed the Jordan River. The mood was celebratory as people poured out to welcome them. But less then two months later, the atmosphere had changed.

On December 30, 1991, Faisal planned to address a rally in Tulkarm, one of a series of speeches he was giving to drum up support for the peace process. Tulkarm is located on the "green line" that separates Israel from the West Bank. Even in the days of the Ottoman Empire it was a traditional marketplace for the Jewish towns and villages along the border. Later, Israelis bought their fruits and vegetables in the Arab markets. But in recent years the 40,000 Palestinians in Tulkarm have become increasingly divided between supporters of *Fatah* and supporters of the Islamic Resistance Movement, whose acronym in Arabic is *Hamas*, or "zeal." In the past, religion and politics always coexisted here. The railroad that took believers to Mecca, the *Haj al-em* ("Route of the Haj"), ran through Tulkarm. But its abandoned tracks now seemed a silent reminder of the city's position straddling the extremes of Palestinian politics. One of Tulkarm's two large refugee camps, *Nur-Shams* ("Sunlight"), sits astride the tracks and is a hotbed of *Hamas* support. Here Taqi al-din Nabhani, the founder of the Islamic Liberation Movement in Jordan, was reared. But here, too, Hilmi Hanoun, Tulkarm's mayor, serves as the longest pro-*Fatah* mayor still in office in the West Bank.

For Faisal, the task of trying to unite all the factions behind his leadership is a daunting one. The opposition from PFLP and DFLP-Hawatme followers is political and secular. But the opposition of *Hamas* is rooted in religion and fanaticism. Accord-ing to the fundamentalist interpretation of Islamic law, the entire land of Palestine belongs to the Muslims. Therefore any attempt to negotiate a territorial compromise with Israel is treason: Israel must be replaced by an Islamic republic. "I went to Tulkarm a little early because I was worried about the whole business," admits Faisal. He traveled in a car marked with the insignia of the Red

Crescent, the Arab Red Cross. When a few rocks were hurled at his car as he neared Gamal Abdel Nasser Square, his concern changed to fear. "I came back and told our people, 'Go and control the whole area. If more preparations or additional safeguards need to be made, let's cancel it.'" But Adnan Dmeiri, the pro-*Fatah* organizer of the rally at Tulkarm's theater, a large, square building with light-blue metal doors, wasn't worried. "We have taken all the necessary precautions," he told Faisal.

Adnan Dmeiri, a short, slim, slightly balding Palestinian with a black mustache, was experienced in politics. Between 1975 and 1981 he was imprisoned throughout the West Bank, in Nablus, Tulkarm, Janin, and Faryouna. The chain-smoking Dmeiri had also served three terms of administrative detention at Ansar 3 near Ketziot in the Negev desert. There he was elected by the other prisoners *shawish of the shawishes* ("sergeant of the sergeants"), the chief Palestinian authority in the prison camp. He felt he could handle any disturbances at the theater. To ensure a fair airing of the issues, he even promised a Birzeit professor, a *Hamas* supporter, equal time to respond to Faisal's speech. But the trouble began when *Fatah*'s security patrol began admitting only people it recognized, people who were known supporters of the mainstream PLO group. A protest erupted outside the theater, near a wall scrawled with graffiti that read, "No For The Conference," a reference to the Madrid peace conference, and was signed "*Hamas*." Finally, a compromise was reached. *Hamas* supporters would sit upstairs in the loge and *Fatah* supporters downstairs in the orchestra.

Everything seemed under control. Faisal began his speech, but catcalls began being yelled at him from the balcony. "Surrender! Surrender!" the *Hamas* supporters screamed. "You have sold out Palestine to the Jews!" Faisal had enough. "Let us end it now," he told Dmeiri. But there was no more time. "Suddenly someone in the balcony started smashing the neon lights and throwing them on the people downstairs. Then they pulled the seats out, broke the cement under them, and started throwing rocks. In the beginning I did not believe it," recalls Faisal. "They were free to do whatever they wanted. No one could reach them. They were controlling the whole place." His bodyguard tried to shield him and the others on the stage. "We had to put chairs over our heads. There were so many rocks. If there were no chairs, I would have been killed." Finally Faisal extricated himself and got to his car. As he sped off, he looked back in horror. "There were fights everywhere."

The next day, December 31, the score was settled. Jaber Dmeiri, a *Hamas* supporter and a cousin of Adnan Dmeiri, was murdered by a *Fatah* stalwart as he left the mosque in the Tulkarm refugee camp. Both the attacker and his victim were only nineteen years old. Israeli newspapers said the attack was ordered by the Black Panthers, *Fatah*'s strike force. But both Faisal and Adnan Dmeiri deny it. "This man wasn't ordered by *Fatah* to fight this man from *Hamas*. He did not have any orders to kill," says Faisal. According to *al-Quds*, the Jerusalem daily, the murder was the result of a family feud. "The reason was not political. It was a personal matter between the two youths," insists Adnan. "It wasn't even connected to events in the cinema." Adds Faisal, "The amazing thing is that Jaber Dmeiri is from a family of *Fatah* supporters, while the other man is from a family of *Hamas* supporters."

But the family of Jaber Ali Dmeiri, the dead *Hamas* loyalist, does not accept this explanation. In an unusual step, Jaber Dmeiri's father purchased an ad in *al-Quds* the next day. It said: "The death of our child was politically motivated and had nothing to do with family squabbles, as was claimed in the story. There are no family conflicts between us and the family of the youngster who is suspected of killing our child Jaber, and there were no personal conflicts between the killer and the martyr."

Faisal suspects that Israeli authorities may have sanctioned the riot to discourage him from addressing similar rallies throughout the territories. He says that the Israeli military commander for the Tulkarm region refused to issue a permit for the rally until the eve of the event. "When he finally called, he said 'Okay, we are giving you permission. But just so you know, *Hamas* will do something against you and we will not interfere.'" The Israelis, contends Faisal, "don't like my visits and the visits of others in the delegation. By allowing such things to happen, they strengthen their goal of prohibiting these meetings in the future. They say, Look, when we permit you to have public meetings, they degenerate into a riot."

This is the weight that Faisal must carry as he tries to lead his people out of the desert, where they have been wandering without a homeland since Israel was created in 1948. He faces internal and external rebellion, having to confront divisions within *Fatah* at the same time he faces the growing power of Islamic fundamentalists and other factions unafraid to use violence against Palestinians and Israelis to sabotage the peace process. There are disagreements between the Gazans and the West Bankers on the delegation; there is tension with a restless population that expects rapid progress; there are disputes with the Jordanians on the joint delegation; and there is constant struggle with the PLO leadership in Tunis. While dousing these fires of discontent, the Palestinian delegation has to negotiate across a much wider gulf with Israel.

Thus it is hardly surprising that Faisal greeted the news of Yasser Arafat's miraculous survival from a plane crash with unabashed glee. "You can't imagine the happiness," he told reporters when he first found out. "People, young and old, are weeping and congratulating each other." For Faisal the celebrations meant that, because Arafat had lived for another day, the peace process would survive. So would Faisal Husseini. Arafat is the glue that holds the rival factions together. The two of them are Siamese twins, of a sort: Arafat needs Faisal as his bulwark against *Hamas* and the extremists inside the territories; Faisal needs Arafat, because without his support there can be no final political and territorial compromise with Israel. Only Yasser Arafat can make palatable for the Palestinians the bitterest dish of all—abandoning the dream of going back to their homes in all of Palestine. And no one realizes that more than Faisal Husseini, who has long been committed to a two-state solution: "There is no alternative to Yasser Arafat. Yasser Arafat is the history of the Palestinian people. He is the story of the Palestinian people, and he will go on with his work."

But Faisal instinctively seems to recognize that an era is ending. The days are over when he could rely on his power as Arafat's surrogate to delegate authority. Palestinians are tired of the one-man rule and the corruption that has dogged the PLO; they demand a more democratic system in which leaders are held accountable and in which institutions—not individuals—hold the bulk of power. They are looking to Faisal to lead them, but they want him to mold more responsible institutions. "I am comfortable with my role," he says. "I have the feeling that I am in the right place at the right time."

Israeli officials insist they are quietly doing their part to encourage this process, citing the hundreds of political rallies they have permitted in the territories. Although the Shamir government continued to imprison Israeli peace activists such as Abie Nathan and David Ish-Shalom for their contacts with the PLO, it seemed to be somewhat more tolerant toward Faisal's links to the Tunis leadership. When Hanan Ashrawi flew with him to meet Arafat in Algiers after the Madrid conference, the Israeli police pressed for both of them to be arrested for violating the law. But the government refused to press charges and the case was dropped. Says Faisal, "They know very well that nothing can happen without the PLO. When [former Minister of Health] Ehud Olmert was asked, 'Did Faisal and Hanan take a plane to Algiers?' he said, 'We know that they went there, but it seems better for us not to know.'" One of the first acts by Prime Minister Yitzhak Rabin after his election in June 1992 was to change the law, permitting contacts with PLO officials provided they do not jeopardize Israel's security.

Of course, Israel's attitude towards Faisal is rooted in the old desire to undermine Arafat. But at least some officials are beginning to appreciate the fact that Faisal Husseini can be a partner for peace. "Surprisingly enough, even people from the defense establishment will tell you discreetly that he is taken to be a real moderate," says a senior Israeli policymaker. "They regard him as a leader with a great deal of influence." Faisal himself says there is no reason for Israel to fear him or his policies. His vision of a state, he says, is one that would not threaten Israeli security. "We may need an army as a symbol of our national identity, but I don't believe an army will be able to protect our security," he explains. "We can never build an army that can face the Israeli army or even the Jordanian army! They could kill us merely by starving us. I would like to see the whole area with a minimum number of armed forces and weapons. What we need are international guarantees that no one will attack us. So maybe we are better off with no army at all!"

Faisal also says the new state could be linked to Jordan and even one day to Israel. "A Palestinian state must be able to issue passports and citizenship. But I prefer a confederation, a Palestinian state [existing] as a confederation, not a federation," and he explains why: "In our lives as Palestinians, we have been a part of three experiences: the Israeli experience, the Jordanian experience, and the Lebanese experience. As Lebanese we saw freedom without authority; in Jordan we experienced authority without democracy; and in Israel we experienced democracy without equality. We hope our state will be a state of freedom, democracy, equality, and only the authority that is required to protect them."

He is ready to assume the burden of negotiating the limits and restraints that Israel would demand, provided statehood remains the goal. "I have sent more than one message to [Israeli Prime Minister] Yitzhak Rabin that he can be the savior of Israel if he wants to be. He is more pragmatic than Shamir." In an August 1992 interview with *Ha'aretz*, Faisal said: "They told us this is a chess game, but Shamir didn't play chess. He was boxing. Rabin wants to play [but] this won't be an easy game." A quarter of a century ago Yitzak Rabin and Abdel Kader fought in a war against each other. Rabin was the commander of the Harel Brigade, which was responsible for the region that extended from Lydda and Ramleh all the way to Jerusalem. Rabin's forces were later nicknamed Kastel because it was at that fortress that they killed Faisal's father. Not long after, Rabin became a member of the Israeli team that negotiated an armistice agreement at Rhodes, formally ending the 1948 war of independence. Today, almost a half century later, Faisal believes his father Abdel Kader Husseini, the Arab war hero who fought to prevent the birth of the Jewish state, would be proud of his son for negotiating peace with Yitzhak Rabin. In fact, says Faisal, "I believe if he were here today, he would do the same thing."

Sari Nusseibeh

━━━━━━━━

As a teacher, Sari Nusseibeh is a pragmatist. He tries to persuade his students to deconstruct their world, to disassemble the myths they have accepted wholesale, and to reconstruct their thoughts so they can discover their own identities, their own way of thinking, and find out who they really are. "They see only the outside part, what is happening to them every day, every hour. The experiences and the hardships of the moment affect their emotions, and they nurture hatred and hostility and vengefulness. They are not free. They are the prisoners of the occupation," says the Oxford-educated professor.

At forty-three, Sari Nusseibeh, his bushy gray hair and bifocals a sign of creeping middle age, has emerged as the reigning intellectual activist of the occupation, a philosopher king whose self-confident, dissident style, organizational skills, and support among the *shabiba* have given him a pivotal place in the forefront of *Fatah* supporters inside the West Bank and Gaza Strip. "I am different from many of my people. I am free in my mind." His popularity is easy to understand. His message is one of self-reliance, of getting on with the business of building the infrastructures of a state, not waiting for the negotiations to yield an "expanded" autonomy. He is impatient and impetuous, even slightly imperial, but he is respected even by those who disagree with him. Eyebrows were raised, for example, when Sari boycotted the Madrid conference. But his absence was more than symbolic; he was home creating the support group for *Fatah* among the masses, the "political committees," to help institutionalize the gains being made at Madrid and, in the view of at least one critic, to anoint himself as the undisputed leader of the next generation of Palestinian insiders.

In unilaterally forming the committees and confronting the Palestinian delegation with a fait accompli on their return from Madrid, Nusseibeh and Ziad Abu Zayyad "tried to create a coup, a bloodless coup" within *Fatah*, charges Riad Maliki, a Popular Front for the Liberation of Palestine (PFLP) supporter in the territories. But even Maliki, an outspoken opponent of the peace process, concedes that "after what happened, he [Nusseibeh] has become more influential than before." Today Sari directs his own research center, called MAQDES, with offices in Ramallah, having quit his professorship at Birzeit University after the school was closed down by the Israelis in 1988.

Few Palestinians have such a sophisticated understanding of the psychology of occupation: the teetering balance between dreams and reality; the visions of one's own homeland along with the banal existence in another's; the quest for independence; the struggles of submission. Like his students' lives, Sari's past is a conflict between two realities, the one he has fought for inside the classroom, and in his dreams, and the one that confronts him outside in the street, determining the daily routine of his life. In his dreams Sari negotiates an understanding between Arabs and Jews. In reality he is beaten up for daring to try to do so. In his dreams his state has open borders, and Palestinian products are purchased in places from Petah Tikvah to the Persian Gulf. In reality he is jailed for being an Iraqi spy. In his dreams he teaches Islamic philosophy to innocent Israeli students at Hebrew University. In reality his students are the same Israeli soldiers who stop him at checkpoints and demand to see his identity card. In his dreams he travels freely between Arab and Jewish quarters of Jerusalem. In reality he has a hard time persuading a taxi to cross from East Jerusalem to West.

"I lived on the border all my life," says Sari, who was born in 1949 in Jerusalem. This was only one year after his mother had been forced to flee from Ramle near Tel Aviv "as the result," says Sari dryly, "of the establishment of the state of Israel." The roots of the Nusseibeh family, like those of the Husseinis, stretch back hundreds of years. They were once wealthy landowners, but in the late 1800s "the [Ottoman] Turks, they massacred a lot of my family," says Sari, and the Nusseibehs lost their lands. "I feel a very strong sense of belonging to the city of Jerusalem and to the country of Palestine. I've always been brought up to feel unhappy about the fact that Israel came into being in the first place," he concedes.

Sari remembers what the Holy City was like in the 1950s, when Jordan ruled the West Bank and when he lived only a few blocks from the high stone wall that divided Jerusalem into sharply delineated Arab and Jewish sectors. It was before King Hussein appointed Sari's father, Anwar, as the Hashemite kingdom's ambassador to the Court of St. James, before Sari was enrolled in British preparatory schools, when he was growing up in the old-world luxury of his parent's elegant home on Nablus Road, with its Oriental carpets and crystal decanters, across the street from the stately American Colony Hotel. Although he was cut off from the Israelis and reared to resent them, they held a strange fascination for the young Nusseibeh. He could look out of his upstairs bedroom window, across the no-man's-land where there had been fierce fighting during the 1948 war, and see the Jews in the western part of the city. Sometimes, without telling his parents, he would wander into the deserted area and play in an abandoned United Nations building that had once served as a halfway house for diplomats crossing back and forth between the Arab and Jewish parts of Jerusalem. Near the decaying building, with its broken windows and bullet-ridden walls, were vineyards; Sari often stopped to pick grapes and bring them home as booty from the Israeli-Jordanian border.

When he was feeling really adventurous, Sari would try to get a closer glimpse of the Jews, skipping down Salah al Din Street and slipping into the Old City through Damascus Gate, the Crusader archway built by Suleiman the Magnificent on foundations that were originally laid in the Herodian era. Sari knew his way around, particularly in the Christian Quarter; since the twelfth century, when Salah al Din captured Jerusalem from the Crusaders and returned it to Muslim rule, the Nusseibeh family had held the keys as custodians to the Church of the Holy Sepulchre, one of the holiest shrines in Christianity, built on the site where tradition says Jesus was crucified. "It's a key plus," says Sari, noting that the Nusseibehs open the church for one of the most solemn

Christian rituals, the night before Easter Sunday, when the Holy Sepulchre is ablaze with thousands of votive candles.

But Sari knew he could not enter the ancient Jewish Quarter, so sometimes he would walk in the shadow of the high stone walls, all the way from Herod's Gate, the entrance to the Moslem Quarter, past Damascus Gate, and down Jaffa Road to Jaffa Gate. There, at the westernmost entry to the Old City, where the Citadel of David stood as a watchtower along the path to the Western Wall where Jews worshipped the only remnant of the biblical Temple of King Solomon, Sari would stop and stare. "At the end of the walk, at Jaffa Gate, you had to turn back, because beyond that was the end of the world," he recalls. "It was very strange. I remember you walked up towards it, but then you saw this thing that was there: a gate into nothing. When you are ten or twelve, it is like Alice in Wonderland to have a gate that is locked and you couldn't go through it."

His childhood expeditions trying to penetrate the wall made such an impression on Sari that when Israel conquered the West Bank in 1967, unifying Jerusalem, he felt a sense of relief. "I was very aware that there was a wall, because I lived close to it. So the thing that really grabbed me was that there was no wall and it was suddenly one country. And in a strange way, although we were beaten and had come under occupation, there was a sense of satisfaction that the country was finally reunified." Adds Sari: "Now there's a wall again. I've created it. Now I rarely dare go across."

It was not always that way. When Sari permanently returned to the West Bank in 1978, after more than a decade abroad, he accepted a position as visiting professor at Hebrew University, teaching Islamic philosophy to Jewish students. He sent his own sons—Jamal, Absal, and Buraq—to an Israeli art school, where they learned to paint with Jewish boys and girls. And later he enrolled them with Israeli musicians, who taught his children how to play the violin, the cello, and the piano. At one point, when Jerusalem was holding its municipal elections, Sari even suggested that Palestinians run for office, though that would have meant helping to govern the city that Israel had annexed as its capital. And in July 1987, when he was approached by a Likud politician who sought to open a dialogue with the pro-PLO leaders on the West Bank, it was Sari who persuaded Faisal Husseini to join the talks with the Israeli right-winger.

Reality, however, reared its ugly head again in the fall of 1987 when Sari was badly beaten by a gang of Palestinian students as he was leaving Birzeit University. He had delivered a lecture on tolerance, expounding the views of English philosopher John Locke. As an assistant professor of philosophy, he knew his courses were popular and well received. As a quasi-diplomat, he had also had some high moments over the past few months. Even though the peacemaking effort had failed and Husseini had been arrested in late August, it had proved that progress could be made toward an agreement for mutual recognition. The meetings with Moshe Amirav, a member of the governing Likud Party's central committee, were supposed to have been a secret, but somehow word of them leaked to the press.

Now, as Sari stepped into the hallway on this warm September day, he moved from Lockeian dreams of coexistence to a Hobbesian nightmare of hate. Suddenly, out of the dark, five masked men appeared and silently surrounded him, pounding his head with bottles and pummeling his stomach with sticks. Without a word they beat him, then ran away, leaving him alone, sprawled out on the floor, with a gash in his head, his body bleeding, and his arm broken. Later on he was told this beating was a consequence of his meetings with the Zionists. There are those who think he was punished by some group within *Fatah*. Sari says he does not know who was responsible for such beatings. "We were attacked on both sides of the fence," he says, in his British accent. "It could have been a small group who took it upon themselves, or they may have been working on orders from somebody outside. I don't know."

But Sari did know that some of his recent comments had been taken out of context and misunderstood. He had gained attention for advocating that Palestinians both recognize the permanence of the Jewish state and demand that Israel annex the occupied territories, on condition that full citizenship be granted to the 1.7 million Arabs. That would force the Israelis to decide whether they wanted a binational state of Arabs and Jews or preferred giving the Palestinians their own independent state. "When I said, 'Let

Israel continue the annexation,' I wasn't talking in vain," Sari had explained to a Peace Now rally. "I was describing an evolutionary-behavorial process that existed in reality."

But the only reality that confronted him on September 21, 1987, was the sterile emergency room at the Israeli hospital and the dozens of stitches required to mend his head wounds. "I was extremely cautious then. It doesn't make a difference," he insists, shrugging off the beating. What does make a difference, he says, "is my fear of the Israelis. Wherever I go, whenever I come back I'm living in a state of permanent terror. I'm living under the scrutiny of an enemy I believe to be extremely intelligent and very unscrupulous. I have to watch my every move and every step and every word. I walk with my head turned backwards."

Sari Nusseibeh grew up the son of an aristocratic family in Jerusalem. His father, Anwar, was a distinguished statesman, a member of the first and only Government of All Palestine formed by Haj Amin Husseini in Gaza after the 1948 war and of the Arab Higher Committee in Cairo, a leader in the Jordanian parliament, Jordan's ambassador to Great Britain, and the Jordanian Minister of Defense. The young Nusseibeh inherited his father's intellect and acquired, as well, his father's ability to interact with the Jews. He had the educational advantages associated with wealth: he finished his undergraduate work at Christ Church College at Oxford and received his doctorate in Islamic philosophy at Harvard. But he also had the intellectual curiosity of a true scholar.

Anwar Nusseibeh was never reluctant to push his son toward involvement with the Jews. One morning during the summer of 1968 the elder Nusseibeh led a group of the Higher Islamic Council to inspect digging being conducted under Jerusalem's Temple Mount by a team of Israeli archaeologists. As the Arab group stood on a promontory near the site, Meri Ben-Dov, the leader of the Israeli team, motioned them to come closer and see the dozens of Islamic artifacts being uncovered. The group declined. Only one man came forward. He asked who all the people were who were digging, and was told they were volunteers from all over the world. The Arab asked whether a Moslem would be accepted if he volunteered. Ben-Dov replied that he would be welcome. The man who asked the question was, of course, Anwar Nusseibeh.

The next day he sent his son, Sari, then nineteen years old and home for a vacation after completing his high school term in Britain, to join the Israeli excavation.

In many ways Anwar Nusseibeh set the example for Sari. A proud Palestinian nationalist, he nonetheless believed it was shortsighted to reject the Arab consensus. "My father believed in toeing the official Arab line," says Sari, recalling that when the 1973 Arab summit at Rabat conferred official recognition on the PLO as the "sole and legitimate representative" of the Palestinian people, "my father said the same, not necessarily because he believed in it, but because it was the Arab line. He believed it was important to be an Arab loyalist." His father, he says, believed that "as an Arab, your major objective was Palestine."

His father also taught him another lesson, the importance of using the system, of immersing oneself in whatever system happened to be in power to advance the Palestinian's nationalist aspirations. Sari recalls that even George Habash, the founder of the rejectionist PFLP, tried—unsuccessfully—to be elected to the Jordanian parliament "just like my father." Between 1948 and 1967 half of the population of the West Bank was employed by the Jordanian civil service. "Today 2 million people are living in Palestine. If the way to do that is through carrying Israeli identity cards or passports, then so be it," says Sari.

But a quarter century after the Israeli conquest of the West Bank and Gaza, Sari is no longer sure that his father was right. At times, he says, he sees the Palestinian people moving in a surreal trance, their bodies marching straight into the reality of Israeli life while their heads turn toward the dream of a Palestinian state. The Palestinian dilemma, explains Sari, is a discrepancy between consciousness and reality, a chasm that grows wider every day. He describes the consciousness as the growing Palestinian national identity, and the reality as an increasing immersion in the Israeli system.

"What is the system?" asks the professor rhetorically. "It is everything. It is taxes, trade, television, the radio station you listen to, the clothes that you wear, the people you register with, the court system you deal with. It is everything—from buying trousers, to selling kippers in the Old City, to working on the construction of settlements, to writing articles. Ninety percent of what we consume is Israeli made. Everything we have done is not for the sake of Israel but to survive, and we do it by entering the system." Not only have the Palestinians come to accept the reality of life under Israel, he says, they have become part of the life of Israel. "When the [Israeli] Egged bus first started coming to the West Bank, people didn't use it," he explains. "We wanted to support our Arab buses." Now, he says, they not only use it, but "many of the drivers are Arabs from the West Bank."

Similarly, the Palestinians reluctantly succumbed to the system of censorship. When the war was over in 1967 and the West Bank belonged to Israel, there were no longer any Arabic newspapers to serve the people. At the time, he says, there was a debate about whether to publish a paper in Arabic. "The pragmatists said, 'We need a newspaper in Arabic.' The ideologues said, 'If we bring out a paper, it means we have to go to the authorities and ask for permission, and to do that is to legitimize the authorities.'" The pragmatists agreed that the authorities should be rejected, but more importantly, they saw a need for a newspaper of their own. Now, says Sari, not only is their own paper published, but the most extreme ideologues are going to the censors to get their articles stamped and approved. "It means there has been a slow immersion," he says. "There has been a slow acceptance, a slow acclimitization to the system."

But Sari believes a contradiction has been growing between what people are doing and what they are thinking. He mentions the Palestinian child who buys a can of paint. The label is clearly marked: it is manufactured by Tambour, an Israeli company. Yet the lad does not think twice before using the paint to scrawl anti-Israeli graffiti on the walls. "While people, in reality, were becoming part of the system, in their consciousness they were developing something totally different: an independent kind of national identity." But the paradox could not continue. "Sooner or later one of the two had to happen: either consciousness was brought down to reality or reality was going to be changed to fit your consciousness." In practical, political terms there must be "equal rights in a single state," or there must be a separate Palestinian state. The failure to achieve either of these was the pyschological spark that ignited the *intifada* and gave the uprising its internal logic, he says.

The *intifada* strategy, he explains, was conceived from the beginning as having two complementary sides. One was "the so-called disengagement" from the authorities by ceasing to show up for work, refusing to pay Israeli taxes, boycotting Israeli goods, and refusing to pay for routine things such as Israeli drivers' licenses. "It was basically holding a pair of scissors and cutting off all these links that had been established over the past twenty-two or twenty-three years," says Sari. But then you reach a stage, he adds, where having cut too much you need to create an alternative, and "the alternative in people's minds was the creation of a state, of a structure. So on one side of the same idea [the rationale of the *intifada*] was disengagement and on the other side was construction."

Indeed, Sari believes that entering negotiations for a five-year period of autonomy, or self-rule, could lead to a new quisling status for the Palestinians. Autonomy, he says, is "an unacceptable and dangerous idea. It will relieve the Israelis from the concern of running everyday life in the territories without losing control of the territory and without giving any substantial authority to the Palestinians." He believes the Palestinians should have moved much sooner to take contol of their own lives. "We should have anticipated the present negotiations by unilaterally seizing autonomy and by creating a provisional government. We shouldn't have made it an object of negotiations. We should have created it two or three years ago."

When the Palestinians inside the territories proclaimed their declaration of independence, which he helped author, explains Sari, it was a fait accompli; the outside leadership had to reconcile itself to the new reality. "The leadership outside was suddenly seized with the fact that the inside leadership, the leadership of the *intifada*, were somehow all in favor of the declaration. It caught their imagination at the right time," says Sari, "and the people outside seized the idea."

Similarly, he defends the formation of political committees, which were created without prior approval from the PLO leadership in Tunis and without the knowledge of the Palestinian delegation to the Madrid peace conference. "Faisal was a bit surprised by the announcement [when they returned from Madrid] and, as I was to find out later, understandably so, because he apparently didn't have any clue to the whole thing," says Sari. "You might find it surprising in this day and age but it was a problem of communication." The people he sent to the Allenby Bridge to inform Husseini and the other delegates never reached them. "They thought it was polite to inform him and good to inform him, but not necessary. Nobody thought it would provoke the kind of reaction that it did," he admits.

All of the excluded factions—including the People's Party (the former Communist Party) and the Yasser Abed Rabbo wing of the Democratic Front for the Liberation of Palestine (DFLP)—protested loudly. Sari concedes that the main purpose of creating the committees was to unite the *Fatah* supporters in the territories and to "create a link, some kind of dialogue, between political activists on the grass-roots level and the negotiating team." There were hundreds of local leaders who felt they should have been involved in Madrid, particularly veterans of the refugee camps who felt there were too many affluent members and academics. "We started these committees," says Ziad Abu Zayyad, one of the cofounders with Sari Nusseibeh, "to satisfy people who felt they were ignored or isolated or insulted because they did not have the role to which they thought they were entitled. We tried to get them involved and engaged in the political process."

But the other factions believed *Fatah* was merely trying to wrest control of the process away from them. "It was a fait accompli in a sense," admits Sari. "Ours was ours. We told them, create yours and then we can integrate. It doesn't work otherwise. If you set up something, if you try to set up something in conjunction with others, it never works. If we had sat down to discuss things more than we had, it would never have happened," he says, citing the earlier effort to create a provisional government. That failed, explains Sari, because "the discussion took place with too many people involved."

Israelis saw the Nusseibeh-Abu Zayyad move as a challenge to Husseini's authority and as an effort to preempt the *Fatah* leader in the territories by creating their own popular base of support. "The Israelis tried to represent this as a fight similar to the fight between Levy and Shamir; they set Sari and Ziad against Faisal," says Abu Zayyad. That is nonsense, he adds. "We are working in full harmony." There are 200 political committees throughout the West Bank and Gaza, and despite Israeli efforts to outlaw them, claims Abu Zayyad, "they meet all the time."

Sari's ideas about disengaging and constructing a new reality to replace the old one have taken hold, however. Technical committees, twenty-eight of them, have been set up by *Fatah* supporters, to prepare the way for replacing the Israeli-run civil administration of the territories. Palestinian experts are employed in fields as diverse as health, finance, law, and the environment. Sari is the chairman of the committees and Abu Zayyad is one of four members on their governing board. He concedes they "represent a sort of infrastructure of a future [Palestinian] administration," the embryo of a provisional government. And he adds, defiantly, "We are not seeking permission from the Israelis."

"I was telling some people the other day, including my wife, people think I'm a political animal, but I'm really not interested in politics at all. If you ask me, I'm totally disinterested. If you took me out of here and you could put me in the Champs-Elysées or anywhere . . . ," Sari says in his flawless English as he relaxes on the veranda of his two-story home in Abu Dis, a village on the outskirts of East Jerusalem. Instead of the Eiffel Tower, the Louvre, and fashionable bistros, from his porch you see the Dome of the Rock. Like everything else in his home, it is a reminder of the present reality that he cannot escape. Next to the rattan chairs on the veranda are potted flowers, petunias, rhododendrons, bleeding heart. The entrance to his living room is as visually chaotic as his life. There are books everywhere, a stack of videotapes, including the film "Mad Max," two cordless telephones, a videocamera, and a pair of binoculars. There also are flowers on the coffee table, which is inlaid with red mosaic tile, and on every table gifts from friends and relatives. The Nusseibehs—Sari's wife, Lucy, is a tall, fair-complexioned, almost ivory-looking Englishwoman—are celebrating the arrival of their fourth child, their first girl. Sari and Lucy, who speaks fluent Arabic, have named her Nuzha.

"It's exhausting and I feel the exhaustion personally," says Sari, who tries hard to fulfill his obligations to his family. It is a constant battle between becoming absorbed in the politics of occupation and maintaining an identity that is not completely defined by the Israeli-Palestinian conflict. "I was talking to someone in the street today and he's totally consumed. I was telling him, 'So what. It's not so important at all.'" But he admits that life has played strange tricks on him and that he's been unable to escape the grip of politics. "It's not because I'm interested in politics. It's because you feel there are certain needs which have to be addressed and you can't get out of it."

At one point in his life, after getting his undergraduate degree at Oxford in 1971, Sari was so discouraged when a professor he was studying with left to teach at Harvard that he briefly considered chucking it all for the good life. "I wanted to be a millionaire," he recalls. Abandoned by his professor, an Egyptian scholar in the history of science, Sari admits, "I was lost academically. I felt poor financially. I wanted to get married and felt I couldn't as a student." So he succumbed to the entreaties of relatives in Abu Dhabi who had invited Sari to come to the Persian Gulf sheikhdom. "You have a job waiting for you here and an apartment and a car," he recalls their saying.

Once there, he went to work in the public relations office of the Abu Dhabi Oil Company and wrote a weekly column for the *Abu Dhabi News*. "I was making more money than I made even after my Ph.D. and after teaching for several years at Birzeit. I wasn't content with merely earning an income. I was on the lookout for opportunities to make money, big money. I thought to myself, if I stay here I must find a way to make a million in five years or it's not worth it, regardless of how much money I make a month. I couldn't find a way to make my million so I decided I'd leave it."

In 1974 Sari applied to Harvard University, asking for a scholarship to pursue his doctorate in Islamic studies. It was the only place he applied. "I told myself, 'If I don't get both, I'm not going anywhere.'" He was admitted and won a scholarship, but still supported himself by doing some student teaching—as a nonresident tutor at Quincy House—and with odd jobs that ranged from doing night watch with the Harvard police patrol to washing dishes in a local restaurant. David Pollack, a classmate who today is chief of the Near East Research Bureau of the U.S. Information Agency, remembers Sari as "less of an activist and definitely inclined toward scholarship." He says Sari was "serious, solid, and thoughtful, with a good sense of humor but never goofy. You couldn't tell whether he was seized with the Palestinian issue."

In 1978 Sari obtained his Ph.D. and returned to the West Bank, where he began teaching at both Birzeit University and Hebrew University. In the early 1980s he was active in organizing the teacher's union at Birzeit and was elected to three consecutive annual terms as president of the Union of Faculty and Staff there. He also was cofounder of the Federation of Employees in the Education Sector for the entire West Bank.

With the beginning of the *intifada*, Sari found himself again relentlessly pulled toward involvement in Palestinian politics. After his beating at Birzeit for helping to initiate a dialogue with Moshe Amirav, he became a target of both the Israelis and some Palestinians. In May 1989 his name appeared as an unindicted coconspirator in a trial of four Palestinian activists. The military court alleged that he was a leader of the Unified National Leadership of the Uprising, the underground group that had coordinated the rebellion. Prosecutors also claimed he was helping to finance the uprising, allegedly having channeled more than $150,000 from the PLO to *Fatah* stalwarts in the territories. Sari denied the allegations. However, no charges were brought against him because, according to the Israeli press, the U.S. government filed an official protest.

The publicity the affair received did not help Sari with his own community. Nor did the fact that he was never brought to trial. Shortly thereafter, an unknown group calling itself the "Popular Palestinian Army" issued a leaflet charging he had used the PLO funds for a luxurious vacation in Europe. The leaflet branded him "the academic doctor, Lord Sari Nusseibeh." It claimed that his holiday was "an escape under the cover of the Zionist Shin Bet after it was known that money he received for submitting to the Strike Forces disappeared." The leaflet said Nusseibeh's hands were "white and not stained by stone-throwing."

A few days later another leaflet appeared, claiming that the first one was a forgery and had been written by the Shin Bet to discredit the Palestinian professor. Within a week an article appeared in the main PLO organ, *Falasteen al-Thawrah*, supporting Sari and accusing the Israeli secret service of having drafted and circulated the original attack. "The Sun Has Shined and the Truth Has Come to Light," was the headline in the weekly PLO newspaper. But Sari's troubles did not end.

On June 15, barely a month after he was named in the court indictment, the Israelis themselves cracked down on him. Acting under a military order, the Jerusalem police seized papers and welded shut the doors of the Holy Land Press Service, a news service Sari was running for foreign correspondents and diplomats. The court order charged that he used the office to channel illegal funds to the uprising. The move came three weeks after the Israeli authorities had banned publication of his *Monday Report*, a weekly newsletter in English that provided analysis of events in the *intifada*. The news agency was ordered shut down for two years.

In an interview with *Ha'aretz* correspondent Gideon Levy, Sari was asked about the charges that his hands were too white. "I don't think that anyone's hands can be too white. They can always be whiter," he replied. The reporter asked if he planned to emigrate to another country. "From a personal point of view, it could have been possible, but it's out of the question for me," Sari said. "I'm stuck here, for better or worse. I don't have a choice." But the personal attacks against him apparently had left their mark. "I have to see myself just like everyone else, and I shouldn't allow myself to do things that others cannot do," he told the Israeli newspaper.

He was also asked whether he had changed his mind about trying to alter Israeli society from the inside rather than through the creation of a separate state. "When I was looking at processes that were taking place in the West Bank and Gaza during the first twenty years of occupation, I saw a process of integration into Israeli society, which was contrary to the stated aims of the Palestinian strategy that called for disintegration," he replied. "I believed that this schizophrenic situation cannot continue for a long time. In order to brigde the gap, there was a need to change one of the two components: either to disconnect from the Israeli system—something that has already happened in the *intifada*— or to change the declared strategy, and to make an effort to integrate into the Israeli system, consciously. I think that is still applicable," he said. "In other words, I believe that if the strategy of disintegration will fail, then maybe the Palestinians will change direction and say: We couldn't do it, therefore let us make the best out of integrating into the Israeli system." He was asked whether that would inevitably lead to a binational state. "By definition," Sari replied, "if we don't reach an agreement on a two-state partition in five to six years, then what happens in fact—no matter what you call it—is a nondemocratic binational state."

Sari made those comments to *Ha'aretz* in the fall of 1989. According to his timetable, the Palestinians must achieve their independence by 1995 or face Israeli annexation. And, he warns, the psychological clock is ticking. "The entire populace is becoming radicalized as the result of continued Israeli occupation," he explains. "The symptom of this [shift] is that more and more people are turning to Muslim fundamentalism. One shouldn't overestimate its importance," he cautions, but one should draw the appropriate conclusion.

The message is that while an independent Palestinian state is still attractive to most Palestinians, both inside and outside the territories, it may not be for very much longer. "Today, you could sell this to the people, not that they would fall in love with the idea," says Sari. He cautions: "The national psychological readiness for a two-state solution is not a permanent fixture of the Palestinian psychology. It's in the Palestinian heart now, but it can quickly fade if there is no response to this feeling of opening up. It's like a star or a comet that comes close by and then goes away. One has to catch it when it is close to your quarters."

Nothing prepared Sari Nusseibeh for his most recent brush with the Israeli authorities. He was putting his children to sleep when the border police knocked on the door of his Abu Dis home. It was nearly 11:15 p.m. on January 29, 1991, almost two weeks after Iraq had begun firing Scud missiles at Haifa and Tel Aviv. There had been twenty-six firings on seven occasions over those twelve days, killing four Israelis and wounding nearly 200 more. A dusk-to-dawn curfew was in effect, but the police were taking no chances; their detachment was augmented by soldiers of the Israeli Defense Force, which took the unusual step of also surrounding the Abu Dis house and blocking off all civilian traffic. When Sari opened the door he was confronted by the arresting officer, who gave him a typewritten sheet of paper, the administrative detention order, signed by Defense Minister Moshe Arens. Sari knew what it meant: he was about to go to jail and could be held, without charges being issued against him and without the right to a trial, for six months or longer. "They waited while I put my things together. They were very quiet. They didn't shout or scream or anything. They were very polite," Sari later told the *Washington Post*. Lucy volunteered to help him pack, making sure to include his favorite plaid shirts, a sports jacket, and a heavy sweater for the cold winter nights. Jamal, Absal, and Buraq, as well behaved as ever, stood silently watching, tears welling up in their eyes. "They were very upset. I told them to regard it as one of my trips abroad," Sari recalled.

The next morning the government issued a statement charging Sari was, in effect, an Iraqi spy. The statement alleged he had been involved in "subversive activities," among them "collecting security information for Iraqi intelligence." It also accused him of channeling information to PLO "elements abroad" who were working in the employ of the Iraqis. "For me, it was a deep shock that this fuzzy-headed professor from Birzeit was accused of being a spy," recalls *Ha'aretz* correspondent Ori Nir. "If it wasn't tragic, it was comic!"

Sari issued his own statement, from Ramle Prison, categorically denying that he had ever engaged in any intelligence gathering "on behalf of any government or organization," and specifically refuting the charges that he had gathered or provided information to Iraq. "It was clear to me," says Mark Heller, an Israeli scholar who coauthored with him the book *No Trumpets, No Drums*, "that Sari had just done something stupid rather than something really criminal." The Israelis apparently had monitored a telephone call to Nusseibeh from the Iraqi ambassador in Tunis, the headquarters of the PLO, and allegedly had overheard him describing the locations where the Scud missiles were landing in Tel Aviv. Nusseibeh identified the sites of the missile impacts with "pinpoint accuracy," claimed Raanan Gissan, a military spokesperson. He told reporters that the forty-one-year-old Palestinian had, in effect, acted as a spotter for the Iraqis, enabling them to correct their aim with the next volley.

There was an immediate outcry and it stretched across the oceans. Amnesty International declared Nusseibeh a "prisoner of conscience." Editorials critical of Israel appeared in hundreds of newspapers, including the *New York Times*, *Washington Post*, and the *Los Angeles Times*. In Israel, right-wing leaders criticized Prime Minister Shamir, saying Nusseibeh should have been expelled, not just sentenced to several months in prison. Ephraim Sneh, the former military governor of the West Bank and currently a deputy foreign minister and close adviser to the Israeli negotiating team, said that if there was hard evidence against Nusseibeh, the government had an obligation to bring him speedily to trial. "If not, this means the intention was political," Sneh chaffed. U.S. State Department spokesperson Margaret Tutwiler took up the same theme. "The charges against Dr. Nusseibeh ought to be made public and a chance given to him to defend himself in a court of law," she said. A British Foreign Office spokesman also demanded that Nusseibeh be given the right to a trial so that he could hear the charges against him. Meanwhile, Saeb Erakat, a Palestinian professor at an-Najah University in Nablus, put it bluntly: "This is a message to us Palestinian moderates. The message is, 'You can forget about negotiations after the war because we are going to make sure there is no one to talk to.'"

But like the 14,000 other Palestinians who had been jailed without charge since the start of the *intifada*, Sari never was given the specifics of the allegations against him or brought to trial. On the eve of his arrest, his activities did not seem consistent with an effort to undermine Israel's security. Sari had spent the afternoon with Galia Golon and other members of the Peace Now movement, who had gone to his house to persuade him to denounce the Iraqi missile attacks. "Sari said he was ready to condemn the killing of civilians anywhere, whether in Tel Aviv or Baghdad," Mordechai Bar-On told Anthony Lewis, the *New York Times* columnist. "The idea was to have an exchange of letters about how we see the future," he added.

It may never be known whether Sari was called by the Iraqi ambassador in Tunis and, if he was, whether he deliberately channeled data on sites struck by Iraq's Scud missiles or was merely describing the scene that was being broadcast on Israeli television. His prison term, however, was cut short. In February, shortly after the end of the Gulf War and the defeat of Iraq, the Jerusalem District Court ordered Sari's detention reduced to three months. The court cited the nature of the evidence in the secret police file on him but said nothing more about its contents. He was freed on April 29, exactly ninety days after his arrest.

While in jail, Sari says, he worked on the galleys of his book. It is difficult to make any judgments about the impact of the prison term on him, but he seemed more committed than ever after his release to reversing the public relations debacle suffered by the Palestinians during the Gulf War. In November 1991, in assessing the results of the Madrid conference, he told a Washington, D.C., symposium organized by the Center for Policy Analysis on Palestine that the "olive-branch strategy . . . is a very smart strategy for the Palestinians to pursue, and I think they should pursue it more intently." He added that all forms of dialogue should be accelerated. "One of &ouré major concerns should be to focus on trying to influence Israeli public opinion through joint actions, demonstrations, statements, or meetings. The Palestinians in the occupied territories have to demonstrate that they are really serious and genuine about achieving peace," he told the group.

A few weeks later Sari appeared with Israeli defense analyst Mark Heller on the PBS-TV program "The MacNeil-Lehrer News-Hour." "I look at the Madrid conference as something that will perhaps change the entire political map," he said. But he cautioned, "It will happen slowly." On the program, Sari provided his own vision of what coexistence could be like. The idea of a Palestinian state "has been demonized in people's minds and it's all to do with psychology," he explained. "I think the more it is shown to them, how a future Palestinian state would coexist side by side with Israel, how it is possible, what the different bits and pieces of the Palestinian state would look like, the more it becomes known to them, I think the less afraid they would be of it."

He explained that in trying to reach an accommodation with his coauthor on the requirements for Israeli security, they tried to go beyond the traditional concept of a border as the clearly delineated fence between states. Their discussion was reminiscent of Robert Frost's admonition that before he put up a wall, he'd make sure to know what he was fencing in or fencing out. "We tried to think about the nature of the relation that will exist across the border . . . and the extent to which you're able to draw up a border which was permeable or porous, which allowed for a free flow of services, goods, people, capital—to that extent you find it easier to agree on a location."

Having grown up on the border between Israel and Jordan, and having spent much of his life crossing the transparent fence that divides Jerusalem, Sari understands the importance of openness. He recalled that even before the start of the *intifada*, fear created its own barrier between the Israelis and the Palestinian people. Someone had called him from West Jerusalem to let him know that United Parcel Service (UPS) was holding a package for him. "We'll leave it at Ben Yehuda [the central post office] and you can come and collect it," the voice on the other end of the phone said. "What do you mean, leave it at Ben Yehuda? Are you crazy?" Sari replied. He told the agent he would pick it up at the UPS office in East Jerusalem. "I'm sorry. We don't have any service to East Jerusalem," the Israeli said. In that case, Sari said, send the package back to whoever sent it or put it in the mail. The agent said he could not post it because his instructions were to give it to him by hand. "So I said, give it to me by hand. But I'm not coming to West Jerusalem to pick it up. I didn't order it, so why do I want it? Why did you accept it in the first place if you don't want to give it to me?" Finally, Sari suggested a compromise: bring the package to the American Colony Hotel on Nablus Road, just a couple of minutes' drive from the imaginary border. The agent laughed and said he would call him back. That was five years ago. Sari is still waiting. The days of Alice in Wonderland are long gone. And yet, in his eyes, as in his childhood, a gate still divides the city of Jerusalem.

Zahira Kamal

In the town and village meetings where Zahira Kamal, a member of the negotiating team, often discusses the progress of the Israeli-Palestinian peace talks, men file into the meeting place first, then teenage boys. Finally, young girls and then women enter, almost hesitantly, to stand awkwardly in the corner. It is symbolic of women's subordinate status in Arab society, and the scene is reproduced daily, over and over again.

Along the crowded Salahadin Street in East Jerusalem, within the narrow channels of the Old City, women in their forties and fifties bargain with shopkeepers and peddlers for a kilo of beef or pistachios. They wear the traditional Palestinian dress: solid cotton with colorful embroidery running down the length of the garment's sides and a complementary geometric pattern reproduced above the waist. Between marketing and tending to their children and household duties, they meet with one another to discuss their lives. Amongst themselves they find a comforting camaraderie derived from a common experience. They will tell you, sometimes with a hint of regret, how they married when they were young and had children soon thereafter. Since then their lives have been routinized, almost always directed outward to others, whether husband, children, or neighbors.

Then there are the daughters, young women sometimes dressed in Western-style clothes surveying the latest fashions. In the American Colony Hotel in East Jerusalem it is not uncommon to find free-thinking young women, wearing jeans and T-shirts, gathered in the courtyard sipping a cocktail, discussing their jobs, their families, and their boyfriends. They complain of how restrictive their parents are, how their brothers are given freedom but they are bound by a set of implicit rules, how they would prefer to be living independently but resist such maverick acts for fear of society's censure. They are educated and liberal and conceive of a different life, one apart from their mothers', apart from the monotony of domestic work. They believe in having an identity not derived from their husband's name but from their own set of accomplishments.

Zahira Kamal has played a large part in this modernization of Palestinian society. Starting from the traditional role of woman as teacher, she become a political activist, aligned with the leftist Democratic Front for the Liberation of Palestine (DFLP), and since the 1970s has been in the vanguard of the Palestinian women's movement.

She is one of the three women (along with Hanan Ashrawi and Suad Amiry) on the Palestinian team participating in the Middle East peace talks. She is outspoken and direct but, to date, less well known than those delegates to whom the media gravitate. She is concerned with substance, and shies away from the TV cameras. While Ashrawi was a familiar image on television, articulating the Palestinians' position on the progress of the talks, Zahira was much harder to find. She says she shuns the spotlight, believing it takes time away from her work. "If you want to follow the media," she says, "you couldn't work. What I prefer is to have some time to read, to discuss, to have meetings."

Zahira's almost aloof disposition should not be mistaken for indifference, however. She is intensely committed to two issues—womens' rights and liberation from the Israeli military occupation. Her noncomformist choices have been challenged and criticized, both by her society and by her family, and perhaps it has been this pattern of struggle that has strengthened her sense of herself. She speaks without hesitancy, as a woman confident in her personal choices and values. When she talks about the women's movement, she speaks about solidarity, sisterhood and the need for collective action, and the simple truth that progress in women's rights will come only with struggle. Zahira is aware that Palestinian women must emancipate themselves from two binding forces, occupation and male domination, and that one cannot be subordinated to the other. This dual encounter with patriarchy and subjugation has been complicated still further by the widening influence of Islamic fundamentalism in the Arab world.

As she sits on a modern-style sofa in the sitting room of her mother's home in Shu'afat, overlooking the mountains outside Jerusalem, Zahira is dressed in a knee-length paisley skirt and a soft-pink turtleneck sweater. Her mother, Fakhrieh, is wearing the more traditional *hijab*, her pink robe completely covering her legs and a white scarf over her head. The contrasting lifestyles are noticeable. "We are looking," Zahira says, her dark eyes unblinking, "at completely changing the role of women in our society."

Zahira was born in 1945 in the Wadi Joz district of East Jerusalem, into a middle-class family. Ahmed, her father, the son of a Jerusalemite merchant, was a geography teacher and later taught math and religion at Rashidiah School. The Kamal family dates to the time of Salahadin, in 570 A.D. Ahmed married Fakhrieh, a young Palestinian woman, just seventeen years old, when he had reached his early forties. They had eight children—six girls and two boys. Zahira is the eldest.

Ahmed was a progressive man, thoughtful and concerned with the issues of the day. He invited friends to his home to socialize and to talk about everything, from the mundane to serious political discourse. As a teenager Zahira would often be included in their bantering. She would sit in the living room with all the men and sometimes even offer her opinions. It is slightly ironic, then, that this feminist who seeks to mobilize women, to empower them economically and politically, would derive her single-mindedness from her father's example. Ahmed was the person she cast as her role model.

Zahira was deeply marked, too, by an earlier incident that cost a young girl her life. It was in 1956, less than a decade into the Jordanian occupation of Jerusalem and the West Bank. One day a local mob rushed down the Kamals' usually quiet street near the Rockefeller Museum. Made up mostly of students, the group was conducting a protest—carrying placards and shouting political slogans. The protesters stopped at the Turkish Consulate, where the protest intensified. One eighteen-year-old high school student, Raga Amashah, climbed up the facade of the consulate, grabbed out at the Turkish flag, and set it ablaze. As she did this, the local Jordanian police fired at her. Amashah fell from the building; when she landed on the ground, she was dead.

Zahira and other members of her family witnessed the entire event from their balcony. "I have never forgotten it," says Zahira now. For her, it was the first display of Palestinian nationalism. "The Turkish flag," she says, "was the symbol of imperialism as such"—though the Ottoman Turkish rule of Palestine was but a forty-year memory, and though the British, too, had relinquished reponsibility over their Mandate of Palestine in 1947.

The imprint Raga Amashah's death left on Zahira was the undeniable truth that nothing could come without sacrifice. This introductory lesson was reinforced during her five years in Cairo between 1963 and 1968, when she received her bachelor's degree. Whereas during the 1980s, before the closure of Palestinian universities in the West Bank and Gaza, women composed roughly 40 percent of the student body of Birzeit University, in Jerusalem in the 1960s, Zahira was one of only five out of her class of thirty to continue her education. As she recalls, "At that time, even if you are from a bourgeoisie family you didn't go. They waited for the man to come and marry them." Zahira aspired to more. When she reflected on her mother's life, she could not envision herself in the same role.

Fakhrieh was a literate, intelligent woman. She was sensitive to her children's needs. But she also married as a teenager—she was "like a daughter" to her husband, says Zahira, "and not like a wife." Fakhrieh conformed to the traditional woman's role. In keeping with her culture's norm, she had not attended college; she had married at a young age, had borne many children, and had remained at home while her husband worked to support the family. The six Kamal girls were expected, too, to marry and raise families—attending university was not part of the calculus.

But after Zahira passed her matriculation exams, she convinced her father to permit her to continue her education. Over the objections of his wife and relatives, he backed his daughter, enabling Zahira to attend college abroad. As a teacher himself, he understood the value of education. His daughter says simply, "He wanted me to go on studying." At the Egyptian university Zahira attended formal lectures and discussions on the theater; she joined a Palestinian student union—this, at a time when the Nasser regime had outlawed political organizations; she attended seminars where accomplished and new writers discussed their works. "Cairo," she says, was a "very wide bookshop. Whatever you wanted to find, it was there."

By 1968 the Jerusalem that Zahira returned to, after graduating with her bachelor of science degree, was vastly changed. Israel's victory a year earlier in the Six-Day War brought the newly unified Holy City under Jewish control. In order to return home Zahira was compelled to obtain special permits from the new civil and military administrations. This was her first taste of Israeli occupation. When she arrived, she learned that her father, by then in his late sixties, was seriously ill; he would die a year and a half later. Out of necessity, Zahira assisted her mother and her younger sisters in managing the household. It was her first brush as a university-educated woman with the routine obligations of domestic family life. "I made sure then," she told *Ha'aretz* in 1990, "that no one else would get involved in making our decisions. Basically, I was responsible for a large family comprised mostly of adolescent kids."

Zahira also began working as an instructor at the Teachers Training College in Ramallah, a position she still holds. The training institute was run by the United Nations Relief and Works Agency (UNRWA). Zahira prepared the students for careers in teaching, physics, and science. Her students included poor residents of the nearby refugee camps. As part of the curriculum, they participated in the Host Schools program, in which they worked as student teachers in schools near their homes. "I visited them there," Zahira recalls. "I visited their houses in the camps and such. When I saw the women—the miserable life of a woman, the high number of children they have . . ." She sighs. "Sometimes they have nine girls and they are looking for a boy. To me, it meant we should work on that." As a science teacher Zahira quickly began drawing up plans for conveying the most elementary facts of life to her female students. Her courses included what would appear to Westerners to be basic lessons on genetics, on "who is responsible for the sex of the child, from the scientific point of view." Her aim, she says, was to help her students understand "that it is the man who is responsible."

The teacher's experience with the refugee camps was the germ that brought forth more wide-ranging plans for transforming the role of her gender in society. Still, this activist is uncomfortable with the label of "feminist." She puts the matter into its simplest human rights terms: "When we are talking about feminism, it is the right of women to work and get an education." With these, women can acquire the skills for economic independence, to move freely, to read and to study, and therefore to achieve some quotient of self-fulfillment.

But she has been bucking tradition. There are fundamental social, societal, and religious obstacles to confront in Palestinian life. First and foremost is the patriarchal base, from which the other obstacles derive. The role of man as the protector has evolved from the rural villages, where the culture emphasized the extended family unit. The family stood above the individual, the wife deferring to the husband and the sister to the brother. In this rigid social structure the woman was bound by her father's will, then, after marriage, to her husband's.

Throughout recent Palestinian history, women's roles ebbed and flowed with the political current and the changing times. The roles, to be sure, did evolve over the course of decades, together with the rise of Palestinian nationalism. Indeed, the women's movement even predated the national movement. As early as the 1920s, during the British period, women banded together for charitable purposes. But charity was accompanied by an air of patronage. Works were administered mainly by upper-class women on behalf of their less fortunate sisters. As the British-Arab-Jewish conflict intensified, so did the activism of Palestinian women. In 1929 the Arab Ladies Committee was formed in response to the killing by British soldiers of nine Arab women—out of 120 Arabs—at Jerusalem's al-Aqsa Mosque.

A turning point occurred in 1948, the year Israel proclaimed statehood and Arab refugees streamed across the land. Many in the upper class left the Jewish state. Middle-class women began assuming the roles in the "charitable organizations" that had previously been handled by wealthier women. Since they, too, had lost a great deal of their property, they were imbued with a strong motivation to fight back politically. But because they were women, their outlets remained limited. They carried on the welfare work of the organizations, though the recipients had by then changed.

Instead of just the economically underprivileged, the beneficiaries of their welfare work were now prisoners and the families of prisoners, especially other women.

In 1964 the Palestine Liberation Organization (PLO) was founded, and in 1965 the General Union of Palestinian Women was formed. The General Union quickly recruited members by tapping the vast personal contacts of women themselves—in the villages, in the families, in the towns. Women were brought out, through the General Union, to attend political gatherings commemorating national events, for example, the anti-Israeli demonstration held annually on the anniversary of the Balfour Declaration, the British document drafted on November 2, 1917, that recognized the right of Jews to establish a homeland in Palestine. But once a demonstration ended, participants dispersed and returned home. There was no follow-up, no framework, no structure with which to generate long-term projects and strategy on the women's agenda. And the group's raison d'être remained to help, not to organize; to run orphanages and hospitals, not to raise consciousness.

Another turning point occurred after the 1967 defeat, coinciding with the Israeli occupation of the territories. Palestinian women began joining men in military operations directed at Israel. The Israeli forces subsequently began arresting women in increasing numbers for the first time. As a result, women were exposed to prison life. When they emerged, sometimes charging they had been sexually abused, they were inflamed with the passion of revolt. For them, the do-good structure of charitable organizations no longer sufficed as an outlet. Nor were the charitable societies sufficiently flexible to reflect the new political realities. They were intimidated by the stronger, more politically conscious women emerging from the prisons. The organizations lacked the ability to keep up with this new generation of revolution-minded women.

Zahira became a member of the In'ash al Usra Society in the town of al Bireh, close to Ramallah. In'ash al Usrah is the largest charitable organization in the occupied territories. Established in 1965 by Samiha Khalil, an indomitable woman, it is led by a group of women whose families were urban traders and landowners. It concentrates on training women in traditional roles, such as sewing, cooking, and secretarial skills, and employs them and then sells their products in bazaars and through a distribution network. Samihah Khalil, affectionately known as *Umm*, or "mother," Khalil for being the foster parent to so many widows and children of martyrs killed in the *intifada*, once viewed Zahira as a protege. But in recent years, Samihah, who is a supporter of a rival political faction of the Democratic Front, has objected to Zahira's willingness to meet with American officials and also criticizes, along with other committee members, her attempts to press women's issues.

Though the society emphasizes training, it does little to empower women politically or to improve their social status. Zahira found her work frustrating. "We didn't change the role of the woman in society. It was just very selective women sharing in that kind of work." She found the mentality governing the leaders of In'ash al Usrah not progressive enough. "They accepted their [women's] national role, but they didn't want them to be socially active and get positions in every place." As Islah Abdul Jawwad, a Birzeit University scholar, says, the task of the charitable organizations "is not to organize women. It is not to raise the consciousness of women or to fight for women's causes or agenda. It's mainly helping." Zahira was part of a new generation that found the structure of the charitable organizations inadequate. "We have two generations now," she says: hers, which believes the issue is urgent, and the "other one, feeling that it is not the time" to press women's issues, believing that the need exists but that the right time to pursue it is "after the liberation."

So in 1974 she and her colleagues began planting the seeds for a more effective self-help apparatus that grew into the Women's Work Committee (WWC), founded in Ramallah in 1978. The WWC later split, following the pattern of the trade unions, producing four organizations that mirrored the political divisions within Palestinian society. All the four major political groupings established committees to enlarge their parties through women: the Federation of Palestinian Women's Action Committee (FPWAC), which Zahira heads, is the largest and is aligned with the DFLP; the Union of Palestinian Working Women's Committees was established on March 8, 1980 (International Women's Day), and is aligned with the People's (formerly Communist) Party; the Union of Palestinian Women Committee was established in March 1981 and is affiliated with the Popular Front for the Liberation of Palestine (PFLP); and the Women's Committee for Social Work was established in June 1982 and is associated with *Fatah*. Zahira aknowledges that progress has been delayed by "the competition between different committees" and concedes that "this affects the programs they are doing. Now, I think, they have come to accept the idea of . . . not *unification*, but I could say *united programs*." She adds, "Hopefully this will lead to a united women's movement."

Since the 1960s Zahira has supported the DFLP. While *Fatah* as an organization used to deny differentiations within society, it was the leftist groups that were concerned with women's issues. For the mainstream *Fatah*, the primary objective has been to end Israeli military occupation, so workers, peasants, and women had to subordinate their own cause to that of national liberation. In contrast, the leftists, such as the DFLP and the communists, claimed to help the peasants and the poor, and because women are oppressed they had to pay attention to women's issues.

The DFLP was established in February 1969, when it splintered off from the PFLP. Based on Marxist-Leninist ideals, it was founded by Nayef Hawatmeh as a movement that sought grassroots support in trying to mobilize the masses. In 1970 it pursued a strategy of attempting to unite Palestinian villages in northern Jordan with those in the Jordan River Valley in hopes of launching joint offensives against Israel. But later that year the operation was crushed as a result of King Hussein's bloody Black September campaign to liquidate the Palestinian guerrilla cells.

The DFLP subsequently split into two. The new wing, headed by Yasser Abed Rabbo, adopted a more Maoist line. In August 1973 the Abed Rabbo faction broke new ground in Middle East politics. It spoke of establishing a Palestinian state in the West Bank, in addition to the state on the Jordanian eastern side of the river. The Palestinian entity would exist alongside Israel. To most Israelis, however, this ideology, while appearing moderate, was a more refined version of the old threat: to them, coexistence was merely envisioned as an interim phase, a step toward ultimately supplanting the Jewish state with a democratic, secular Palestinian state. It is the Yasser Abed Rabbo wing of the DFLP that Zahira supports.

Abed Rabbo, former deputy to DFLP chief Nayef Hawatmeh,

is a polished, chain-smoking activist-turned-diplomat who was the chief Palestinian negotiator in the talks that the United States held with the PLO in Tunis in 1989-1990. Hawatmeh, based in Damascus, opposes the Madrid peace talks and the "expanded" autonomy that they are aimed at creating; Abed Rabbo supports the peace process and the Israeli-Palestinian talks, leading one senior Israeli official to jibe that his DFLP faction is "the little *Fatah*." Zahira Kamal, says the Israeli, is a "salon activist," implying that she is a descendant of the "ladies of the salon" who ran the charitable organizations in an earlier era. The Israeli says that the Abed Rabbo faction of the DFLP does not have a mass following. Hawatmeh has the troops in the streets. "He has the rank and file. Abed Rabbo has CNN." Zahira, however, is used to such sniping. She won't let it deter her. She stresses the need for a two-state solution. The Jewish settlers, however, must leave the West Bank; she claims they are there illegally. "We believe, in our committee, that we should work for both—the national and the social work. This is the reason why we started the committees, because charitable societies are not working for the women's issues as women's issues," she says. The FPWAC aims at reaching the majority of the women. "So we go to the villages and the camps and we work at the grass-roots level with housewives. It is part of the national movement in the West Bank and Gaza Strip, looking for our self-determination." At the same time, she adds, it stands for "changing the role of women in society."

The FPWAC strove first and foremost to eliminate female illiteracy among housewives—beginning with the basics. "And not just reading and writing," asserts Zahira, "but also to discuss, to let them be open-minded, to accept ideas. Then we could go on." Second, the organization instituted an intensive job-training program. "We had to train them," says Kamal, "with some kind of skills so that they could get proper work" and earn their own wages. She explains the premise as one aimed at "taking women out of the house, the first step toward social liberation." For example, a Gaza program taught participants to mass-produce biscuits and dairy products. In Ramallah, women were taught to sew and to work with copper. The new skills themselves were supplemented with courses in business planning and marketing. Slowly, the women were becoming cooperative entrepreneurs.

Zahira also introduced family-planning classes. She brought discussions of birth control out into the open, although she considers birth control as a more effective family planning. In Zahira's view, parents should spread out the births of their children to be no closer than three years apart. "From the health point of view, the general health of the mother and the psychological health of the child, it is needed to have spaces between the children," says Zahira. Furthermore, she considers enlightened child-bearing as not inconsistent with Muslim doctrine. To those Islamicists who question her sincerity, she cites a passage in the Koran that, she maintains, sets family-planning standards.

Finally, the FPWAC began organizing such basic support services as day care for the new working women. It established twenty-six kindergartens and six nurseries. It offered health care and circulated a health bulletin. It even taught courses in time management, aimed at helping women balance the pressures of outside work with their cooking, cleaning, and laundry duties at home.

One thing it was not necessary to offer was current affairs or education on the internal situation. Politics were, and are, covered in lessons as events dictate and as interest demands, she says. But the day's events hit so close to home that formal group instruction is superfluous. Zahira says the people "are living the situation. They don't need education politically."

Establishing the work-study programs brought Zahira into contact with a cross-section of Palestinian society throughout the territories. She had to walk the thin line between conveying enlightened progress and posing a threat, between political correctness and radicalism. In the *Ha'aretz* interview, she recalls the initial effort this way: "We developed local cadres in villages, refugee camps, and towns. When we'd get to one town, we'd try to form a cadre of local women, bypassing the town elite. We tried to support them and give them ideas. And we tried to educate them, but not to compel them. We also tried to involve the men, even the clergy—but not to go against the tradition, but rather with it." Zahira admits candidly that the issues she raises have no easy answers. When asked how she balances family planning against women's assumed obligation to produce Palestinian offspring, she replies bluntly, "I couldn't say that we resolved this."

Although Zahira's advocacy has not led to consequences more severe than heated arguments with her own people, it has, from time to time, caused her trouble with the Israeli authorities. In 1979 she was held in administrative detention for over four months for alleged security violations. "They didn't tell me why," she recalls of the officers who came to her house to bring the news. "They didn't say anything." But they did attempt, she says, to scare her by threatening to extend the detention in six-month increments. To the Israelis, she represented a dual threat. They were suspicious that she was using her frequent trips to leftist conventions abroad to funnel money from the PLO to guerrilla groups inside the territories and suspected that she supported the DFLP, which advocated an ideology, the Israelis believed, that sought to replace Israel with a binational, secular state. Thus, to many Israelis, particularly in the security service, her organizational skills were a threat to everything Jewish about the Zionist nation.

Zahira maintains that her imprisonment was unjustified, that she was merely engaged in the day-to-day activities on behalf of the WWC. Perhaps, she infers, her arrest was part of a general attempt at silencing Palestinian leadership. Indeed, the authorities never asked or demanded that she sign a confession. They were always trying to to wrangle a confession from the other prisoners. "But for me it was, I know, that I didn't do anything." She believes her arrest was politically motivated, a consequence of her outspokenness against the 1979 Camp David accords, which were signed just months before she was apprehended. Zahira says she was "not afraid then to tell anyone that I'm against Camp David" for, in her view, neglecting the Palestinians.

The period of administrative detention placed Zahira in Moscobiyah, the Russian compound, in the center of Jewish West Jerusalem. The first ten days of her imprisonment in mid-1979 were "something difficult," she says, filled as they were with day-long and night-long interrogations. Ever the student, Zahira had prepared herself for what she knew would be an inevitable prison stay. She expected "not to find a hotel there; it's a prison." She perused books about prison life. She read the reports of noted Israeli lawyers Felicia Langer and Leah Tsemel, two Jewish women who earned their reputations representing Palestinian detainees before the Israeli military authorities. The prospect of prison experience left Zahira "I wouldn't say scared, but [with] a kind of fear inside." It was a fear of the unknown, of what awaited behind the prison walls. But Zahira was subjected to no physical abuse during her incarceration. Besides, she says, fear is normal—and a prerequisite in the struggle. "If there are no fears, there are no brave people."

Zahira was so incensed at what she believed to be the Israelis' attempt to quiet her that she appealed her sentence. On December 12, 1979, one day prior to the scheduled court date, she was released—forty-five days short of the full six-month sentence.

As the books and writings prepared Zahira for administrative detention, the initial experience served as a precursor to a longer term of confinement. Like prison, it was a period of restriction, one that lasted six and a half years but also meant regular contact with the Israeli authorities in and around Zahira's own home. It was what the Israelis called "town arrest," an experience Zahira calls "very difficult, even more difficult than prison." For five of the years under town arrest, Zahira's routine was planned around her registering twice a day with the Israeli authorities. At one hour past sunrise she would venture from her home into East Jerusalem, to her old stomping grounds at Moscobiyah, and sign in. She would then drive to work in Ramallah. She'd return to West Jerusalem for the 2:30 p.m. sign-in.

At the beginning, the routine interfered with Zahira's UNRWA classes. She adapted by leading classes from her home—"the first time," she says, "that physics was taught by letters from the teachers and the students." Each morning she sent over the lessons to be taught, and each afternoon the students' homework was brought to her home. Every two weeks she would travel to the school and teach the lessons personally. At the same time, her FPWAC work demanded Zahira's attention. She would devote herself to her projects in her home during the day, and would encourage friends and colleagues to drop in on her there. By so doing, Zahira prevented herself from being cut off from her work. "All the time that I was at home I was so busy with work that I didn't feel that I'm isolated," she says. "I had a lot of friends that I didn't know I had before."

Far from creating a vindictive radical out of her, the experience altered some of Zahira's preconceptions and broadened her perspective. The Israeli guards with whom she regularly signed in at Moscobiyah were not what she expected. They were among those whom she says she had "a lot of [preconceived] ideas about" but who "are totally different when you meet them. I am not scared at all of security people," she asserts now. "I deal with them . . . with anything, as two equal people. I don't feel that they are above me. I feel that I am one, that I have rights."

Because of articles in the Israeli press as well as international attention—Zahira was twice cited as Amnesty International's Prisoner of the Month—the "town arrest" prisoner received welcome moral support. Even Israelis came to her home in solidarity. Some told her: "We believe what you believe." All in all, says Zahira, the encouragement she received from some Israelis proves "it's not the problem of the people," but rather of some of the leadership who cynically "want the situation to be like this."

Zahira manipulated her situation to convey a point. Having broken the stereotypes, she made it a lesson of sorts for her two young nieces, Maha and Sheren. She meant for the experience to be "a training for them, so they would not always be afraid of such things." Before several early-afternoon sign-ins, Zahira stopped by the kindergarten of little Maha, then four, and Sheren, just three. Their aunt packed sandwiches and the three ascended the hill to Moscobiyah. The nieces at first found the pilgrimage to be anything but the field trip Zahira planned. The younger girl was taken aback the first time she saw the armed prison officials standing alongside her Aunt Zahira as she signed in. But both girls changed. On one field trip to Moscobiyah, with the West Jerusalem lunch crowd going about its business, Maha turned to Zahira. "Oh, Aunt," mewed the niece, contrasting the free scene before her with the measures carried out on occasion in the West Bank, "we hear on television that everywhere there is a curfew. In Ramallah, in Nablus, everywhere a curfew. Why is there not in Moscobiyah a curfew?"

Nowadays, with her nieces approaching adolescence, Zahira sits astonished at their early insight, particularly their ability to attune themselves at such an early age to the different nature of Palestinian and Israeli society. The aunt, single and childless— her mother, Zahira notes with a chuckle, is "worried" about that state of affairs but has no choice but to accept it—describes how

Hanan Mikhail at about age five in Amman, Jordan.

The Mikhail family (from left to right): Nadia, Daoud (father), Muna (standing), Huda (sitting), Abla (standing), Wadia (mother), and Hanan (at age eight).

Hanan Mikhail at her wedding to Emile Ashrawi on August 8, 1975, at St. George's Cathedral in Jerusalem. Hanan was born on October 8, 1946. She says, "Eight is my lucky number."

Hanan Ashrawi and her four sisters present a gold plaque to Wadia and Daoud Mikhail on their parents' fiftieth wedding anniversary. (Daoud Mikhail, a physician, died a few months later.) From left to right: Muna, Hanan, Huda, Daoud, Wadia, Nadia, Abla. Photo Credit: Emile Ashrawi

Protestant Archbishop Samir Kafeity greeting Hanan Ashrawi, her husband Emile, and daughter, Zeina, after Easter mass at St. George's Cathedral in East Jerusalem. Photo Credit: Rula Halawani

Faisal Husseini, age twenty, with his wife, Najat.

Faisal Husseini sitting on the veranda of his home in Wadi Joz, overlooking East Jerusalem. Photo Credit: Rula Halawani

Faisal Husseini clasping hands with peace activist David Shlomo after the Israeli was sentenced to prison for meeting with PLO Chairman Yasser Arafat. Photo Credit: Rula Halawani

Sari Nusseibeh in the garden of his home in Abu Dis, a village on the outskirts of East Jerusalem. Photo Credit: Rula Halawani

Zahira Kamal as a student at the University of Leeds.

Zahira Kamal with her mother, Fakhrieh, at her home in Beit Hanina, a suburb of East Jerusalem. Photo Credit: Rula Halawani

Ziad Abu Zayyad playing Monopoly with his teenage daughters, Lamah (on left) and Hibbah (on right). Photo Credit: Rula Halawani

Ziad Abu Zayyad at age eighteen (third from left, standing) with his father Kahlil (seated) and his mother Aminah (seated) and brothers and sisters.

the two girls play-acted. They sat on opposite sides of the room and one called to the other: "Could you come to visit me?" The other called back: "I'll come, but I'll be a little late because I have to go to the police and sign in." And then she likes to tell about the niece who, in the innocent ways of children, responded to her teacher's asking for an example of a habit. "To go and sign in with the police," came the answer. "If you are under town arrest like my aunt, and you have to go there two times a day, then it becomes a habit." Their aunt's delicately exposing them to the realities of Israeli-Palestinian existence seems to have had a long-lasting effect, making the nieces, in Zahira's eyes, "perhaps much bigger than their age." After the *intifada*, the girls instituted their own personal boycott of Israeli products—extending even to such usually ideology-free childhood pleasures as ice cream and cookies. Not even Aunt Zahira matches their example. She buys Israeli-made clothes on occasion.

In order to keep the FPWAC accounts on what Zahira calls "the right and safe side," the committee maintains an account at Bank Leumi's branch in Ramallah. She knows that since the *intifada*, the archives of the women's committees have been closely watched by the Israeli authorities. Thirteen members of the FPWAC have been arrested since the start of the *intifada*, and hundreds more have been intimidated by the Israeli authorities into skipping committee meetings. They have tried all sorts of tactics, says Zahira. "Since our committee was set up, our offices have been continually raided and names taken from the files. Then the women are called for interrogation," she charges.

The Israelis, she says, also will try to exploit the traditional nature of Muslim society by "not calling the women themselves but by calling their father or their brother or their husband." If he is a merchant, they will threaten to stop his merchandise from crossing the Allenby Bridge into Jordan. "You won't see your produce until you stop your daughter from going to these committees," is what they warn them, she says. "We try our best to go to the families and convince them not to yield to this kind of pressure. Sometimes it works. Sometimes it doesn't. In a country like ours, with its traditional cultural mentality, sometimes the women have been forced to skip the meetings. This is the kind of stress we have to constantly put up with. You know," she says seriously, "I didn't prepare myself for these situations. But when it happens, you find that there is something special going on."

The words of the husky woman with the short black hair echo with as much relevance in the 1990s as they did in the 1960s, as thought-provoking in the West Bank as in developing countries throughout the world. "The logic behind this work," Zahira told *Ha'aretz*, speaking of her initial involvement with women's causes in 1968, "was to take women out of the house. Our basic premise was that taking her out of the house was the first step to social liberation." There was more: "We can't struggle for national liberation without it being accompanied by ongoing achievements in the social realm. One of the building blocks of our state is the creation of a healthy, just society. And in order to do so, we have to liberate the woman."

Yet Zahira also recognizes the shortcomings: "If we are talking about the women's movement, we should involve all sectors of women in it. And if we want to make the change, we should reach also the young in age. We didn't concentrate on students. You'll find we struggled, for instance, for education and work and these kinds of things. The age that is younger than us, they thought things are paved for them and they are used to not struggling for getting these things. And because of this, you could see differences, like forcing women to put on veils." In Palestinian universities, such as an-Najah in Nablus, Hebron, and Islamic University in Gaza, it is common to find women wearing the the veil, a practice many of their mothers have rejected. Zahira does not oppose the veil, "if they are convinced to put it on, if they are believers." She objects when many are intimidated and wear a veil to escape social censure. It is closely related to other rights, Zahira believes, "other rights that are related, work, the right of choosing their husband, not to marry in a young age, all these things are related together. The veil is only one part of it. If you look to the whole it makes the difference."

She considers the Islamicists part and parcel of a conservative, male-dominated Muslim society. She maintains that restrictions on women demanded by fundamentalists, such as ultramodest dress and avoidance of compromising situations, are in fact not based on Islam but on deeply rooted sexism within her society. The fanatical attraction to religion, too, she says, is merely a by-product of poverty and hopelessness. "Not every Muslim," she says, "is a fundamentalist." They only gain credibility in a conservative society when political and economic conditions worsen and people turn to God. The result is that religion finds a fertile breeding ground.

Having made the point, Zahira then proceeds, surprisingly, to deny that the fundamentalists have had any negative effect on the national movement. "In general," she asserts, "we don't find that their influence prevents people from participating" in political activity. She says that after the Madrid peace conference, the fundamentalists participated in broad-based community meetings and made no move to block Palestinian participation in the talks. To underline what she sees as the woman's growing emotional, if not yet actual, liberation, Zahira cites the recent grass-roots backlash against fundamentalism. She mentions that women have been distributing leaflets in Gaza, calling for resistance to wearing the compulsory long, loose-fitting dress, with the head covered. "Women started to fight. I myself saw two fights," she says. "One woman during Ramadan, an annual month-long period of meditation and fasting, was eating an apple. A man said, 'You are not shy? You are eating an apple?' She cursed him and insulted him. Then some youths came and started beating up the man."

Zahira also says it is important to place Islamic fundamentalism in the context of global events. In the last ten years, she says, "we saw an extension of right-wing movements all over the world, and every time they achieved more and more representation in different places," including Western Europe, the United States, the Arab countries, and Israel. "It's Islamic, it's Christian, it's Jewish," she insists. "It is all over the world and we are part of that movement. So it reflects itself on us."

Fear of women's regressing is backed up by recent history. According to Ori Nir, the Washington correspondent of *Ha'aretz*, who covered the occupied territories for four years, the *intifada* marked the first time Palestinian women asserted their independence. Even in the villages, they joined the demonstrations against Israeli rule. The FPWAC and its sister committees organized women to join rallies, to visit wounded demonstrators, to distribute food during curfews, and to collect financial aid for prisoners' families. But there followed a male backlash that relegated the women to their long-held roles. That regression fueled women's fears that national aims would outpace their own gains, fears of, once again, being left behind. The observation led Amal Khreisheh, a leader of one of the four women's committees, to say, "We are heroes in the street and servants in the house."

In March 1989 Zahira predicted that once they have achieved their liberation, Palestinian women will never permit themselves to be relegated in the manner that Algerian women were, regressing from the revolutionary battlefields to the drudgery of housework. In Algeria, she says, the women made a major contribution to the struggle against French colonialism, but then their efforts did not translate into a change in their status in society. "The women of Palestine," she asserts, "will not be like the women of Algeria; that is, they will not be homebodies." For Zahira, however, both roles are indispensable. "If you compare these two things, domestic work at home and activities in the street, you could say the women are heroes in the street and servants in the home. But the role at home is the continuation," she notes, of the battle in the streets. "What's the alternative?"

When the Israeli and diaspora Palestinian press reported on the regression of women during the *intifada*, the Israeli civil administration commissioned a special report, says Nir. It found that despite women's participation on the front lines of the uprising, their social status had indeed not changed. Nor did women's organizations in the territories refute the report's conclusions on the return of the old order, says the Israeli correspondent.

The *intifada*-induced economic slide has taken its toll on the women's movement, too. Zahira speaks of a link between worsening economic conditions and a declining marriage age for Palestinian women. As conditions deteriorate, fathers are shifting responsibility by marrying off their daughters. In addition, she relates the decline in the marriage age to the educational crisis caused by the Israelis' periodic closure of West Bank universities. With education and the consequent employment opportunities threatened, the daughters' opportunities are set back once again. The FPWAC has tried to respond to these newer challenges by offering women social and legal aid in its new Jerusalem office.

Zahira demands, then, that the Palestinian leadership, a closely knit group of men, yield a fair share of influence to women—and not begrudgingly, either. To date, she maintains, the leadership manipulates women's nationalist activism while stifling their progress as women. Finally, the various women's committees must, in her view, unite under the banner of female liberation. An attempt was made in December 1988 to unify the four politically aligned committees in the Higher Women's Council. The Council sought to prevent a backsliding of the gains women had made by presenting a united front of the main politically aligned committees. But that required a degree of cooperation among the women of the DFLP, the PFLP, *Fatah*, and the communists that the men themselves had never achieved. Today the prospects have improved, she says. "There's agreement of all sides on the grass-roots level while on the leadership level it's still being discussed," she says.

As she sits in the restaurant in the foyer of the Grand Hotel in Washington, D.C., during a break in the December 1991 talks, the seemingly uncompromising Zahira Kamal now finds herself as one of three women on the Palestinian team negotiating with Israel. She says she was chosen not for her sex but because of her experience and politics; she admits that her support for the DFLP-Abed Rabbo wing helped broaden the range of representation on the delegation, and she talks of a meeting she and Hanan Ashrawi held before leaving for Washington. They spoke to several hundred women at East Jerusalem's al-Hakawati Theatre. The women represented many different groups and committees. They had come to pass on their recommendations—and hopes—to the two women who had been chosen, together with Suad Amiry, to be on the predominantly male Palestinian delegation.

Says Zahira proudly, "I have been playing a political role since I was a student. I've been struggling inside and outside the family. I'm respected politically for the party that I'm representing in the delegation and I've been accepted by the community, as a people, for whom I've worked on the grass-roots level." She expects and demands that the talks will pave the way for complete equality between the sexes. She cites the 1988 Palestinian Declaration of Independence as providing equal rights for her sex. Although there still are no women on the fifteen-member executive committee of the Palestine National Council (PNC), she says that in any self-government scheme, women must be a vital part of the decision-making process. When the Palestinians finally get their state, she adds, women must be able to attain ministerial ranks and serve equally in a national armed force. "If we are calling for equality, you should be part of everything," she insists.

More than two decades as a physics teacher and an activist in the teachers' union have helped make her name a household word in the territories. "Because of this," she adds, "I've been accepted as part of the delegation and become known as one of the national persons in the country." It has been a long, hard struggle. Says Zahira: "This didn't just happen overnight." But now that the process is under way, it may not take two decades to see a woman leading the Palestinian people.

Ziad Abu Zayyad

It was in early June of 1991, six months after the Gulf War, when, Ziad Abu Zayyad says, he received a phone call from Yossi Sarid asking him to set up a meeting with Faisal Husseini. The balding Ziad, his wisps of hair and mustache slightly grayer after six months in prison for allegedly being a member of the Unified Leadership of the *intifada*, was surprised by the request. His Palestinian colleague Husseini and the Israeli Sarid had been friends for years; ordinarily, they would have had no need for an intermediary like Ziad to arrange a meeting between them.

But Husseini was still smarting from Sarid's bitter attack against him in the liberal Israeli newspaper *Ha'aretz* almost a year earlier. Sarid had written a column telling the Palestinian leader to "get lost" after he voiced support for Iraqi leader Saddam Hussein. Usually, it would have been easy to ignore such an attack, but this one came from the parliamentary conscience of the Israeli left, the Knesset member who had devoted his political career to persuading the Israeli public that Palestinians could be trusted and deserved a state of their own.

Yossi Sarid had also been rebuked by the leader of his own left-wing party, Ratz, for the damage he had caused to the progressive movement in Israel. Sarid and Husseini had not talked for months. It was easy to understand why. The column that appeared on August 17, 1990—two weeks after Iraq invaded Kuwait—was unrestrained in its criticism of the Palestinian response to the invasion. "One has to wear a gas mask to try to overcome the poisonous and repulsive smell of the PLO's position towards Saddam Hussein. The hugs and kisses between Yasser

121

and Saddam cause disgust, but also fear," Sarid wrote.

Like many others who had advocated direct talks with the PLO, Sarid felt betrayed. He had invested a lifetime in the peace movement, turning his back on a more conventional career in the Labor Party, where Golda Meir was grooming him for a future leadership role. Spurning the party's establishment, he had joined Ratz, a small party that advocated recognizing Palestinian rights, quickly gaining a reputation as a man of principle, a deeply committed dove who preferred peace to personal power; even his critics respected his dedication.

So when Sarid's column appeared, it had a devastating impact in Israel and abroad. Israeli embassies, seizing the unexpected opportunity, distributed reprints throughout the world as proof of the bankruptcy of the peace camp, hoping Saddam Hussein had been able to accomplish what Shamir and Sharon had so far failed to achieve: silencing the critics of their hardline policy. Sarid's column was titled "Let Them Come Looking for Me," *them* being Yasser Arafat, Faisal Husseini, and Abdul Wahab Daroushe, an independent Arab member of the Knesset. The Hebrew expression used in the headline, *sheyechappesu otti*, was far more dismissive than its literal translation would indicate. In its colloquial meaning, the Sarid's admonition to the Palestinians was "get lost."

The West Bank leadership should not have been too surprised. Within hours of Iraq's invasion on August 2, 1990, photographs of Saddam Hussein appeared in mosques, shops, and homes in the occupied territories; pro-Iraqi graffiti were scrawled on the ancient stone walls of Jerusalem, and leaflets were circulated extolling the virtues of the Iraqi leader. For Palestinians, emotions, not reason, ruled the day. Here was the heroic figure they had been waiting for, a modern-day Saladin; not since Gamal Abdul Nasser had there been anyone who so brazenly threatened Israel. He vowed he would actually use chemical weapons against the Jewish state if it continued to defy the United Nations resolutions that called for immediate withdrawal from the West Bank and Gaza. If the Western world wanted Iraq to comply with U.N. resolutions demanding it withdraw from Kuwait, it would first have to coerce Israel into complying with the "international legitimacy" it had ignored for a quarter of a century.

Even if Saddam was using the Palestinian issue to cloak his

lust for more oil and land, that mattered little to the inhabitants of the West Bank and Gaza; they applauded his linkage to their cause and cheered his reckless threats of chemical and nuclear blackmail. For them, Saddam's daring had put the stateless Palestinians back on the map; his brash behavior mirrored their own outrage at a world that for too long had tolerated Israeli occupation and was deaf to their loud and painful pleas for help.

The Israelis, of course, saw things differently. Palestinians, in refusing to condemn Iraqi aggression against Kuwait, and in cheering from the sidelines, were revealing their true colors. If a picture is worth a thousand words, the photo of Yasser Arafat's affectionate embrace of Saddam Hussein spoke volumes. How could any Palestinian be believed anymore when their leader, the guerrilla chieftain who had renounced terrorism and recognized Israel, was hugging the madman who vowed to obliterate the Jewish state? "You have to understand what the attitude was at the time," Israeli defense analyst Mark Heller told the *Washington Post*. "There was a great deal of anger and outrage and a sense of betrayal on the part of a lot of Israelis who had been inclined to think positively about direct negotiations with the Palestinians. And now, at the first opportunity, they had gone and tossed their support to somebody like Saddam Hussein. A lot of people threw up their hands and said, 'These are the people we're supposed to be making peace with?'"

Yossi Sarid had framed the issue squarely in his column. "If it is acceptable to champion Saddam Hussein, who has murdered tens of thousands of his regime's opponents without batting an eye, who unleashed poison gas on Kurdish men, women, and children," he wrote, "then maybe it's not so terrible to support the policies of Shamir, Sharon, and Rabin; compared to the crimes of Saddam Hussein, the sins of the government of Israel are as pure as the driven snow." He noted that he still supported the right of Palestinians to a state of their own, "because it is my right to get rid of the occupation," but served notice that "Arafat, Husseini, and Daroushe should not be surprised if the moral outcry about the horrors in the occupied territories is reduced to a whisper," adding that "until further notice, as far as I am concerned, they can come and try to find me!"

The fallout between the Israeli left and the local Palestinian leadership was so profound that Ziad was genuinely surprised when he received that phone call from the Israeli politician seeking his help. But he was also pleased that he might be able to help Sarid and Husseini reconcile their differences. It was a role Ziad had been playing for more than two decades, ever since he graduated from law school at Damascus University in 1965 and soon found that he had an uncanny ability to think and speak like an Israeli. He also was exposed to them: he had made his first contact with Israeli bureaucrats in 1965 in his job with the Jordanian Government, as supervisor of the Department of Passports and Immigration in Jerusalem.

After Israel conquered the West Bank in 1967 and annexed Jerusalem, the twenty-seven-year-old Ziad attended an *ulpan*, a school where Israelis teach recent Jewish immigrants the Hebrew language. The intensive course was given at Beit Ha'am, "The House of The People," in the center of West Jerusalem. Ziad was the first Arab to enroll. For a few years after the occupation, he served as a Hebrew translator for *al-Quds*, a pro-Jordanian newspaper; then, in 1977, he began editing a Hebrew-language edition of *al-Fajr*, a pro-PLO newspaper. When *al-Fajr* stopped publishing the Hebrew edition in 1986, Ziad decided to publish his own Hebrew-language Palestinian newspaper, *Gesher*, "The Bridge." It was a personal effort to reach out to the Israeli public.

It was through Ziad that Palestinian and Israeli journalists made their first contacts. Some people joke that journalists and criminals are the only ones who cooperate across the "green line," the border that divides Israelis from the Palestinians. But it is no joke: the bonds that Ziad helped establish between Israeli and Palestinian correspondents are real and enduring. They were the only lines of communication that remained intact during the Gulf War. They often go out on stories together, even when that entails some risk. Two Israeli writers, Danny Rubinstein and Meron Benvenisti, teamed with Ziad on *The West Bank Handbook: A Political Lexicon*, the first book to be jointly penned by Israeli and Palestinian authors. And when Palestinian reporters want to bypass the strict Israeli censors, they occasionally provide the raw data to an Israeli colleague, who publishes the story; the following day the report appears in an Arab newspaper translated from the Israeli press.

Ziad is no stranger to reaching across forbidden lines. Even his home town, Bethany, site of the biblical cave where Jesus is said to have raised Lazarus from the dead, sits astride the border with the West Bank. Part of Bethany, called Ezariya by the Arabs, is within the municipal boundaries of Jerusalem and part of it is outside Israel, in the West Bank. Arabs who live in the part of Bethany that is inside the "green line" have yellow Israeli license plates on their cars; those, like Ziad, who live in the West Bank part of Bethany have the mandatory blue plates. Ziad has operated on both sides, in Israel and in the West Bank, a human seam who has striven to explain to Israelis what binds the Palestinians together and what gives them identity as a people and as a nation. Ziad also understood Jewish suffering, having often spent evenings giving lectures at kibbutzim and having made pilgrimages of his own to Yad Vashem, the Holocaust memorial.

When Ziad spoke to Sarid, he says, Sarid told him he felt his article had caused damage, and that he wanted to "start seeking a compromise." Sarid, however, says that it was the Palestinians who sought the reconciliation. "One day I got the message that Faisal Husseini wants to see me, and I said, 'I'll be happy to see him.' I didn't view it as a reconciliation meeting. I didn't have anything to reconcile about," he insists. Adds Sarid, "I didn't fight with anyone. I just expressed my view. I still stand behind it."

After the conversation with Sarid, Ziad called Dr. Ahmed Tibbi, an Arab citizen of Israel who was close to Faisal Husseini and who was often sought out himself by Israeli politicians and journalists as a channel to Yasser Arafat. Tibbi, a respected Palestinian gynecologist, suggested that the three of them—Sarid, Husseini, and Abu Zayyad—meet at his home in Dahiat al-Barid, a neighborhood just beyond East Jerusalem on the road to Ramallah. There, on a hot June day, behind the glass walls of his front veranda, where Tibbi had installed metal bars to protect his sun room from assaults by the Israeli police, the two Palestinians and the Israeli politician began to make amends. "The aim was just to break the ice, to start, to see if we were still friends and if we could still socialize together," explains Ziad. Most important, they wanted to put the personal bitterness that had arisen after the *Ha'aretz* article behind them.

"I think the evening was very successful," says Ziad. They pointedly avoided talking politics. When Sarid wanted to take some photographs to prove to his critics that he had restored relations with the Palestinians, Husseini and Ziad demurred. "We were there as human beings and there was no need for publicity. So I asked that there be nothing in the press. That would be clear evidence that we had not stage this meeting to score political points," says Ziad, adding that "Sarid was very understanding about that." It had taken almost a year, from August of 1990 to June of 1991, for both sides to cross the gulf that had divided them. Ziad, the human bridge, suggested they expand the contacts. "We started planning a bigger meeting with some Knesset members," he says. But passions remained so strong from the Gulf War that the meeting never took place.

Ziad, however, continued his own efforts. In August 1991, a year after the Iraqi invasion, he appeared on a panel with Faisal Husseini and two Israelis, Shlomo Lahat and Mordecai Gur, at Tel Aviv University. Gur is a prominent Labor leader in the Knesset, is a former minister of health and the general who commanded Israeli forces when they reunified Jerusalem in June 1967. Lahat, also a retired army general, is the mayor of Tel Aviv. He is a political maverick who is a member of the Likud but supports the Palestinian right to statehood and direct talks with the PLO. Security was very tight in the university's Gilman Hall. Outside, protesters demonstrated from Israel's most militant factions, the Gush Emunim, Rehavam Zeevi's Moledet, and Meir Kahane's Kach. "Luckily, we arrived forty-five minutes late," says Ziad. "Some of them thought we were not coming, and left. We sneaked in through a back door." Inside, an audience of more than 500 students had gathered for the debate. Among them Ziad noticed four girls dressed in traditional Islamic clothes, their heads covered in *kaffeyahs*, their bodies covered in *jalabiyyas*, garments that reach down to the ankles. "It demonstrated the level of self-confidence that the Islamic movement has reached," says Abu Zayyad. "Here, in the middle of Tel Aviv University, in a large auditorium where you had a mostly Jewish, Israeli audience, here you had four Arab girls studying at an Israeli university and coming and sitting there and asking all kinds of questions of the panel."

The most common question asked by the Israelis was how the Palestinians could have any moral basis for condemning the occupation when they had applauded Iraq's occupation of Kuwait and cheered when many of the thirty-nine Scud missiles that were fired at Israel hit populated areas, killing several civilians? "You should not judge us by the emotional reaction in the street," Ziad tried to explain. The important thing, he stressed, was that the Palestinian political position had not changed and that it remained committed to the November 1988 resolutions of the Palestine National Council, which accepted a two-state solution. "Since the PLO did not pull back or withdraw from this position," Ziad told the Israeli audience, "you do not have the right to tell us how we should feel about Iraq or Kuwait. That is a dispute within the Arab family and we must be free to express our emotions. The support for Saddam has nothing to do with Israel, nor was it real support, because we believed the PLO was in a very difficult position: they were forced to choose whether you are with us [Iraq] or against us."

The PLO, he insisted, tried to remain neutral and to mediate a solution between Iraq and Kuwait, but it failed. Ziad accused the Israeli government, and its media, of trying to equate the PLO with Iraq and of deliberately exaggerating the use of the photo of Saddam Hussein greeting Arafat on his arrival in Baghdad. "This was a campaign for the character assassination of the PLO and of Arafat himself," Ziad charged. But he did not disguise, even in front of an Israeli audience, that the PLO leader made a grievous error. "In the end, we are here to decide what to do about the future. This is all part of the past. Even if it was true, even if Arafat made a mistake, every politician makes mistakes and you cannot continue to judge me by my mistakes. We have to learn from our mistakes but also go on and take future steps together."

Ziad occasionally spoke to the students in Hebrew. "We think of him almost as an Israeli," says Ori Nir, the Washington correspondent of *Ha'aretz*. "Ziad speaks Hebrew so well, he knows so many Israelis and how they think, that we tend to treat him like one and lose respect for his Palestinian sensitivities. He is a very sensitive man." In fact, Ziad was motivated to learn Hebrew when an old friendship was rekindled between an Israeli and his eighty-three-year-old father, Khalil, a peasant and a landowner. "He experienced the Turkish period, the British period, the Jordanian period, and the Israeli occupation. His generation represents the Palestinians who never had a happy day in their lives; they are still reliving World War I, World War II, the British mandate, the 1948 war between the Arabs and the Jews, and now the Israeli occupation." On a mid-June summer day in 1967, after Israel had captured the West Bank from Jordan, Ziad was at home standing in the courtyard of his family's two-story house in Bethany. He saw a soldier patrolling in that area suddenly approach his father as he was sitting in front of the house. The Israeli, on reserve duty, studied his father's face, and his father studied the Israeli's face. Hesitantly, they asked each other's name. Now, absolutely sure that they were not mistaken, that they were the two old friends who had worked together but had not seen one another for twenty years, the men hugged in joy. The soldier, Shimon Spiegel, was invited in for coffee, and the friendship was reborn. They talked of their days working side by side in the Jerusalem municipality during the British mandate and how their paths had separated after the 1948 war. It was impossible to travel from Bethany to Jerusalem because of the curfew, so Spiegel asked if he could bring Khalil something from the city. "I remember," says Ziad, "he said to me, 'Jerusalem will be open to the Arabs and you can come into West Jerusalem. Here is my telephone number. Call me and I will take you for a drive and show you all around.'"

Ziad kept in touch with Spiegel. And when the curfew was lifted a month later, he called the Israeli, a well-known building contractor, at his office. But the secretary who answered the phone could speak neither Arabic nor English, and Ziad could not speak Hebrew. "I said to myself, 'This is nonsense. Here we are living with these people and we cannot communicate, not even on the telephone.'" Ziad vowed to change his life.

Spiegel introduced him to a professor of Arabic literature at Hebrew University who helped Ziad enroll in the intensive Hebrew course for new immigrants at the *ulpan* Beit Ha'am. Before long thirty more Palestinians had joined the class. Ziad developed a close personal relationship with the school's director, Ruth Alon, whose husband, Menachem, was a supreme court judge and would later run against Chaim Herzog as the Likud candidate for president. "Some of the teachers complained that the Palestinian students in the classes were preventing them from doing their Zionist duty, and they asked to divide the classes into some for the Arabs and some for the Jews," recalls Ziad. "But Ruth Alon refused. She said, 'If Jerusalem is unified, I will not allow my classes to be divided.' She was a very wonderful lady. She insisted that the Palestinian Arab students and the Jews must continue to be in the same classes."

The Alons' three sons represented the Israeli political spectrum: one was a member of the extremist religious party Gush Emunim, one was a lawyer and a moderate, and the third was a secular liberal. Over the years, Ziad would spend many evenings with the Alon family, both at their house and at his. At one point, too, when the Palestinian's brother was in trouble with the Israeli authorities, Safi Alon, the lawyer, would represent him in court.

With his knowledge of Arabic, English, and Hebrew, Ziad took on three jobs, acting as a translator in each. In the morning he taught science at a local school. In the afternoon he worked for the Jerusalem District Electric Co., the Arab utility that supplied electricity to the Jews. His job was to translate letters, ranging from complaints to requests for additional service, written by Israelis in the Jewish quarter inside the Old City and by Israelis in French Hill and the other new suburbs around Jerusalem. Ziad's evening job was working as a translator for *al-Quds*.

"I thought I was going to be a lawyer or a judge," he says, but the Israeli occupation changed his career. "I could not become a judge. I found myself slowly dragged toward journalism. I found out I'm addicted to this journalism business. This was the major change in my life which I did not plan for." His loyalties were changed too, torn among his Palestinian heritage, his Jordanian citizenship, and his Israeli occupiers. Each—Jordan, Palestine, and Israel—had a claim on Ziad, demanding he give a part of himself in order to survive. "I found I was unable to liberate myself from it," he says. But as a journalist he could link all three.

Although his legal career was limited, as a lawyer Ziad again was faced with the strange dilemma of occupation; he represented Palestinian clients in Israeli military courts, using the legal system of the British mandate. His most memorable case may have been the one in which he represented his brother, Khalil. In 1970 Khalil Abu Zayyad was arrested by the Israelis for being a leader of a *Fatah* guerrilla group. Although Ziad claims that Khalil was not responsible for any direct attacks against Israelis, he explains, "some of the group confessed that Khalil was a partner in their activities and carried messages between them and their commander in Amman." Khalil was sentenced to ten years in prison and served them all. For three or four years Khalil was kept in Ramle Prison, and then was transferred from one jail to another, the Israelis' way of weakening the Palestinian networks that form in their prisons. Says Ziad, "He began touring all the jails, from Tulkarm to Beersheba to Ramle to Ramallah to Hebron. We were laughing about it with my mother, Aminah, telling her that because he is transferred from jail to jail, she will have the opportunity to visit all the parts of the country."

Finally released in 1980, Khalil continued to show himself a leader and organized a committee to look after the welfare of the people still in prison. He provided everything, from clothing to money to bus trips for family visits—activities that soften the harshness of imprisonment and, therefore, infuriate the Israelis. A year later he became involved with an effort that angered the Israelis, this time by helping the Druze: a number of Druze villages in the Golan had demonstrated against the Israeli government and were under siege and curfew. Khalil arranged for several vans, filled them with food, and arranged for them to be driven to the villages. Not long after, he was placed under town arrest.

In August 1985, after a hiatus of several years without deportation, the Israelis began the so-called "iron fist" policy and ordered Khalil deported from the country. He was the first to be deported, and the Israelis wanted to make him an example. At this point Ziad called on his old friend Safi Alon, who quickly prepared papers to appeal the case. Two other Israelis, both noted correspondents, offered their help: Danny Rubinstein, of *Davar*, and Yehuda Litani, of *Ha'aretz*. Working closely together, Ziad and the three Israelis approached Ephraim Sneh, the head of the Israeli civil administration, with this compromise: Khalil, acknowledging that he was a leader of *Fatah*, would leave the country for three years, of his own free will, with the commitment not to engage in activities against Israel during his time outside the country. In exchange, after the three years he would be allowed to return like any ordinary visitor. Sneh recommended to the military attorney that it be approved. "So they cancelled the deportation order and he left the country. He took a cab to the Allenby Bridge and went to Jordan," says Ziad. In 1988 Khalil came home.

"The funny thing about this," says Ziad with a smile, "is that we signed an agreement between the state of Israel and Khalil Abu Zayyad. Israel insisted on putting down all the accusations against him, so the agreement stated that he was a member of the PLO and the leader of *Fatah* in the West Bank. It seems to me this was the first agreement that Israel signed with the PLO, because if they insisted that he is PLO and he is the leader of *Fatah* on the West Bank and, in spite of that, they signed an agreement with him, between the government of Israel and Khalil Abu Zayyad, it is a precedent: it is the first agreement with the PLO."

Many Israelis see Ziad Abu Zayyad, in the words of a June 1985 *Jerusalem Post* headline, as a "wolf in dove's clothing." He concedes that "some of them say that I am PLO, that I am extremist. However, I see myself as a reasonable, realistic man, a practical man. I have my views." Those views received widespread attention in a 1986 editorial Ziad wrote for the charter issue of *Gesher*. The PLO cautiously embraced his views. "I am after coexistence on the basis of mutual recognition and mutual respect," Ziad said in an interview when the editorial was published. "Force cannot solve the problem," it declared. "Neither the Arabs nor the Jews can solve their own problem by defeating the other side. There is no way but a political, peaceful settlement." *Gesher* envisioned two possible solutions: a secular, democratic state with both Arabs and Jews, versus a Palestinian state alongside the state of Israel "and not to replace Israel."

In those days the concept of a two-state solution contradicted PLO policy, which demanded Israeli recognition of Palestinian rights before the PLO would accept Israel's legitimacy. After the *Gesher* editorial was published, Ziad was invited to give a lecture at the Van Leer Institute, a liberal think tank in Jerusalem, and he repeated his preference for a two-state solution. By then the editorial had been reprinted in *al-Fajr* and Ziad was being attacked by Palestinian extremists. But the PLO intervened to defend him. After the lecture, he recalls, "an Israeli came to me and showed me the main mouthpiece of the PLO, which had published the full text of the editorial." The PLO organ, *Falasteen al-Thawrah* ("Palestinian Revolution"), carried an introduction making clear the PLO did not agree with everything Ziad had written. But the magazine, published in Cyprus, reprinted the entire text. "For me this was a very clear sign that they were not against what I was saying or what I was doing," says Ziad. Israeli officials believe the PLO subsequently decided to finance the Hebrew-language newspaper, but Ziad denies that. He insists the money to run *Gesher* comes from a news service he runs for Arabic publications in Europe and other parts of the world.

But Ziad does not refute Israeli allegations that he has maintained contact with the PLO. As early as February 1976, almost a year after he had made a trip to Lebanon, Ziad was arrested by the Israeli police, who accused him of having contacts with high-ranking PLO leaders while on a trip to Beirut. They charged that among those he met was the number-two man of the Popular Front for the Liberation of Palestine (PFLP), which had masterminded a series of airplane hijackings in the early 1970s. Ziad did not deny the meetings, but he told the police that the people he had met with were school friends; the reunions were neither about Israel nor against Israel.

Although the army legal adviser ultimately decided there was no offense and the case was never brought to court, Ziad was still held in prison in Hebron. For more than two weeks, during the winter of 1976, he was kept in solitary confinement, alone in a bitterly cold cell on the top of the prison, where melting snow dripped in from a broken window in the roof. "I'll never forget the cold there," he says. "I was turning all the time from one side to the other so as not to get frozen. It's like fire: when you touch fire and it's very hot, you turn to the other side so you won't get burned. I discovered that cold could be like fire. Sometimes you touch it and it gets to the point that you can't continue touching it because you get your hand so hot." After eighteen days in the cell, he was transferred to the general prison and sent to a room with twenty-three other Palestinians. For Ziad it was like a homecoming. "I felt as if I was released, because when you go there you are part of a very big family." The other prisoners gave him pants, a T-shirt, and some soap and put him at the head of the line for a shower. "When you are inside the jail, you feel as though you are inside your family," he says.

Unlike many Palestinians, Ziad has not spent years in jail. Twice he was arrested and held for a week, harassed, and released;

in Hebron in 1976 he was imprisoned for two months. But his most recent arrest was the most frightening, because he was isolated from his wife and his eight children during the Gulf War. In the six weeks of the war, he never stopped worrying that the Scud missiles fired by Iraq contained chemical weapons and that they would fall short, hitting a Palestinian neighborhood on the West Bank.

Ziad's children, four boys and four girls, were not even aware that he had been arrested. Around dusk on November 12, 1990, the military governor of the Bethlehem district called to invite Ziad Abu Zayyad to stop by the next morning for coffee. The Palestinian journalist always obeyed such summons; in the past the governor, a man he only knew by the nickname "Dudu" (for David), had been polite to him, asking him a few questions and exchanging gossip about who's in and who's out of the local leadership. But this morning when Ziad arrived, promptly at ten o'clock, the governor's secretary ushered him into an adjoining room. Waiting for him there were three Israeli officers. They handcuffed his wrists while one of the officers started to read the order for his arrest. The papers were on the table in front of him and, of course, they were in Hebrew. "Before he read the first line, I had already read the whole page," says Ziad. Under the military laws governing the occupied territories, he could be held under administrative detention, without charges being formally brought against him, for up to one year; the term could also be automatically renewed without his having the right to a trial.

Ziad was never sure why he was arrested. He suspected that the government was under pressure to do something after three Israelis were stabbed in the Bak'ah area of Jerusalem, one of the few nonreligious enclaves that previously had been immune to violence. "The only accusation was that I am involved in the Unified Leadership of the *intifada*," he said, shrugging off a role the Israelis see as a threat to their national security.

After the officer finished reading the order, alleging that Ziad was dangerous and that his imprisonment was required to safeguard the public order and security of the state, the prisoner was taken to a dark, damp cell in the basement. As he began to walk down the stairs, one of the guards turned to him and offered to take his expensive camel-hair coat. "If you like, I can keep it with me so it won't get dirty," said the guard. Ziad turned and said, "You care more about the coat than you do about me!" and took it with him.

He spent two and a half hours in the cold basement before being transferred to Jneid, the central jail of the West Bank, in Nablus. His cell there was a twelve-foot square and housed eight people. They slept on four double-decker beds. In one corner was what the Israelis euphemistically call a WC but is really a hole in the floor; there was a basin and a small faucet, which occasionally had hot water. Every morning the 720 inmates at Jneid were allowed thirty minutes of physical activity, and later in the day they were permitted to walk around the courtyard for an hour and a half. Unlike other prisoners, Ziad was able to visit other sections, teaching Hebrew to a group of student prisoners and literacy to a group of older inmates. During the long hours inside, he played *sheshbesh*, a Turkish version of backgammon.

The food varied in substance but rarely in taste; the soup was a mix of hot water, butter, and spices. "Sometimes they added a few lentils, but you had to swim to find some of these things," says Ziad. If there was a surplus of tomatoes in Israel, "you could expect to have tomatoes every day; otherwise, you could spend two or three months and not see the tomato." He was able to get tea, but it was a weak brew. "They would boil seven cups of water with one tea bag for half an hour," he recalls. The experience left Ziad without much of an appetite when he was finally freed. "Even though it's been almost a year, I still have a hard time with any luxury. I still remember many of those people who were with me, and mentally I can't help but compare what it's like outside and what it was like inside the jail."

Ziad will never forget the blare of the air raid sirens that sounded whenever an Iraqi missile attack was under way. The prisoners heard the first alarms on a transistor radio inside their cells. "In the beginning we were really scared because we really believed Saddam Hussein had chemical weapons and he would shoot them at Israel. None of the Palestinian prisoners were given gas masks or access to a sealed room, and the windows at Juneid were broken between the bars so "if he had fired any chemical weapons, we would have died immediately," says Ziad.

But the most humiliating experience during the war was

listening to the announcements whenever a Scud attack was imminent: loudspeakers instructed the Israeli guards to put on their masks and to proceed to the sealed room inside the prison complex. Ziad tried to explain to the officer in charge of the jail that "he should find a way to have his men put on their masks and go to the sealed room without making us aware of what he is telling them to do." He says he told him that when the instructions are broadcast on the speaker system, "we feel nobody cares about our lives and that we are worth nothing." During the first few attacks, when no one knew whether the Scuds had chemical warheads, "we were sitting just waiting for death," he recalls.

He worried most about his children. Family visits were permitted only every other week. And after the Gulf War began in January, curfews were slapped on most of the towns and villages of the West Bank and Gaza. So weeks went by without any news from home. During the war even their lawyers were barred from seeing the prisoners. "As the father of eight, I didn't know how they managed their lives—if they had a sealed room, if they had enough food and enough money, or how they were managing." Ziad's oldest daughter, Joumaneh, is, at this writing, a senior at Hebrew University, majoring in English and international relations. Like her father, she is fluent in Hebrew. Two of his sons are in the United States: Tariq is studying engineering at Brigham Young University; Ali, almost twenty, is studying computer sciences. Ziad has three other girls: Nissren, a high school senior, Lamyah, who is in the ninth grade, and Hibah, a fifth-grader.

But the two children Ziad worries most about are his two youngest sons: Sari, who is almost fourteen years old, and Ammar, who is ten. Although his daughter Nissren was arrested and spent forty-eight hours in jail for being involved in a stone-throwing melee and his eldest daughter, Joumaneh, criticizes her father for being too moderate, the real radicals in the family are Sari and Ammar, born under Israeli occupation and raised during the *intifada*. By the time Sari was ten he was pleading with his mother to be allowed to go out on the street and throw stones at the Israeli soldiers. Time and again his mother told him that his father would be held accountable and would be sent to prison. But Sari insists that he would take responsibility. "If they ask me who's your father, I will not tell them," he swears innocently. "I know in jail they torture people, the food isn't good, and things are bad. But still," says Sari, "I want to go."

"Sari is at a very tough age," says Ziad. "This stage of life is very difficult for parents and teachers." The fiercest fighter in the household, however, may be his ten-year-old son, Ammar. The youth has spent much of his life in Al-Amari, a Ramallah refugee camp, where he was taken care of during the day while his mother, who grew up in a camp in Gaza, worked as a teacher. The wretchedness of the camps has made a strong impact on Ammar, whose Palestinian consciousness is even greater than that of his older siblings. When he was only six, one of Ammar's favorite pastimes was to draw the outlawed Palestinian flag and to hang his work on the walls. He strung six of the red-green-and-black-striped flags on each side of his bedroom, Ziad says somewhat proudly, and "wants everybody to come see it." The father recalls his son's excitement when he announced, "I liberated my room!"

Ammar was born in 1982 during the worst two weeks of the siege of Beirut, and although his parents say they never told him, he was named after Abu Amar, the code name of Yasser Arafat. "It was not clear whether the PLO would be able to get out or not," says Ziad, "so Ammar himself, his fate, was a question mark. That's why we gave him this name, Ammar, after Abu Amar, to commemorate it just in case anything happened to him." Since he was six, Ammar has known the identity of his namesake and feels passionate about him. On one occasion, when the family drove by a high-walled detention center, the children asked who was inside. Told that the jail held Palestinian prisoners, seven-year-old Ammar announced, "I will go to Yasser Arafat, bring him with his men, and we will bring guns and blow up these walls. We will free all the prisoners who are inside." Says his mother, "He was quite serious about it."

For all the children, the PLO chairman is larger than life. "Arafat is a symbol, not a person," Ziad explains, "and when those kids speak about Arafat, I think they speak about an imaginative thing. For them he represents the leadership of the PLO. When they see him on television, they say, 'This is our president.' They are used to seeing him, and they like how he looks. They are not like the Americans who want to see him shaved, with a suit and a necktie."

Ziad tries to refrain from influencing his children politically, and, like any parent, he is happiest when they are doing their homework. "As a parent you always want your son to be safe and secure. But you can never tell what your son is going to be involved in because he never tells you what he is going to do."

The biggest difference between his generation and that of his children, he concedes, is that "I know the Israelis much better. I have personal friends among Israelis. There are some things which I understand about the Israelis or at least which I am prepared to understand." For example, says Ziad, if you tell an ordinary Palestinian that the Israelis are afraid of them, he will never believe that. It is simply incomprehensible, because their own experience has been one of harassment and beatings at the hands of the Israelis. Palestinians see them as their tormentors, too strong to be vulnerable, too brazen ever to be afraid. In their minds, Israel is a superpower, with the fifth-largest army in the world and possessing nuclear weapons. "For me, with my experience and my contacts with Israelis, I would say there are many Israelis who are really afraid when they speak about security," he adds. Ziad notes that Arab schools do not teach much about the murder of 6 million Jews in the Holocaust. "Maybe we, here in the occupied territories, could learn something from the Israelis about their suffering in the Nazi period." But, he adds, Israelis can also learn something from the Palestinians. "They have to understand that now we are playing the same role they played during the 1930s and 1940s, before they had their own state. We are the Jews of today."

Today Ziad Abu Zayyad is the chairman of the Political Committee of Jerusalem. Like his Hebrew-language newspaper, *Gesher*, he believes these committees—there are 200 of them throughout the West Bank and Gaza made up strictly of *Fatah* supporters—can be an important bridge between the masses and the tiny, select group on the Palestinian negotiating team. He defends the need for the committees because these Palestinians, particularly those in the refugee camps, felt alienated by the selection of erudite and educated Palestinians to negotiate with Israel. Whether they were justified or not is beside the point, he says. "They felt they were ignored or isolated or insulted or whatever," but the bottom line was that they felt "they did not have the role to which they thought they were entitled."

Ziad believes the activities of these committees, on the local level, can be a useful precedent for the evolution of political parties. He is angry that the Israelis continue to ban such parties. "We felt there was a need for a bridge between the delegation and the people to communicate in both directions. We thought that by declaring these political committees in a demonstrative and open way, this will give legitimacy to these committees and to the peace process itself," he explains. They are also needed as a bridge between his generation and the next one, the generation born under Israeli occupation. They were brought up under different conditions, he says. "The moment they open their eyes and start to know the facts of life, the first thing they see is the Israeli soldier in the street, the soldier who tries to harass them or provoke them." The children learn quickly that their people, the Palestinians, are living under different conditions than the Israelis. "They grow up with this mentality of confrontation," he says.

Ziad concedes that if the peace process fails, the next generation will be more extreme. "But *radical* is not the right word," he says. "I would say, more committed. They are more aware of their national identity, more committed to the national struggle, and more willing to sacrifice, because they live in daily confrontation with the occupation." He has already lived the major part of his life and has learned from experience, both good and bad, about the Israelis. He also has "family responsibilities," says Ziad, and knows that however much it hurts, "sometimes you have to bow down until the storm is over and then you can erect your body. For the young generation, for someone who is sixteen or seventeen, who doesn't have any other responsibilities, he thinks he is the strongest, he thinks he is the bravest and the most courageous, so he doesn't care about the things that I, in my age, care about."

The sense of invincibility that comes with youth has passed for Ziad. He has matured politically, avoiding extremism and avoiding total disengagement from Israeli Jews. He has broken the linguistic barrier between Arabic and Hebrew, the physical barrier between Israel and the West Bank, and the psychological barrier that leads many Palestinians to live in a state of siege.

Meanwhile, he is glad that the United States is acting as a bridge between the Palestinian leadership inside the territories and the PLO in Tunis. Senior advisers to Yasser Arafat like Nabil Shaath and Akram Hanieh now travel regularly to Washington to help advise the Palestinian delegation; as a result, important new ties are being forged, links that Israel long sought to obstruct. "The peace process has provided the opportunity for the people inside and outside to communicate more freely and more deeply. It has allowed us to get to know each other better and to work together as a team. As a result, the gap between the outside and the inside is disappearing. We are acting as a team," says Ziad.

This is good for the peace process, he explains, because in the end it is only the PLO that will be able to "decide the future of the Palestinian people" and to ratify any settlement reached by the local leadership. When Arafat's plane went down in the Libyan desert and he was feared lost, there was panic because the aging guerrilla leader has been the glue that holds the process together. Until real progress is made in the peace talks, he will remain the indispensable link, says Ziad. "Anyone from the occupied territories who does not have the support of the PLO—and the cover of the PLO—is worth nothing; he cannot make a single decision." But the dynamics are changing; "by providing facilities for members of the PLO from Tunis to travel to Washington, the Americans are actually helping to make this process meaningful," says the Palestinian journalist. By changing the law to permit Israeli citizens to meet with the PLO in Tunis or anywhere else, the Rabin-led government in Israel has taken the first step toward recognizing the centrality of the PLO. What is unspoken, of course, is that if the peace process succeeds, the resulting ties between Israelis and Palestinians, and between the Palestinians inside and outside the territories, will form their own bridge, permitting West Bankers such as Ziad Abu Zayyad to assume new roles as leaders of the Palestinian electorate.

Sami Kilani

When most Americans recollect their early adolescence, they may recall their first date or their first drink and they remember their idols, singers like the Beatles or the Beach Boys, or boxers like Cassius Clay. Sami Kilani, a somewhat rounded, balding figure who wears a wry smile like a cloak of invincibility, has decidedly different memories of his childhood. He recollects giving half his pocket money to a special fund to help the student radicals in Algeria. "This was the awakening of my political activity," he says. He remembers, too, how he joined with thousands of other students in 1967 to demonstrate against King Hussein after the Jordanian ruler did little to fend off Israeli attacks against Palestinians living in the West Bank. His heroes were not rock stars or even pugilists in the ring; they were life-and-death fighters, the young revolutionaries who forced General Charles de Gaulle to give independence to the French colony of Algeria; they were the Marxist guerrillas of the National Liberation Front in South Yemen who fought the Royalist forces of the British colony of Aden. Teenagers growing up in the Jordanian-occupied West Bank idolized anti-imperialist figures such as Fidel Castro and Ernesto "Che" Guevara in Cuba, Ho Chi Minh in North Vietnam, and Mao Tse-tung in Communist China.

Sami Kilani was born in 1952 in Ya'abad, a large rural village near Jenin. His mother, Aisha, and his father, Mohammed Zigil, a tobacco farmer, had made their home and raised their five boys and two girls deep in the agricultural heartland of the West Bank. The village they lived in, seemingly insignificant, had become widely known because of the fate of an Arab leader, Izz Din

Kassam. This Arab hero who fought against the British had been discovered hiding in Ya'abad and had been turned in to the authorities, ensuring not only the fame of the town but the fate of its youth. The role of revolutionary would become synonymous with being a Palestinian.

Kassam, a Muslim sheikh, was one of the first to preach *jihad* ("holy war"), often complaining that *waqf* money was being squandered on the repair of mosques. He offered his people a radical alternative—revolution—to combat what he saw as the inevitable result of burgeoning Zionist immigration: the establishment of a Jewish state in Palestine. As president of the Haifa Muslim Society and an early proponent of Muslim *fundamentalism*, Kassam organized the dispossessed Arab fallahin in the shantytowns on the northern coast of Palestine into secret armed cells. He first came to public attention in December 1932 with a hand grenade attack on a house in the Nahalal, one of the first Jewish agricultural settlements in the Yizrael valley of the southern Galilee. Kassam was killed less than three years later, says Sami proudly, "as a martyr near my village," when he refused to surrender to British troops. "His name is connected directly to Ya'abad. Sometimes they call it Ya'abad al-Kassam."

After Kassam's death, support for militant action gained even wider popularity; and with the outbreak of the Arab Revolt in 1936, Ya'abad became synonymous with resistance. Moshe Dayan, Israel's defense minister during the Six-Day War, even asserts that the violence espoused by the "terrorist-zealot" Izz Din Kassam had a long history in Ya'abad. "It was here, some 3500 years ago," Dayan writes in his memoirs, that the biblical Joseph narrowly escaped murder at the hands of his brothers and "was sold to Midianite merchantmen," slave traders, who took him to Egypt. Dayan also describes one of the fiercest attacks of the 1967 war, for control of Ya'abad, which he says he ordered because of the town's strategic position on a hilltop overlooking the Valley of Dotan. Many Israelis were killed in this battle with the Jordanians. It was such a bitter memory for the Jewish state that a song eulogizing the victims of the "Battle of the Valley of Dotan" and sung by the Lehakat Hanakhal, a chorus of the Israeli Armed Forces (IDF), became very popular after the end of the war.

Despite his pride in being on the Palestinian negotiating team,

Sami stands apart from most Palestinian revolutionaries. He has fought not with guns but with words, as a teacher, as a writer of short stories, and as a poet. His roots, however, are not in academia but in the land and in the suffering of those who have spent the bulk of their adult life in Israeli jails. At forty, Sami has been under detention for much of the last decade. He has traveled on a Cook's tour of the prison world, from Jneid, the central prison of the West Bank, at Nablus, to the interrogation center at al-Farah, to Dahariyah, the military camp near Hebron, to Ansar III, the desolate desert camp near the border with Egypt. His family are not strangers to trouble: at one point four of the five Kilani boys—Sami, Salim, Khalid, and Adnan—were all in prison at the same time. It was while Sami was in prison that some of the most significant events in his life have occurred. He was in jail when his father died; he was in jail when a brother was martyred in the *intifada*; and he was in prison when two of his three children were born. Even his freedom has had its invisible bars. As an ordinary citizen, he sought to leave the West Bank, but the Israeli authorities banned him from traveling. "I came out for the first time in sixteen years," he says, his lips curling to underscore the irony, "when I was appointed a member of the Palestinian delegation."

He sees himself as different from many members of the Palestinian negotiating team: they come from affluent families; they have been educated and have traveled extensively abroad; and they seem polished, easily able to intermingle in the West. Sami Kilani is somewhat rougher around the edges, an earthy man, a farmer's son who has struggled to feed his intellect; a jolly man who nonetheless often looks bemused by all the attention his more sophisticated associates are getting. Unlike his pro-*Fatah* colleagues, he supports the wing of the Democratic Front for the Liberation of Palestine (DFLP) led by Yasser Abed Rabbo, because, he says, his party has not been corrupted; it has ties to the Palestinians in the refugee camps and "depends on the masses." Political activists, he insists, must have "deep roots with the people, a clean national history, and proven leadership."

Scavenging out an empty room at an-Najah University, where he now teaches physics, Sami sits down to reminisce about his high school days and the peer pressure of the older boys who wanted to follow in the footsteps of Sheikh Izz Din Kassam, their native martyr. In 1962, when he was ten, Sami recalls, those with the biggest following in school were the members of a clandestine group, *Harakat al-Kawmiyyin al-'Arab*, the "Movement of Arab Nationalists." It was established by leftist students at the American University of Beirut (AUB) a few months after Israel achieved independence, to organize the masses of Arabs against the Zionist incursion. "They were active in this village," says Sami, "and we [the younger boys] were trying to imitate them and to follow them." The older brother of one of his best friends belonged to the group, he recalls, and every day Sami contributed half of the money given him by his parents. It was exciting to know someone who belonged to the *Harakat al-Kawmiyyin al-'Arab*, a group that advocated the overthrow of the conservative and corrupt Arab regimes; what's more, it promised the creation of a pan-Arab nation, a single socialist state that would unite all of the Arab peoples.

Among the organization's original founders at AUB was George Habash, a charismatic Christian Palestinian who later formed the Popular Front for the Liberation of Palestine (PFLP). Like its sister organization, the PFLP espoused the use of violence to rid the Middle East of Western influence, including Israel and the Arab regimes the West helped to support.

The PFLP was not the only group calling for all tactics, including terrorism, to be used against the Zionists. In May 1964, when Sami was twelve years old, the Palestine Liberation Organization held its founding conference in Jordanian-administered East Jerusalem. Led by Ahmed Shukeiry, the new PLO vowed to destroy the Jewish state through armed struggle and said in its charter that this was "the only way to liberate Palestine." Sami remembers that although he was barely old enough to help his father shuck tobacco, he was excited enough to help collect funds for the new liberation group. Even after relations soured between the new PLO and the occupying Jordanians, "we continued trying to raise money [for the PLO]."

By March 1965, when Sami was thirteen, a new underground group, which called itself *Asifa* ("The Storm") but was connected to *Fatah*, had already staged ten guerrilla raids and sabotage operations against Israel, seven from the Jordanian-administered West

Bank or across the river from the East Bank of Jordan, and three from across the Egyptian-held Gaza Strip. By the end of the same year, thirty-five such operations had been launched, twenty-eight from the West Bank alone. The Israelis considered their sabotage targets—setting explosives in water pipes, on railroad lines, on craggy roads, and in border settlements—to be attacks on civilian areas and therefore beyond the rules of warfare. Several different groups of Palestinian fighters, grandly named the "Heroes of the Return" or the "Palestine Liberation Front," took credit for these operations, but the most active seemed to be *Fatah*. Israeli officials were aware that the leaders of three of the Arab countries rimming Israel—Hussein of Jordan, Nasser of Egypt, and the Christian-led government in Lebanon—were doing their best to stop these reckless guerrilla groups. But their best was not good enough.

During the summer of 1966 alone, fifteen guerrilla attacks took place inside Israel, most of them emanating from the West Bank. When in October Palestinian commandos dynamited three homes near the central bus station of West Jerusalem, wounding an elderly woman, and a month later detonated a mine near the Jewish settlement of Nehosha, killing three Jewish soldiers and wounding six others, the Israeli government felt it had been pushed too far. On November 13, 1966, in broad daylight, heavily armed Israeli units crossed the mountainous border near Hebron and, in less than a day, shot down a Jordanian air force plane, destroyed several Jordanian army posts and a police station, and, as a message to the guerrillas, demolished dozens of houses in the Arab village of Samua, where the fighters were based.

The Israeli operation, involving tanks, artillery, air-support, and infantry, was the biggest retaliatory raid since the 1956 war in Suez, and was intended, according to Yeshayahu Gavish, the commander of the southern region, "to force Jordan to close the area of the Hebron mountains for *Fatah* activity." But it had the opposite effect, severely embarrassing the Jordanian regime, which hardly even tried to confront the attacking Israeli forces. Many Palestinians, including fourteen-year-old Sami Kilani, were left with the impression that Jordan could not defend the residents of the West Bank and that the Palestinian fedayeen were their true saviors. "We thought the fedayeen were supermen and paid every respect to them," says Sami. He recalls that they imagined the feda' to be much stronger than they actually were, but nevertheless, they were real heroes. "All we were thinking is, how can we be fedayeen?" says Sami.

He was not old enough to join a *Fatah* or PFLP cell, but after the Israeli invasion of Samua, Sami joined the tens of thousands of West Bank Palestinians who poured into the streets. From Jenin in the north to Hebron in the south, they demanded that Jordan give them the weapons to fight Israel. "I participated in those demonstrations," says Sami. They started around November 17, and five days later reached the Old City of Jerusalem. On November 26 the Jordanian army, trying to contain the violence, killed four Palestinians and wounded fifteen others. Their funeral turned into a giant anti-Jordanian protest: 4000 people chanted slogans calling for the overthrow of King Hussein.

The long-term impact of the Samua raid, and the Palestinian reaction, was to strengthen the position of Ahmed Shukeiry's PLO. At the same time, it increased the national consciousness of Palestinians in the West Bank and severely strained Jordan's relations with Egypt, Syria, and the PLO. On January 3, 1967, King Hussein, faced with a growing insurrection from a large part of his population, ordered the PLO offices in Jerusalem closed. "Then things changed," recalls Sami. On May 30 Shukeiry came to Amman, returning with King Hussein from Cairo, where the Jordanian monarch had signed a defense pact with Gamal Abdul Nasser placing his troops under the command of the Egyptian forces. "We were very happy that the Arabs finally were collecting the momentum to face Israel," says Sami, "and then we were frustrated with what happened."

Sami was fifteen years old on June 5, 1967, when the war began. Rumors abounded that there could be serious fighting at night, because Israeli and Jordanian gunners had exchanged some artillery fire earlier in the day. Sami had gone to visit the Jordanian troops on the East Bank and had returned to Ya'abad to find that no one was at home. Upon asking the neighbors, he was told that his family had gone to a cave near an orchard of fig trees on their farmland. As he reached the cave, he found his father, Mohammed Zigil, hurriedly shoveling dirt out of the walls to widen the hideout. His mother, Aisha, was there, along with twenty-five other people, all huddled together. "It was very crowded. There was no place to sleep. We were practically sitting on top of each other," recalls Sami.

During the night a fierce battle took place around them. "We were in the middle between the two armies, the Israelis and the Jordanians," he says. Inside their temporary shelter they could hear the burst of bombs dropping from Israeli warplanes and could see the bright lights of heavy artillery shells exploding all around them. When dawn broke, all was quiet. The Israelis had not discovered their hideout and the Kilanis made their way back to Ya'abad. The village had been virtually leveled by the all-night bombardment. "Many houses were bombed. Electricity lines were on the ground. We heard that some people had been killed from the shelling and that there had been a kind of massacre in the main square, the main marketplace, of the village," says Sami.

Back at his house, Sami turned on his transistor radio to try to hear what Egyptian leader Nasser was saying. "We respected that man very much. We considered him a symbol," recalls Sami. He could not get the Egyptian Radio frequency; all he heard was Kol Israel, the Voice of Israel, instructing the inhabitants of the West Bank to raise white flags over their homes and promising that they would not be harmed.

Within six days the war was over: an extraordinary victory for the Israelis, a brutal humiliation for the Arab states. For King Hussein the loss meant utter shame: the Hashemite ruler had lost the Arab land that his grandfather Abdullah had worked so diligently to save in 1948. In addition, Jerusalem, holy city for the Muslims and hallowed symbol of the Sharif of Mecca and the Hashemite dynasty, was gone.

But for Sami the swift Israeli victory had a more personal and permanent impact. When he returned to Ya'abad early that June 6 morning, he found that one of his best friends had been badly injured by the Israeli shelling. Naif Assad told Sami that he had been rounded up along with all the teenagers and young men in the village. They were ordered to stand together under the blazing June sun, their arms tied behind their backs, in the market square. The midday heat was so strong that one of the men tried to get into the shadow of a nearby building. "The Israelis thought he was escaping, so they opened fire: five were killed in that instant and several injured. My friend was one of those injured.

Others died from the shelling, and two of them were my age," says Sami. "That experience put the fingerprints on all my life," he adds. He resolved to act in revenge.

A year later Sami Kilani had his own encounter with the Israelis. His father already was in trouble with the new occupiers, who cracked down on illegal tobacco growers just as their Jordanian predecessors had. Manufacturing cigarettes at home "is illegal because the government considers it something taxable and you cannot sell it without those taxes," explains Sami. He adds with a slight smile, "We were followed very furiously by the Jordanians and after the occupation by the Israeli customs forces."

Sami longed to be one of the fedayeen, "but I was not old enough to be one of them." Instead, he decided to write some anti-Israeli pamphlets, to distribute them in the streets of Ya'abad, and to demonstrate against the occupation. "We had to do something," he says. With the help of two of his high school teachers, Sami wrote placards that read "Palestine is Arab" and "Away with Occupation." They organized a student march through Ya'abad, thumbing their collective nose at the Israeli military presence there. A dozen people were arrested, including Sami and his teacher Hamad Fadal Tahr. They were summoned to the Jenin police station for interrogation. "It was the first time I faced torture, because we were whipped with electric cables and slapped in every kind of way," he says. His teacher was deported to Jordan. Sami's father, Mohammed, was summoned to Jenin. "He was forced to sign a kind of guarantee that I am not going on any more demonstrations," says Sami, and the budding fifteen-year-old activist was released.

For the next several years Sami managed to stay out of trouble, concentrating on his studies. He graduated from high school in 1970 and obtained his bachelor of science degree from the University of Jordan. After working for a year in Amman, he returned to the West Bank, where he obtained his master's degree in 1976 from an-Najah University in Nablus, then a teachers' training college. For the next year he taught physics at the university, quickly developing a following among the younger, more politicized students.

But in November 1977 an event of cataclysmic proportions rocked Sami Kilani's world. Egypt's Anwar Sadat, the successor to his childhood hero Gamal Abdul Nasser, whose country had been at war with Israel for almost thirty years, journeyed to Israel. For Sami this was the ultimate betrayal of the Palestinian cause: the leader of the largest and most powerful country in the Arab world traveling to Jerusalem, the capital of the Jewish state, and addressing the Israeli people from the seat of their nationhood, the Knesset. Once again he vowed to resist; it was his duty to his people. "We distributed pamphlets saying we are against this partial step at the expense of the comprehensive solution. I helped write the pamphlets," admits Sami.

In 1977 Sami, no longer a child, was also no longer so fortunate as to have his father bail him out. He was arrested and sentenced to three years in jail for "incitation," a charge, says Sami, that "has stuck with me all my life." Sami was first sent to Jneid in Nablus and then to Jenin Prison. For the first two years his father came to see him for the alloted thirty-minute visit every month. In his third year, however, his father stopped coming, and Sami would quiz his mother about the reason. "I was asking, 'Why doesn't he come? What's up? Does he have something against me?'" Sami thought his father blamed him because he was the oldest of their six children and his parents depended on his modest teacher's salary to support them. He recalls that it was hardest on Aisha, his mother, when he was first arrested. "I'm the eldest son and I returned from university and I started helping the family. Suddenly I was away three years in jail. It was a shock for her, visiting me in jail. I could see at the time she is trying to show me another profile, that she's handling this, but I knew she was suffering, because my other brother, five years younger than me, was not making a living and my father was beginning to fall ill. She started collecting thyme—doing anything to help the family."

Then, two days before his release from prison in 1980, Sami received the news. It was "one of the very drastic and tragic events in my life," he says. No one in his family had told him that the reason his fifty-five-year-old father no longer traveled to see his son in prison was due to an illness: a rare form of blood cancer that gradually sapped his strength and finally killed him. Sami will never forget how he learned of his death. The warden ordered that he be moved to a special cell, one he thought was to prepare him for his release forty-eight hours later. "He came, speaking in Hebrew. I misunderstood him," says Sami. "I thought he was talking about some disturbance or something that happened in another room, and since I was one of the leaders of the jail, I thought he wanted to talk about this." Sami told the Israeli that he had nothing to do with anything of the sort, that since he only had two days left to serve on his sentence, he was keeping his nose clean. The warden said, "No, that was not it," and then, says Sami, "I understood that he had spoken with the military governor of Jenin." Since the warden spoke Hebrew only, however, and Sami's Hebrew was hardly fluent, the warden summoned a prison guard, an Israeli Arab, to speak to him in Arabic. He said it was difficult for him to impart bad news but added that he had been ordered to do it. Sami recalls that he said he "is feeling for me," and then he told him, "Your father is dead." Suddenly aware of why his father had not been able to see him for the past year, Sami felt guilty. "I cried silently," he says.

At first the authorities were unwilling to release Sami to go to the funeral. But representatives of the International Committee of the Red Cross (ICRC), for whom he had been acting as interpreter in prison, prevailed on the Israelis to let him go. "They came and took me to the village. I went out with two military jeeps; the policemen handcuffed with me," he recalls. "I went the whole way from my home to the cemetery with the policemen attached to me and the jeeps going in parallel to the funeral. They took me to the house where he was laid. Then I went back to spend the two days in jail."

During his first three years in jail, Sami had time to reflect on how he could serve his family, and the Palestinian cause, more effectively than he had. "I consolidated my thoughts, and I began to understand the struggle from a humanitarian point of view." Curiously, he says he was filled not with revenge but instead with a desire to make a more lasting contribution to the struggle for self-determination. Those years, between the ages of twenty-five and twenty-eight, when other young men were getting married and raising families, Sami says, forced him to become more pragmatic. "I don't say moderate or extremist, I say I became realistic."

His father's death, he believes, made his mother and the whole family stronger. "My absence for three years helped in shaping them," says Sami. "We are tobacco farmers," he adds proudly. "This kind of farming needs the wife, the husband, and the whole family to work together. After I was released, my brother Ahmed started to become involved in the struggle and was arrested. I was beside my mother at that time so I gave her some strength. Then the whole family started going to jail, including one of my sisters. This made her strong."

The method Sami used to fight back was not the sword but the pen. Less than a year after his release, he published his first book of short stories. They were based on the land and on the sacrifices he had seen his mother endure. The volume is entitled *Al Zaatar al-Akdhar,* "The Green Thyme." By then, the summer of 1981, his stories had already emerged as a thorn in Israel's side, a prickly one that irritated the authorities every time a poem or a piece of fiction appeared in a local Palestinian newspaper.

Sami remembers when he was summoned for interrogation by the "military governor himself," a badge of honor that was better than any rave review of his work. "Do you know why you are here?" the governor asked. At first Sami thought it was to hear the good news that he would be allowed to travel to Turkey to obtain his doctorate. He had been accepted in the Ph.D. program at the Middle East Technical Institute at the University of Ankara. But his earlier requests for a laissez-passer had been turned down. Maybe the decision was being reversed. Why else would the governor himself want to see him? "I hope you will have a positive reply for me," Sami told him. The Israeli official looked surprised. "No, that's none of my business," he said. "That's a matter for the intelligence service, the Shin Bet." Sami told him he had no idea why he was summoned. The governor asked him whether he had written *Al Zaatar al-Akdhar.* Sami said he had, and that he had also provided sworn statements on two occasions to the police in Jenin when they charged him with writing stories that incited unrest and hatred of the Jews. "Yes, I know, and they found nothing that could be used to formally indict you in it," the Israeli said. "But I am also telling you clearly and very explicitly: we want you to stop writing this dangerous mixture of literature and politics."

Sami told the governor that several of the stories had previously appeared in Arab periodicals that were forced to submit their contents to the Israeli censors. The Jerusalem publishing house that brought out his book also had to submit the contents for official clearance. "This is literature and I have the right to write it," he said, adding wryly, "even if it [the book] is guilty, it is not me" but the publisher who should be brought to heel. "Yes, we know. You are operating inside the law," the governor said. "But inside this circle, you are playing against us." And, added the Israeli, apparently threatening Sami with town arrest, "we can punish you without holding you," without placing formal charges against you, and without "your having recourse to your lawyer, Felicia Langer." "What do you want me to do?" asked Sami. "We want you to stop writing. What is your reply?" Sami answered that it was impossible to predict what he would do. "Perhaps now I will be zealous and unafraid and say, 'Yes, I will write,' and when I leave here I will be afraid and stop writing. Or, on the contrary, maybe I will be afraid of you and promise I will not write, and when I leave here I will write. I don't have to give you an answer," he snapped. "You will find out if you keep following the papers." Sami says he knew he was being impudent and he was truly afraid. "At that time, really, he could have punished me."

But Sami did not cease writing or publishing. A second book, a volume of poetry, appeared in August 1982. It was called *Wa'd Jedid L'Azidin Al Kassam*, "A New Oath for Azidin al Kassam." This time, says Sami, "they came to my house in Nablus to arrest me. I was newly married. They confiscated two or three copies of my book." He was not taken to the governor's office this time but to the military headquarters in Jenin, where he was interrogated by an Israeli officer, Moshe Elad. "He called himself the consultant to the military governor for Arab affairs," says Sami; Elad's was a name he would come to know well. The Palestinian poet-cum-activist was placed under town arrest, and every week for the next thirty-six months he had to report to Moshe Elad, or, as he came to be known in Sami Kilani's next book, "Uncle Moshe." Moshe Elad became the military governor of Jenin. He was, according to most reports, a somewhat unusual ruler, a scholarly, soft-spoken, well-educated military man who held a master's degree from Haifa University, and, according to *Ha'aretz* correspondent Ori Nir, was—"unlike others—very pleasant."

But there was nothing reassuring to Sami Kilani about the next three years of his life, the period from 1983 to 1985, when he was under town arrest in Ya'abad and had to report regularly to Uncle Moshe. "I think this was the worst period in my life," he says, preferring imprisonment to the loneliness and helplessness of town arrest "away from my work and my home in Nablus." In jail, says Sami, there is a camaraderie among the prisoners; your family visits every week or two, and even though you are shut off from the outside world, the isolation makes it easier to bear. When you are placed under town arrest, he says, "you are confined to this village without any activities, no work, you are doing nothing, and at the same time you feel you are responsible for your family. You have to do something. In jail you are excused because you can't do anything, but when you are out of jail you feel you are responsible, you have to do something for them."

The winter months are the most difficult, he says. Sami's wife, Nuha, is a teacher; she taught at a school in Anabta, a small village near Nablus. Nuha lived with her parents in order to conserve her modest salary, the only monies being earned while Sami was under detention, so she could feed and clothe their first child, their daughter Zoya, named for a sixteen-year-old Ukrainian resistance fighter who'd been hung by the Nazis. Nuha and her family visited him once a week, "like when I was in jail," says Sami. Those visits were painful, because, he recalls, there was always some problem with their child, "and you are supposed to help in solving it but you yourself need help in this very difficult situation. It was," he reflects, "very much more difficult than the prison time itself."

Sami used his time in Ya'abad to tutor high school students needing help in physics and other sciences, and he helped form a new union of tobacco farmers. But most of the time he wrote. "Almost all my short stories are part of my own experience: some of them talk about jail and prison life, some of them of life under town arrest, some of them about life in the village. But in every short story you can feel the fingerprints of my experience on them."

One of his favorite stories is *Huna al-Anbaa*, "Here Is the News," written during the period when Sami had to report every week to Moshe Elad. "He thought that my presence in the village was the source of every disturbance and therefore was trying to do everything to make life difficult for me," says Sami. "By the way, his character left many touches on my literature," he adds, "because it really was a personal challenge with this man, between me and him."

In the story, Sami disguises his own identity. The leading character is the secretary of a small trade union in a rural village. One day, on his way to the post office in the village square, a mailman greets the union secretary with the news that the military governor's office called to inquire about him. "They want you to go there," says the postman. When he returns home to tell his wife, she gets very upset, worried that he may never return. "Don't worry, I'm just going for a good lunch with Uncle Moshe," says the Palestinian trade unionist. "I insisted on not leaving before letting her laugh," says Sami, continuing to recount the story as if he were the leading character which, of course, he is.

When the Palestinian arrives at the Israeli military headquarters, the governor is incensed. He starts to shout at him, "You are the source of every problem I have," and goes on and on. He orders him to surrender his I.D. card and informs him that he will henceforth have to report every day, regardless of the weather, to the police station at Jenin. To punish the Palestinian activist, the police keep him there until late at night, always releasing him, but never asking him a single question. His character tries to pass the time by counting the tiles on the floor, the stairs, and the bars on the window. "What are you doing?" asks another Palestinian who has been summoned there. "I'm passing the time," he replies. "Save your time," the second detainee says. "Someone has already counted everything and it's inscribed on the wall."

Sure enough. There is the list: the exact number of tiles, of stairs, and of bars on the windows. The trade unionist starts to reflect on his predicament. Most of those summoned to the police station expect to be arrested and to go to prison for months or years. They are prepared to accept the fact that they will not see their families, and yet they occupy themselves with counting the number of tiles, stairs, and prison bars. "The human being is strong indeed," he thinks to himself. One by one, each of those ordered to report goes home, all except Sami's hero, the trade unionist. It is nearing midnight, and he thinks the delay is due to the fact that the authorities are preparing the arrest warrant for him and are about to cart him away. But the police chief arrives and says he can fetch his I.D. card and go home. "I heard him tell another officer, with a big laugh, 'How's he going to get home in this cold winter night!'"

When the Palestinian leaves the station, he tries to find a taxi, but there are none at that hour. He hails a private car, a "service," the kind that sometimes is available for hire. Although the driver saw him exit the police station, and sees from his disheveled appearance that he probably will be unable to pay, he agrees to take him home, all the way back to Ya'abad. "When I tried to pay him, he refused. He said, 'No, I know you and I know what happened to you.'"

The trade unionist first goes to say hello to the neighbors. He does not want to see his wife right away because he is sure she thinks he has been imprisoned far from home. As he enters the living room of a nearby house, the news bulletins are being broadcast on radio. One of them reports that Lech Walesa, the Polish leader of the Free Trade Union Solidarity, was summoned by the communist authorities to the Gdansk police station. The bulletin says that Walesa was released after two hours of questioning. The irony does not escape this unknown Palestinian. He thinks to himself, "What kind of world is this? It is international news that Lech Walesa was brought to the police station and interrogated for two hours. Meanwhile, I am being brought there day in and day out for all these weeks and months of suffering."

Although Sami is a board member of the executive committee of the Palestinian Writers Union, and has had four of his books published, to critical acclaim, his reputation has not helped keep him out of prison. "I have spent much of my life paying for my writing," he says, adding with a note of irony, "in Europe and in the West writers are cashing checks for their books, but here we cash charge sheets."

In mid-November of 1987, just two weeks before the *intifada* was to begin, Sami Kilani was arrested again, together with five other Palestinians, on two charges: incitation, and membership in a hostile organization. "Once they called it the PLO, once they called it the Democratic Front for the Liberation of Palestine," he scoffs. He was initially sentenced to six months of administrative detention. "Of course, you can't defend yourself, because the prosecution will say he has classified material," explains Raji Sourani, head of the Gaza Center for Rights and Law, a branch of the International Commission of Jurists. Sourani, who won the 1991 Robert F. Kennedy Prize for human rights, says it is "like confronting a ghost." The accused has no access to the file provided to the prosecution by the Shin Bet. Palestinian lawyers do not "have inspiration from God," says Sourani. "They need concrete material, evidence, charge sheets, etc. Nothing like this exists. So you can't defend your client. It's like a lottery."

After Sami had completed the first six months of imprisonment at Jneid, his sentence was extended for an additional six months. In August 1988, ninety days after he had begun his second term, the Israelis decided to transfer Sami and almost 100 other prisoners to Ansar III, the military encampment at Ketziot in the Negev. The day before he was due to be transferred, Sami's wife was to bring his daughter and his newborn son, Mohammed, for the first time. "I was preparing myself for the visit, to have neat clothes—we have no ironing, but you put them under the mattress in a certain way—and I bought some bonbons for Zoya. Then suddenly, a day before they came, they transferred us to Ansar III. I left some unfinished works of literature there," says Sami.

Three large buses were brought to Jneid. The prisoners were assembled in front of their cells at nine in the morning, handcuffed and blindfolded, and boarded an hour later on the waiting buses. For four more hours the vehicles stood motionless in the torrid August heat before beginning the five-hour trip to their new home. It was a tinderbox, recalls Sami. There was not even any water to drink, and there was continuous shouting as the restless Palestinians protested their helplessness. "Everything was going to explode," he says. In an effort to end the disturbance, several of the prisoners were removed from the bus and forced to sit outside. In whispers, those remaining colluded in removing their blindfolds, en masse, by brushing their cuffed hands against their foreheads. "We were cuffed with our hands in front of us, not behind us, so we could push them off," says Sami. To end the minor insurrection, the guards finally agreed to let those outside back onto the buses; those aboard the buses agreed to put back their blindfolds, and they all began the long trip to Ansar III.

Ansar means "supporters" in Arabic. It is the name used by the Palestinians for the desert compound located in a closed military zone about forty-one miles south of Beersheeba. The Israelis call it, simply, Ketziot Detention Center. Two days after it was opened on March 18, 1988, to house offenders of the *intifada*, a military order relaxed restrictions on the use of administrative detention, permitting any district commander to automatically renew the six-month term and freeing the armed forces from having to present the detention order to a military judge within ninety-six hours. The roman numeral stems from the evolution of such centers: the first, Ansar I, was in South Lebanon; Ansar II (Katiba) was in Gaza; Ansar IV was in Khan Yunis; and Little Ansar, so named because it held minors, was in Anata (Jerusalem).

Ansar III, or Ketziot, is divided into sections and subsections of white tents, all arranged in carefully laid-out rows. Each subsection has eight to ten tents enclosed by double barbed wire and separated by a narrow corridor only six yards wide for the soldiers to patrol. Each tent has room for twenty to twenty-five prisoners; outside each subsection a warden is on guard twenty-four hours a day. "He has live ammunition," notes Sami.

On arrival the prisoners are asked to remove their civilian clothes, and each of them is given one blue or brown uniform and several sets of underwear. The ICRC provides the Israeli authorities with a limited number of white hats designed to protect the inmates from the scorching desert heat. "When we arrived, there were no hats. They had run out," says Sami. Anyway, he adds, "we were not allowed to put them on under the sun."

Every day, three times a day, the Palestinians are assembled in rows of ten and ordered to stand between their tents to be counted. "Sometimes it's more than an hour," says Sami, before the authorities arrive. The procedure also is constantly altered. Sometimes each subsection is free to return to its tent as soon as the prisoners have been counted; on other occasions it is forced to wait until the entire process is complete. In addition to the three daily times of attendance-taking, there also are emergency sessions when "they wake you up at two in the morning," says Sami. As each name is read out, each inmate has to call out his number.

"I had four numbers. Once I was 45024. The latest one was 13000," he says. Then there are the general searches, which can last as long as three hours. "You have to take everything outside the tent: the mattresses, the pieces of sponge, the wooden boards of the bed, and the blankets. You take it outside in the hot sun, pile it up, and they come to check."

Among the things the Israelis are looking for, says Sami, are the stone pendants they sculpt, engraving on them, with a small nail, the likeness of a daughter, a wife, or a mother, to give as presents on visiting day. Transforming these rough stones into necklaces requires enormous patience, says Sami. "We smooth the face of the stone by going to the bathrooms. The floor is flagstone, and you keep scratching it, for hours and hours." Eventually the surface is clean and the stone is formed into a triangle or square. After the portrait is etched onto the stones, a small hole is bored near the top for the necklace. The thread of a sock is removed and "you spin it with a heavy object like a bar of soap. When it's a colored sock, it's a very marvelous string," says Sami proudly. "They are very artistic. Sometimes we spend more than a month sculpting one stone. It is something that I can claim I was the first to do in jail," he adds. The pendants are so popular with Palestinian women that a friend of Sami's four-year-old daughter admonished her father because she did not have one. "Why don't you go to jail and give me presents like Zoya's father?" the child demanded. Sami told Zoya that her friend's father does not have to go to jail for her to get one. "I'll make another for her," he said. But it is not easy: the Israelis constantly confiscate the pendants. "We discovered that many of the soldiers give them as presents to their girlfriends or wives," he says.

Some Palestinians are such gifted artisans that they can make handicrafts out of empty tubes of toothpaste or shaving cream, old cigarette boxes, or disposable plastic lighters, the kind that Marlboro used to give away with their filter tips. "I thought of cutting the lighter in two and filling it with a picture," says Sami. At first he tried filling the space behind the clear plastic with bread, which he used as a tiny canvas, "but it was wet and spoiled, so the drawing was destroyed." He says he tried something else. "I made a mixture of toothpaste and bread. The toothpaste killed the fungi and algae. But it was also wet, so it affected the drawings." Eventually he found another technique that allowed the mixture to dry. "I'm not an artist," he insists, "but I became an artist. I could make a very good drawing of a flower on one side of the lighter, and on the other side I would write some of my poems or Palestinian songs." For Sami Kilani it was the perfect fusion of a life devoted to science, literature, and politics. The stone became a metaphor for resistance and beauty, the poem a parable of his own effort to give meaning to his struggle of existence.

> Get up and stop
> Listen and turn your ear
> This is the song that rises
> This is the whisper of the stone
> This is the shadow above our heads
> The shadow of the flag
> The fusion of the precious blood
> With the precious land
> Which the women kneed at this moment
> With henna for the bride whose dowry
> Is the stone.

From the poem *The Festival of the Stone*

Sami's temperment and training helped shorten the long days at Ansar III. Every morning the inmates were aroused at five a.m. for their first attendance report, and they had to be back in their tents by ten o'clock at night. They were not allowed to have lights in their tents, so no one could read. If anyone was caught talking past midnight, they were hauled off to an isolation cell. The daily routine was divided between playing games of *sheshbesh* (backgammon) or chess and attending classes in which they could learn Hebrew or improve their Arabic. The food was plain: a small quantity of beans in the morning, some rice with a cup of soup for lunch, and a boiled egg or some jam in the evening. The soup usually contained a piece of meat, some chicken or fish, but it was often raw or stale, says Sami. Even though their Israeli guards were eating the same food, Sami says Palestinians simply have higher standards. They are used to eating staples such as stuffed vegetables and various Arab delicacies, so, he concedes, to the

Israelis the food may not have seemed so bad.

During the day and at night, each faction—*Fatah*, DFLP, PFLP, and the communists—organized its supporters in secret seminars under a single tent. There would be two or three speakers or a question-and-answer session. One of the favorite activities was a game called "Know Your Homeland." Each night a different Palestinian would talk about his hometown or the village his family came from in Palestine, before the existence of the Jewish state, and others would grade him on his performance. They had to be careful, says Sami, "because being in a group, even inside the tent, was forbidden."

The tensions between the various factions outside Ansar III were reflected inside the compound as well. The tents of *Fatah* supporters were the most unruly, says Sami, because they were mainly shabiba, teenage activists "who are emotionally with *Fatah* because of Abu Amar [Yasser Arafat], not because they are politically mature enough." He says, with "these kind of people, you can't tell them we are going to have a strict program; we are going to have three lectures today." The DFLP supporters are generally older, in their mid-twenties and thirties, and are better behaved. They were able "to convince the youths [of the *intifada*] to adhere to a specific daily schedule," he says. As disciplined as the leftists were the *Hamas* supporters, the Islamic fundamentalists who are "people of the religion" regardless of their age.

Although he is not a deeply religious person, Sami admits he is superstitious. He no longer makes stone pendants, because, he says, "it's related to a very bad experience in my life. The first time I thought of sculpting occurred at a very tragic time for me," in October 1988. There are no radios or televisions permitted in Ansar III, and the newspapers arrive a week late. But when prisoners are transferred from other parts of the West Bank, occasionally someone will smuggle in a small transistor radio. With it, the several thousand Palestinians have organized a network: someone is responsible for secretly tracking the news bulletins, writing them down, and circulating them among the different sections of the camp. Sami was in the tent of a friend who was reading the latest bulletins. They noted that a young man from Ya'abad had been killed by the Israelis. There apparently had been a stone-throwing incident, and the Palestinian youth, who was near the demonstration, was shot in the chest by an Israeli sharpshooter, from the Israeli's jeep. Sami left the tent worried it might have been someone he knew. He asked a friend, "Do you know how I can find out the details of this?" The friend knew but stopped short of telling him. "I know you are a patient man. We were trying to think of a way to tell you that the name is so-and-so. From the name it isn't yet clear. Maybe there are other Ahmed Kilanis in the village. Kilani is a big family and Ahmed is a common name among Palestinians," he said. The next six hours were brutal for Sami. "I didn't know whether he was Ahmed, my brother, or someone else."

Finally, another Palestinian returned to the camp from visiting his lawyer and told Sami, "Yes, he is Ahmed, your brother." Ahmed was the only one of the five Kilani brothers who was free at the time. He had just completed a seven-month jail term and been released two weeks earlier. Sami's four other brothers were still in prison. One of them, Khalid, was in another section of Ansar III. "They didn't let me see my brother in order to be in this moment together," he recalls, nor was Sami temporarily released, as he had been when his father died, to attend his brother's funeral. Later, he found out more about Ahmed's death. "They couldn't take him to the hospital because the village was seized," says Sami. So they tried a back road to reach Kufr-Kara, a nearby Arab village just across the "green line" inside Israel. But when they reached the medical center there, the doctor sent them to a neighboring hospital. "When they reached the yard of the hospital," says Sami, "he was dead." It had taken two hours from the time he was shot to reach the hospital; Ahmed died from massive internal bleeding that Sami says could have been controlled if he had reached the hospital sooner.

A portrait of his brother Ahmed hangs in the center of the wall of Sami Kilani's study in his Nablus home. His death has transformed Ahmed into a *shahid*, a martyr. Martyrdom acquired its own mythology, its own sad ethos, during the *intifada* as hundreds of young men died in clashes with the Israeli army. Palestinian society had to find a way to cope with this phenomenon without deterring others from participating in the struggle. The

ethos of the *shahid* is rooted in the Islamic tradition of holy war—
not *jihad*, but a sacrifice of self that brings one closer to God.
Families who have lost their sons in the *intifada* enjoy a special
status in Palestinian society; in many homes, both Muslim and
Christian, there are portraits of the *shuhada*, or martyrs, in the
most hallowed place of the home; their family names are
enshrined in the Palestinian equivalent of the Jewish Book of Life.
Nor is it entirely an Islamic concept. During the December
holidays, hundreds of pictures of men and women who have died
in the *intifada* are hung from the branches of Christmas trees,
instead of the more traditional ornaments.

The death of Sami's brother in 1988 has had a profound
impact on his work. "Being a writer helped me so much, because
when you feel this very difficult time, you can express yourself
in writing," he explains. Much of his poetry is affected by the ethos
of martyrdom and its accompanying imagery—the earth, the
stone, the blood, the wedding. In the poem "The Basil," Sami
writes,

> The basil gives life above the grave.
> To your grave, to your last way,
> To all that is said concisely,
> To the piece of land which gave blessing
> to your wedding party.

Sami Kilani has been preparing for his new leadership role
all his life. The most explosive situations at Ansar III, those that
tested his capabilities as a leader, occurred when the Palestinians
were ordered to work directly for their Israeli captors. "In principle we refused to work for the soldiers; we worked only for
the facilities which served us," he explains. At the signal, everyone
would leave their tent, start marching in a military formation, and
shout their anti-Israeli slogans. "In these kinds of times, everyone
was united, all groups together, no problem," he says. The Israelis
would surround the section, firing tear gas cannisters at the Palestinians and shooting live ammunition into the air. "Some of the
detainees who are experienced in the streets pick up the cannisters
and hurl them back on the soldiers, throw the food plates and
the stones and the wood," says Sami.

Before he arrived, there had been a serious outbreak of violence. An Israeli commander had ordered everyone back into their tents. "There was someone at the edge of the tent, at the side of the tent. He told him to get in. He didn't get in. Then the commander himself shot him in the chest and he fell down. When this news spread to the next section, it was boiling and they started throwing every object they had at the soldiers. Then another martyr was killed." In these crises, says Sami, "you don't want your friends to feel they are weak, that they have to obey humiliating orders such as 'Go back to your tent, you donkey ass.' So you look for a chance to show them that they are strong. You have to balance this and avoid, if at all possible, the spark which will lead to a killing." That, he says, is the responsibility of a mature leader. "You have to compensate between those two sides, to show you are strong, to show your people, the detainees, that you can confront the others, and at the same time refrain from reaching that point of the spark, of something deadly."

Today, Sami Kilani spends a lot of time with villagers in the rural areas around Nablus and Ramallah, visiting refugee camps and speaking at symposiums, always deflecting criticisms of his involvement in the peace talks with Israel. An old woman, a refugee from Haifa, asked the entire Palestinian delegation at a recent seminar in Amman if they were going to negotiate away her right to return to her homeland in Palestine. "It was an emotional scene," recalls Sami. Everyone tried to answer her, but, he says, they all responded by evading the thrust of the question. "If you lived in Jenin, which is closer to Haifa, that would be better than Amman," one of the panelists replied. Another told her that if the Palestinians get their state in the West Bank and Gaza, it will help resolve her problem. "It's not the solution," she was told. "The solution will depend on the U.N. resolutions, which say you have the right to choose between return and compensation."

Sami says the efforts to placate her bothered him. "We have to be frank with them," he says. "They can't accept it overnight; and even if we construct our state in the West Bank and Gaza, they will ask it again. It's the dream and the possible. Sometimes I accept the possible, but that does not mean I am ready to abandon the dream. That is something that is very difficult for the Palestinians. Even if I build my state on the West Bank and Gaza,

I will not stop putting the lace on the map of Palestine [a reference to the common Palestinian practice of embroidering a map of the pre-1948 Palestine]. I say Palestine is my homeland but I'm sharing it with another state. It's a dilemma but you have to break through. The breakthrough is being a realist."

Mamdouh Aker

███████████

In "The Death of the Hired Man," the American poet Robert Frost writes of a New England farmer and his wife who are arguing over whether they should shelter a homeless man they had hired many years earlier to help them "hay the meadow." The elderly workman, explains the farmer's wife tenderly, has come "home" to die. The inhospitable farmer, annoyed that his wife is questioning his generosity, ridicules her comment. "Home is the place," he says, "where, when you have to go there, they have to take you in." No, she replies. "I should have called it something you somehow haven't to deserve." For Mamdouh Aker, a silver-haired surgeon and senior member of the Palestinian negotiating team, *home* was a concept he did not think about very much when he was growing up in the 1950s in Nablus. In fact, he could not wait to get out.

Nablus, in the northern part of the West Bank, not far from Jenin and Tulkarm, has always been one of the most straight-laced, religiously conservative places in Palestine. Through centuries of Turkish, Jordanian, and Israeli occupation, Nablus has remained unchanged. In the center of town are the familiar sights of Palestinian culture: the carts filled with elongated circular cakes, breadlike pieces covered with sesame seeds, and the vendors mechanically scooping falafel and dipping it into the skillet of hot oil. In the air are the pungent smells of *shawirmah* roasting, and on large round metal pans, the orange-tinted *kunfafah*, a Palestinian dessert made of wheat, filled with cheese, and covered with a sticky, sweet syrup. Nablus is an industrial town, a soap-manufacturing center since the medieval ages, where the local political leadership is still dominated by an older generation of landowners and merchants with names like Masri, Nabulsi, Tuqan, Shaka, and Abd al Hadi.

When Mamdouh was growing up in Nablus, there were no nightclubs, and only a few groceries sold wine, so there was very little drunkenness. "We used to call Nablus the 'cemetery of the educated,' because if someone wanted to do something with his life, he had to leave Nablus," recalls Mamdouh. Which is what he did. Like hundreds of other bright Palestinian teenagers, Mamdouh was on a fast track to earning a comfortable living somewhere else in the Arab world. He received straight A's at an-Najah high school and graduated *al awal*, first in his class. When at age nineteen he was admitted to the University of Cairo to study medicine, the tall, handsome Palestinian did not disguise his joy at leaving the provincial Arab town for the cosmopolitan Egyptian capital.

It was in Nablus that Mamdouh's grandfather had established a large tannery, shearing the hides of cattle, sheep, and goats, which had grazed on the Palestinian lands for centuries. It was here that his grandfather had achieved the status of a *shawish*, a wise man in the Arab community; families would come to his home and invite him to theirs to adjudicate quarrels between rival clans and within families. It was also in Nablus that his father had met his mother, when her Syrian parents, trapped in Nablus by an earlier outbreak of British-Arab violence, had settled at his aunt's house. It was here, too, that in 1925 his father had established his thriving trading company; he traveled regularly to the Orient to buy carpets, returning a week or so later with luxurious and exotic merchandise to sell to the wealthy Arab landowners. But none of that mattered at the time to the nineteen-year-old Mamdouh. He left the West Bank in 1962 for Cairo and did not return for almost twenty years, finally going home in 1981, when he was almost forty years old.

Ziad Aker recalls that his brother Mamdouh originally wanted to be a cardiologist. "I asked him once why he became a urological surgeon, and he told me that once you begin studying medicine, the most complicated area is urology." Mamdouh has always loved the challenge of taking things apart and putting them together again, says Ziad. When they were youngsters and their father went on business trips, he would ask what they wanted him to bring them. "I always said a football or a gun," recalls Ziad. Mamdouh always asked for Mechano, a Lego-like construction set that you could assemble into a car, a truck, a house, or hundreds of other things. "I remember once he built a big boat, and the ship had engines and could load and unload things. I thought he was going to be an engineer," says Ziad.

Mamdouh did not set out solely to become wealthy, but, like other Palestinians, he was trapped outside his homeland when the Arab-Israeli war broke out in June 1967. Not allowed to return to Nablus, by Israeli law, he completed medical school, then took the advice of several friends and relatives and went to Kuwait. The former British protectorate was beckoning the Palestinians, the most educated and accomplished people in the Arab world, to help transform their desolate stretch of sand in the oil-rich Persian Gulf into a gushing oasis. Along with Yasser Arafat, who earned his first million dollars as an engineer in Kuwait, tens of thousands of Palestinians arrived in the newly independent emirate. Like Arafat, who also graduated from the University of Cairo, Mamdouh believed Kuwait would be the new land of opportunity. There the homeless Palestinians could turn their university educations into lucrative positions, teaching the less educated Bedouin sheikhs how to pry their fortunes from pearls that clung to the seabeds and from petroleum that oozed from the earth. But Kuwait also was like a magnet that attracted the Palestinians and would not release them. "I thought I would spend two or three years there and then go back, but you get lazy and dragged down by the life in Kuwait," particularly by the materialism and the conspicuous "American-style" consumption, says Mamdouh.

Mamdouh spent five years in Kuwait before leaving for England in 1974 to advance his career as a urologist. He won a coveted fellowship to study in England and, a year later, was awarded a position in surgery at the most noted hospital in Edinburgh, the Royal College of Surgeons. Two years later Mamdouh returned to Kuwait, remaining there until 1979, when he was offered a staff position at Kings College Hospital in London.

Though Mamdouh was earning more money than he ever thought he would, he began to realize that the search for a professional challenge and the good life were leading him away from a part of himself, away from his identity as a Palestinian, and away

from his roots in Nablus, where his family had lived for generation after generation. Those two decades abroad had been
dramatically different from his strict Moslem upbringing. He had
escaped the Six-Day War and its aftermath, the forced intermin-
gling of Palestinian and Israeli societies. For Mamdouh there had
been virtually no mixing with the Jews—in Cairo, in Kuwait, or
in Edinburgh.

This was not the way it used to be. He remembered from his
childhood that his father had preached religious tolerance. The
Akers shared their two-story home in Nablus with a Christian
family, who lived downstairs; on one occasion, when the mother
of that family passed away, the Muslim Akers opened their home
to receive condolences for them. His father also had generally
spoken well of the Jews, several of whom were his customers.
Thus, as a child, Mamdouh had little reason to hate the Jews. He
was only five years old when Israel won its independence and
the West Bank came under Jordanian occupation. But he was old
enough to know that life for Madhat, his father, had become more
difficult with the creation of the Jewish state. For one thing, his
father's rug business depended on regular trips to Damascus,
where he would shop for Persian carpets in the Hamidiyeh souk
and bring them back to sell in his Nablus store. The shop, Novotel
Laila, was located in the new Exhibition Center and was a source
of much pride to the Aker family. Before the 1948 war it was easy
to travel back and forth from the British mandate of Palestine to
Syria, Egypt, or Lebanon; trains ran regularly between the Arab
capitals, and there was continual commerce and tourism.

After the war, travel became more difficult; there was tension
between Syria and Jordan, and the new boundary between the
Jewish state and the Hashemite kingdom meant that Jews no longer
came to Madhat's store. In fact, Mamdouh remembered his father
telling him once that on the eve of the 1948 war, a good friend,
a Jewish rug merchant, had called his father to ask a favor.
"Madhat, I can't get to Nablus because there's a problem on the
highway. I have some notes, some promissory notes, which I need
to pay to the bank. They are due today," the merchant told him.
He asked if his Palestinian friend would go to Barclay's and pay
off the notes for him, adding "When I come tomorrow, I'll pay
you whatever is due." Madhat paid off the notes and put them

in a safe place to return to his Jewish friend when he arrived with the money. "He never saw him," says younger brother Ziad. But about a month after the Israeli victory in the June 1967 war, when the West Bank fell under Israeli occupation, two Jewish soldiers showed up at the Business Center in Nablus inquiring about Madhat Aker. "Nobody told them where he was," says Ziad, because they were afraid that Madhat, who had been forced by the travel restrictions to abandon his carpet business and to sell clothes and then fabric, was in trouble with the Israeli authorities. However, one of the soldiers said he was the son of a friend of the Palestinian and had been instructed by his father to find him. Having finally convinced Madhat's associates that they had not come to arrest him, the Israelis were given directions to his spacious home in Rafidiah, the parklike upper-class neighborhood in the al-Muntazah section of Nablus. There they were told how to reach Madhat's store. When they arrived, the younger of the two soldiers told the Palestinian that his father had asked him to pay off the twenty-year-old promissory notes. "He knows he still owes you the money," said the soldier. "But he's very old and he would like to meet you in person to give you the money back himself," his son said. When the two elderly men met several weeks later, there was some discussion about the interest owed on the 2000 *jeneh*, or pounds, an amount equivalent to about $6000. But Madhat saw that the intervening two decades had not been kind to his Jewish friend, "so my father refused to take any interest," says Ziad.

Like his father, Mamdouh has a "big heart," Ziad says. When they were children, it was his younger brother who was the troublemaker, the one who liked to pick fights with the older boys. Even when it was not Ziad's fault and someone else started the fight, Mamdouh would intervene and tell him that his brother did not really mean it. "Whenever there's an area where people are suffering, he likes to understand what's going on and to talk to people about it," explains Ziad. Ziad remembers a time when he was six years old riding a scooter with eight-year-old Mamdouh and the younger boy saw his disciplinarian father standing at the bottom of the hill. Sure that his dad would punish the two brothers, Ziad jumped off, even though they were going straight downhill. Mamdouh was left alone on the scooter but could not control it. He crashed into a wall, luckily escaping serious injury. But when he got up to inspect his cuts and bruises, his father was waiting for him. "He didn't see me," recalls Ziad. Mamdouh took the rap for him.

Several of the boys in the Aker family—there are seven brothers and two sisters—were politically active, recalls Ziad. After the Six-Day War, while Mamdouh was studying in Cairo, Samir was walking home from school when he was ambushed by an Israeli patrol. "Some Israeli soldiers were waiting for them, and they put a bag over my brother and carried him to jail," says Ziad. He was accused of being a student activist and inciting others to violence. "Samir has been the one most in trouble with the Israelis," adds Ziad, "but Mazzin [a younger brother] has also spent a lot of time in jail." Today Samir is an orthopedic surgeon at the Palestinian Red Crescent Hospital in Cairo, and Mazzin, who was deported by the Israelis, is an engineer in the United Arab Emirates.

Mamdouh, on the other hand, has always shown a more cerebral interest in politics. Before television arrived in the West Bank, he used to spend hours and hours listening intently to the radio. In the mid-1950s, when he was in elementary school, he would race to his father's store as soon as the last bell sounded. There he would sit and sip tea or Turkish coffee with the visiting Arab businessmen and "tell them what's going in the world," recalls Ziad. "He talked about [Patrice] Lumumba, Suharto, Sukarno, and always he had some poetry about discrimination, about the violence in Africa and South Africa," his brother recalls. "Maybe he was ten or twelve at the time," he adds.

While a university student in Cairo, Mamdouh was also a member of the General Union of Palestinian Students (GUPS). Like other students, he was enthusiastic about the creation of the Palestine Liberation Organization in 1964 and supported the PLO charter calling for armed struggle to destroy the Zionist state and replace it with a democratic, secular state. Mamdouh did not remain on the sidelines of the Palestinian struggle, but this part of his life is still shrouded in mystery. "He was active, but I don't know in what way," says Ziad. It was in Cairo, also, that another friendship was forged, one that would much later bind Mamdouh to an important Palestinian insider, Faisal Husseini. Husseini, who is three years older than Mamdouh, was traveling back and forth between Cairo and Jerusalem in the early 1960s. They met in the course of GUPS activities. The student union, developed by Yasser Arafat, was at the time headed by Husseini. It was through him that Mamdouh first became acquainted with Arafat who, in the mid-1960s, had already begun to organize the underground guerrilla struggle against Israel.

Mamdouh was more interested, however, in furthering his medical career than in joining a revolutionary liberation movement, and in 1969 he left Cairo for Kuwait. There Mamdouh did not have to wrestle with the thousands of inconveniences for Palestinians living under Israeli occupation. With his Jordanian passport, he did not need the orange I.D. card issued to Arabs in the West Bank or the red one issued to Arabs in Gaza. Nor did he need to ask the Israelis for a *laisser passez*, a beige passport-sized document, when he wanted to travel outside the territories. He would, of course, occasionally reflect on how humiliating these bureaucratic encumbrances were for the Palestinians he had left behind. They were more than mere impediments to free movement. They were a denial of identity. The space reserved for "citizenship" on their laisser passez reads "undefined"; it is a constant reminder of their homeless, stateless condition. Mamdouh, in moving to Kuwait, became a part of a larger group, the 3.5 million Palestinians in the diaspora. Political activity was barred for Mamdouh and other "foreigners" in Kuwait, even though the tiny Persian Gulf sheikhdom gave generously to the PLO coffers. Even if he did not understand all the implications of his decision, like many of the Palestinians he had left behind, he too was now a stateless person. Mamdouh says that while life in Kuwait was materially and professionally satisfying, the discrimination he felt as a foreigner, and as a Palestinian, was almost unbearable. "They used to treat the Western experts they recruited better than the Arab experts, engineers, and doctors. I felt not only that I was a foreigner but I felt like a second- or third-class foreigner," he says. Both his boys were born in Kuwait. But like the majority of foreigners living there, they were never able to obtain Kuwaiti citizenship. A 1959 law defines a Kuwaiti as one who is a descendant of those in Kuwait since 1920. A 1960 law allows naturalization but restricts the number to fifty per year. "You can work there for seven, eight, nine years and you are still a foreigner," says Mamdouh. Nor were his children allowed to attend the same schools as Kuwaiti children. "They had to go to expensive private schools," he says. If a Palestinian wanted to buy land or own his own business, he had to find a Kuwaiti who agreed to take a 51 percent share. Nationality was the sine qua non to economic wealth and social equality.

The Civil Service law of 1960 also reserved senior posts and pensions for Kuwaitis. The political and social system was structured so as to create a three-tiered system. The first tier was exclusively for Kuwaiti citizens, the second was for Western expatriates, and the third was for non-Western expatriates, including Palestinians, Indians, and Filipinos. Privileges and salaries were commensurate with one's place on the social ladder. "I remember in 1978, after returning from the fellowship at the Royal College in England and working as a surgeon in Kuwait, I found the Kuwaitis who were junior to me had much higher salaries, and the British, German, and American doctors had special contracts," says Mamdouh.

But it was the personal prejudice he experienced that was the most irritating. "They don't consider you a human being," says Ziad, who worked for a while in the Gulf Bank in Kuwait. He recalls an incident that took place on his second day in the country. "Mamdouh was driving, and a Bedouin almost hit us. He stopped the car and was cursing at us—very bad words, like 'fuckin' foreigners'—and cursing my father and mother in Arabic." "I was very mad," says Ziad. "So I got out of the car, grabbed him, and started hitting him. My brother was hitting me. He told me that if the Bedouin cursed me, it's all right. He told me, 'If they [the Kuwaiti authorities] catch you, they are going to give you hell. I can take it—I'm a troublemaker, I expect it. But not you.'" Mamdouh told his brother that it made no difference whether the Bedouin had run the light or who was at fault—the punishment would be the same. "They take their shoes and hit you. Anywhere. Without having a reason. Why? Because if you didn't leave your country and come to Kuwait, this accident would never have happened."

Ziad says that a cousin, Khaled Aker, had a similar experience while working as head of the department of dentistry at al-Ahmadi

Hospital. A Kuwaiti bigshot walked into his office and demanded an immediate appointment. Khaled explained that he could not refuse patients who had been waiting for weeks and months for their surgery but offered to take him after office hours at five o'clock. "He refused and he hit my cousin," says Ziad. "The Kuwaiti considers himself God, because when they were born, they were living on camels; then suddenly they had everything, everything," he adds. It makes no difference to the Kuwaitis that Palestinians like the Akers helped turn the backwater colony into a modern nation-state. "They see it the other way. This guy, he came and built the country. No. We appointed him to do this," says Ziad. Mamdouh says that a distinguished physician who spent thirty-five years working in the Ministry of Health wanted to have his employment extended. "They extended it for two to three years after that; then he was given two weeks to leave the country," he says. "Imagine, going to Jordan. He will feel like a complete stranger because he doesn't know anyone there." Even in England, says Mamdouh, he did not feel discriminated against. In Kuwait, "there always is this feeling, that at any moment you can be thrown out of the country; or your contract, whether government or private, can be terminated. They always make you feel that you lack control. At any moment anything can happen," explains Mamdouh.

This is why, he adds, if you want to understand the initial Palestinian reaction to the Iraqi invasion of Kuwait, "you have to go back to this sort of relationship." After the 1991 war in the Persian Gulf, most of the 400,000 Palestinians in Kuwait were forced to flee to Jordan, the only country that would accept them. On the personal level, says Mamdouh, "I had very fine Kuwaiti friends, some of the most brilliant intellectuals. But when you consider the collective atmosphere created by the government, it is very ugly, very poisonous."

He finally decided to leave Kuwait after an incident that involved a Palestinian friend who was the chief pharmacist in the Ministry of Health. The man had spent twenty-six years working for the Kuwaiti government. His older son had gone to the United States to study engineering and wanted to return home to spend the summer holidays with his family. "The father had to apply for a permit for him. It took him quite a long time to obtain permission," says an exasperated Mamdouh. "His son was born there; he had completed all his schooling in Kuwait and now his father had to run from one office to another to get permission for him to come home. He spent twenty-six years as the head of a department in the Ministry of Health. His children know no home except Kuwait. And now they are treated as foreigners. So I made the decision, this will never happen to my children. I wanted to be in a place I can be proud of." Mamdouh took his family back to England in 1979 and was offered a post in Saudi Arabia "with a much better salary" than he was receiving in Kuwait.

But Mamdouh says he did not want to return to the Gulf. Furthermore, his two boys, six-year-old Muhannad and eight-year-old Nidal, were starting to say, "We are Palestinians, but we don't know Palestine." Mamdouh said, "Okay, we'll go to the capital of Palestine." When asked whether it was the land that drew him home, Mamdouh responded, "By the late 1970s, I had started to realize that our national movement—and the armed struggle—was not getting us anywhere. I realized it would take time and that the occupation will go on and on. Finally, I reached the conclusion that the most important thing for our people is to stay on the land and to endure and sustain ourselves there no matter what."

But Mamdouh was not drawn to the olive groves or the vineyards of his youth. He hesitated to return to Nablus because he felt it too provincial. After Edinburgh, London, and Kuwait, the conservatism of Nablus, with its xenophobia so common to mountain communities, might hem him in. Instead, it was Jerusalem, with its worldliness and its rich history in Islam, Christianity, and Judaism, that attracted him. The holy city, with its thousands of tourists making their daily pilgrimages to religious and cultural sanctuaries, breached the provinciality of most Arab towns. There, he was certain, he could make the adjustment, satisfied with his decision to return. When he found out there was not a single qualified urologist in the West Bank, he knew he had to return. "I said, okay, I'll go back home, but I'm not going to get involved in politics. I'm just going to be there to help the people who badly need it." In the fall of 1981 Mamdouh accepted a position at Maqassad Hospital in Jerusalem, although the salary was less than a third of what he had received in Kuwait. "I felt that to be outside the country while your people are suffering was not right. Really, I felt guilty," he says of his days in Kuwait. "Just to be there [in Jerusalem] as a specialist, this is by itself a national obligation."

Mamdouh describes the experience of returning home after an absence of almost two decades as a "process of metamorphosis." This, he says, "was my first contact with Israel as a reality and with the Israeli people. I started to get in touch with Israelis in my profession." Whenever he traveled to Tel Aviv or even just to the western part of Jerusalem to meet with other physicians, Mamdouh says, he was struck by the fact that "we can't ignore it"—Israel—anymore than the Israelis could ignore the reality of the almost 2 million Palestinians in their midst. He realized things that he had never thought about before. "I started to feel how crucial it was to the Israeli people to keep the Jewishness of the state. They don't want this binational state, and even listening and watching and sensing the Israeli feeling and mentality, I started to realize the paranoia behind it," says Mamdouh. For the first time, he says, he understood why Israelis felt they needed to maintain a Jewish majority in their state and that anything short of that would "threaten their very existence." Mamdouh says he concluded therefore that "the only way is to share the land. That is why I was one of those from the very beginning to say we have to accept the two-state solution. Before the intifada, it was very difficult to pronounce that, except in Israel, because when you say 'two states,' you have to accept the existence of the Israeli state. It was very obvious that there had to be a compromise. But a compromise means offering a concession, and offering a concession when you are weak is very difficult." The *intifada* gave the Palestinians the strength to adopt the two-state solution as a necessary compromise.

But peaceful words such as these were suppressed by Palestinian moderates, who feared they would bring swift retribution from Palestinians opposed to compromise. Mamdouh had seen one of his close friends gunned down only a few months after returning from his self-imposed exile. In early March 1986 Zafir Masri, the Palestinian mayor of Nablus, was assassinated. He was shot from behind and in the head in broad daylight as he walked to his office, by a member of George Habash's Damascus-based Popular Front for the Liberation of Palestine (PFLP). The assassination was carried out by three students at an-Najah University, one of them a young woman. Masri's crime was his willingness to serve under the Israeli civil administration. The murder exposed the internecine battle between rival PLO groups in the territories, but also became an opportunity for *Fatah* cadres to flex their muscles. Masri was an extraordinarily popular figure, a member of one of Nablus' most notable families, a supporter of *Fatah* who also was close to Jordan. His funeral, however, became a mass demonstration of support for Yasser Arafat and a protest against King Hussein, who a month earlier had called for the PLO leadership to be replaced in the West Bank.

For Mamdouh, Masri's death was a bitter personal blow. They had been classmates in high school and had remained very close. "People were consoling Mamdouh, calling to express their sympathies and to say how sad they were that you lost your friend," recalls Ziad. Mamdouh knew, says his brother, that Masri had been murdered "because he started saying we can make peace with Israel. His death helped convince Mamdouh that his place was at home," says Ziad. "Once he came back to the West Bank, he never left again." Says Mamdouh, "I think one of the main lessons we Palestinians learned, although we learned it the hard way, is that whatever might happen, we have to stay on the land. We have to stay because anybody who experiences what it means to be in exile or a refugee—this is one of the most humiliating experiences. Here, irrespective of the hardships and the difficulties and the sufferings of being under occupation, still the main point is to be on the land and face the occupier."

But he was still not very eager to get involved in politics. It was Muhannad, his youngest son, who was the catalyst for Mamdouh's conversion. In 1986 Muhannad volunteered to work at the Palestinian Center for the Study of Nonviolence, headed by Mubarak Awad, a Palestinian peace activist. People who had various headaches with the Israelis would come to their East Jerusalem office and Muhannad would interview them, taking careful notes, "trying to understand why these things happened," says Awad. These were not political problems, he explains, but "social problems: difficulties with the Israelis," which included the uprooting of trees and denying permission for a well to be dug any deeper because it would deprive a neighboring settlement of water. Other Palestinians complained that their family had increased in size and they could not get permission to build onto their house. "So they would build a house, and the Israelis would come and destroy the whole house because they built it without a permit," says Awad. Or someone would come to the center trying to locate a relative who had been imprisoned somewhere in the territories. For the next two years Muhannad would go home every night and tell his father the details of the stories he had heard during the day.

Finally, in mid-January of 1988, less than three weeks after the *intifada* had begun, Mamdouh decided he could no longer remain silent. He wrote an "open" letter to "a central figure in the Labor Party," a man who was committed to a political settlement and who was defense minister of the Likud-led coalition government. That man was Yitzhak Rabin. "That was his [Mamdouh's] first step in politics. His son was the fellow who changed him," says Awad. In the letter, Mamdouh wrote that he was addressing Rabin instead of Labor Party leader Shimon Peres or Prime Minister Yitzhak Shamir because "you represent to us the iron fist of the Likud philosophy. You therefore represent to us, more than Mr. Peres or Mr. Shamir, the official nonpartisan Israeli position towards us." He says he decided to write Rabin because it was "very insulting" to listen to him continually describing the stone-throwing incidents as "riots" and denouncing the Palestinians as "terrorists." Mamdouh said to himself, "Hey, wait a minute. Watch it. That is not right. This is a popular uprising. You see in it the masses, all ages, all women, the elderly, schoolboys, and teenagers."

But bringing his open letter to Rabin's attention proved harder than he thought. Mamdouh wrote it in Arabic, because he wanted to publish the letter in *al-Quds*, the pro-PLO East Jerusalem newspaper. But the editor was not interested. "It's great," he told Mamdouh, "but I can't publish it as it is. You'll have to change this and that." Mamdouh was incensed. "I didn't come here asking to write an article. I have a message and I wrote it out in this form because I want it to be published as a letter. I'm not going to change a letter of it," he said. The editor still would not budge. "They'll shut down the paper," he said. "I can't." Mamdouh called a friend, an Israeli journalist, who suggested that he rewrite it in English and promised to try to get it published in the *Jerusalem Post*, which at the time was a liberal Israeli newspaper often critical of the government. "He phoned the editor for me, and he said, of course, he would publish it," recalls Mamdouh.

The letter is an unusual document, particularly considering that it was written in the very early days of the *intifada*. In it Mamdouh cautions Rabin that in medicine, "making the correct diagnosis is more than half of the treatment." Without the right diagnosis, it is impossible to understand the "underlying causes," Mamdouh writes. He cautions Rabin that he is making a "grave mistake" in believing the outbreak of the *intifada* reflects "a state of despair" among the Palestinian people. It is precisely the opposite. "In my lifetime, which spans more than forty years, I have never seen our people with as high a spirit and confidence as I am seeing today," Mamdouh writes. The correct diagnosis, he says, is that the Palestinians in the West Bank and Gaza lost hope in the ability of others—institutions such as the United Nations and even the two superpowers—to help them "and therefore have chosen a different route." He cautions Rabin that what is taking place in the territories cannot be dismissed as "disturbances," "unrest," "riots," or "acts of violence."

> If you really want to understand what is taking place, you have to agree that it is a revival. It is a qualitatively different phenomenon, reflecting a Palestinian rebirth. No description that neglects this is worthy of your attention. This determination, this courage, this spirit, this comprehensive sustained movement indicates no less than a popular uprising. . . . If you are seriously interested in identifying the source, it is the occupation. Do you expect us to throw roses on your soldiers? Did your people do that when they were persecuted in Europe?"

Perhaps the most enduring part of the letter to Rabin was Mamdouh's foresight in predicting that the *intifada* would strengthen indigenous Palestinian leaders like himself, who were the natural partners for a peaceful dialogue with Israel. "In the diagnosis, it is also imperative to note that this uprising returns the focus of Palestinian activism to its proper place, and returns the emphasis of a Palestinian national movement to the 'inside,'" Mamdouh wrote. He added, of course, that nothing could detract from the "unity of our people or the primary role of the 'outside' leaders."

But the major thrust of his letter was a call on Rabin to initiate the dialogue:

> One does realize your obsession with security, but in all objectivity and without provocation, allow me to say that we the Palestinians are the only party that can grant you security and tranquility. If you really want peace, it will only be accomplished by talking to us, and through our legitimate representative, the PLO. Security can't be reached by your army, regardless of how strong it gets. No Arab country or international force, including the U.S., can provide you with security. Only a negotiated peace, freely reached by you and our genuine leadership, will provide a context for such negotiations.

Mamdouh concluded his letter by asking prophetically, "Why do you need to rediscover that the earth is round? Denying the central and basic fact only means a continuation of this cycle of suffering for you and for us."

The exchange marked a turning point in Mamdouh's life. He would no longer remain on the sidelines of the Palestinian struggle. "Apparently it was a daring letter. There was quite a response—positive and negative—from the Palestinians," he admits. Many of his friends told him he would now be targeted by the Israeli right wing. "They felt scared that the settlers might harm me," says Mamdouh. But he also received many encouraging responses from ordinary Israelis, although he never heard directly from Rabin. "Without intending it and without planning it, [the letter] put me into the middle of the dynamics of the *intifada*," he says. "I was searching for a role because I felt this [the *intifada*] is a historic event and I had to be part of it," he says.

Other letters followed. They were published in the *Jerusalem Post* and in newspapers in other countries as well. In March 1988 he helped to create the organization Israeli-Palestinian Physicians for Human Rights. "Then I started to get involved in medical relief activities," he explains, because most of the Arab villages in the West Bank and Gaza had no emergency clinics. "When you see the injured in the hospitals, it really is ugly," says Mamdouh, who is on the board of the Arab Medical Welfare Association. He has recently launched a campaign to obtain ambulances with mobile operating rooms, because, he says, "many people die on the way to the hospital."

His involvement in helping to heal the wounded made him realize that he should extend his task beyond those with physical afflictions. "I started feeling that I had a responsibility to convey the message of the *intifada* to the Israeli public, so I started to accept invitations from Israeli peace groups. I attended dozens of meetings, where we argued about how to find a solution," says Mamdouh. One of those groups was the "21st Year," an Israeli-Palestinian organization that held meetings in Jewish homes. "We conducted informal sessions," says Haggith Gor Ziv, the coordinator of the Jewish-Arab Council for Peace Education. "There we witnessed the beginnings of a real dialogue of equals on highly controversial questions," including Palestinian and Israeli terrorism, Ziv recalls. "Even today," says Mamdouh, "I don't consider what I am doing is political. I'm doing this as an intellectual and as a nationalist."

When the *intifada* spread to remote rural parts of the West Bank, he says, "we started to know the names of new villages, villages that I never heard of before. This is when I started to be restless. I have to be part of this," he told himself. "I sensed it, from the very first week or two, that this is different, this is different. I am always grateful to my profession: being a physician allows you to keep your hand on the pulse." The unique thing about the *intifada*, he explains, is that its roots stretched into all levels of Palestinian society, including the refugee camps, and involved all age groups and religions and men, women, and children. "With the *intifada*, we moved into the stage of active resistance—not only resisting occupation but saying that we are not afraid anymore. The barrier of fear was broken forever."

The Israelis claim Mamdouh was not just one of the people helping the *intifada*, he was one of the people running it. He was arrested on February 27, 1991—during the period when Iraq was shelling Israel with Scud missiles—and brought before an Israeli military court on March 13 for a hearing. The Israeli media quoted official government sources as saying he was being interrogated in relation to unspecified disturbances: inciting violence, the issuing of leaflets hostile to the authorities, and alleged contacts with illegal organizations, including the PLO. A senior Israeli official was more blunt. "He was a member of the Unified National Command [UNC] of the *intifada*," states this military source, who says there were well-founded "suspicions" that Mamdouh took part in writing UNC leaflets. He was interrogated for forty days and forty nights. "At the beginning he denied any connection to the Unified National Command; then he admitted that he wrote part of it [the UNC leaflet], a medical chapter. He was a part of the UNC—fully," claims the Israeli.

This official charges that Palestinian leaders like Mamdouh wear two hats. Their twin roles, as political activists in the territories and as members of the negotiating team, which gives them diplomatic status if not total immunity, pose a serious dilemma for the Israeli security services. Their job during the day is to negotiate with Israel for Palestinian autonomy; their "night job," contends the Israeli, is "to secretly give instructions for riots and public disorder." Because Israel wants to encourage a peaceful political process to replace the violence of the *intifada*, this is a "gray area," says the official. "We are in a catch here what to do."

On March 13, the day Mamdouh was brought before a military judge to hear the charges against him, he began a hunger strike. It lasted for three and a half days. There was little doubt what the Israelis wanted: a full confession of his alleged role as one of the principal organizers of the *intifada*. Mamdouh was held in a cell three feet long and five feet wide. "It was very dirty," says Ziad. "They humiliated him in every way possible. Even when he had to go to the bathroom, they would not let him. And the food they gave him—it's like a dog. In the interrogation they put him in a box, called *tabut*. It was exactly his size—only your head protrudes from the top—and they prevented him from sleeping for a long time, for five days or a week."

The confinement took a toll on the forty-eight-year-old doctor and his family. Mamdouh was not permitted to see his relatives or his lawyer, Jonathan Kuttab, until March 25, when his counsel applied to the Israeli High Court and obtained a writ allowing the visit. When Kuttab finally saw his client, Mamdouh had lost a lot of weight. He had suffered chest pains and heart palpitations. Through his lawyer, Mamdouh issued a public statement, in which he described himself as a "Palestinian nationalist and a doctor who feels the pain and suffering of his people." Said Mamdouh, "I have always advocated peaceful solutions and dialogue and coexistence with Israelis. I continue to believe that this is the only way to ensure justice and security for Israelis and Palestinians alike. I have always believed in nonviolence and the moral force of a just position, rather than the use of weapons and violence." Although he denied any involvement, "even indirectly," in inciting unrest or violence in the territories, Mamdouh acknowledged that "during the [Persian Gulf] war, I felt it my duty as a Palestinian to advise my countrymen in matters of civil defense, self-help, preparations for medical emergencies, and care for the needy and suffering during the time of the prolonged curfews."

His arrest aroused worldwide attention. Among those protesting his imprisonment were Amnesty International, Middle East Watch, the Nelson Mandela Institute, the Palestinian Center for the Study of Nonviolence, the National Council on U.S.-Arab Relations, the American Friends Service Committee, Americans for Peace Now, the Jewish Peace Fellowship, the British Association of Urological Surgeons, and the Royal College of Surgeons at Edinburgh. Mubarak Awad, who was deported by Israel after being similarly charged with a leadership role in the *intifada*, organized an International Committee for the Release of Mamdouh Aker, in Washington. Dr. Jonathan Fine, the executive director of Physicians for Human Rights, wrote Israeli Defense Minister Moshe Arens and U.S. Secretary of State James Baker. He had met Mamdouh "on more than one occasion" in Israel, Fine wrote, describing the physician as "a man of moderation who has consistently sought a peaceful solution to the Arab-Israeli conflict. He is highly regarded professionally. Furthermore, he is an unusually gentle person who would offend no one."

Finally, on April 7, a week after he had begun another fast (for the month of Ramadan), and ten days before the prosecution was required to present an indictment against him, Mamdouh was released on $10,000 bail and placed under house arrest pending trial. But the trial never took place. Apparently in response to the international outcry, the Israeli prosecutor never pressed charges against him. On April 11, however, the Israeli embassy in Washington, which had been deluged with mail from a letter-writing campaign on Mamdouh's behalf, sent a response to everyone who complained about his confinement. The Israeli letter said Mamdouh was arrested "on suspicion of promoting hostile terrorist activity" as well as "maintaining connections with terrorist organizations in the region and abroad." The letter added that "in the course of the investigation, Mr. Aker admitted to taking part in hostile activities and to having connections with terrorist organizations." Said one Israeli official, "From what we knew about his activities, the judge could have easily sentenced him to at least two years in jail."

Mamdouh did not have the opportunity to confront his accusers until the following October, when he was chosen as one of the fourteen members of the Jordanian-Palestinian delegation to the Madrid peace conference. He was one of two guests on a special Madrid edition of the Cable News Network program "Newsmaker Saturday," hosted by CNN's White House correspondent, Frank Cesno. The other guest was Zalman Shoval, the Israeli ambassador to the United States. "I was quite excited when I found out we would meet here," Mamdouh said, jumping at the chance to address the Israeli official directly, "because during my detention, in response to letters received on my behalf, Mr. Shoval described me as a 'hostile terrorist activist.' Here I am. Do I look like a hostile activist?" asked the mild-mannered, distinguished-looking Palestinian diplomat. Shoval shot back, "I am happy to hear you have not been a terrorist." But the Israeli then said that all Palestinians had behaved irresponsibly during the war in the Persian Gulf. "The only thing I was involved in," replied Mamdouh, "was to give guidelines to my people from a medical perspective." No charges had ever been filed against him, he said, and after forty days and nights of interrogation, and having been released on bail, "everything was lifted," said Mamdouh.

He went on to challenge his Israeli counterpart. "The first step," he said, "is to treat me as an equal. I am a people. This is the cry of our people—that we are people. We are not residents or inhabitants of Judea and Samaria. We are the Palestinian people. The moment you recognize me as an equal, the whole atmosphere will be different.'' Before Shoval could respond, Mamdouh added: ''I recognize you as a people, the Israeli people—and as a nation and as a state. This is the spirit with which we have come to this conference, with an open heart and an open mind and trying to reach out. I am not denying you any right I am claiming myself. Let us treat each other as equals entitled to the same rights.''

Mamdouh's performance in Madrid, his refined appearance and air of self-confidence, made him something of an overnight television sensation. Shortly after appearing on CNN, he was asked by Barbara Walters to appear on ABC-TV's popular ''Nightline'' program. Several other network news shows, including PBS-TV's ''MacNeil-Lehrer NewsHour,'' also invited Mamdouh to square off against their Israeli government guests.

His private Ramallah clinic in the nondescript Hanania Kharaz building, its waiting room of brown vinyl chairs filled with anxious patients, seems a world away from the drama and glory of Madrid. But as Mamdouh reflects on the future of his struggle, the two realities seem somehow linked, perhaps by the suggestion on the walls of his clinic, covered with murals of a forest, that it is the land, after all, that will determine the outcome. ''It is not just a matter of freezing the [Israeli] settlements,'' he says. ''It is important to stop all settlement activity while the peace talks are going on and all through the interim phase of autonomy. We cannot negotiate while the main issue, the land, is being confiscated every day.''

This thin, handsome man with the bushy black eyebrows, short-cropped hair, and furrowed brow also has another aim: to persuade as many Palestinian physicians as he can to return to the land that he hopes will become the nucleus of a Palestinian state. ''There are a sizeable number of Palestinians who have their I.D. cards and can come but who hesitate,'' says Mamdouh. ''I believe that deep inside them they feel the guilt.'' Even his immediate family is not spared the pressure. Says Ziad, who lives near Washington, D.C., in a plush new development with its own Olympic-size swimming pool and tennis courts, ''Mamdouh always is after me to come back. Now he is also trying to persuade our younger brother, Samir, and his wife—they are both doctors—to go back and work in Nablus."

Mamdouh is clearly overworked. Between his medical duties—he divides his time between three hospitals in Jerusalem (Saint Luke's, Saint George's, and Saint Joseph's) and two in Nablus (Women's College Hospital and al-Ittihad)—and his new diplomatic and political chores, he has little time for anything else. "I make it a point to save one night a week to spend with my family," he says.

But for Mamdouh, his two roles—as the healer of the sick and as a key negotiator trying to mend the wounds with Israel—are closely intertwined. "I have many patients from the refugee camps. I make it a point always to talk to my patients and they talk to me, particularly since I was named to the [Palestinian] delegation. Every one of them, without exception, talks about their hopes, their dreams, their suffering." These Palestinians are Mamdouh's patients, but they are also his future constituency, the people who may vote for him if the autonomy talks lead to elections for a national assembly and he decides to run for office. For the moment, this *Fatah* supporter is an important link between the exiled PLO leadership in Tunis and the emerging generation of West Bank and Gaza leaders that is gradually gaining the respect and support of a worldwide audience. "The legitimacy is coming from outside the territories, but the credibility is coming from inside," says Mamdouh. "Credibility," he says, underscoring his own considerable following. "The people chosen—people know them, they respect them." One thing is certain. He is not leaving the West Bank again, at least not until the state of Palestine is a reality. "We'll die here," he says speaking for himself as well as his people. "We're not going to move anywhere."

Sameh Kanaan

Sameh Kanaan is a walking paradox: a Jew who allies himself with the Arabs, an Arab who could be counted as one of a family of Jews. Ask any Israeli official about Kanaan, and a grimace comes across his face. True, Kanaan's grandparents were Moroccan Sephardim, Jews from the Orient, who fled North Africa and settled in Jerusalem; and true, they were observant, orthodox Jews. True, Kanaan speaks fluent Hebrew, reads the Israeli newspapers, watches the Israeli news, admires the democratic Israeli Knesset, and understands the mentality of modern Jews. And true, Kanaan is one of the people currently negotiating for peace between Arabs and Jews. But to the Israelis, Kanaan is an anomaly, an absurdity, an insult: by *halakha*, the Jewish religious law, he is a Jew; but in the real world, he is a Muslim, an Arab, and an active supporter of the PLO.

Sameh Kanaan is a cultural hybrid, a mix between a father who was a Muslim and a mother who was a Jew. As children his parents lived next door to one another in El Musrara, a Jerusalem neighborhood just beyond the Old City walls. It was then late in the thirty-year period of the British mandate—a time, his elders say, of an open society in Palestine. Despite their competing claims to the land, and occasional outbursts of violence, Arabs and Jews in Jerusalem mingled freely and lived amongst each other. It was an era, Sameh's family told him, when the physical and psychological barriers that were to divide the two peoples following Israeli independence in 1948 had yet to be erected.

Throughout the 1940s the Maimans, a Jewish family that had emigrated from Morocco, and the Kanaans, their Muslim neighbors, paid little attention to each other's affairs; little did they think that a son from one house and a daughter from the other would fall in love. But in 1946 Mazal Maiman and Taleb Kanaan announced they wanted to marry. The bride's father, a religiously observant man, refused to condone his daughter's marriage. "It was not easy to give his daughter as a wife to a Muslim," says Sameh. For an orthodox Jew, to see his daughter marry out of the Jewish faith is a tragedy: it is even the custom to sit *shiva*, that is, to sit in mourning for the girl as though she were dead. For the Kanaans, however, the coming marriage was a joyful event as they helped their future daughter-in-law prepare for her new life. Taleb's family taught Mazal the Muslim traditions of cooking and keeping house. Although Islam, unlike Judaism, does not forbid intermarriage, it does insist that the bride become a Muslim; Mazal had to convert to Islam before the couple could marry. The conversion was performed by Abdul Hameed Sayeh, then sheikh of Nablus and current president of the Palestine National Council. Sameh speaks of Mazal as being absolutely devoted to Taleb, enough to risk alienating her own family to marry him. "In love, nothing is difficult," Sameh says. "She sacrificed everything for my father—her religion, her family."

The Kanaans left Jerusalem for Nablus, where Taleb's extended family, ensconced for many generations, had acquired property throughout the town. Taleb, who had manufactured bus seats as an employee of the bus company in Jerusalem, opened his own shop in Nablus. For two years the couple lived a quiet life; but when the Jews declared their new state in 1948, the Arabs attacked and the area was at war. Jordan seized control of the entire West Bank, including Nablus and the eastern part of Jerusalem; the Israelis retained control of the western section of the city. For the first time in its history, the holy city was divided. It would be nineteen years before Mazal saw her own family again.

But in Nablus Mazal had become part of the community. The religion of her birth sowed no ethnic discord in the Arab town. The family lived its Muslim identity unambiguously. "Because we were living in a Muslim area and in a Muslim family," says Sameh, "we were brought up by Arabic tradition. Because [my mother] was Muslim, her traditions now converted to Muslim." Although Taleb was not a religious man, the family's home life unmistakably followed his faith rather than his wife's. Muslim holidays were celebrated in the Kanaan home; Jewish holidays were not. Arabic was spoken; Hebrew was not. The Jewish line of the Maiman family, in effect, had ended with Mazal. The Kanaan children were Muslims. Nevertheless, under Jewish law all offspring of a Jewish mother are considered to be Jews—rendering Mazal's children, at least technically, Jewish.

In 1954 the Kanaans, struggling to make a living, left Nablus, traveled across the Jordan River, and settled in Irbid, a town in the eastern part of the Hashemite kingdom of Jordan. That year Sameh, the last of Taleb and Mazal's seven children, was born. Like his four brothers and two sisters, Sameh was raised in a traditional Muslim manner. He was taught the religion and culture of Islam, both at home and in the state school he attended in town. Ten years later, still seeking better economic conditions, the Kanaans crossed back over the Jordan and returned to their family in Nablus. Then, in 1967, the Six-Day War erupted, and Jordan again attacked. This time Israel captured the West Bank and controlled all of Jerusalem.

Suddenly, for the first time in two decades, Mazal was reunited with her family. Tears flowed the day the Kanaans welcomed Mazal's brother and brother-in-law to their Nablus home. Sameh, then 13, still remembers the excitement of meeting his Jewish uncles for the first time. Sameh's maternal grandmother, by then a widow, did not make the trip to Nablus for the emotional reunion; twenty years of separation had left her unprepared for a sudden reconciliation. Still, Mrs. Maiman gave her blessings to the meeting, and mother and daughter soon reconciled privately in Jerusalem. "Nothing can prevent a mother from searching for the heart of her baby," says Mazal's youngest child.

But along with the picture of joy came another image as well: the military unification of the West Bank with Israel brought Jewish soldiers to Nablus. When young Sameh first laid eyes on Israelis, his vision was one not of family but of the enemy. "The flags of the Arab countries were raised over these tanks," he recalls of the confrontation with Israeli troops in 1967. "It was the trick from the Israelis to understand they were Arab tanks." Sameh thinks the ruse was meant to draw Nablus residents from their homes and allay resistance to the new military forces. It worked, even with bullets rattling and Israeli fighter jets roaring overhead. Friends told Sameh of others who ran to the tanks, cheering them in welcome. The friends said that some who approached had their weapons confiscated and were encouraged to leave town. Four years later, the seventeen-year-old Sameh had a more personal view of Israel's soldiers. They were the ones who took him into custody at the Damya Bridge.

Growing up in Nablus, Sameh spent much of his spare time playing soccer; as a young boy he was named "Best Goalkeeper in the West Bank, Sixteen and Under." But the constant presence of Israeli soldiers and the pressures of occupation soon displaced the joy of playing ball. As a teenager Sameh felt strongly that Israeli control of his town was wrong, and he decided to take to the streets in protest.

Although Sameh says he could have supported a number of different groups, it was *al-Fatah*, the popular Yasser Arafat–led wing of the Palestine Liberation Organization, that claimed him. "For me at that time," he says, "the most important thing was the struggle against the occupation. The umbrella wasn't important. So I think at that time, accidentally I was recruited to *Fatah*. . . . The important thing was to struggle against occupation. *Fatah* had the principle to struggle, so I agreed immediately to be recruited to the *Fatah* organization." In fact, he says, a friend drew him in to the group. "I think that *Fatah* was a very important name at that time. Its name attracted me, so when he told me '*Fatah*,' I was interested in getting in." Although he did not conceal his belief in armed struggle against the Israelis, and admits he "was recruited to the *Fatah* organization in order to struggle by military means," he insists that "I was not engaged in anything but some demonstrations against the occupation. But," he acknowledges, "my friends were involved in some military activity."

In 1972 Sameh was returning to the West Bank after a visit to Jordan. Crossing the Damya Bridge over the Jordan River and re-entering Israeli-controlled territory, he and three of his buddies were apprehended and charged with membership in an illegal organization: *Fatah*. Someone, perhaps an informant, had passed on word of the cell's activities to the Israeli authorities. Sameh admits to training fellow Palestinians in the use of explosives. But to this day, he denies involvement in any acts of terror. Senior Israeli officials confirm his general account but contend that he was hardly an innocent traveler across the Jordan. "He was involved in transferring weapons, automatic machine guns and explosives, from a cell that tried to organize a terrorist attack against Jews. In the end they did not succeed. The intentions were there. The weapons were there. But he is right. He did not personally kill anyone with his own hands," explains an Israeli familiar with the Kanaan case.

After his arrest, Sameh was taken immediately to the Nablus jail and placed in a two-foot by seven-foot cell. "It was a very dirty cell, with voices of a lot of mice," says the exprisoner. "Actual mice and dirty blankets." For twenty-one days he was kept in the Nablus cell and interrogated by Israeli intelligence officers. Occasionally he was beaten and slapped around, and he remembers, too, the discomfort of the cold showers. He was repeatedly interrogated. The Israelis said to him, "We know you are this and you did this. Confess!" He replied, "I don't know who informs about me. At the end I confessed that I was a member of one of the Palestinian organizations," which was illegal under Israeli law. He says it was *Fatah*.

Sameh spent the next year in a holding pattern in a larger cell with many other prisoners before being put on trial by the military court. The three military judges sentenced him to twenty-one years' imprisonment and fined him 5000 Israeli lira (then about $1500). He was moved to the prison near the southern Israeli city of Beersheba, where he spent the bulk of his thirteen years in jail. In 1985, during the massive prisoner exchange of 1150 Palestinian activists for three Israeli soldiers, Sameh was freed, fortunately for him, eight years before his sentence was due to expire.

His memory is still sharp with images of Beersheba. He calls it a "very, very bad jail. I was put by the Israeli jailers in one section which is called Section 7, consisting of about forty-five cells." Each five-by-seven-foot cell held two prisoners. For seven years these living conditions grated on Sameh and his fellow inmates. "When we were in prison they brought us beds, two-story beds, and the beds were in every room: beds, beds, beds. You cannot go in the room. You eat and sit in your bed. We had no space. When the officer comes to count you, you must get down from the bed and stand in front of the officer." He reaches into his memory bank to create a detailed picture of his tedious prison life: 500 prisoners; he was number 47. One pair of pants for summer, one for winter. Six a.m. roll call, noon and evening roll calls, emergency roll calls. But "we have dignity. Some of us were rational persons." They agreed to make a stand. "So we told the director of the prison about the crowding."

He found Beersheba's southern climate difficult, at best. The extreme heat, unexpected chill, and unpredictable desert winds were nettlesome. He remembers that, at times, over 100 prisoners would line up to take a bath after spending hours in the summer sun. Still, during his Beersheba days, Sameh discovered his Jewish guards were also human. He points to two immigrants from the then–Soviet Union with whom he cultivated brief friendships. One, Sameh recalls, cheered the prisoners during their basketball and volleyball games. Another confided in Sameh his unhappiness with his duties and said he "did not like this life." "He told me," says Sameh, "'Do you know the meaning of a guard?' I said to him, 'Yes, to guard a person.' 'No,' he told me, 'I am like a dog. The dog guards.'"

Partly to relieve the boredom, Sameh pursued his intellectual interests, and prison became his "university." He participated in political meetings of Palestinian activists. He read newspapers and cheap novels. And he learned Hebrew. "I want to understand my enemy, because the prophet Mohammed says always, 'If you want to be safe from the enemy you must learn his language.' Sameh began studying the language in Beersheba. The prisoners themselves created a lingual chain. Israeli Arabs taught the language of the Jewish state to their Palestinian brothers: one taught another, who taught another, etc. Sameh's teacher in Beersheba was Muhammed Azhar, who led a class of twenty students. The grass-roots Hebrew instruction program, like the political meetings, was sanctioned by the Israeli prison authorities.

Sameh devoured every bit of Hebrew material he came across. He read books and magazines given to him by his guards. He listened to Israel's Hebrew radio stations, in addition to the Arabic ones. For a while he even maintained a subscription to Israel's mass circulation daily *Yediot Acharonot*. He says he is unsure whether he was the only Palestinian prisoner in Israel's history to have paid for a subscription to a Hebrew newspaper. Mostly, he devoted himself to the Jews' language because of a desire to penetrate the Israeli psyche, to grasp the mechanisms that help make Israeli society tick. True, his mother could speak Hebrew fluently. But after her wedding, she never spoke it at home. Sameh had no advantage over the other inmates, although he may have had more interest to delve into his roots. (Even now, every night he's at home Sameh makes sure to position himself in front of the television for Israel's 9 o'clock "Mabat" newscast. In that way, he echoes the habits of most every Israeli at home at that hour.) He knew that mastery of Hebrew could help him satisfy his burning curiosity about the other side—the side against which he campaigned in *Fatah*, the side represented by his prison guards, the side that had its own street signs and Declaration of Independence and currency—and, although he does not say it, the side that had cut off his mother from her own people.

But Sameh insists that his intensive study of the Hebrew language merely reflects his general inquisitiveness into Jewish culture. He reads up on the latest trends in Israeli life and can quote liberally from the great medieval Spanish Jewish philosopher Maimonides. Ask him why he dedicates himself to the Palestinian cause and he'll respond in Hebrew with the famous statement on personal responsibility by Hillel, the renowned Second Temple–era Jewish scholar: "If I am not for myself, who will be for me?" Asked about the Muslim holy period of Ramadan, he will talk about the story of Purim, the Jewish holiday that, too, falls in March. Or of the story of Shavuot, the Jewish springtime holiday. Or of how he ate Passover matzoh in prison—and enjoyed it. "The holidays are interesting to me because it shows how Israelis think," he says. "It shows how they preserve their traditions."

But probing the strangers' culture serves, too, to underscore the gulf he sees between the two peoples' worlds, between the worlds of his own grandparents. "I'm astonished at how they preserve their religion but prevent others from observing theirs," he says. "I'll give you an example. In Ketziot [the Negev prison where he served six months in administrative detention], we were forbidden to make prayers outside our tents." The reason may have had less to do with Israeli bars on religious observance than with the fact that all kinds of gatherings of more than a handful of

Palestinians were barred because the Israelis were afraid they would turn into an organized rebellion. Sameh also remembers being struck once by a news report of the Israeli traffic streaming northward for the Passover holiday. The report resonated with bitterness because it made him think, "The Israelis go for picnics. They go everywhere, but we have curfews."

For nineteen years under Jordanian occupation, West Bankers like Sameh saw no signs of Israeli life. There were no windows between the peoples, and they were offered no such contrast between the nationalities. There was none of the direct, day-to-day Israeli-Palestinian enmity that was to eventually characterize the relationship. The absence of contact served as a thick, blank wall. After the Israeli victory in 1967, that invisible barrier toppled and each side saw the other for the first time.

But Israeli occupation bred anger, and with the anger came violence and fear. Sameh admits that his greatest worry is falling victim to the random, and sometimes not-so-random, violence resulting from the often heated confrontation between the two sides. "I know of a man, a bus driver for the Arab buses in the West Bank. He drove into one of the bus stations in the West Bank. And he took a recess, a break, and went inside and used the lavatories. And while he was inside the station, the [Arab] guard from the station went onto the bus and just sat down on the driver's seat. There were no passengers on the bus at that time— the bus was empty. The guard just sat down in that driver's seat, maybe just to rest. And he was shot and he died. There was noise because of the shooting. And the driver returned, and he knew that he might have been this victim." While Sameh agrees that the incident could have been a random violent act that was not politically motivated, it underscores for him the fragility and unpredictability of West Bank life. It reminds him, too, of those violent flare-ups directly related to the Israeli-Palestinian conflict.

In traditional Islam, you must be prepared to meet your creator, says Sameh. But during the last five years of the *intifada*, that was not something you could put off for tomorrow: you had to be clean physically before venturing anywhere. "Everyone in the West Bank," he says, "washes themselves before going outside on the street. Why? Because in case they are killed and they die and become a martyr, they will be pure." He pauses, then adds,

"Yes, when I go out of my house, I feel insecure, because bullets are normal. And I also wash myself." It is, he says, part of the mystique of the *intifada*, part of a force that dictates that someone is probably going to die whenever there is a demonstration.

Today Sameh is dogged by dreams of Israeli soldiers and of the effects of Israeli occupation on the routines of day-to-day life. He points, first, to the nagging, depressing bureaucracy. He cites the high and all-encompassing taxes. He mentions the Palestinians' obligation to carry the identity cards that must be produced on demand. Even though he knows Jews and Arabs in Israel proper also are subjected to high taxes and Israelis must also carry identity cards, both are annoying symbols of the constant Israeli intent to subvert the Palestinians to their will. They are daily reminders of the fact that Palestinians do not yet have their own state, with their own tax system to support it, and their own passports. It is that denial of their identity as a people that gnaws at him.

Then there is his anger over what he sees as the Israelis' assignment of collective guilt to the Palestinian nation in their midst. "If I am young or small or old—there is no difference for the Israelis," he says; there is "collective punishment against all the Palestinians." Such penalties as townwide curfews are meted out against everyone. "All Palestinians are the same."

However, it is the randomness, the feeling that they can never plan anything, that they never know what is going to happen to them, that helps explain the impromptu Palestinian reaction when Iraqi Scud missiles fell on Israel. To many Palestinians it was the sense of satisfaction they felt that Israelis were finally experiencing the same kind of random attacks and not the fact that Israelis were dying that caused such elation. A Scud could fall at any time; a curfew could be called without prior warning and, just like the Palestinians, the Israelis would be confined to their homes. It is this feeling that there is a force out there you cannot control, that can change your life at any moment; the fear that in the middle of night soldiers can knock on your door and search your home, that is one reason, he says, Palestinians feel they are being punished—as a people. "And all the Palestinians are against this treatment, not [just] the terrorists of the Palestinians. They [the Israelis] are against the Palestinians as a people because they don't distinguish between the Palestinians," says Sameh.

But he does distinguish between the Israelis' treatment of Palestinians in Nablus and those in Jerusalem. In Nablus, he says, "There are no positive contacts. All the contact with the Israelis here is negative, unlike in Jerusalem, for example. In Jerusalem, I think they treated the people unlike they treated them here in Nablus. Why? Because [Jerusalem] is a holy place, so it is very important to make the people feel comfortable."

Today Sameh still lives in Nablus with his wife, Rueda; their three daughters, Samah, 4, Hind, 3, and Zein, born about the time of the Madrid peace conference; and his mother, Mazal. The sixty-three-year-old woman's other children are scattered across the world. Her daughters live in Jerusalem. Two sons live in Sweden, one in France, and another also in Nablus. "We are like the Palestinian people," jibes Sameh, who works as an English–Hebrew translator for the Nablus Chamber of Commerce and Industry. "Everyone, everywhere." Near his home sits one of the old Kanaan properties, which he intends to renovate soon. He refers to the long-vacant structure as "the ancient house" and says that one day it will be used as a *diwan*—a place to hold family events, both celebrations and sad occasions.

Of course, who will come depends on the political winds. Just before the start of the Palestinian *intifada* in December 1987, Sameh began meeting again with the Jewish family members he had never really known. Most still live in Jerusalem. Until the *intifada* split the fragile seams of the two nations' coexistence, the Kanaan-Maiman families' relations were warming. "Now," though, says Sameh, shaking his head, "there is nothing. Only telephone calls." The extended family walks the delicate line, recognizing the improbability of maintaining a unified family, of gazing beyond the politics, of coming to terms with their diverging destinies. Despite the hardships, he says, "I'm proud that my mother was a Jew. Always, my mother, on her lips, says, 'Peace.'"

The man who spent thirteen years in prison for his activities with *Fatah* says he still sees the PLO as his people's brightest hope for progress on the peace front. He shrugs off Israeli fears of a PLO-controlled Palestinian entity in the West Bank. While conceding that the PLO advanced its agenda through bloody, violent attacks against Israelis, he asserts the organization has changed more than just its stripes. In Sameh's view, the Palestinians "are not contrary to other nationalist movements. The PLO is not a terrorist group but a national movement, like the African National Congress and the Vietnamese movements. It doesn't exist just to kill Israelis. It has changed. It's not the same PLO, it's a government. Now we'll leave the PLO aside—let the Israelis make peace with us."

Sameh Kanaan speaks with some authority. He has been chosen as one of the fourteen people on the Palestinian team negotiating with Israelis in the Middle East peace talks. He believes his reputation as an honorable man preceded him from prison, and he thinks it is responsible for the call he received last year from Palestinian leader Sari Nusseibeh requesting that he join the Palestinian team to negotiate peace with Israel. Harking back to his athletic days, and grinning ear to ear, Sameh calls himself the "goalkeeper of our delegation"—the one who will "not let the Israelis score goals."

The road to peace, he believes, requires preliminary building blocks. For starters, he looks to the Israelis to continue reaching out with confidence-building measures. Such efforts, he says, help "convince our people that we are going to peace," and must go beyond a freeze on new settlement activity, the release of political prisoners, the reopening of Palestinian schools and universities, and a cessation of curfews—all of which have been ordered by the new Rabin-led government. When asked about simultaneous Palestinian-initiated confidence-building measures, however, he is less forthcoming. "We acknowledge that Israel is in need of security. But we are the weak and they are the powerful. We have no tanks. We need security more than the Israelis. Believe me, this is the feeling of all the Palestinians on the West Bank." Nonetheless, Sameh says, once Israel proves its good intentions and halts the building of all settlements, Palestinians may consider reciprocal measures, such as temporarily suspending the *intifada*.

He sighs deeply and rubs his right eye with his palm as if to wipe away an ugly vision. "Listen," he continues in English. "We know Israel is afraid of Masada and a Holocaust. We know everyone needs security. So we're willing to sit with the Israelis for five years, under an interim self-government arrangement—

to give Israelis [the opportunity] to find out that we're not terrorists, that we'll agree to peace."

The Palestinian proposal, the "Model of Palestinian Interim Self-Governing Arrangement (PISGA)," envisions Palestinian elections for a 180-member legislative assembly. The elected body would in turn select a twenty-member committee handling the day-to-day ministries of government. After a two-year period of Palestinian self-rule, Israel and the Palestinian leadership would, according to the plan, negotiate over the next three years the final status of the West Bank and Gaza Strip. The document was submitted by the Palestinian delegation to the Israelis in January 1992. But the plan was rejected by Israel, which considers PISGA a blueprint for a Palestinian state. The new Rabin government has instead proposed elections for April 1993 for a more limited, 18-member administrative council.

Now Sameh sees time running out. He knows that lack of progress strengthens the hands of Palestinian hardliners. His words come across as a friendly warning to the Israelis. "If they want real peace," he says solemnly, "they [must] encourage the moderates, just like us, in order to give us courage to go to our people and say: 'Look, the Israelis really have good intentions to make peace with the Palestinians.' "

Sameh is apprehensive, too, about hot heads on both sides seeking to torpedo the peace process. As an example he cites the then-upcoming election in Nablus for the town's Chamber of Commerce and Industry. As in other West Bank towns holding such elections, the Nablus vote offered two predominant lists: the Islamic fundamentalist group *Hamas* and the nationalist leadership backed by the PLO. *Hamas*, known also as the Islamic Resistance Movement, rejects the concept of Palestinian participation at the peace table with Israel. "I think they [*Hamas*] are becoming strong because of the frustration of the people with the situation," Sameh says. "We are living in fear, in frustration, and [the people gravitate] to God. This is a psychological feeling. So they go to *Hamas*, and *Hamas* gets stronger. Also, they exploit the feeling they must be a Muslim. They use the mosques for their activities." Because the PLO supported Iraq, he says, "I think after the Gulf War they [*Hamas*] were paid by the Gulf countries with a lot of money. And I heard from outside they gave money before the Gulf War to compete with the PLO. The money is very important. Now they are paying for many people to get into the Chamber of Commerce. For example, they say that 'after we get into the Chamber of Commerce we will build Islamic institutions.'"

Sameh's wariness of *Hamas'* new-found strength proved prescient in the West Bank town of Ramallah, although not in Nablus. Ramallah, ten miles north of Jerusalem and traditionally a nationalist stronghold, saw *Hamas'* surprising near-sweep to victory in March 1992, with the fundamentalist group winning ten out of eleven seats. The PLO regrouped in time for the Nablus election on May 21, 1992, and captured nine of the board's twelve seats. It took to the offensive, responding both superficially and tactically—it campaigned as the Nationalist Muslim Coalition. *Hamas* candidate Imad Kanaan told the *Mideast Mirror* on May 21, 1992, that the nationalist opponents succeeded by sowing confusion and throwing into question "which is the true Muslim group." When *Hamas* responded with its own appeal to religious values, Sameh Kanaan would later say: "Islam might be the solution, but *Hamas* is certainly not."

Hamas' infiltration into the West Bank, as well as its subsequent success at the polls, seems to Sameh to reveal more than merely its geographic progression from the neighboring, nondemocratic Arab countries. He accuses Israel of slyly egging on *Hamas* so as to block the natural course of peace. Some Palestinians "think *Hamas* is right in saying 'We are against the peace process.' And this is the role of Israel—to make it longer, longer, so our people will be convinced of the Islamic [fundamentalist] groups. So the Israelis can say, 'Yes, we are going to peace, but the Palestinians are not.' So this is the game. The [Israeli-run] civil administration is encouraging *Hamas* to be in the Nablus Chamber of Commerce. They encouraged them, although they [*Hamas*] want Palestine from the River to the Sea. This is the contradiction."

Indeed, says Sameh, the Palestinians' new-found moderation offers Israel its best prospects for making peace with residents of the territories. "If [the Israelis] do not exploit this opportunity, they will lose it." Otherwise, he says, the moderates will be unable to hold off the fundamentalists and hard-liners in the Palestinian camp. But while on the one hand he warns of these dangers, on the other he argues that they are a natural part of the political growing process. "We have opposition. Not all the opposition is in the democratic way. We are like any other people, and we are not primitive people. We are educated people, and this will help us in order to have our own democracy."

It is a late afternoon in early March 1992, the last of eight grueling days at the Middle East bargaining table. The final session at the U.S. Department of State concluded just a half hour ago, and Palestinian diplomats are returning to the Grand, the luxurious Washington hotel they call home during their landmark meetings with Israeli representatives. While his colleagues enjoy a well-earned siesta upstairs or smoke cigarettes in the lobby, thirty-seven-year-old Sameh Kanaan, dressed in a fashionable navy pinstripe suit and kaleidoscopic red tie, sits relaxedly in the darkened hotel restaurant, sipping from a glass of water. Nearly two weeks of intensive talks with the Israelis, meetings fraught with disagreement and frustration on both sides, have not sapped the color from his round face or removed the ever-present grin from his lips. He has sharp features, and his short, pronounced jaw reminds one of the American comedian Jay Leno. As one of the fourteen Palestinian negotiators, he contemplates the results of the just-completed third round of Middle East peace talks, and the progress made since the Madrid conference the previous October.

The mood is very different now than it has been during past efforts at peace negotiations. "I think everything is changed," he says, "and politics is the science of changing. In 1970 I wanted to struggle against the occupation by my own means. But now the situation is different for me because I am now engaged in politics, engaged in analyzing the situation after the Gulf War, after the *intifada*. At that time my fight was by armed struggle; now I fight by engaging in the peace process. And engaging in the peace process is [more] difficult than the armed struggle, because we want to exchange words, not bullets."

What the Israeli-Palestinian peace negotiations ultimately come down to, in his view, is ethical human beings sitting together and airing their differences—great as those may be. Indeed, the former explosives instructor has come to the negotiating table still citing his mother's teachings. "My mother brought me up in a very strict way," asserts Sameh. "I learned how to behave properly. I became the *shawish* in prison, you know. That means that I was responsible for the others in prison."

Even after his long prison sentence, even after two periods of administrative detention, even after his house was searched in 1990 while he sat watching an Israeli basketball game on television, there is much the rookie diplomat admires in Israel. He sees it as providing fodder for a future, independent Palestinian government. "I'm fond of the Israeli democracy in their society. I would like to have [a similar democracy]. When I saw the Knesset—and I know Hebrew—the Knesset discussions, I understand what they said. They insulted each other, they attacked each other, but at the same time they sit beside each other. At the time of danger all of them are united, and that means for me something good for democracy. And the [Israeli] elections also are going in a good way, without attacks, physical attacks."

Still, the question remains—for the world, for the apprehensive Israeli populace, and, ultimately, for the Palestinians themselves: are the bitterly factionalized Palestinians capable of instituting a similar democracy? Says Kanaan, unequivocally: "Yes. I say that we are able, and I will give an example. In prison we were able to have democracy, good relations between each of us, I think because we have a thing in common. And I think in Palestine we have in common the general interest of all the Palestinians. And if you look at this objective positively, we'll have our own democracy."

As the Palestinian negotiator speaks, he plays with the ice in his glass. His face puckers and, without warning, his broad mouth breaks into an even bigger grin. He says he sees in his own, unique background a kernel of hope for future Palestinian-Israeli cooperation. "After all," says Sameh, "there's a Jew on the Palestinian delegation—me!"

Abdul Aziz Rantisi

As sixteen-year-old Walid sat with his family watching Tom and Jerry chase each other across the television screen, he could hear the voice of the muezzin calling the faithful for late afternoon prayers. The religious wail was drowning out the shrieks of the cat and the mouse. Walid was enjoying the cartoon, but, as one of the *shabab* in Gaza, he knew he was supposed to report to the mosque. His home in Jabalya, the largest refugee camp in the Gaza Strip, was under curfew; even the mosque was off limits. But Walid knew it was important to attend afternoon prayers; the mosque was the only place in the overcrowded camp, where 60,000 people lived in conditions of appalling stench and poverty, that Israeli forces were forbidden to enter. It was, thus, a sanctuary for the *shabab* to plan their anti-Israeli activities.

Walid was a tenth-grade student at Khalid ibn al-Walid High School, a school named for a general in the Muslim army of Prophet Mohammed that had defeated two tribes of Jews in 628 A.D. His high school, like the rest of Gaza, had been kicked back and forth, like a soccer ball, between Israel and Egypt. The school's curriculum, established by the Egyptians during their rule of the Gaza Strip from 1948 to 1967, included English, mathematics, chemistry and religion. There was, however, no course on Palestine or Palestinian politics. The Israelis had banned such. Since conquering Gaza in the Six-Day War, the Jewish state had tried to discourage a separate Palestinian identity. They had even encouraged the Muslim fundamentalists to build mosques, as a means of undermining the PLO. But none of that mattered now. On this warm, damp day in early December of 1987, Khalid ibn al-Walid School was closed, and Walid wanted to reach his friends at the mosque. Running down a narrow dirt path, Walid met up with several of his buddies; together they ran toward the mosque in whose enclosed yard they could hide in preparation for the approaching showdown.

The battle had started earlier that week, at about noon on Sunday, December 6, 1987, when Shlomo Sakal, an Israeli plastics salesman, had been stabbed to death on the main street of Gaza. Sakal had been removing merchandise from his van when he was murdered by a member of the Islamic Jihad, a shadowy group of militants who modeled their ideology on Ayatollah Khomeini's revolutionary Iran. Two days later, on Tuesday afternoon, December 8, an Israeli truck smashed into a car carrying Arab laborers home from their jobs in Israel to the Gaza Strip. Four of the Arab occupants were killed; others were badly injured. One of the injured was Walid's father, Mahmoud, a Bedouin who had worked for almost twenty years as a construction worker at a nearby Israeli settlement. Rumors swept Gaza that the "accident" was no accident, that it was a deliberate act of revenge by the family of the Israeli salesman who had been stabbed to death in the marketplace two days earlier. As the mourners returned from the funerals, they were joined by thousands of Jabalya camp residents. The large group of refugees hurled stones at the Israeli soldiers who stood inside their fortified outpost, protected by a barbed-wire fence. The soldiers fired shots into the air, but this did little to dampen the anger of the crowd. "The ground will be burned from underneath the feet of the infidels!" the protestors chanted. Others called out, "Jihad! Jihad!" By early the next day, December 9, a new, unidentified group had circulated a leaflet denouncing the killing of the four Palestinians and calling for a mass uprising. The Israelis, meanwhile, had decided they could not tolerate any more disturbances and ordered two armored personnel carriers (APCs), preceded by a jeep, to enter Jabalya to restore order.

Walid had reached the mosque by the time the group of fifty soldiers arrived. He picked up a rock and hurled it in the direction of one of the Israelis. Within seconds tear gas was fired into a window of the mosque, and the rhythmic chants of "God is Great!" escalated to screams. Women, their heads covered and a few wearing veils, stood at their doors and began to wail hysterically. The *shabab* fled to the roof of the mosque. There they pelted the Israelis, who had already been hit by Molotov cocktails. The Arab boys fired stones from their slingshots and threw jagged, broken bottles at them. A few Palestinians hurled themselves onto the APCs, forcing the drivers to swerve out of control, while others tried to grab the machine guns from their turrets. Walid ran from the roof out of the mosque to a friend's house. There he knew he could find a handkerchief that had been doused in perfume to get the irritating sensation of the tear gas out of his eyes. But the door was jammed.

By now the Israelis, who had been using rubber bullets, switched to live ammunition. "You could see them kneeling and taking aim," recalls Walid. "They were sitting on their haunches and they were shooting. They wanted to fire straight at us," he says. But instead, keeping to their military orders, the Israelis fired at the legs of those they thought were the ringleaders. "I didn't feel the first shot," says Walid. "The soldiers were around the corner. I didn't see them. Then while I was running, I felt as though I had lost my right leg, as if it was paralyzed. I looked at it, and suddenly I saw blood coming down my knee." He collapsed and was picked up by two of his friends, who carried him to the house of a camp doctor. A nurse adminstered first aid and telephoned for a Red Crescent ambulance. Walid had been shot in an artery, causing massive bleeding in his thigh. The bullet had entered the soft tissue of one leg and then gone into his other leg, where it had smashed the femur and shattered his kneecap.

On the same day that Walid had been wounded at Jabalya, hundreds of students had gathered in schoolyards at Rafah and other refugee camps, taunting the Israelis by cursing at them in Hebrew and tearing open their shirts, baring their chests, and challenging the Jewish army to shoot them. Later that evening, on December 9, 1987, a military spokesperson announced on Israeli Radio that three Arab youths had been killed and twenty wounded. In the painful chronicle of the Arab-Israeli conflict, the events of those four days in December marked the start of the popular uprising known as the *intifada*.

The Israelis should have expected trouble. Only a few weeks earlier, in November, support for the Islamic Jihad at al-Azhar, the

Islamic University, had risen dramatically. Supporters of the militant underground movement had won three times the number of seats in the student council than in the elections a year earlier. A few days before the December incidents there had also been a huge demonstration in Gaza in support of the Islamic Jihad. When Israel subsequently arrested its leader, Sheikh Abdul Aziz Odeh, more than 2000 Palestinians had stormed the Israeli outpost at Jabalya.

"On the first day of the *intifada*, December 9, 1987, I was with Sheikh Ahmed Yassin and five others and we decided to establish *Hamas* at that time," boasts Abdul Aziz Rantisi. The forty-five-year-old pediatrician says *Hamas*, the acronym for *Harakat al Mukawwamah al Islamiyya* (Islamic Resistance Movement), was deliberately created to demonstrate that the Muslim Brotherhood was among the principal initiators of the uprising. "We changed the name [from the Muslim Brotherhood] to *Hamas* because not all the Muslim Brothers are sharing in *Hamas*. It's one branch of the Brotherhood," he explains.

Rantisi claims that *Hamas* issued its first leaflet on December 9, the first day of the *intifada*. "The decision was to start the *intifada* under *Hamas*' name. We were preparing for that for a long time," he adds. Although there is no firm evidence to support his contention—none of the first three leaflets were signed—the Israelis have no doubt about the identity of Abdul Aziz Rantisi. They know he was one of the original founders of *Hamas*. In March 1988 he was convicted on charges of establishing the group and of having written its first leaflet. Abdul Aziz Rantisi served two and a half years in Israeli prisons, including eight months at Ansar III, before being released on September 4, 1990. Two months later he was sentenced again to another year in prison.

As he sits in an office at the Islamic University in Gaza, the husky, bespectacled Palestinian looks more businessman than theologian. He keeps a green Koran with gold arabesque lettering on his desk; but dressed in a conservative navy suit and boldly striped tie, he hardly looks like a religious fanatic. At the university, he teaches courses in science, genetics, and parasitology. He admits that he did not expect to lead this kind of life. But for Abdul Aziz Rantisi, as for almost three-quarters of the 750,000 residents of Gaza, life did not give him a choice. Like the more than half a million other Palestinians in Gaza, he, too, is a refugee.

His own life parallels that of the 16-year-old high school student Walid. Born in October 1947 in Yibna, a small town between Ashkelon and Jaffa, Abdul Aziz was only six months old when the Rantisis fled to Gaza. Like all refugees after the 1948 war, his family believed they would return home shortly. But instead they joined the 200,000 other Arabs displaced when Israel was created and the 80,000 Arabs already living in the Strip. The Rantisis settled in Khan Yunis, the second-largest of eight U.N.-administered camps in the Gaza Strip.

Less than seven miles wide in the south and narrowing to only four miles wide in the north and at its midsections, Gaza's steamy twenty-eight miles of sand could never contain the passions of its inhabitants. Gaza is bordered on one side by the sea, on the other side by a barbed wire fence with Israel. The strip has been compared to a long, narrow bottle. Its only opening is the congested Erez roadblock, where Israel monitors traffic in and out of the dusty, sun-drenched dirt roads of the main city. This narrow opening at its top is the only way out; it is blocked off at its southern end by the border with Egypt. So whenever Israeli security is threatened, Gaza is sealed shut, forcing the bottled-up mixture of hatred and poverty to transform into vapors of violence and death.

It was here, amidst the open sewers and constant buzzing of flies, near the huge mounds of garbage and cesspools that turn into squalid wintry rivers, that Abdul Aziz grew up. He was one of eleven children, nine boys and two girls, a typical-size family in the refugee camp. By the time Abdul Aziz became an adult, the population of Gaza had more than doubled to almost 650,000 Palestinians, an average of 1800 people per square kilometer, making the Gaza Strip the most densely populated area on earth.

But despite the crowding and the cramped conditions, Abdul Aziz will tell you, his family always maintained its identity. In fact, for Abdul Aziz and other refugees, the term "camp" is a misnomer; it implies impermanence. However makeshift in appearance, the camps have proved durable. They are a constant reminder, a thorn on the conscience of the world, that between 4 million and 5 million Palestinian people remain homeless and stateless. In the camps, families expand inward, not outward: each generation builds literally on top of the previous one; the concrete additions rise upwards, not only because this is the Arab style but because they have nowhere else to go.

Ask teenagers in Khan Yunis or Jabalya or Rafah where they are from, and they will not give you their street address or postal box number. Nor will they tell you they are from Block 3 or Block C or even from the camp at Khan Yunis, Jabalya, or Rafah. They will tell you they are from Yibna or Kharatia or another town in Palestine, even though they have never seen it and there is no country called Palestine.

Abdul Aziz Rantisi's mother still lives in Khan Yunis—forty years after she fled Israel. For her and thousands of others, the camps have accomplished a purpose: maintaining the mental presence of the homeland. The families from a particular village or town still live together, and marriages are arranged between their sons and daughters. Even the old hierarchy is still in place: the elderly Arab who was the *mukhtar*, the traditional religious leader, of Yibna or Kharatia continues to be the *mukhtar* of Block C or Block 3. It is all intended, of course, to keep the memory alive.

Abdul Aziz Rantisi was raised in the camp. He played among its sandy alleys and exposed, shallow sewer channels, and received his health care from the medical facilities of the U.N. Relief and Works Agency (UNRWA). His family lived in a tent. When he was four years old, he recalls, the winter was so harsh they had to move to an old school to escape the cold. UNRWA subsequently built mud houses for the refugees but the Rantisi's mud house was nothing like the beautiful home his parents told him they had abandoned in Yibna. When he was six, he had to work during the summer, earning the equivalent of one cent a day, which he gave to his father to help buy food for the family. "I will never forget that I had no shoes. I had to go to school with bare feet and torn clothes. I never had enough to eat." During the October 1956 Suez crisis, when Abdul Aziz was nine years old, the Israelis bombed Khan Yunis to deter the Palestinian guerrillas from using the refugee camp as a base of operations for commando raids into Israel. He remembers hiding in an underground shelter and being very scared. "When I got home, I heard my mother and father screaming. I was told that the Israelis attacked my uncle's house and had killed him."

But the biggest crisis in Abdul Aziz's young life occurred in 1957, just after his tenth birthday. "I borrowed some money from my relatives and bought some goods to sell in Egypt," he recalls. It is only a few miles from Khan Yunis to the Egyptian border, and it was easy in those days to cross and come back on the same day. Abdul Aziz never got to the border, however. "Some thieves stole my goods and ran away with them. I had to go home empty-handed. I was crying because I knew my parents were very poor and, of course, they did not have the money to pay my cousins back."

Abdul Aziz attended an UNRWA secondary school at Khan Yunis, where he and his sisters wore the blue-and-white-striped uniform required by the international organization. In 1965 he graduated from high school. "I was from a very poor family and we had to struggle, but I was the top in my class," he says proudly. Education, he explains, has always been the only way to escape. When he left Khan Yunis later that year to begin taking courses at the University of Alexandria in Egypt, he was preparing for a career in medicine; neither religion nor politics was on his mind. "I was concentrating on my medical studies," he says.

Throughout his childhood, and even before Egypt took over the administration of the Gaza Strip in 1948, Cairo enjoyed a special relationship with Gaza. This was due in part to Egypt's physical proximity and to the ease with which one could travel back and forth across the border at Rafah. But there was more than human traffic; Egypt and Gaza also traded in goods and ideologies. Gazans became familiar with Egyptian television and books, Egyptian culture, dialect, and food. Although Egypt never annexed Gaza or gave its residents passports, the Egyptians greatly improved the educational system in Gaza, opening many new schools and requiring compulsory attendance for every child over the age of six. Egypt also opened its own universities to talented students like Abdul Aziz, offering college education to several thousand Palestinians a year, most of whom could not afford to pay tuition.

When he reflects on those early years, Abdul Aziz says he was strongly influenced, although he was unaware of it at the time,

by a sheikh he had first met when he was ten years old and starting to go to the mosque in Khan Yunis. The sheikh's name was
Mahmoud Eid. "I always felt that he was a very wise and smart
man," he recalls. When Abdul Aziz began college in Alexandria,
he again ran into Eid, and the young man and the older sheikh
started to attend prayers together. "Of course, Mahmoud was the
sheikh of the mosque there," recalls Abdul Aziz. It was Eid who
taught him about the Muslim Brotherhood and who filled his
impressionable mind with the "truth" about Egyptian president
Gamal Abdul Nasser and his pan-Arab philosophy. "I began to
understand the failure of the system in the Arab world and why
the Arabs had such bad leaders. At the same time, the Muslim
Brothers were suggesting that Islam could solve all the problems
in the Arab countries. It was because of Mahmoud Eid that I eventually became a faithful follower of the Brothers," he says.

In fact, it was while he was studying in Alexandria, Abdul Aziz
says, that he experienced a "psychic shock," brought on by Israel's
sudden and surprisingly swift victory over Arab forces in the 1967
war. He was twenty years old. He listened to the hourly reports
of the fighting on a transistor radio and watched the more infre-
quent television news summaries. He could not believe what he
heard and what he saw. In six days the Arabs had lost the Golan
Heights, the Gaza Strip, the entire West Bank of the Jordan River,
and Jerusalem, the third-holiest city in all of Islam. The defeat
had a profound impact on him. "I sat by myself for a long time.
I did not talk to anybody for weeks. I just sat there all by myself.
Then for six months I suffered from psychogenic dyspniea—
sighing, a heavy sensation pressing on my chest. I was so irritable.
I spent all the nights unable to sleep, and after that I became
interested in religion," he says.

Sheikh Mahmoud Eid suggested that Abdul Aziz read the
works of two great Islamic scholars: Sheikh Hassan Banna, who
founded the Muslim Brotherhood in Egypt in 1929 and was its
"Supreme Guide" until he was murdered twenty years later, and
Sayyid Qutb, a theoretician and writer who was hanged in 1966
for allegedly plotting to assassinate Egyptian president Gamal
Abdul Nasser.

It was not unusual for university students like Abdul Aziz to
turn to the Muslim Brotherhood, particularly after the crushing

Egyptian defeat in the Six-Day War. By the mid-1960s the Muslim Brotherhood had been at the center of Egyptian politics for almost a generation; and in the period Abdul Aziz was in Alexandria, it dominated the headlines in the local papers.

Even though Nasser owed a big debt of gratitude to his fellow "Free Officers," who had toppled King Farouk and installed him in power, he was less grateful to the Muslim Brotherhood, which had also helped overthrow the monarchy. Sixteen months after he took over, Nasser banned the Brotherhood following a power struggle with Mohammad Nagib, the Egyptian general who helped mastermind the 1952 coup and who had lobbied with Nasser for a more lenient approach to the Brotherhood. In October 1954 the Muslim Brotherhood was blamed for a plot on Nasser's life, and nineteen of its leaders were charged with treason in a widely publicized "show trial." Six of them were executed, and the Brotherhood was again forced to go underground.

It was not until the mid-1960s, when Abdul Aziz arrived in Alexandria, that the Muslim Brotherhood resurfaced as a major irritant. In 1965 and 1966, after another reported attempt on Nasser's life, thousands of Muslim Brotherhood supporters were arrested and hundreds tried. Three leaders, including Qutb, were sentenced to be hung in the fall of 1966. By executing the sixty-one-year-old Qutb, after he had already served more than a decade in prison, Nasser had unwittingly conferred on him the status of *shahid*, or martyr. Nasser further enflamed fundamentalist opinion by sentencing Sheikh Hassan Ismail Hudeibi, who had succeeded Hassan Banna as the Supreme Guide of the Brotherhood, to a lengthy prison term. Hudeibi is believed to have died in prison shortly thereafter.

By 1968, following the Egyptian defeat in the war against Israel, there was a new wave of student unrest throughout Egypt. Nasser, already on the defensive, again blamed the Muslim Brotherhood. Abdul Aziz, however, blamed Nasser: the Arabs had lost the war because they had not been good Muslims. "Surely, Islam is victorious not only because God stands side by side with Muslims but for many other reasons," he says. Nasser and his government were internally corrupt and too dependent on foreign social and political models, particularly Arab socialism. "Nothing can be called Arab socialism. It was Marxism with some cosmetic to create the impression that it belonged to us. In reality, it was a foreign seed implanted in the Islamic world. Nasser's government was not faithful even to the Egyptians," he charges.

Islam "means to be faithful in your fight, to be faithful for the sake of your country. It means preparing yourself both religiously and from the military standpoint," explains Abdul Aziz. But Nasser failed to prepare his soldiers to sacrifice for the sake of Egypt. He badly underestimated the strength of the enemy and overestimated the ability of Syrian and Jordanian forces to meet the challenge. "The soldier in Islam is prepared to sacrifice for the sake of Islam," he insists. "He accepts that and believes in that and feels that his sacrifice will give him paradise in the next world." The Islamic soldier "trusts his leader so he will do his best to achieve victory." But no one trusted Nasser or his government. Thus the Egyptian Government was doomed to fail, he says. "We heard all the time that everyone around Nasser were thieves. How could I trust them? How could I sacrifice for the sake of my country, and face being killed myself, when I regarded my leader as a thief?" Nasser's Egypt, he concludes, was not only "far away from Islam" but erred when it tried to graft political models from the East and the West—the ideologies of socialism and nationalism—onto an Islamic culture. "Nationalism was a Western attempt to shift us away from Islam as a nationality. Socialism, too, was completely unsuitable for the Islamic peoples in our countries," he explains.

Only Islam, with its promise of fulfilling God's trust "in all the branches of our life, in the home, in the school, in medicine, in engineering, in how to deal with others," can realize the potential of the Arab people. Islam "means science and development. It means all the best manners in your life and, above all, values," he says, citing an excerpt from Sayyid Qutb's principal work, *Ma'alim fi'il Tariq,* "Signpost on the Road." Humanity, wrote the martyred Muslim leader in 1964, "today stands on the brink of the abyss because of its bankruptcy in the domain of 'values' under which man could have lived and developed harmoniously."

For Abdul Aziz, as for Qutb before him, neither the East nor the West has the answers. In the period from 1948 to 1967, he says, the pan-Arab nationalists failed to make any tangible gains. In the next two decades, secular, militant nationalist groups such as the Palestine Liberation Organization, with its Democratic Front for the Liberation of Palestine (DFLP), Popular Front for the Liberation of Palestine (PFLP), and pro-communist factions, failed in the struggle to regain Palestine. In the 1990s the demise of Marxism in the Soviet Union and Eastern Europe discredited the leftist ideologies.

Abdul Aziz, the devout believer in Islam, is not surprised. "What did you expect when the region did not have a single Islamic leader?" he asks rhetorically. "The communists failed. The nationalist leaders failed. The secularists totally failed. Now the field is empty of all ideologies—except Islam." Again, the physician cites his mentor, Sayyid Qutb, who wrote in the mid-1960s that "both individualist and collectivist ideologies have failed. Now at this most critical time when turmoil and confusion reign, it is the turn of Islam, of the *umma* ["community of believers"] to play its role. Islam's time has come."

The real credit for the religious rebirth belongs to Hassan Banna, says Abdul Aziz. "He was the 'renewer.' Before Hassan Banna you would not see a single religious person in the street or the mosque. You would only see old men. You would never see a young man in the mosque. But after Hassan Banna it was different. He put Islam in all the branches of our life."

After seven years in Egypt, Abdul Aziz returned to Gaza in 1972. Much had changed. Gaza was now under Israeli occupation. The Six-Day War and King Hussein's 1970 campaign to rid Jordan of Palestinian guerrillas who threatened his throne, known in Palestinian lore as Black September, had forced thousands of new refugees to Gaza. The majority of the people were still living under the wretched conditions of the camps, and the appeal of the outlawed PLO was irresistible. Thousands of youths joined its militant wings, including *Fatah*, and many joined George Habash's extremist PFLP, an outgrowth of the Arab National Movement.

With no hope of a political solution to grant the Palestinians a homeland, acts of violence were occurring all over the world, aimed at the Israelis but killing and wounding dozens of American and European civilians. Backed mainly by the PFLP, terrorist groups hijacked commercial airliners in Europe and the Middle East, taking passengers as hostages. *Fatah* carried out sixty

Sami Kilani with his daughters Sahar (on left) and Zoba (on right). Photo Credit: Rula Halawani

Sami Kilani (on left) with his brother Ahmed.

Mamdouh Aker, a urological surgeon, in his clinic in Ramallah. Photo Credit: Rula Halawani

Mamdouh Aker discussing a medical report with a patient in his Ramallah clinic. Photo Credit: Rula Halawani

Sameh Kanaan with his Jewish-born mother, Mazel. Photo Credit: Rula Halawani

Sameh Kanaan with his children Samah (on right) and Hind (on left). Photo Credit: Rula Halawani

Abdul Aziz Rantisi, Hamas cofounder, teaching a class of female students at al-Azhar, the Islamic university in Gaza. Photo Credit: Rula Halawani

Abdul Aziz Rantisi greeting some of his religion students in front of a painting of al-Aqsa Mosque in Jerusalem, the third holiest site in Islam. Photo Credit: Rula Halawani

Riad Maliki discussing a civil engineering project with a student. Photo Credit: Rula Halawani

Riad Maliki at his desk in a classroom at Birzeit University, where he teaches civil engineering and transportation planning. Photo Credit: Rula Halawani

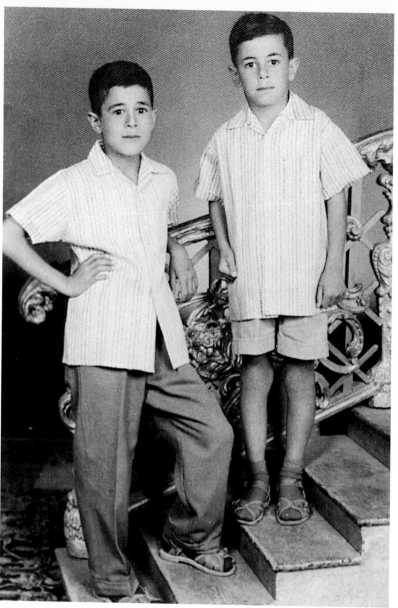

Ghassan Khatib (on left) at age eight with his brother Waddah, age seven.

Ghassan Khatib addressing the residents of the village of Kufr-'Ein, seeking support for the Palestinian–Israeli peace talks. Photo Credit: Rula Halawani

Ghassan Khatib at his Ramallah home with his two children, his daughter Rasha and his son Abed. Photo Credit: Rula Halawani

Radwan Abu Ayash with his daughter Sheda, after her sight was saved by an Israeli eye surgeon at Hadassah Hospital. Photo Credit: Rula Halawani

Radwan Abu Ayash at his office in the Arab Media Center in East Jerusalem. Photo Credit: Rula Halawani

different acts of sabotage inside Israel, and thousands more that originated inside Jordan. In Gaza itself, PLO activists conducted a reign of terror, murdering local Arabs they considered collaborators. Anarchy prevailed; shoot-outs between Arab youths and Israeli soldiers took place almost every week in the narrow alleys of the refugee camps.

The twin defeats of the 1967 war and Black September had also bolstered the appeal of the Muslim Brotherhood to the Palestinians in Gaza. But, ironically, it also had appeal to the Israelis, who were faced with the difficult task of having to govern the lawless territory and who regarded the religious fundamentalists as a useful counterweight to the PLO.

In 1974 Abdul Aziz returned to the University of Alexandria to complete his master's degree in pediatrics, which he was awarded two years later. He returned to Gaza in 1976 and began an internship at Nasser Hospital, the main medical facility in Khan Yunis, the camp where he had grown up.

The frustration of the Palestinians in Gaza did not peak until 1978, when Egypt and Israel signed the Camp David Accords, pledging to end their state of war and to negotiate a formal peace treaty. Left in the lurch were the million and a half Palestinians in the territories, who were offered what they believed was only a humiliating form of autonomy that would indefinitely perpetuate Israeli occupation. The real losers, however, were the Palestinians in the Gaza Strip.

Anwar Sadat, who had succeeded Nasser in 1970, did not want to face the same kind of trouble his predecessor had experienced from the fundamentalists. The Muslim Brotherhood had condemned his willingness to make peace with Israel, calling it a gross capitulation to the Zionist entity. So Sadat reacted decisively. He sealed the border with the Gaza Strip, putting the Palestinians there entirely at the mercy of the Israelis. No longer would Palestinian students be able to pursue higher education at Egyptian universities. Sadat also expelled the members of the Muslim Brotherhood who were known troublemakers. He sent them to Gaza. How ironic that only three years later Sadat himself would be murdered by an Islamic zealot.

"Now, in 1978 those activists who were thrown out of Egypt and others came to the civil administration and asked to register a *jama'ah*, a nonviolent association," recalls an Israeli official who served in Gaza. "They told us they wanted to make a *mahw l'ummyya*, [fight against illiteracy] and wanted to build kindergartens for their children, to open a new set of stores for their people, and encourage social activity among the older generation. They started to flourish," the official says. "They built one mosque, then a second and a third mosque. We tried to find out where the money was coming from. It was coming from Saudi Arabia and from Jordan and from a lot of internal taxation and *zakat* [charitable contributions]."

The chief architect of the Islamic revival movement was Sheikh Ahmed Ismail Yassin, a thin man with a round face who was almost totally paralyzed as the result of a childhood illness. Yassin, a scholar on Muslim law, did not disguise his belief that Israel was an illegitimate state, but he urged his followers not to rush into a *jihad* before they knew they could win. Instead, he urged them to pursue *tarbiyeh* [education] and *da'wah* [preaching].

The popularity of the Muslim Brotherhood, explains Ze'ev Schiff and Ehud Ya'ari in *Intifada: The Inside Story of the Palestinian Uprising*, was partly a backlash against the materialism and permissiveness that had spread to Gaza from Israel and partly a result of the need for communion to share one's suffering. Yassin was like a father to his flock, they note. "When all doors are sealed, Allah opens a gate," the cleric said. But the fundamentalist groups also "offered a special kind of activism that combined patriotism with moral purity and social action with the promise of divine grace," explained the two Israeli authors. "Sheikh Yassin offered the young Palestinian something far beyond Arafat's ken: not just the redemption of the homeland but the salvation of his own troubled soul."

Yassin had nothing but contempt for Arafat and the leadership of the PLO, who he reviled as "pork eaters and wine drinkers." So when the sheikh approached the Israeli authorities, as the "supreme leader" of the Muslim Brotherhood in Gaza, to register charitable organizations to propagate Islam and to recruit supporters for the faith, the Jewish state willingly agreed to register the society and provide the appropriate tax-free licenses. Eleven Islamic clerics, led by Yassin, chartered *Al Mujama'a al Islami*, "The Islamic Assembly," in Gaza. In Nablus, *Tadammun*

["Solidarity"] was established; in Jenin, "The Elderly Society"; in Hebron, "The Islamic Societies"; and in Jerusalem and Hebron, "The Muslim Youth Societies." But by far the most important was the Islamic Assembly in Gaza, which had over 2000 members and held control of Gazan mosques.

The Israeli policy in Gaza was visible, says Ori Nir, a correspondent for *Ha'aretz* who covered the territories for several years. "In the mid-1980s Israel had a clear policy of letting money come in to build mosques and to build an Islamic infrastructure and give them a kind of laissez faire environment, a network of libraries, mosques, schools, and kindergartens," explains Nir. Through the mosques' network, the Islamicists were able to distribute recorded speeches and books, extending their influence. Through the orphanages, clinics, and libraries, they provided alternative social, health, and educational facilities, and hence challenged the authority and credibility of the secular Palestinian factions. Nir recalls attending a briefing in mid-1987 with a senior civil administration official in Gaza at which the Israeli boasted: "We have a good relationship with the Islamic Assembly. We work very well with them."

A secret study commissioned by the Israeli Government and issued in a classified report in April 1987 reveals the extent to which the Jewish state deluded itself into believing that the Muslim Brotherhood did not constitute an immediate security threat. The study, completed eight months before the start of the *intifada*, totally failed to predict that there was any risk of a violent uprising or that the Palestinian revolt would be ignited by Islamic fundamentalists. Entitled *The Gaza Strip Towards the Year 2000*, the study was shared with only twenty agencies, including the Israeli Defense Forces (IDF), the Mossad, and the Shin Bet. The foreword by General Shayke Erez, the military governor of Gaza, noted there had been an escalation in religious fervor among the eight different Muslim factions and that the political aspirations of all of them "focused around the creation of an Islamic state like Iran on the whole territory of *Eretz* ["Greater"] Israel." But the study concluded that "all of the Islamic movements want to focus first on the process of winning the hearts and minds of the Islamic camp and only later begin the active struggle against Israel. An exception to this is the Islamic Jihad, which emphasizes the priority of a struggle to liberate Palestine in parallel with a process of converting the Muslims."

Explains Nir, "the significance of this is that although they were aware of the fact that these groups had a radical ideology and at least a potential at some point to start implementing it, they chose a policy of encouraging them in order to counterbalance the PLO, which had the opposite policy—a more pragmatic ideology but a conduct of using violence. This was very, very shortsighted." Emile Sahliyeh, a Palestinian professor, reaches a similar conclusion in his book *In Search of Leadership: West Bank Politics Since 1967*, published by the Brookings Institution: "An Islamic movement that was hostile to the PLO's secular orientation and opposed to the formation of a nationalist, secular Palestinian state complemented Israel's policy of striking against all facets of Palestinian nationalism."

In the decade between Camp David and the beginning of the *intifada*, the Muslim Brotherhood had made its influence felt in Gaza. Women no longer appeared on the street without the traditional *hijabs*, or veils over their heads and floor-length dresses. Dozens of new mosques were built to accommodate the surge in the number of believers. Men grew beards, and at the beaches it was rare to see either sex in a Western-style bathing suit. If they dared to wear one, they risked being beaten up by an overzealous believer.

When Sadat shut the border with Gaza in 1978, the independence of the Muslim Brotherhood in Gaza was reinforced. But with the doorway to Egypt closed, the Brotherhood also became more dependent on Jordan. The Allenby Bridge became the only exit to the Arab world, which meant that Palestinians from Gaza had to traverse Israel and the West Bank. When they started to cross through Jordan they became susceptible to the influence of both the Hashemite regime and the Jordanian *Mukhabarat*, its intelligence service.

According to a key Israeli analyst, nowhere was the maxim that "the enemy of my enemy is my friend" more apt than in King Hussein's sudden new appreciation for the Muslim Brotherhood. He used the Islamicists against the Israelis in the West Bank, this official says, but he also used them for subversive activities to destablize the regime of Hafez Assad in Syria and against the new breed of nationalist-minded, pro-PLO activists in the territories, who were as anti-Hussein as they were anti-Israeli. "The Muslim Brotherhood defended Jordanian interests in the universities and in the clashes between the four pro-PLO blocks: the PFLP, DFLP, *Fatah*, and communists," he adds. But perhaps the greatest appeal of the Brotherhood for King Hussein was as an instrument to help validate his own authority. "The British took his grandfather [Abdullah] and made him the ruler of the Palestinians, saying he was their king," he explains. "What right did they have to do that? Because he said, 'I represent the Sherif of Mecca.' Who is the best one to legitimize such a thing? A religious movement. This was the Muslim Brotherhood. Consequently, the Muslim Brotherhood in the West Bank became pro-Jordanian."

But the divorce from Egypt, and new access to Jordan, proved an unexpected headache for the Israelis. In 1984, says the Israeli official, "we discovered the biggest arsenal of weapons that we had ever captured in the territories. It was something like sixty different kinds of weapons." They included M-16 rifles, Uzi machine guns, and hand grenades, all of which had been purchased through the criminal underworld in Israel. In Sheikh Yassin's home alone, Israeli soldiers found a cache of sixty rifles.

The entire leadership of the Muslim Brotherhood was sentenced to lengthy prison terms; Yassin received thirteen years. In the course of arrest, "We discovered that the money to purchase these weapons had come from Jordan. I remember the sum of 22,000 dinars. It had come from two of the main leaders of the Muslim Brotherhood and a member of parliament, Youssef Asan, who is still in parliament today. That was the first time that we got the green light that the trends were changing, that the Muslim Brotherhood was not as connected to the Egyptians anymore, and that the Muslim Brothers in Jordan had become a real source of authority for the Gazans as well as the West Bankers."

Even more astonishing to the Israelis was the fact that "they had the weapons for over a year and never shot a bullet at us. They had a policy not to confront us until they were ready," he explains. The Muslim leaders testified that the weapons were not intended to be used against the Israelis. "They said their ideology was first to organize internally to fight the other camps, such as *Fatah*, PFLP, DFLP, mainly the left, and then when that was over to recruit the masses to fight the Zionists. But don't go fighting unprepared," the official recalls.

After Yassin was arrested, Abdul Aziz Rantisi took up the cause, helping to organize the Muslim bloc in student council elections in al-Azhar, the Islamic University. Yassin was released in 1985 as part of the exchange engineered by Ahmed Jabril, the leader of the Damascus-based General Command of the Popular Front and under which six Israeli soldiers captured in Lebanon were traded for 1000 security prisoners in Israel. Not eager to return to prison, Yassin gave up the chairmanship of the Islamic Assembly, which Israelis suspected was the cover for the militants. Instead, he resumed the reins of the Muslim Brotherhood, devoting his time chiefly to improving health and education.

Soon the reasons for amassing the arsenal of weapons became clear. Under Yassin's guidance, but without his direct involvement, Abdul Aziz Rantisi and two other disciples of the sheikh organized a campaign in the spring of 1986 to rid the Islamic University of the PLO. Under the passive eyes of the Israelis, they targeted supporters of the Popular Front and the communists, who were not only atheists but propagated the godless ideology of Marxism. The communists also were in the vanguard of a new Palestinian readiness to settle for a two-state solution, pressing *Fatah* to recognize Israel's right to exist in return for Palestinian statehood. That was anathema to the Islamic believers.

Using the Islamic Assembly as cover, the three academics— Abdul Aziz Rantisi, Mahmoud Zahaar, and Mahmoud Siam— organized the 700 students and teachers at the university into a small religious army. For the first time they were prepared to defend themselves against *Fatah* and other PLO factions that taunted the Muslim Brotherhood for their refusal to participate in the national struggle and derided them as being "babies of the Zionists" for obtaining Israeli licenses that had been denied to the PLO.

The resulting fracas resembled the civil war in Beirut: people were beaten and killed; there was a wave of brutal stabbings and acid attacks. The infighting among the factions went on for several months before Israeli forces intervened to stop it. By then the Islamic Assembly had won 80 percent of the backing of both men and women, who under Islamic law voted separately, at al-Azhar. The fundamentalists had flexed their muscles and won a decisive battle against the PLO—notably without Israel having intervened until the war was almost won.

But by the mid-1980s, another group, *al Jihad al Islami*, the Islamic Jihad, was flexing its own muscles. Its members were unhappy that the Muslim Brotherhood was making the liberation struggle take a back seat to the re-Islamization of Palestinian society. That could wait. The Muslim Brotherhood was wasting its resources fighting the PLO for control. It should follow the example of the nationalist groups that were practicing armed struggle and even coordinate with them. The fight against Israel had to be a "holy war." There would never be a complete rebirth of Islam, the Jihad doctrine said, until the Jewish state was destroyed. Why work through charitable societies or existing institutions? Public education and mass propaganda were useless. The only way to foment an Iranian-style revolution in Palestine was through a network of clandestine cells that would be well hidden from the Israelis and strike at their most hallowed symbols.

The Islamic Jihad got its inspiration from two graduates of Zakazik University in the Nile Delta, a breeding ground for Muslim fundamentalism. They were Fathi Abdul Aziz Shqaqi, a physician from Rafah, and Sheikh Abdul Aziz Odeh, an expert in Muslim law who preached at the Sheikh Izz al-Din al-Kassam Mosque in the village of Beit Lahiya, near Gaza. Both men returned from Egypt in 1981. In 1985 the Israelis jailed Odeh for eleven months for inciting the public to armed struggle through his sermons in the mosque. Shortly after his release, Shqaqi was jailed for smuggling weapons and similarly inciting violence. But it was too late.

The first terrorist attack publicly attributed to the Islamic Jihad took place a few months later. In October 1986 its members hurled hand grenades at relatives attending the swearing-in of a brigade of Israeli infantry recruits at the Western Wall in Jerusalem. The attack took place in a parking lot adjacent to the wall, but this did not disguise the fact that the Jihad had struck close to one of Judaism's most venerable sites or that the attack was against civilians, not soldiers. The father of one of the soldiers was killed and eleven others were wounded. There was something else different about this attack. *Fatah* and the Islamic Jihad had planned it jointly: the PLO provided the money and the weapons, the Jihad the manpower.

Between 1986 and 1988 the Jihad escalated its terrorist activities. Unlike the Muslim Brotherhood, the Jihad has cooperated with the PLO, although it is not a member of the *intifada*'s ruling Unified National Command (UNC). In 1988 Yigal Carmon, Prime Minister Yitzhak Shamir's adviser on terrorism, charged that one of the PLO's military units, known as "Committee 88," was directly responsible for operations of the Islamic Jihad in the territories. "The first one to join the *intifada* was not the *Fatah* of Arafat; it was the Islamic Jihad—they were the first to know, the first to jump on the bandwagon, and the first to promote it," says the Israeli official.

In fact, to reinforce their claim to having triggered the uprising, the Jihad calls on shop owners to strike by closing their stores on a different day than the PLO or *Hamas*, which observe December 9 as the anniversary of the *intifada*. The Jihad asks the public to observe the sixth of every month as the anniversary because it considers October 6, 1987, as the first day of the *intifada*. On that day, four Palestinians were killed in the Shajaiyeh quarter of Gaza City. Israeli authorities alleged that the four were members of the Islamic Jihad. Two M-16 rifles, two pistols, a hand grenade, and a number of magazines of ammunition and explosives were found in their possession. General Yitzhak Mordechai, the Israeli commander of the southern region, claimed the cell was preparing to launch a large-scale military operation against Israeli targets in the region.

But Abdul Aziz Rantisi disputes the claim by the Islamic Jihad. "The decision was to start the *intifada* under *Hamas*' name. We were preparing for that for a long time," he insists. Israeli officials have yet another version. They believe both *Fatah* and *Hamas* were playing catch-up to the Islamic Jihad. Within weeks of the December 1987 incidents, *Fatah* recognzied the danger that their *shabiba*, their youth wings, would desert to the Islamic Jihad if they did not allow them to join in the street battles. First came the stonings, then the Molotov cocktails.

"Then in 1988 we saw a dramatic shift in the policy of the Muslim Brotherhood," explains the Israeli official. "We thought they had learned the lesson of 1984 when we imprisoned their leaders. After they were released a year and a half later, there was no effort to organize themselves again as a terror group. All we saw were civilian and religious activities in the mosques." But with the *intifada* gathering steam, says this Israeli, "suddenly, in February 1988, they said, 'Just a minute, let's build an armed branch, an armed arm like *Fatah* has.' You know, *Fatah* has a political branch and an armed branch. Sometimes it is the same people who do both things, for example Abu Jihad [the PLO commander inside the territories]. They said, 'Let's build a system that's in charge of violent activity, civilian violence and terror violence. That was *Hamas*." This Israeli claims that Sheikh Yassin was forced in February 1988 to yield to the demands of his followers to create the militant wing after the nationalist groups had created the UNC that asserted its right to run the *intifada*. It was at a meeting that month in Sheikh Yassin's home that the infrastructure was created for the new underground movement whose name, *Hamas*, means literally "zeal" or "courage."

At first the Israelis tried to countenance the organization, believing that the new popularity of *Hamas* would help undermine the PLO. Schiff and Ya'ari, in their *Intifada: The Inside Story of the Palestinian Uprising*, point out that the Israeli army rarely interfered with *Hamas* strike stewards, who saw to it that shopkeepers would keep their stores closed during precisely those hours when the UNC instructed them to remain open. The authors also reveal that while the PLO was prohibited from getting funds from outside the territories, the civil administration did not interfere with the flow of money from Jordan to *Hamas* "and even permitted high-level emissaries of the Muslim Brotherhood to come from Amman for consultations." The Israelis, conclude the authors, were successfully sowing suspicion among the UNC leaders, who believed that *Hamas* was deliberately being allowed to flourish and to gather strength so that it could be unleashed against the PLO, "turning the uprising into a civil war."

Consistent with Israel's initial lenient policy toward *Hamas*, when the Israeli authorities began their crackdown on the fundamentalists they started with the Islamic Jihad. In October 1987 the military government accused Sheikh Abdul Aziz Odeh of incitement during Friday prayers in Beit Lahiya, north of Gaza City. He was formally charged a month later and deported in April 1988.

The crackdown on *Hamas* did not come until the middle of the summer, when the Israelis were left with no other choice. At that point, Israel realized for the first time that their efforts to create a nonviolent alternative to the PLO in Gaza had failed. The bubble had burst; they no longer had any illusions about the Islamic fundamentalists. "In August 1988 we arrested the first group of Muslim Brothers for terror in Gaza: they had put detonators and explosives in an area north of Gaza," says the Israeli official. The Shin Bet also discovered that a new military arm, *mujahedu Falastin*, "holy fighters of Palestine," had been set up, comprised of over 200 youths, and were preparing caches of arms and explosives. The distinction between *Hamas* and the Muslim Brotherhood that Sheikh Yassin had tried so diligently to maintain had become, at least in Gaza, almost irrelevant.

From July through September of 1988 more than 100 *Hamas* leaders were tried and sentenced. Several months earlier, apparently convinced that he was one of the main ringleaders, the Israelis had imprisoned Abdul Aziz Rantisi. On January 15, 1988, he was sentenced to a prison term of two and a half years. He served eight months at Ansar III (Ketziot Detention Center) in the Negev and the balance in Gaza Jail and Kfar Yonnah. He was released on September 4, 1990, but two months later was returned to jail. Neither move appeared to dampen enthusiasm for the new fundamentalist organization.

With its leadership incarcerated at Ansar III, *Hamas* still managed to issue its *Mithaq*, the "Covenant of the Islamic Resistance Movement—Palestine." Proclaimed on August 18, 1988, the forty-page typewritten manifesto set forth the group's ideological position. It proclaimed *jihad* was the "personal obligation" of every Muslim because Palestine was the "soil of the Islamic trust till the end of days." Liberation must be total "from the [Mediterranean] Sea to the [Jordan] River," the covenant said. The Israeli official contends it spelled out that *"Hamas is the branch of the Muslim Brotherhood movement in Palestine which is responsible for the military activity. That means every Hamasnik is a Muslim Brother but not every Muslim Brother is a Hamasnik!"* He mentions Sheikh Bassam Jarrar, an Islamic leader in Ramallah, as an example. "He sits on the fence between the two, and that's why, for a while, he was not arrested or detained."

But the *Hamas* covenant, explain Schiff and Ya'ari in *Intifada*, represented much more than a rallying cry from the imprisoned leadership. It was, they note, "tantamount to waving a red flag in front of the nationalists, for it meant the renunciation of the long-standing Palestinian covenant together with the formal institutionalization of the Islamic Resistance Movement as a separate political entity with a doctrine distinctly its own." On September 21, 1990, *Fatah* and *Hamas* signed a "code of honor" pledging to end the fighting between them. The ink was barely dry before reports of violence began coming in from Gaza.

Less than two months later, on December 14, 1990, Abdul Aziz was sentenced to another year in prison for allegedly inciting the violence. He was returned to Ansar III. There, he says, he shared a narrow cell with his mentor, Sheikh Ahmed Ismail Yassin, who had been arrested along with some 260 more activists in May 1989. Abdul Aziz recalls that the two of them were separated from the other prisoners because, he says, "the Israelis felt I was very effective among the prisoners, teaching and so on." In October, November, and December of 1991 he was put in solitary confinement: "I refused to stand up for the [Israeli] leader of Ansar III because of my religious convictions. Our religion prevents us from standing for anyone except God. This is Jewish justice," he adds bitterly. He was released on December 12, 1991, and two months later was elected to the Gaza Medical Association.

Abdul Aziz does not disguise the fact that his support for *Hamas* continues to take a personal toll. As an opponent of *any* peace talks with Israel, Abdul Aziz today worries more about the welfare of his children than he does about the ever-present danger of being jailed himself. "I'm afraid that someone may attack my children or force them to become informers," he says. "It's so easy for the Mossad or Shin Bet," he complains. "So day and night I keep my children under strict supervision. I watch them. I take them to school and back home again. Then after that, I close their doors myself. Can you imagine what kind of life this is? It's very, very hard. My mother constantly spends sleepless nights, because she hears the sounds of jeeps passing in the streets" and thinks they are coming to arrest him again. "What kind of existence is this with children being killed, elderly people being shot, and homes constantly being destroyed?" But the personal suffering has not diminished his zeal for the fundamentalist cause.

The dispute with the PLO, Abdul Aziz explains, centers on its acceptance of a two-state solution. "The land of Palestine is an Islamic endowment, and it is not permissible to cede any part, any group, or any generation of it at all," he says. "To establish a [Palestinian] state on a part of Palestine is accepted by *Hamas*, on the condition that this would not be at the expense of the other parts." But he adds decisively, "*Hamas* does not accept recognizing Israel." He says that in contrast to Islamic Jihad, which cooperates with the secular nationalist groups and is pro-Iranian, "*Hamas* is the real expression of Muslims in Palestine." The long-term goal of *Hamas*, he adds, "is a pan-Islamic state, but its immediate goal is to demonstrate the inhuman behavior of the Israeli authorities."

"We are living in circles," adds Mahmoud Zahaar, the Islamic scholar at al-Azhar. "Minor circles inside bigger ones and all included in a large Islamic circle. There is no contradiction between being Palestinian, Arab, and Islamic, because Palestine was always a part of the larger Arab lands. For 1400 years, the Arab has been a very important part of the heart of the Islamic land."

Says Abdul Aziz, the Nasser regime fell because it was *nizam al jahiliyya* ["the ignorant regime"]. All the Arab states—except Sudan, which has an Islamic regime—fall in the same category, he adds. The rebirth of Islam will come when "Islamic movements all over the world, in Egypt, in Jordan, in Algeria, in Yemen, obtain a wide popular base and succeed in spreading Islam throughout all the different sectors of Arab society despite the presence of communists, national leaders, and others," he explains. History, he says, is on Islam's side. "The first nucleus was in Sudan. The second in Algeria. These nuclei will coalesce." Democracy is a threat to Arab leaders, he adds, and suggests that if democracy had prevailed in early 1992 in Algeria, that nation would already have become an Islamic state.

Democracy, predicts Abdul Aziz, will bring Islamic leaders to power, even in towns of the West Bank that have traditionally been Christian. He points to the March 1992 elections in Ramallah where the *Hamas*-dominated list of candidates won ten of eleven seats on the Chamber of Commerce. That victory, the most serious defeat for the pro-PLO nationalists in a city that was always considered their stronghold, reflected the increasing birth rate among

Muslims in the West Bank and the rise in emigration by Christians. But the results also ratified the growing strength of *Hamas* throughout the territories. Even *Fatah* activists admit that the Islamic group today is second in popularity and catching up fast. One sign of its growing power was the reconciliation accord that the PLO felt it had to negotiate with *Hamas* after several days of renewed violence in Gaza claimed one life in the Shate refugee camp and threatened to explode into a civil war. Haidar Abdul Shafi, the venerable and highly regarded leader of the Palestinian team negotiating with Israel, signed the July 1992 accord on behalf of the PLO. It was signed on behalf of the Islamic fundamentalists by Abdul Aziz Rantisi, a clear sign of his growing personal power.

Hamas believes that the Israeli-Palestinian talks will fail to provide Palestinians with real independence or statehood and thus that the territories will remain a fertile ground for recruiting support. Mahmoud Zahaar even predicts the current peace process will suffer the same fate as the Nasser regime, and "the shock [when it fails] will be as great as the 1967 defeat." Autonomy, he says, is simply "not acceptable to the majority of Palestinians." It is an Israeli proposal, he adds, that is simply intended to perpetuate Israeli rule. "They consider our land is the Land of Israel. So how can they give us a true transition period [to a Palestinian state]?" he asks.

To the fundamentalists, of course, an Israeli-Palestinian accord is a matter of real concern. It can only set back their ultimate objective, particularly if Palestinians on the ground begin to feel that their own lives are being transformed and materially improved. Predicts Abdul Aziz, no matter how much authority Palestinians obtain when they receive self-government, the consequences will be a calamity for the Arab people. The *intifada* will be brought to an end, hundreds of Jewish settlements will remain in the West Bank and Gaza Strip, and the weak regimes of the Arab world will have no choice but to establish "good relations" with Israel.

In the process, the Palestinians would again be betrayed. "We are the true owners of the land. The only solution is for us to have our rights," declares Mahmoud Zahaar. "We are going to establish a pan-Islamic state." Adds Abdul Aziz, even if the peace talks succeed, they will codify the existing imbalance between the Jewish and the Arab peoples. "Israel will be strong. The Palestinians will be weak." That, however, is only a temporary phase, because God has promised in the Koran "that Muslims will be gathered in a pan-Islamic state and only after that will Palestine be returned." This is not simply a prophecy. It is, he says, the word of God.

Riad Maliki

███████████

Arriving at the office of Riad Maliki, you are surprised to see a group of Israelis saying goodbye to the unofficial spokesperson of the Popular Front for the Liberation of Palestine (PFLP). You are also surprised to hear the Israelis warmly thank the youthful thirty-seven-year-old for taking the time to meet with them at his refurbished apartment on quiet Zahra Street in East Jerusalem. It is there that Riad greets visitors to Panorama, his research center for foreign journalists and diplomats. In leaving, the Israelis tell Riad they would like to meet again. He asks that they call him in two to three weeks, after he returns from Geneva where he plans to attend a United Nations Conference on Trade and Development (UNCTAD). They shake hands, and the visitors and Riad go their own separate ways—the small band of citizens of the Jewish state and the supporter of the group that advocates a guerrilla war to destroy their state, the nation the PFLP calls "the Zionist entity."

Riad makes sure the waiting reporter overhears his plans to fly to Geneva. For several years, indeed up until January 1991, he was banned by the Israeli authorities from traveling anywhere. They said he was a leading member of the Unified National Command (UNC) running the *intifada* and a key PFLP leader in the territories who helped write the clandestine leaflets giving daily instructions to the *shabiba*, the young, stone-throwing troops in the field. For one month, in October 1990, the Israelis locked Riad up, keeping him in solitary confinement at the Moscobiyah Jail in Jerusalem.

At first sight it is hard to reconcile the appearance of this personable, self-assured, and smooth-faced engineering professor with the spectacular terrorist acts of the PFLP: the September 1970 hijacking to Jordan of three passenger planes, a Pan Am 747, a TWA 747, and a BOAC jumbo jet; the April 1974 murder of sixteen Jews, eight of them schoolchildren, in the northern Israeli town of Kiryat Shmonah; the March 1986 murder of Nablus mayor Zafir Masri; the more recent murders of seventy suspected Palestinian collaborators by PFLP "Red Eagle" assassination squads.

The PFLP has never disguised its support for the "armed struggle," and has been uncompromising in its demands that all of Palestine, from the Mediterranean to the Jordan River, be restored. When the Palestine National Council (PNC) declared in 1974 that it would accept a ministate on any part of Palestine that could be "liberated," the PFLP withdrew from the PLO's executive committee to protest what it regarded as a move toward a two-state solution. It formed its own Rejection Front and did not rejoin the PLO until 1981.

Today, it would seem, there are two Riad Malikis, a private one and a public one. Publicly, Riad is one of the leading spokespersons for Palestinian opponents of the current peace process. He tells the media that it makes no sense for the Palestinians to be negotiating when all the cards are stacked against them: the PLO is isolated politically and economically; the Arabs are divided in the wake of the Iraqi defeat in the Gulf War; the Soviet and Communist bloc have disintegrated; and the only superpower left—the United States—is able to impose its will. "It's the best time for the Americans and the worst time for the Palestinians," says Riad, noting they were even forced to form a single delegation with Jordan, "as if we are not mature enough to represent ourselves." In fact, he adds, he cannot think of any time since World War II when the Palestinians were in a weaker position than after the Gulf War. America has dictated the terms, he says, and they are humiliating terms: the PLO has been excluded from the process; no East Jerusalemites are allowed to participate; the Palestinians are treated as two separate people, shutting out three and a half million in the diaspora; and, worst of all, the outcome is predetermined. In the official letter of assurances that the Bush administration provided to the Israelis and the Palestinians, says Riad, "the Americans said the best solution is confederation with Jordan. They said no to an independent Palestinian state. They said no to Palestinian self-determination." Even the fourteen members of the Palestinian negotiating team had to be preapproved by Israel, he adds. "This is something that has never happened in history—your enemy selects your own negotiating team."

The Palestinians want a solution but not just "any" solution, insists Riad. More than a thousand people have been killed in the *intifada*, and tens of thousands more injured, many of them maimed and crippled for life. These sacrifices, he states, were not made in vain and certainly not for some form of limited self-rule that will perpetuate Israeli occupation. "They didn't give their lives for autonomy. Nor to be annexed to Jordan," he says. "My son or daughter or brother or my father died raising the Palestinian flag in order to build on their dead body a state—an independent Palestinian state!"

In newspaper and television interviews it is this vehemence that comes across, a willingness to accept nothing less than a total, absolute solution, or, as he says himself, only "a comprehensive and durable peace that leads to justice for the Palestinians." That is what drives Riad Maliki's principled stance against the Arab-Israeli peace talks. Why should the Palestinians, he asks, be forced to accept less than any other ethnic or nationalist group in the world? "Apartheid is being dismantled. Namibia is gaining independence," he says. "The wars in Angola, Mozambique, and Afghanistan" have liberated those nations too. "The only people still striving for independence are the Palestinians and," he warns, with characteristic flair, "the Palestinians will be the last ones. We will be the pain in everybody's back."

That is the public PFLP Maliki. Behind the scenes is another Riad Maliki, one that materializes in less noticeable places, such as the Jerusalem salons where Palestinian decision making takes place for the next round of negotiations with Israel. Surprisingly, Riad Maliki is there, too. What he tells Faisal Husseini in the privacy of their frequent discussions is somewhat different from his public stance against the peace talks. "He tells us he will join if the conditions change," says a leading member of the Palestinian delegation. Riad "attends all our meetings, the meetings where we discuss political matters. He is there, Hanan [Ashrawi] is there, Ghassan [Khatib] is there, Faisal is there." Riad is cautious, however. He hedges his bets. He keeps his options open. "I don't believe this is going to work," he says politely. Or he suggests, "If you do this, it might work; but don't do that," says the Palestinian participant.

Nor does the private Riad Maliki limit his involvement to the prenegotiation sessions at Faisal Husseini's home. According to sources in the Palestinian delegation, Riad, the PFLP spokesperson, asked for and regularly received verbatim "notes" of who said what to whom when the Husseini-led delegation met with U.S. Secretary of State James A. Baker III. He received a readout on each of the Baker-Husseini sessions, "meeting by meeting." Afterwards, Riad briefed his own PFLP followers on the contents of the official talks with the United States, and then issued a public statement that was usually very critical. "But when we sit together," notes a delegation source, "he says, 'Okay. Whatever you can bring—bring! We will not join, of course, unless new conditions are created for the peace talks, because we have promised that to our people.'" The PFLP role, he explains, "is not black and white. Let me put it this way: they have negative power. They can make a problem for someone. They can't stop it [the peace process], but they can create a problem."

Even the Israelis are noticing a change. The public Riad Maliki is appearing more often at joint press conferences and lectures with representatives of *Fatah*, the DFLP-Abed Rabbo wing, and other factions that support the peace process. Says one *Fatah* leader, "We care to appear together more since Madrid than we did before." He adds: "We have two different ideologies, but we appear on the same platform." Unlike *Fatah*, however, the stated platform of the PFLP, as spelled out from its headquarters in Syria, remains uncompromisingly anti-Israeli:

- *Fatah*, the mainstream faction of the PLO, headed by Yasser Arafat, accepted the existence of Israel in December 1988. The PFLP does not recognize the existence of a separate Jewish state.
- *Fatah* accepted U.N. Security Council Resolutions 242 and 338, which recognize Israel's independence and security within its 1967 borders provided the Jewish state relinquishes territory in the Golan Heights and in the West Bank and Gaza Strip. The

widely held interpretation of 242 would permit territorial adjustments required to safeguard Israeli
security. The PFLP rejects 242 as the sole basis for
negotiation, maintaining that the document treats
the Palestinians as refugees and does not guarantee
them the right of self-determination. Therefore, the
PFLP demands the implementation of all earlier
U.N. resolutions, including Resolutions 181 and 194,
which decades ago committed the world body to
give the Palestinians a state in what is today part of
Israel, and promised Palestinians the "right of
return" to their homes in Palestine. The PFLP calls
all three resolutions—181, 194, and 242—the "international legitimacy."

• *Fatah* has publicly renounced the armed struggle to
destroy Israel. From its headquarters in Damascus,
the PFLP still clings to the doctrine that armed
struggle—namely, the use of violence against both
military and civilian targets in Israel—remains the
only way to ultimately liberate all of Palestine.

One senior Israeli official believes West Bankers such as Riad
Maliki are tired of the old sloganeering and are looking for a new
foundation for the PFLP platform. The Israeli points to an article
written by Riad in July 1992 and published in *al-Quds*, the largest-
circulation Palestinian newspaper in the West Bank and the only
one, says this analyst, that refuses to side with any Palestinian faction. Riad wrote the article during the showdown between the
Israeli army and six armed "Black Panther" terrorists who were
disrupting the elections for a new student council at an-Najah
University. The four-day standoff was resolved when the Israeli
army agreed to lift its siege of the 4000 students and the six *Fatah*
guerrillas agreed (1) to leave the Nablus campus, (2) to be turned
over to the International Red Cross, and (3) to be deported to Jordan (after being disarmed) for a period of three years. "If his byline
was not on the article, I would have thought it was written by
the Israeli Minister of Information," chortles the Israeli
policymaker. "This is a very important article," he says.

In the article, Riad condemns both the activists who smuggled weapons onto the campus and the *Fatah* supporters who helped them do it. He denounces both groups for threatening the Palestinians organizing the elections as well as the students who were trying to vote. "How can we allow people who are armed to compete in elections?" asks Riad. "How can we demand recognition as an independent state if we cannot prove we are capable of organizing free, peaceful, and democratic elections?" he continues. In a separate article in *al-Wasat*, Riad faults the Palestinians who allowed the Israelis to deport the six, accusing them of being complicit in their forced exile. He singles out Faisal Husseini, charging that Faisal had effectively helped Prime Minister Yitzhak Rabin "climb down from the top of a tree [by providing him with] a staircase." The deal, the article goes on, had stripped the PLO of a major card it used to mobilize world public opinion against Israel's deportation policy. But Riad also underscores that, of all places, a university campus must be free of all force and threats of violence.

The Israeli analyst says, "Okay, Maliki is PFLP and he enjoys attacking *Fatah*! But there is much more to it than that, because you would expect the PFLP to take a much more supportive position of the activists, namely, [to declare] that as long as these are Palestinian weapons, let them in." Instead, "he recognizes there were armed people inside the campus and not only blames those who entered with their weapons but also those who allowed them to enter." That is hardly consistent with the PFLP's support for armed struggle. "Even if he was talking about the principle [of nonuse of force], it was a milestone," adds the Israeli. "I think Riad Maliki is going to turn in a new direction. I don't want to say there is a split in the PFLP. But undoubtedly there is a new trend that could in the future lead to a split and to the creation of a much more pragmatic faction than even the *Fatah* of Arafat."

The shift away from traditional Marxist-Leninist ideology did not happen overnight. There has been a gradual evolution toward a more pragamtic policy since the start of the *intifada* in 1987. The main change has been in the realization that although the Israeli-Palestinian conflict is by nature existentialist—that is, an independent Palestine must exist *instead* of an Israeli state—there is a new recognition that this kind of absolute solution cannot be implemented now.

Israeli journalist Ori Nir suggests the shift is most noticeable when you examine PFLP leader George Habash's declarations before and after the *intifada* began. In 1976 Habash said, "Peace will not exist as long as the Zionist state exists." In 1983 he asked the rhetorical questions "Can we—even if we wanted to—live together with Zionism? Can we make a distinction between Israel and the Zionist movement? Isn't Israel the physical, military, economic, and political embodiment of the Zionist movement? Can you defeat Zionism without defeating Israel?" Answering his own questions, Habash asked, "Were the Nazis defeated without the defeat of the Hitler regime?" In 1985, following the signing of an accord between Arafat and King Hussein, Habash concluded, "We will not be able to secure the future of our generations if the Zionist germ continues to exist on Arab soil." In November 1988, toward the end of the first year of the *intifada*, Habash began to make a distinction between "a just solution" and "a comprehensive solution." He told a press conference that "I hope you feel that I'm not talking about a 'just' settlement, because I believe there is no 'just' settlement to the Palestinian problem at this stage, since the only 'just' settlement is a Palestine that becomes Arab again, just like Egypt is Arab and Syria is Arab. A comprehensive settlement, however, would allow the establishment of a Palestinian state and the return of the refugees to their homeland." Nir points out that this was the first time Habash implicitly accepted the reality of Israel's existence by suggesting that, for now, the Palestinians should accept a state. Habash does not say where the state should be, thus leaving the question of borders open for future negotiation. Establishing this state, presumably on the West Bank and Gaza, would be sufficient to achieve a *comprehensive* solution, he says.

Habash elaborated on this theme in a January 1989 interview with *al-Hadaf*, the PFLP organ. He justified the need to establish a Palestinian state even if it did not include *all* of Palestine. "The Arab and the international conditions do not enable us to achieve more than the establishment of a Palestinian state on a part of the Palestinian lands," he said. "We view it as an achievement on which we can rely for the continuation of our struggle. We view it as an achievement on the one hand and the beginning of the suicide of the Zionist project on the other hand. . . . In the last forty years, Zionism has deepened its roots in our Palestinian land, so can we destroy it in one blow? If the answer is negative, then we should be courageous and tell the masses that while it is true that Palestine is Arab and that there can never be coexistence with Zionism or the Zionist entity, it is also true that we simply cannot destroy this Zionist entity in one blow."

Of course, an ideology that seeks to destroy the Jewish state in stages is no more appealing to Israeli policymakers. But they believe it is only a matter of time before PFLP leaders inside the territories assert their independence from the outside leadership and follow the example of the Democratic Front for the Liberation of Palestine (DFLP), which has split into two factions, one supporting the peace process and one opposed to it. Riad Maliki and Raji Sourani, a human rights activist, recipient of the Robert F. Kennedy Prize for human rights (for establishing *al-Haq*, a body that monitors human rights violations in Gaza) and the leading PFLP figure in Gaza, represent a new generation of intellectuals, says a key Israeli official. "They are playing a double game," he explains. "Inside their closed rooms they are saying they are for it [the peace process]. But they are confronting the pressures of the outside. The PFLP is very organized. You cannot have opposite opinions and still stay in the party. But if you ask me, they are lying in wait for the death of the doctor. They do not dare do anything before they know Habash is dead."

Riad Maliki was not even born when George Habash, a Christian descendant of a Greek Orthodox family from Lydda, graduated from medical school at the American University of Beirut and cofounded *Harakat al-Kawmiyyin al-'Arab*, the "Arab Nationalist Movement" (ANM), in the early 1950s. The ANM was a radical underground organization that opposed the established Arab regimes and increasingly adopted Marxist-Maoist doctrines. In the late 1950s their model was the Egyptian revolution, which had overthrown the British-supported monarchy of King Farouk and brought to power in Cairo a nationalist-minded leader, Gamal Abdul Nasser. All the mass movements supported Nasser's brand of anti-imperialist, pan-Arab socialism. Habash's ANM was a suitable umbrella for most Palestinians. But after the breakup of the union between Egypt and Syria in 1961, it became increasingly clear that Nasser's brand of pan-Arabism was at odds with the Palestinian nationalist aspirations to liberate their homeland.

Habash founded the PFLP in January 1968, a few months after the devastating Arab defeat in the June 1967 war against Israel. But it was not until August 1968 that the old ANM coalition that had united George Habash, Nayef Hawatmeh, and Ahmed Jabril finally broke apart and all three established their own liberation groups under the umbrella of the PLO. For Habash, the revolution had to begin by provoking a confrontation with Jordan. He saw King Hussein as the real culprit. Hussein's acceptance of Resolution 242, which ended the Six-Day War, implied Jordanian recognition of Israel within its pre-1967 borders. To Habash, Hussein was offering the unthinkable: a peace treaty with Israel merely for the return of a 2200-square-mile slice of territory on the West Bank and Gaza. The PFLP drew its support from among the poorest Palestinians in the refugee camps; thus its message, that the "proletariat should elect the leadership of the national movements," had broad appeal to the young, impoverished ideologues. Habash, the Christian physician, preached that Arab unity was the necessary precondition for the liberation of Palestine but that Palestine would only be liberated after the masses had revolted and replaced all the corrupt Arab regimes with Marxist dictatorships.

Although Ahmed Jabril did not like Habash's brand of radical Arab politics, most of all he did not believe that Arab unity was necessary before Palestine could be liberated. "The PFLP tried to be a party of all Arabs everywhere," he says. "We were a patriotic Palestinian faction. We needed to have good relations with Syria and Iraq." So in October 1968 Jabril formed his own splinter group, the PFLP-General Command (PFLP-GC).

Habash's split with Hawatmeh, who formed the Democratic Popular Front for the Liberation of Palestine (DPFLP), which later abridged its name to the DFLP, was more profound. "We considered Nasser and the so-called progressive Arab regimes responsible for the 1967 defeat," explains Yasser Abed Rabbo, a DFLP leader. "But we felt the answer was a new organization, based on Marxist principles, which would act as an alternative to Nasserism on one hand and to the traditional, orthodox Arab leftist parties on the other." The DFLP also did not support Habash's desire to topple existing Arab regimes. "While dealing with the bourgeoisie is evil," explains Abed Rabbo, "there is something worse, and that is occupation. We believed unity was essential, so we made alliances with *Fatah* and Syria."

Riad Maliki was only thirteen years old, barely a teenager, when these groups were being created, but his attitudes toward the Israelis were beginning to be formed by the events of his own life. Riad was part of a minority from the beginning, born on May 31, 1955, into what he says was a "lower-middle-class" Muslim family in the Christian town of Bethlehem. His father, an elementary school teacher, became headmaster of a private school in Bethlehem and later was appointed by the Israeli civil administration to a post with the regional department of education. Education was always a priority for the Maliki family. "All of us went to universities and graduated," he says proudly of his two brothers and three sisters. "Two of us even had the opportunity to do graduate work." Saving every dinar to help the family raise the funds for their schooling was the top priority for him, particularly since he was the oldest child, says Riad.

When he was ten years old, he recalls, he had to part with his most valuable posession, a collection of thousands of foreign stamps amassed with the help of his three uncles, who wrote him regularly from their homes in South America. "The stamps had a very special meaning to me, but I was forced to sell them in order to bring some money to my family," says Riad. The experience matured him. "It gave me a very good sense of responsibility. I was able to share the burden of my father to provide the family with a certain income. This makes you grow up quickly, quicker than usual," he notes.

After coming home from school, and during vacations, he sold postcards of Jesus' manger and other religious sites to the thousands of Christian pilgrims and tourists who visited Bethlehem. By the time he completed sixth grade, Riad had accumulated 200 dinars (about $250). Those funds helped his father send him to the best high school in Bethlehem, Terra Santa College, a private Christian academy run by an Italian monastic order, the Franciscan Brothers. There he mingled with the sons and daughters of wealthier parents than his own. "It's not easy," he says now of the experience, "especially if you understood the limitations of my family."

He was eight years old, says Riad, when he started reading newspapers and magazines, including *Time* and *Newsweek*. He would spend two or three hours reading them from cover to cover. Like the exotic, beautifully colored stamps, the publications gave him a window on the outside world and whetted his appetite for history and geography. They helped him learn English and taught him about the social and political revolutions that were taking place in Cuba, Algeria, and Indochina. "They helped me understand why our family could not provide for our basic needs, why my father could not be rich like everyone else, why I had to work to bring in extra money," he says.

Riad's father was never very interested in politics, and they rarely discussed the issues of the day. His father, however, was a good Muslim; he performed the Islamic ritual of praying five times a day and had already gone on the "Haj," the required pilgrimage to Mecca, the birthplace of the prophet Mohammed, and to Medina, the second-holiest shrine in Islam. But Riad was never interested in religion. He was the only Muslim attending Terra Santa, so he skipped religious classes. He also skipped French class, "for no real reason." He even balked when his father insisted that, at age fourteen, he begin accompanying him to the mosque for prayers. But he went, every Friday for an entire year. Then one day he refused. His father tried to persuade him, "but I insisted, and I won," says Riad.

His rearing in his own religion was limited to cramming for the Jordanian-administered *tawjihi,* and exam that tested knowledge of Islam and that Riad had to pass in order to graduate from high school. He does not know why he developed such an aversion to religion. Perhaps it was due to his reading about the oppression of the poor in South American countries, where the Catholic Church was rich and powerful. "I was more interested in social problems, in what was happening elsewhere in the world, than in spending time praying for the sake of praying," he recalls. "Maybe it was because we lived in Bethlehem," adds Riad. "The climate in school was Christian; my friends were Christian and the whole atmosphere was Christian." His father, knowever, has never stopped pressing Riad to return to Islam. "But he knows," says his son, "that he is talking to the wall."

After Riad graduated from high school, his father insisted that Riad, then seventeen, enroll at Saint George's School in Jerusalem to prepare for his British BCE graduation exam, which he needed to pass to be admitted to university. During this period his hero was the most charismatic Arab leader of the time, Egypt's Gamal Abdul Nasser. "When he used to give a speech, we used to be speechless," says Riad. Nasser's pan-Arab philosophy was attractive to Riad, but unlike other teenagers, "I never tried to memorize what he said." He recalls that he used to believe "in the ability of the masses to be mobilized and to rebel against regimes and that through them, we could unite all the Arab people. But I was disappointed with the level of readiness of these masses. I thought that if I wait for them to reach the point where we can start a mass movement towards the liberation of Palestine, I'm going to wait a very, very long time. That was when I started looking for alternatives."

Two events profoundly influenced Riad's life. At age nineteen he would leave for South America to pursue his education, to spend the next five years in Colombia, at a time when guerrilla movements there and in neighboring Argentina and Chile were mobilizing masses of peasants who, unlike the Arabs, were revolting against their regimes.

The other—earlier—event that shaped his attitudes was, of course, the June 1967 war, when Bethlehem and the rest of the West Bank and Gaza fell under Israeli occupation. The six days of fighting made a deep impression on Riad, who was only twelve: the war and his own small role in it, he says, taught him a surprising lesson—that the Israelis were not invincible. "We used to hear about the Israelis, dream about them, but we never saw them," he recalls. "We always figured them to be different from us," he adds, explaining that most Palestinians thought they were supermen who were fearless in battle and ruthless to their enemies. Riad found out differently. When the war began, Israeli troops easily drove the Jordanians out of Bethlehem and ordered the town's residents to fly white flags from their homes. Failure to do so risked having the houses bombarded. The threat was a serious one: all day long Riad heard the screams of jets as they flew their missions, barely clearing the rooftops of Bethlehem.

When the Israeli forces moved in to Manger Square, loud-speakers blared orders for everyone to set up the white flags, leave their homes, and go toward the road to Jericho. "I won't go," said Riad's grandfather. The whole Maliki family had gathered at his house. "If they want to kill us, then I prefer to be killed inside the house. I'm not going to leave. We don't want to see the tragedy of 1948 repeated again." Riad says the family decided to remain there. It was the first act of defiance, of what he calls *sumud*, or steadfastness, that he had witnessed.

But before long, rumors began to fly that the Israelis had started to bomb any house not flying a white flag. Riad's father worried about his own house, for no one was there to put the flag out. "Being the oldest son," recalls Riad, "I was asked by my father to go to the house and to raise the flag in case something happens. I had to walk, crossing Bethlehem, for about twenty to twenty-five minutes." He knew the network of alleys that led to his father's house, but to get to them he had to escape detection by the Israelis. He had only gone a short distance when an Israeli jeep spotted him. "They shouted at me to stop. I panicked, so I ran. They shouted at me again and they followed me." He ran as hard as he could, ducking into passageways and narrow streets, "all the time expecting a bullet to hit my back." Says Riad, "I don't know where I got my courage." He reached his home and put the flag up. But it was late and dark and he was not eager to return. "So I stayed by myself for two days and two nights in the house, alone, while at night watching the crossfire." He says he was horrified by what he saw. But he kept quiet, motionless, waiting for the war to end.

Only after the fighting did Riad learn that a friend, a boy only two years older, had been killed, his head shot off. Riad says he wanted to see what had happened, so he walked to the site of his friend's death, hoping "to find anything related to him." All he saw were pools of blood in the street. He would keep his distance from the Israelis now, but they fascinated him. When a contingent of soldiers turned his elementary school into a temporary encampment, Riad could not keep away. "I used to look carefully to see what they were doing," he recalls. "I kept my distance because they could really hit. They could kill anybody whether they knew him or not and with reason or for no reason at all." The events of those summer days left their mark on him. "It's as if I felt a force inside me that was pushing me towards political activities," he says.

When he was seventeen, Riad had his first opportunity to travel abroad. A friend asked Riad to join him in Austria, where the friend was attending a university in Graz, the neutral country's second-largest city. Riad enrolled in undergraduate courses in civil engineering, but he had a hard time adjusting. German proved a difficult language to learn, and Austrian society seemed closed and remote to the young Palestinian. When he tried to rent an apartment, he was reminded of his status as a stateless person. Worse than that, he was regarded with suspicion. A few weeks earlier, a Palestinian terrorist group affiliated with "Black September," a breakaway *Fatah* faction, had taken Israeli athletes hostage at the 1972 Munich Olympics. Eleven of them were killed in the shootout. The landlord told Riad that she was sorry—he was a Palestinian and she simply could not take a chance. He finally found an apartment, worked for a while in a distillery, and visited neighboring Yugoslavia, where he was impressed by "how people live in a socialist country." But Riad still felt out of place, so when an aunt and uncle visiting from Qatar suggested he return with them to Bethlehem, Riad was glad to have the opportunity.

No sooner had he returned home, however, than another Arab-Israeli conflict erupted, the October 1973 war, and the universities on the West Bank again were closed. Riad wrote to his uncles in Colombia and convinced his father to let him travel there to continue his studies. "My father has a weak point when it comes to me," admits Riad. In Bogota he enrolled in the civil engineering faculty of Pontificia Universidad Javeriana, a Jesuit school. An uncle who had become wealthy in the Caribbean paid the tuition for him. Riad quickly became fluent in Spanish and unlike his experience in Austria found that he was easily accepted, a minority of one among dozens of native minorities and ethnic tribes.

Ironically, it was thousands of miles from home that his identity as a Palestinian would largely be forged. "I saw many things through social and economic eyes—not just political," he says. "I saw how people really live, the rich and the poor, how the multinational corporations exploit the wealth of these countries, and the differences between the colors of human beings." Riad says "the dimensions of the injustice" made a deep impression on him. He says he will never forget seeing the progenitors of South America, the poverty-stricken Indians, begging for food. Today they are "fifth-grade citizens of their own countries. You see the civilization they built and see them on the streets of Quito, Lima, and La Paz begging for charity." Parallels with the Palestinians began forming in his mind. "You don't see much difference being in Colombia or Peru or Bolivia or Ecuador or in Israel," he says.

He familiarized himself with all forms of guerrilla warfare. "I used to read about each and every guerrilla group," says Riad, deliberately pronouncing the word in Spanish: *gue-RI-ya*. He studied the "urban guerrilla and the rural guerrilla," he says, the Shining Path in Peru and the Revolutionary Armed Forces of Colombia (FARC), the *Tupamaros* in Uruguay, and the Movement for the Revolutionary Left (MIR) in Chile. He wanted to learn why each of them "took up arms, for what purpose," and became convinced that without a similar platform for economic and social justice, Palestinian factions such as *Fatah* that waged primarily a political struggle would be unable to respond to the needs of the people. "If you want to reach the level of the people, where they can identify with what you are doing, you must go that deep," he explains.

Riad says he also learned that for a guerrilla struggle to succeed, it had to have genuine popular support. The use of terror to intimidate the people is counterproductive. Speaking of the slaughters that were carried out by the Shining Path and other groups, he says: "I'm not in favor of their system of imposing their own ideology or presence by force. By force I mean cases where out of terror they go to a village and massacre everybody. I detest this." Riad feels as strongly about the murder of Palestinian collaborators on the West Bank and Gaza Strip. A liberation struggle must garner support because the people feel they are protected by it, "not because they are terrified by it," he says. The support must be generated by a social, economic, and political program, "the ideology, the thinking that you convey and that is accepted because people believe in it and you are wanted, you are supported, you are loved." The Palestinian people consider the PLO their sole, legitimate representative, he explains, "not because it was imposed on them but because they wanted it so. The PLO achieved its status as the result of the sacrifices, the struggle of defending the rights of the people and carrying on that struggle for some time." In South America, says Riad, "you are talking about a totally different situation."

After graduating in 1979, Riad left Colombia to spend a year earning a master's degree in civil engineering, transportation, and planning in a combined program adminstered by New York University and Brooklyn Polytechnic. By the time he returned to begin his teaching career at Birzeit University in 1980, he was imbued with the fervor of the many Arabs who lived in Manhattan and were exposed to the strong pro-Israeli sentiments of its large Jewish population. He saw analogies between oppression in South America and what exists in his own homeland, he says. The analogies are not precise, he admits, but "the symptoms are the same."

Riad asserts that the United States props up Israel by providing several billion dollars in annual economic and military aid, much of it to oppress the Palestinians. When flagrant human rights abuses take place, then the United States, Israel, and neighboring Arab nations such as Egypt, Jordan, and Saudi Arabia, which are heavily dependent on American arms, look the other way—just as the U.S. government did when American companies confiscated Latin American wealth, exploited the natural resources and Latin labor force, and provided the military regimes there with the weapons to enforce their dictatorial rule. "If the United States had wanted to, it could have stopped Israel from oppressing the Palestinians by simply suspending financial aid and arms supplies, by making the linkage," says Riad. "The humans who suppress you are the locals; but the equipment, the machines, and the orders come from abroad. And when I looked around and asked why my Arab countries were not coming to my rescue, I found out they were also limited. The Americans were telling them you cannot do this, you cannot do that—because the United States wanted to let Israel enjoy military superiority."

The other similarity he sees between the Palestinians and the peasants of South America is their almost mystical attachment to the land. The land and the person are one. "It's not like in the States, where you are from California and live in Texas or you buy a house and settle in Arkansas. Here your roots are from this village and you always call yourself a person from that village. You teach your children and your grandchildren that you belong to that village. If you speak to the villagers who live on a piece of land, you'll see what this piece of land means to them. It's their life, their culture, their survival, their ancestors, their tradition. Sometimes a farmer, especially the Palestinian farmer, spends more time with the land than with his family. They have a special relationship with the olive tree. They speak to it. They know the history of the tree."

In fact, says Riad, in Palestinian culture, in songs and in folklore, the earth is equated with the primeval force of nature, motherhood. In Arabic the word for a woman's honor, *al-'ard*, and that for the land, *al-ard*, are similar. There is a saying: The two things an Arab cares most about are *al-ard* and *al-'ard*. Riad says, "If a woman is violated, it's the end of the world for an Arab. If his land is confiscated, it's the same thing . . . as if you are trying to kill that person." That's why, although each of the males in the Maliki family—Riad's father, his three uncles, and each of the three sons—owns a part of the family tract, it will never be divided. "It must be united as a single piece of land," he explains, which is why whenever anyone sells their land, "it's as if you are selling your life and your family." Adds Riad, "The last thing a Palestinian would do is sell his piece of land."

In 1983 Riad returned to NYU to begin work on his doctorate degree. He received his Ph.D. in 1986 and returned that fall to continue teaching at Birzeit. The start of the *intifada* a little more than a year later brought his whole life into focus, from the day he sold his stamp collection to the race to outrun the Israelis in Bethlehem to the suffering and pain he had seen with his own eyes in the *barrios*, the slums of South America. For Riad, the *intifada* marked an important stage in the historical determinism of the Palestinian people. They lost their fear of the Israelis, and with that they took the first step toward scaling the psychological wall that had perpetuated occupation. "That a kid, a Palestinian kid, confronts the Israeli soldier knowing he might be killed and still he confronts the soldier," says Riad, was a spiritual breakthrough of immense proportions. It gave the Palestinians pride, but it also gave them a new sense of equality with their adversary. "The Palestinians were able to remove all the artificial barriers that existed as a result of so many Arab defeats. Individuals and communities were able to achieve what Arab governments and Arab armies had failed to achieve; indeed, they were able to reverse what the Arabs had indirectly created as a result of their defeats—the Israeli occupation."

On another level, says Riad, the *intifada* taught the Palestinians that the Israelis are not supermen. "They don't have a greater will to fight than the Palestinians. Right now the Israeli soldiers confront the kids because they know they have the submachine gun and they are ready to use it to kill. He knows the Palestinian facing him is unarmed. Give me, as a Palestinian, the same weapons and I will guarantee you that the Israeli will run when he sees me. The moment he sees an armed Palestinian, then his own behavior—his own response—will be different." Nature has not made the Israelis stronger or braver or more determined than the Palestinians. "I don't think they have any greater will to fight or to be killed or to live," he says. Therefore, it is illogical to believe that a nation of 4 million people will always be able to defeat 200 million Arabs. It is the artificial conditions, including the arsenal of weapons the United States supplies to Israel, that has made the difference between the two societies. The *intifada* has made the Palestinian realize that Israel is an "inflated giant, and if you punch this giant you can reduce him to his real dimensions. This is new," says Riad, underscoring that PFLP doctrine has always dictated that Israel will one day be reduced to its natural size. "We have learned that the only reason Israel is a giant is because others want him to be one. They have inflated him. So your fight is not only with this giant but with the ones who are behind him, who have blown him up. This," says Riad, "is how I see the situation."

In fact, Riad believes that in joining the negotiations on Israeli terms, the Palestinians squandered much of the gains of their five-year-old uprising. "At the first moment when the Palestinians decided to meet with Mr. Baker, before they went to Madrid or to Washington," he says, "they should have thought about their position and not accepted the Israeli conditions. Mr. Baker said it very clearly—without the Palestinians there will be no peace process." Riad blames the PLO and its *Fatah* leadership inside the territories for capitulating to pressure from the other Arabs. "I'm not waiting for the Arabs to come and liberate us," he says cynically. Instead of yielding to the humiliating Israeli conditions, says Riad, the PLO should have recognized "that *our* presence is vital to the convening of the process so our participation should be as vital as our presence. We should never have accepted merely a presence. We should have insisted on real participation." If the United States and Israel and the rest of the Arabs were unwilling to meet these demands, he says, the Palestinians should have said, "Okay, if you don't want us, then we won't go. And *khalas*, that's the end!"

Falling back on his larger view of the world, and its Marxist roots, Riad, the PFLP supporter, says that once the conditions were accepted—that the Palestinians could not represent themselves as an independent delegation, the PLO was excluded, no Jerusalemites could participate, and the diaspora was shut out—the die was cast for the outcome. "The Arabs are defeated. The socialist states have disappeared. The PLO is isolated politically and economically and we come and negotiate!" he says contemptuously. "We selected the worst time ever to enter the peace process." Riad dismisses the notion that the Palestinians in the territories can improve the conditions of their daily lives, ridding themselves of the outward manifestations of the occupation, such as the presence of Israeli troops in their towns and villages, and gaining the right to elect their own local leaders and to run their municipal affairs. "That's bullshit," says Riad. "This is a political process that depends entirely on the balance of power in the world, which is weighted strongly against the Palestinians. The new world order, he says, is in reality "the new American order." Therefore, the results are preordained. "I know that the outcome will be nothing else but autonomy," contends Riad, "just the way the Israelis want it."

He says entering the negotiations has revived the *Fatah*-led PLO by giving it power to dictate the terms of the talks to Palestinians inside the territories. "The leadership is sitting there in the palaces and villas in Tunis thousands of miles away and directing the struggle from there," says Riad. "The weight is outside while the struggle is inside. The weight should be where the struggle is," he says. "The occupation is daily, the struggle is daily, the

suffering is daily, and you have people who live outside in complete comfort," he adds. Riad rarely disguises his contempt for
the continual power struggles within *Fatah*, which remind him
of the preoccupation of Japan's governing party with maintaining a large enough coalition to rule. "It's always a struggle, always
a competition, always people trying to bring other people together
to get power for themselves. This is *Fatah*. It's a movement based
on individuals who can become very powerful in a very short
period of time. It's not an orderly kind of process."

Creating a process that would provide legitimate political
authority for insiders like himself—through free and fair
elections—is one of the few gains Riad believes could justify the
Israeli-Palestinian peace talks. It is one of the reasons why he has
tempered his opposition to them. Right now, he explains, on the
West Bank and in Gaza, "everything is illegal: political activities
are illegal, political parties are illegal, everything is underground.
We have to work in the absence of a real infrastructure."

If the Palestinians succeed in wresting real responsibility for
electing their own leaders in the territories, Riad says, he may eventually change his view. He is not wasting any time, however.
Panorama, the organization he started in 1991, is offering
workshops on democracy. "The participants are the leaders of the
grass roots," the local politicians Riad apparently hopes will form
the nucleus of a future PFLP constituency. Panorama, he says, also
plans to begin public opinion polling. He defends his speeches
criticizing the peace talks, suggesting they are part of the new process of educating the masses in how to resolve their disputes
peacefully instead of through violence. "To start with, I'm a very
peaceful person. I'm a person who detests violence and counter-
violence and bloodshed, because I do not believe that any person has the right to kill another person," says Riad. Occasionally,
he says, a national liberation movement must depart from
established codes of conduct, "but I'm a pro-peace person." He
adds: "I still believe that one day we will reach a settlement in
this area, and that's why I'm in favor of the peace process, of *a*
peace process—but we have to define that process." He explains
that "if it's a process that will lead to justice for the Palestinians
and be durable and comprehensive," it will deserve everyone's support. "I would like to get to the point where there is just one very

clear definition of peace that is acceptable to everybody," he adds.

As the last of several interviews, each several hours long, draws to an end, Riad wants to be sure his interlocutor understands his position. "I'm not saying wait, wait and sit and do nothing." But Riad Maliki remains deeply suspicious of the current negotiating process. In a December 1991 interview, he warned that without an internal consensus on the definition of a just and durable peace and without the legitimacy that derives from being popularly elected, the delegation currently representing the Palestinians "may become our *Wafd* Party, in the full sense of the word." In 1918 the Egyptian parliament appointed a delegation, the *Wafd*, to present the case for Egypt's independence to the Paris peace talks that ended World War I. The delegation came home with nothing more than promises from the British. The Palestinian negotiating team could suffer the same fate if it loses touch with the masses, Riad says.

Meanwhile, Riad acknowledges, there have been heartening changes in the Bush administration's policies toward the Middle East. "American foreign policy has started to take the Palestinian factor into consideration. It has become a permanent factor in the formulating of policy. This is something totally new," he says. "But I believe the American administration still has a long way to go before it reaches a position where the Americans can really enjoy the trust of others—in particular, the Palestinians—or present themselves as fair brokers." For Riad Maliki, the thirty-seven-year-old Birzeit professor, the important thing is to remember his grandfather's attitude by remaining adamant in the righteousness of his cause—even when foreign pressures and internal expediency threaten to weaken his resolve. "Without these elements of *sumud* ('steadfastness'), you are talking about suicide. I don't think I'm advocating suicide," he says, in describing the PFLP's opposition to the peace talks. "On the contrary, I think the worst thing to do is to commit suicide, because you are ending a life without any meaning." The PFLP, he implies, should not commit suicide by remaining unalterably opposed to a peaceful settlement with Israel. Riad Maliki clearly hopes he will one day be a part of an honorable negotiation—one that will give his life, past and present, real meaning.

Ghassan Khatib

███████████

On a clear afternoon in May 1992, shortly before the fifth round of Arab-Israeli negotiations are due to begin in Washington, Ghassan Khatib, a member of the negotiating team, readies himself for a casual talk in the West Bank that may prove as sticky as any he faces at the formal table. Dressed comfortably in a zippered jacket, a collared shirt, and gray slacks, he leaves his Ramallah apartment and, joined by a resident of the village of Kufr-'Ein, sets off in his own car, a white Volkswagen Beetle. He apologizes for the modest, slightly rusty means of transportation and mentions that he almost had to cancel a scheduled meeting with the Canadian foreign minister because the parking attendant at the consulate refused to believe he was one of the invited guests. As Ghassan drives past the stony mountain landscape, he notes that he has been up and down these roads many times, speaking to dozens of local village groups about the peace process. When he returned from Madrid, he says, he appeared at fourteen different gatherings in eighteen days.

Arriving in picturesque Kufr-'Ein, near the top of a small ridge overlooking a valley, Ghassan is met by the local representative of the committee that has organized today's event. He is welcomed to the gentleman's home, and the two men sit down to sip sweet tea and chew on green almonds and beans. Ghassan's host informs him that the village had had some unusual visitors that morning, Israeli soldiers who informed them that in forty-eight hours, two houses in Kufr-'Ein would be demolished, as punishment for allegedly harboring a terrorist. The men finish their refreshments and walk through the simple village, past a few scattered stone houses and some olive trees to the building that is the center of village life, the mosque. In its courtyard, as in so many parts of the West Bank, the walls are brightly painted with graffiti, as if the stones were magnetized for spray paint, the two media an inseparable pair. Scrawled on the walls are the words *Allah Akbar* ("God Is Great") and the slogans of various groups, from *Hamas* to the Democratic Front for the Liberation of Palestine (DFLP) and the Popular Front for the Liberation of Palestine (PFLP). In the middle of the courtyard the branches of a tree are strung with a tattered Palestinian flag, while another flag, also torn, flaps limply on a pole.

Slowly, by ones and twos, men start to trickle into the courtyard until there are about twenty-five people, ranging from teenagers to men in their sixties. At first the women remain outside, grouped together, while the men walk in and sit down on the stone benches built along the side; after they are settled the women will join them. As more people walk in, some of them open chairs, forming a semicircle around Ghassan. Next to him is the *mukhtar*, the village leader, wearing a brown wool pinstripe jacket and under it a long wrap of cotton fabric covering his legs like a skirt. He is sporting dark Ray-Ban sunglasses.

As Ghassan is about to start his speech, he notices two boys not much older than he was when his father died. One of them is wearing a T-shirt imprinted with the Hebrew word *Gali*, the name of an Israeli sportswear manufacturer. Like so many Palestinian boys, he has bought himself this inexpensive T-shirt without understanding the meaning of the word imprinted on it. Some boys even wear sport shirts proclaiming *Beitar Yerushulaim*, not realizing they are promoting the Jerusalem soccer team sponsored by the Israeli hard-line Herut Party. But the other boy that Ghassan spies is wearing a far more menacing T-shirt. It shows a likeness of Nasser Abu Hamid, a member of *Fatah*'s Black Panther strike force. Underneath the picture are the words "You Are Wanted Dead," a reference to the fact that Hamid is one of the most hunted PLO terrorists.

Ghassan begins by talking about the end of the Cold War and the new geopolitical realities that have combined to weaken the Palestinian position: that the United States is now the only superpower, that the Soviet Union is no longer a reality, and that the Palestinians accepted humiliating conditions because their position was weak. Ghassan concedes there are some Palestinian organizations opposing the peace talks, but he minimizes the differences between them, explaining that they disagree on the means, the conditions for engaging in the talks, not the end. Everyone agrees the talks must lead to self-determination and to an independent Palestinian state. He praises the American decision to freeze $10 billion in housing loan guarantees until Israel freezes settlement activity. This is unprecedented, Ghassan notes.

Ghassan then asks for questions. One elderly Palestinian poses a seemingly simple query: will the peace talks be successful? But the question is fraught with danger. What is meant by "successful"? How long will it take before the Palestinians achieve their self-determination? How long will it be before they get a state of their own? Ghassan tempers his response, offering neither unrestrained optimism nor a bleak outlook. He says success is not guaranteed but is worth trying for. Then he is asked about the *intifada*. The *intifada*, he replies, will make no headway unless it is accompanied by negotiations. Violence alone, he knows, is an outlet for rage that will only bring more rage. Stone-throwing and striking out at one's enemy are helpful only if they lead to the two sides' sitting down together and talking.

It is a subdued performance. The reception is warm but not enthusiastic; there is no fanfare or any certain promises to fulfill wild dreams. Ghassan does not speak in hyperbole or seek celebrity status. Neither does he pretend to be a political leader. He has come as an equal, to discuss the current situation openly and honestly, without leaving false impressions or high hopes. He has gained the audience's respect, and they leave satisfied that their concerns are being addressed, if not fully met. As he gets back in the Volkswagen, Ghassan says it is important for the delegation to maintain grass-roots support. "I'll tell you, I'm the kind of person who cares a great deal about the reaction, particularly of the young people, to what I'm doing." The image of the angry young boys in their T-shirts cannot be far from his mind. It recalls a picture of a younger Ghassan Khatib, one who felt far closer to their rage than to his own now far more moderate, response. Ghassan will never forget that he, too, like the "wanted"

Fatah terrorist in the T-shirt portrait, was once considered a terrorist, despised and shunned by ordinary Israelis.

Ghassan was eleven years old when his father died, fourteen when he was beaten by Israeli troops, nineteen when, he says, Israelis broke his jaw and then sentenced him to five years in prison. His crime was belonging to a militant faction of an underground Communist Party-led coalition, the *al-Jabhah al-Wataniyya al-Falastiniyya*, the Palestine National Front (PNF). As painful as all of that was, nothing sears the memory of thirty-eight-year-old Ghassan Khatib as strongly as the December day in 1979 when he was caught demonstrating near Birzeit University, dragged outside the women's dormitory, and, with his hands tied behind his back, smacked with the butt of a rifle, slapped with a night stick, and kicked by Israeli soldiers. "I remember hearing the screams of the girls," he says. "They kept moving me from one place to another in order to make an example of me for the students." But it is not the brutality of the beating or even the injuries he sustained that still cause pain. It is what happened after the incident was over, when the Israeli troops tried to lock him up in the Ramallah Prison.

Whenever a new prisoner is admitted, an Israeli health official must certify that his or her life is not in jeopardy. The official who examined Ghassan refused to provide the document, saying instead, according to Ghassan, "This guy might die any minute. I cannot admit him in his condition." The army officer started shouting at the bureaucrat, but it was useless. So Ghassan was boarded back on the patrol wagon and taken to Beit El, a large military compound that also served as the headquarters of the civil administration for the Ramallah region. He was examined at the clinic by a military doctor who the Israelis hoped would finally authorize Ghassan to be admitted to prison. The Palestinian remembers the physician asking him what he was studying at Birzeit. When told economics, the doctor said that if Ghassan wanted to stay healthy, he should stay out of politics. But after examining him, this Israeli also refused to comply with the officer's request. He suggested that Ghassan be taken to Hadassah Hospital on Mount Scopus. Once the hospital had issued its report, the army could cart him off to prison, he explained.

When they arrived at Hadassah, the lobby was jammed with dozens of patients seeking emergency treatment. Two soldiers held Ghassan under each arm, helping the limp Palestinian take one step at a time. His wrists were handcuffed; there were black and blue marks all over his face, and he was bleeding from his neck. The sight of the soldiers bringing the prisoner into their midst sent instant alarms through the room of ordinary men, women, and children nervously awaiting their own turn with the doctors. As Ghassan moved forward, he says, "they started to whisper, *'hablan, hablan,'* which means 'terrorist, terrorist' [actually, 'explosives expert'] and everybody moved aside." Ghassan was ordered to sit down on a long bench. One of the Israeli soldiers sat next to him while the other went to the admissions office. An infant was at the opposite end of the bench, where his mother had left him while she went to register. Suddenly, two hospital security guards noticed the child and rushed towards Ghassan, shouting to the mother "How can you leave a baby so close to this terrorist? He might kill him." For Ghassan, that moment still hurts. "That was very hard for me. I was twenty-five. I felt I was an ordinary person," he says. The attending physician's report said that Ghassan had three broken ribs and neck and leg wounds and needed a few days of medical care but that there was no threat to his life. Ghassan was taken back to prison in Ramallah, where he was later sentenced to a six-month jail term.

This was not the first time Ghassan Khatib had been behind bars. On May 4, 1974, he was sentenced to five years in prison for allegedly being a member of a secret cell in a militant offshoot of the PNF called the Patriotic Front. He was nineteen years old at the time. "I was recruited for the military wing of the Communist Party," he says. "My tasks were actually armed activities. I was trained to use weapons and explosives." But Israeli officials confirm that despite the training, neither Ghassan Khatib nor the Patriotic Front ever committed any acts of violence. In fact, the Israelis were surprised when, in the spring of 1974, they discovered that the Communist Party had even organized an armed front. The communists were the apotheosis of nonviolence.

In the 1920s, when the Communist party was founded, it was largely a Jewish underground movement aimed at resisting both Zionism and British imperialism. Naturally, it attracted widespread

Arab support for its stance that Jews and Arabs should be included in a single democratic secular state. "The idea was to fight on social levels against the oppressor, which was British imperialism. There was even a plan to start a joint kibbutz," recalls an Israeli who'd been a member of the party. When the United Nations adopted its plan in 1947 to partition Palestine into Jewish and Arab states, the communists followed the example of the Soviet Union, which was the second country to vote for the creation of and to extend diplomatic recognition to Israel. Although several communist Arab leaders had themselves become refugees and did not go along, the party maintained its principled position against the use of force. It opposed the 1948 war, thereby coming in direct conflict with the Arab countries that had declared their aim of destroying the newly formed Jewish state. The *Miflaga Kommunistit Isra'elit* was subsequently set up in Israel, the only country in the Middle East where the Communist Party was legal and took part in elections.

Ghassan Khatib has devoted most of his adult life to finding alternatives to violence. He lectures regularly at Israeli universities and has worked closely with the Israeli Peace Now movement in organizing marches to villages in the West Bank. He has helped stage sit-ins that have been so successful Israeli security officials still use military jargon to describe them: "He has made many *operations* with Peace Now," says one such official. Ghassan also was the prime mover in forging a human chain on Christmas Eve 1989, when tens of thousands of people joined hands around the ancient walls of the Old City of Jerusalem. A year later he mounted an entire campaign to prevent the expulsion of Palestinians and the takeover of their homes in Silwan, a small Palestinian town adjacent to the City of David, where Israeli Housing Minister Ariel Sharon wanted to create a new Jewish settlement. Even Jerusalem Mayor Teddy Kollek joined the protest organized by Ghassan against Sharon's plans.

But today Ghassan Khatib has a new role. He is a leading member of the Palestinian-Jordanian negotiating team, one of two members (the other is Samir Abdullah) of the Palestine People's Party on the Palestinian delegation. A close confidant of Faisal Husseini, Ghassan is a studious, soft-spoken scholar whose persuasive manner, selfless style, and hard work have earned him the trust of all the members of the delegation.

Although the Communist Party per se has ceased to exist—it has split into two groups, the Palestine People's Party, headed by Bashir Barghouti, and the Palestine Democratic Assembly, headed by George Hezboun—Ghassan does not hide his pride in the party or its historic accomplishments. Indeed, he notes that seventy-year-old Haidar Abdul Shafi, the chief negotiator, who delivered the stirring speech for the Palestinians at the Madrid peace conference, was once the most senior and respected member of the former Communist Party in Gaza. Even rival *Fatah* delegates note that the communists play a proportionately larger role in the peace talks than the number of their supporters would warrant. "They have a strong intellectual role within the delegation and are part of the decision-making group," explains a colleague. "They come to every meeting with a prepared list of demands and proposals and choices," he says. "The others just come to talk and to set up an agenda."

But the former communists, the rival adds, would win less than 10 percent of the vote in any West Bank election. Their credibility has been damaged by the collapse of the Soviet Union and, he adds, they have never had much power in the Palestinian street. "When we say 'the street,' what does it mean?" he asks. "It means control on the ground through institutions, members, structure. They don't have this. Where will you find them? Three or four teachers at Birzeit University; three or four people in the administration office; two or three people at a newspaper. But on the ground you don't find them widely like the PFLP or *Hamas* or *Fatah*. There are reasons for that," he adds. "Ours is a religious society, and when you say 'communist,' it's someone who does not believe in God! Communism is something that takes you on an express train to Hell!" The communists, says this *Fatah* supporter, "are a piece of paper and school and ideas, books!" Indeed, in Ramallah, he notes, their library is nicknamed the "Red Library," their books the "red books." Their power derives from the fact that "they have always espoused big principles such as equality and democracy. They were," he notes, "the first to support a two-state solution."

But never underestimate the communists, cautions an Israeli

official. "Don't weigh them by their numbers. Weigh them by their activities. The People's Party," says this veteran policy maker, "is very important. They know how to organize public relations campaigns and they know how to organize the trade unions. They know how to write leaflets. They are very clever. That's why we say, 'One Communist is worth six *Fatah*!'"

Ghassan Khatib grew up in the Jordanian-ruled West Bank. He was born in 1954 in the village of Beit Iba, near Nablus, the eldest of six children, three boys and three girls. His father, Abdelwahab, was a civil servant, a district school supervisor for the Jordanian government. "Because he was a government employee, we constantly had to move from one town to another, which was very disruptive. I didn't live continuously for more than three years in one place," he recalls. Of course, that meant enrolling in new public schools, always being forced to make new friends, and never having a permanent place to call home. But, says Ghassan, it also exposed him to many towns and villages on the east side of the Jordan River, which would be off-limits to him later in life.

The event that changed his life, however, was the death of his father, when Ghassan was only eleven years old. Abdelwahab had not inherited anything from his parents; and because he had neither savings nor saleable land, the family had to go on welfare, receiving benefits from the Jordanian government, as well as occasional handouts from their relatives. The greatest influence on Ghassan came from his uncle Hafez. "He is the one who took care of us," says Ghassan. Hafez Khatib was an activist, an early member of the Arab Workers Congress and its communist front organization, the National Liberation League, which helped to organize Arab trade unions in Jordan. Until 1951, West Bank members of the league supported the creation of an autonomous Palestinian state and opposed the unification of the West and East Banks under Hashemite sovereignty. The Jordanian government, however, declared the league illegal in 1949, and the Jordanian Communist Party was outlawed two years later.

Hafez Khatib remained active in the communist underground in the West Bank, supporting Suleiman Nabulsi's National Socialist Party, which was in the vanguard of the opposition to the Hashemite regime during the 1950s. One of the founders of

Nabulsi's party on the West Bank was Daoud Mikhail, Hanan Ashrawi's father. It was an offshoot of Nabulsi's party that organized the first wave of strikes against Israeli occupation after the June 1967 war. In fact, Hafez was with Ghassan when Israeli tanks rolled into Nablus less than seventy-two hours after the war began. "There were rumors that these tanks might be Iraqi or Algerian," recalls Ghassan, so he ran out of the house and into the street to wave to them. But an old man who lived in the neighborhood and knew better saw him. He swooped up the thirteen-year-old, carrying Ghassan back into the house, telling him: "Those are Israelis. Stay indoors!" The Khatib family lived on the main street of Nablus, which was a Jordanian army stronghold, so when the tanks entered the city and began firing warning rounds, Hafez and Fatima, his mother, sought cover for the six children. "We were about twenty-five people in a small corridor," says Ghassan, when the whole house almost went up in smoke. A stray bullet had ignited a mattress lying on the second-story balcony. "I was crawling on the ground taking buckets of water to put out the fire," he says.

For the next month a curfew was imposed throughout the West Bank. When it was lifted, the Khatibs went to Beit Iba, the village where Ghassan was born, to make sure no one in their extended family had been hurt. On the way, Ghassan had his first real glimpse of the scars of war. "We passed through a valley which had been a battlefield, and we saw several bodies of Jordanian soldiers hanged on the trees, burned bodies, burned trees. That was quite a shocking scene for me at that age," he recalls. In Beit Iba, Ghassan had his first close-up glimpse of Israeli troops. They would regularly impose local curfews, ordering everyone over sixteen to the schoolyard so house-to-house searches could be conducted for secret arsenals of weapons. Almost the entire village of 2000 adults had to congregate at the Beit Iba school. "I was awakened in the middle of the night by the Israeli loudspeakers. I was there with my younger sister and my elderly aunt. I was underage so I remained at home. We were really scared. We didn't know what to expect. At about ten o'clock soldiers came, entered the house, and ordered me to stand facing the wall while they searched everywhere. Of course, they found nothing," says Ghassan.

When the family returned to Nablus, his uncle encouraged the teenager to join a group of other youngsters going from house to house collecting food and money to give to hospitalized victims of the bombing and to the homeless Palestinians who had streamed north from western parts of the newly occupied territory and were living in makeshift refugee centers. "My first personal, direct exposure to Israeli soldiers came a few months later," says Ghassan, when he joined an impromptu protest rally on the main street of Nablus. "I was chased by the soldiers for no reason. They caught me and started to beat me up. I was taken to a hospital, and then they brought me home," he says. Fatima was furious and warned Ghassan to stay away from such demonstrations, because even though he was only thirteen, he had responsibility for the rest of the family. "My mother did her best to prevent me from becoming involved in political life," says Ghassan. He tried his best to obey her and did manage to stay out of trouble. But like most youngsters, the more his mother lectured him on the dangers of becoming politically active, the more attractive it appeared to him.

By the time Ghassan turned sixteen, he was ignoring his mother's advice and was distributing anti-Israeli leaflets and participating in demonstrations. "The source of the attraction was student life," he says. "There were some communist activists in the school. The communists were strong among the workers and among the lower classes. I was approached by these activists," says Ghassan, "and I got involved. I was attracted to the political line rather than the [Marxist] ideology." After the Israeli occupation, the Communist Party of the West Bank had separated from its parent organization in Amman because the Jordanian party was pressing for reunification of the West Bank with the Hashemite kingdom. Many members of the Jordanian Communist Party, however, had remained on the West Bank and went underground to forge ties with their comrades in the Gaza Strip.

By the early 1970s, in the wake of the Black September massacre of thousands of Palestinians in Jordan and their mass migration to Lebanon, the rivalry between pro-Jordanian and nationalist-minded Palestinians in the West Bank was becoming intense. It was reflected in the editorial policies of Palestinian newspapers: the Jerusalem daily *al-Quds* parroted a pro-Jordanian line, while *al-Fajr* promoted *Fatah* and the mainstream PLO. The governing Labor Party in Israel also was flirting with the so-called "Jordanian option," a plan for eventually returning jurisdiction over the Palestinians to Jordan, provided the Hashemite kingdom agreed to territorial modifications in the pre-1967 borders and, of course, to establish diplomatic relations with the Jewish state. King Hussein, meanwhile, was advancing his own proposal to establish a United Arab Kingdom that would reunify the two banks of the Jordan after an eventual Israeli withdrawal from the West Bank and Gaza. To the vanquished PLO in its offices on the Beirut waterfront, these machinations looked suspiciously like an Israeli-Jordanian plot to deprive the Palestinians of their right to a homeland.

Despite generous economic stipends from Amman, West Bank Palestinians were turning actively against King Hussein, partly because of his repression of the PLO and partly because Yasser Arafat was beginning to emerge as a significant political force in the international arena. Inside Israel, Moshe Dayan's "open bridges" policy, which permitted Palestinian institutions to function with a minimum of interference, in hopes that Jordan would continue to play a role in administering them, was wearing thin. Facing new terrorist threats in the wake of the massacre of eleven Israeli athletes at the Munich Olympics, the civil administration clamped down on all aspects of Palestinian life, increasing censorship of school textbooks and newspapers, and tightening control over everything, from health to local government to refugees. Meanwhile, more and more Palestinians were being deported for political reasons. By 1973, even before the October Yom Kippur war, all of these trends were converging to create a strong new sense of Palestinian nationalism and a growing animosity toward the traditional pro-Jordanian elites.

The first manifestation of this new Palestinian attitude surfaced in the summer of 1973 when more than 100 prominent figures from the entire political spectrum on the West Bank and Gaza Strip sent two memoranda to the United Nations. They condemned the Israeli occupation and demanded "the right to self-determination and to sovereignty on their own land for the inhabitants of the West Bank and Gaza Strip." The message for the PLO in Beirut was unmistakable: from now on it had better take the views of Palestinian insiders to heart. The priority of the outsiders should be on ending the occupation and finding some sort of accommodation with Israel that would lead to a separate ministate for the Palestinians. The Communist Party had played a leading role in organizing the insiders; and in August 1973 the PLO was forced to acquiesce in the creation of the first internal organization that was formed as a political base for a future Palestinian state. It was called the Palestine National Front and was formed by a coalition that included the communists, the PFLP, the DFLP, and *Saiqa*, the party of pro-Syrian Palestinian Ba'thists. The National Front declared itself "an inseparable part of the Palestinian national movement represented in the Palestine Liberation Organization." Its creation coincided with a new proposal made by the DFLP's Marxist leader, Nayef Hawatmeh. Achieving the liberation of all of Palestine was "not realistic in terms of the present balance of forces," he said. The PLO therefore should concentrate on "the art of the possible," meaning the more attainable goal of compelling Israel to withdraw from the West Bank and Gaza Strip so that a new "national authority" could be set up in any part of the territories that were "liberated."

Although they quickly declared the National Front illegal, some Israeli officials were arguing that it should be tolerated. They contended that the communist-led group eventually could become a rival to the outside PLO leadership. "There was a strong open debate about this in the PFLP and Communist Party magazines in which the left tried to persuade *Fatah* to let them open an inside leadership," says one senior Israeli official. "They said don't be afraid of this. They are only going to run the day-to-day struggle. They are not going to be the full-scale leadership of the PLO. We wanted it," he says. "*Fatah* did not." Why? he asked rhetorically. "Because *Fatah* always had this unconscious fear that if they let such a small group run the day-to-day life, it will develop over time into a substitute leadership. Their second fear was that since most of the activists who comprised the inside command were the left and not *Fatah*, they were afraid they would gain the upper hand in the very delicate balance between *Fatah* and the left in the day-to-day struggle."

If Israeli attitudes were initially tolerant toward the National Front, they changed dramatically after the October 1973 war. The war was perceived throughout the Arab world as an Arab victory, the first by any Arab nation over Israel. "The Arabs," recalls this official, "were euphoric." They told themselves, he says, "We can beat Israel. Israel has lost its confidence." Inside the territories this mood translated into a new assertiveness, a belief that the Jewish state could finally be forced on the defensive. The National Front was the ideal vehicle to organize the new campaign. The Israeli security services even had their own internal jargon for the activists. They called them *"Khalapniks,"* an acronym formed from the Hebrew for "Palestine National Front"—*Hazit Leumit Falastinit.* "At the beginning they said, 'Let's organize riots,' what I call 'soft violence'— stonings, strikes, protests in the streets," says the Israeli official. "The problem was that our security services noticed very quickly that this was deteriorating into something much more violent: the armed branch of the National Front. You could see how the security services started to deport them, one after another. We deported all of the *Khalapniks*," he boasts, "the biggest sharks to Jordan." Meanwhile, hundreds of Palestinian sympathizers were arrested and detained, including Ghassan Khatib. But the attempt to crush the PNF only inflamed nationalist sentiments, leading to even harsher repressive measures by the Israelis.

It was Bashir Barghouti, a fifty-year-old Palestinian Marxist from the village of Deir-Ghassana, near Ramallah, who rescued the party from near oblivion. Barghouti had spent years imprisoned in a desert detention camp in Jordan after the Communist Party was outlawed by King Hussein. He did not return to Ramallah until 1974. In their book *Intifada*, Ze'ev Schiff and Ehud Ya'ari describe him as a "chain-smoking, balding man" with "an exceptionally keen mind and sharp pen" who devoted most of his time to editing his East Jerusalem weekly newspaper, *a-Tali'ah* ("The Vanguard"). Under Barghouti's guidance, note these authors, the Communist Party "returned to its traditional philosophy, disassociating itself from terrorism and accentuating the principle that had always distinguished [it] from other Palestinian organizations: recognition of the state of Israel within its 1967 borders. These two tenets were drummed into the comrades at cell meetings and through the clandestine organ *al-Watan* ('The Homeland')." A high-ranking Israeli official describes Bashir Barghouti, who is in his sixties and still very influential, as "the communist Godfather, the Haidar Abdul Shafi of the West Bank."

In June 1974 the *Fatah*-led Palestine National Council (PNC), meeting in Cairo, put its imprimatur on the more pragmatic political strategy being urged on Arafat by the DFLP's Hawatmeh and by both Haidar Abdul Shafi and Bashir Barghouti. Although the governing Palestinian body repeated its aim to establish a democratic secular state in all of Palestine, the parliament-in-exile also called for the establishment of a "people's national, independent, and fighting authority on every part of Palestinian land that is liberated." The PLO move was partly intended to preempt efforts by King Hussein, who was trying to coax Henry Kissinger, the shuttling U.S. Secretary of State, to follow up his Egyptian-Israeli troop disengagement accords in the Sinai with a dramatic West Bank deal between Israel and Jordan. Had Kissinger's appetite been whetted—which it was not—such a pact would have guaranteed Israel its security in return for a partial withdrawal that allowed Jordan to regain its influence in the West Bank. The PLO wanted to serve notice that if Israel withdrew from any part of the West Bank, the Palestinians—and not the Jordanians—would claim exclusive sovereignty in that "liberated" area and the right to establish a state. The historic PNC decision, which was intended as a signal that the PLO was embracing a political rather than a military strategy, failed to impress the Israeli government, which denounced the move as a mere tactical shift toward a piecemeal strategy of destroying the Jewish state in stages. The PNC move also was denounced by George Habash, who saw it as a step toward the ultimate acceptance of a Palestinian ministate in the West Bank and Gaza Strip. By the end of September Habash's PFLP had withdrawn from the executive committee of the PLO and formed a "Front for the Rejection of Capitulationist Solutions."

Ghassan Khatib was arrested on May 4, 1974, and charged with being a member of an underground armed cell. Several friends of his had also been arrested, and he suspects they may have mentioned his name to the Israelis. "It is not always easy to know what led them to arrest me," he says. "They thought there were some hidden weapons that I knew about," he adds. For forty days Ghassan was kept in solitary confinement, interrogated almost hourly about the alleged whereabouts of these weapons. "I experienced all kinds of different tortures, to the extent that they broke my jaw by beating me with their fists," he says. "They used to ask me to take off all my clothes, and sometimes they put me under a cold shower, and after that they starting whipping me with a thin, plastic water pipe." Ghassan eventually confessed to membership in the National Front and also to having been trained in the use of weapons and explosives. But he steadfastly denied he had ever been involved in any terrorist or violent activities. That made little difference to the Israeli authorities, who sentenced him to serve five years in the Nablus central prison.

Ghassan is philosophic about his experience. "It gave me a lesson in suffering," he says. But it also created a sense of community, which he acknowledges he had not felt before, with hundreds of Palestinians who had been far more involved in the underground struggle than he. The political affiliations of the 600 inmates mirrored the diversity of Palestinian political thought in the society at large. Among the activists were supporters of *Fatah*, the PFLP, the National Front, the DFLP, and even some of the smaller groups, including *Saiqa*, the pro-Syrian Ba'thist faction, and Ahmed Jibril's splinter group, the Damascus-based PFLP-General Command.

The Israeli jailers, says Ghassan, are tough and humiliating, so, whether they intend to or not, "that consolidates the hatred on our side towards them." He says he will never forget the prison guard who forced one of the Palestinian leaders in the prison to lie down and, putting his foot on his neck, loudly proclaimed that "your parents and your grandparents were servants to us in this land of Israel and you will also continue to be our servants!" Instead of deterring Palestinians from becoming involved in fighting the occupation, prison creates a camaraderie, he says, forging bonds that become almost as important as the family ties that bind these teenagers in their earlier years. "It was a place with the most intense social experience you could imagine," says Ghassan. "You are living, day and night, with a huge number of people, all of whom are from different places and who are of different ages and different classes." Because the Israelis try to discourage prisoners from fraternizing with each other, they constantly move them around, which, of course, means that by the time someone like Ghassan has completed his lengthy sentence, he would know virtually everyone. In the final two years of his term, the twenty-one-year-old Palestinian was chosen to represent the prisoners in negotiations with the Israeli administrators. Whenever there was a general strike, it was Ghassan who helped to relay the prisoners' demands and find a compromise. He also served on the coordination committee in charge of "organizing the life of the prisoners," arranging cultural activities for them and helping to resolve disputes between individuals and factions inside the prison. "It was a very, very rich experience," he says. "If I had not had this experience, I doubt very much if I would have been involved in political life."

The intellectual challenges in prison were to overcome the boredom and to outwit the Israelis. "We often split up into groups or cells and would sit together to talk about cultural, political, and organizational matters. After a little while, the Israelis would enter the room and divide us up. They kept changing the order of the rooms and of the prisoners, constantly moving us from one part of the jail to another whenever they felt a certain group had gained strength and power." Often the guards would institute a cell-to-cell search, looking for any written material that would provide information on a particular faction. Whenever they found something related to "the organizational aspects of our life," says Ghassan, it would be confiscated and the perpetrator put in solitary confinement. But the situation was mildly absurd. In a prison the size of the one in Nablus, it was fruitless to try to prevent political discussions from taking place or factions from emerging, he says. The dilemma "was inevitable for the Israelis. On the one hand, they wanted to arrest people. On the other hand, they could not prevent such a large number of prisoners from organizing. So they had to pay the price," Ghassan explains.

His thirteen-by-twenty-six-foot cell was large by comparative standards, even though he shared it with several other prisoners. They slept on the floor because there was no bed. The two windows were barred but they were not covered; neither was the door. And in winter it was sometimes brutally cold. The cement floor, says Ghassan, was good for his back, but the constant chill made him feel "as if you were sleeping on the street." Each inmate was given five blankets in summer and six in winter. Ghassan would put two or three under his body to serve as a mattress and tuck himself in with the others. At six o'clock every morning the guards paced up and down the corridors, shouting at the prisoners to wake up and rattling their keys along the cold metal doors. In the next thirty minutes they were expected to get dressed, to fold up their blankets neatly, and to stand at attention to be counted by the prison authorities. At precisely 6:30 the central radio would carry the Israeli news in Arabic over the prison loudspeakers and breakfast would be brought to them in their cells. Afterward, "we waited our turn for the twenty minutes which we were allowed to go out into the sun." This part of the daily routine was almost surreal, he says. "Everyone keeps walking in a circle, so all you see are prisoners from all different rooms walking around," he says.

The next three or four hours were spent reading or talking with the other prisoners in their cells. At ten o'clock was another roll call, the second of five each day; and at one o'clock lunch was brought to them and they were counted again. After lunch Ghassan usually took a nap or read. At four o'clock was yet another roll call. But the next three hours, from four to seven o'clock, became the most treasured time of all. This was, says Ghassan, "a very vital part of the day" because it was the only time when the inmates were permitted to socialize. One day someone would present a book report. The next day there would be an open discussion of some issue pertaining to the occupation, or someone would entertain by playing a musical instrument or singing for the other prisoners. This was their only chance to read a newspaper. The Israelis gave each cell one copy of *al-Anbaa* ("The News"). It was, says Ghassan, "the government line, in Arabic." Each day he would pick out the important items and read them aloud to his cellmates. "During this period we also got the last meal of the day," which consisted of soup, an egg, and hummus, he says. "We didn't eat it, because if we ate it at four or five o'clock then we would feel very hungry later. So we kept it until seven or eight and then we ate it," he says.

When he finally emerged from prison, a year before his term had expired, Ghassan was eager to rejoin his Communist Party colleagues. "Most Palestinian youngsters who are released from prison get involved in political activities," he says. For Ghassan, his prison experience was the most valuable school he ever attended. "I learned most of the things I know in my life during those four years," he says. The world he rejoined in 1977 was different from the one he had left four years earlier. During his imprisonment, the Israeli government had waged a new battle to win over the Palestinian public. In October 1975 Defense Minister Shimon Peres introduced a "civil administration" plan that promised greater authority to the local municipalities, including naming Palestinians to run administrative offices. The Peres plan envisaged turning over virtually all authority over civilian matters to the mayors and other officials of the towns and villages in the occupied territories. The initial reaction was overwhelmingly hostile. "The very idea of 'autonomy' in the occupied territories," charged Hikmat Masri, the former mayor of Nablus, "is an insult to the dignity of the Palestinian people, and we refuse it with all our strength."

To implement the plan to turn over even limited powers to the Palestinians, the Israeli government had to organize municipal elections. For the first time the PLO decided that the National Front should field candidates, mainly to demonstrate its strength inside the territories and to deprive the pro-Jordanian merchants and notables, whom Peres saw as his tacit allies, of positions of authority. The April 1976 election consequently became a contest between the PLO surrogates, who campaigned under the nationalist slogan "No to Civil Administration. Yes to the National Front," and the hand-picked Israeli candidates, who owed their loyalties to the Hashemite kingdom of Jordan. When the votes were counted, the pro-PLO nationalists had won a convincing victory, seizing control in Hebron, Beit Jala, Nablus, Ramallah, al-Bireh, Tulkarm, Beit Sahour, and Jericho. The PLO victory was so complete that over the next several years the Israeli government gradually sought to undermine their authority.

Many of these newly elected Palestinians were deported but that only added to the reputation of the National Front, which in Palestinian eyes was beginning to assume almost mystical proportions. "They refused to accept that it does not exist anymore," one surprised Israeli official recalls. "I was in the civil administration of the interim government in 1977," he says, "and I remember reading every week in *al-Hadaf*, the DFLP magazine, how we have a body in the territories called the National Front. I went to my boss and said, 'What's going on here?' He said, 'I don't know. They

ceased their activities a long time ago.' " After a secret investiga-
tion by the security services, the Israelis concluded that the communists and their DFLP and PFLP allies had indeed tried to renew
their activity. "They had already taken the first steps to revive the
Khalap (the National Front)," says a senior security source. "Then
we discovered it was only the intention of the leftists. *Fatah* did
not agree to it, and there was no *Khalap*," he adds. But by the
end of 1978 the leftists had again proved their determination to
carry the nationalist banner for the insiders. They created a new
organization, the National Guidance Committee, to oppose the
Israeli-Egyptian Camp David Accords, which they believed would
deprive the Palestinians of the right to self-determination by
imposing an even more limited version of the Peres autonomy plan
on the West Bank and Gaza Strip.

One of the founders of the committee was Ibrahim Dakak,
a respected Palestinian architect and civil engineer. Prior to the
October 1 creation of the National Guidance Committee at a secret
meeting in the labor union building in Beit Hanina, Dakak had
helped convene a Communist Party gathering that published a
position paper demanding the establishment of an independent
Palestinian state in the West Bank and Gaza Strip within the June
4, 1967, borders. That position was formally adopted on
September 27, 1978, when, at a large gathering of Palestinian
nationalists in Jerusalem, a proclamation was issued that "a stable
peace cannot be achieved in this area without the consolidation
of Palestinian-Arab sovereignty over Jerusalem, the West Bank, and
the Gaza Strip under the leadership of the PLO, the sole legitimate
representative of the Palestinian people."

Despite the nod to the PLO, another bold step had been taken
by the insiders to serve notice that they demanded at least an equal
say in controlling their fate. Support for the National Guidance
Committee was demonstrated when, soon after its founding, 3000
people, including traditional pro-Jordanian elites such as Hikmat
Masri, rallied in Nablus against the proposed Camp David Accords.
Evident in the crowd were hundreds of homemade Palestinian
flags, a portentous sign that the Israelis would not be able to contain the nationalist aspirations of the Palestinians, which a decade
later would explode in the *intifada*.

The committee did not survive for long. Three of its

members—Mayors Basam Shak'a of Nablus, Karim Khalaf of Ramallah, and Ibrahim Tawil of al-Bireh—were the targets of a 1980 assassination attempt by militant underground Israeli settlers, among them the son-in-law of fundamentalist Rabbi Moshe Levinger and his wife, Miriam. Shak'a and Khalaf were seriously wounded and had to have their legs amputated. Two other members, Fahd Kawasme, the mayor of Hebron, and Muhammed Milhem, the mayor of Halhul, were deported to Jordan. Other leaders, including Ibrahim Dakak, were placed under house arrest. Once again the Israelis had managed to suppress a legitimate nationalist organization and to remove the immediate threat to their security. But the price for maintaining the military and civilian occupation of an increasingly restive and desperate population would continue to grow until the unremitting violence of the Palestinian uprising became the only answer to Israeli domination.

In 1977 Ghassan Khatib returned to Birzeit University to continue his studies. These were interrupted when he participated in the December 1979 demonstration near the school, suffered three broken ribs, and was sentenced to six months in prison. Says Ghassan, "You cannot imagine the brutalities that I witnessed at Birzeit. They killed several students while I was there. They even beat up Gabi Baramki, the president of the university, on the stairs to his office." He graduated with a bachelor of arts degree in 1982.

In 1983 Ghassan was admitted to Manchester University in England to pursue a master's degree in developmental economics. He still remembers his excitement when he received the news. "After four years of imprisonment and five years at Birzeit University, it was the first time in my life I was able to leave the country," he says. "I wasn't a child," he adds. Indeed, Ghassan was twenty-nine years old when he started graduate school. The next several years also were an eye-opener for him. Ghassan thought that everybody was familiar with the Arab-Israeli conflict and supported the rights of the Palestinians to a state on the West Bank and Gaza Strip. Instead, he discovered that he could not even introduce himself as someone from the occupied West Bank. "The typical response was 'West Bank of what?'" he recalls.

In England he discovered that the reputation of the Arabs had been badly damaged by the "rich Saudis and Kuwaitis who used to travel to Europe spending money and looking for prostitutes. I felt ashamed by their behavior," says Ghassan. If the average European did not view the Arab as a profligate playboy, he saw him as a terrorist. "I realized that there's a lot to be done to improve the image of the Palestinian people in the outside world," he says. Ghassan blames the deliberate distortions of unnamed groups responsible for spreading "hostile propaganda about us." But he also faults the Palestinians themselves, particularly "individual Palestinians outside the territories," who have tarnished their image. "I learned that we are living in a very small and weak country in the world and that we will never be able to win our independence unless the world understands our rights and our suffering. I thought we, as Palestinians, should try to establish our own reputation, our own vision, our own character and change the view of the outside world," he says. Ghassan vowed that when he returned to the occupied territories he would make it a priority to improve the image of his people. "The idea of establishing the Jerusalem Media and Communication Center (JMCC) first dawned on me when I was studying in Britain," he says.

Today the JMCC has become one of the most respected institutions in the West Bank. The center offers something more than the Western media can obtain in the almost idyllic setting of the American Colony Hotel. Staying at the former pasha's residence and meeting intellectuals from Birzeit while sitting in the hotel courtyard, with its blossoming bougainvillaea and its fish pond, leaves one with a distorted perception, with the falsely reassuring sense that things are not really that bad. In reality, however, Ghassan sees the American Colony as a haven for privileged Palestinians. He believes that for many journalists, occupation becomes something sterile, something spoken but never experienced.

He thought he could break down some of this insularity by taking the press into the field to visit refugee camps and remote villages, by writing reports in English on Israeli settlement policies, on education, on agriculture, and on a favorite preoccupation of his, regaining the rights to the valuable water resources on the West Bank. The JMCC, because it is a bridge between Palestinian society and the foreign media, has also increased Ghassan's own exposure to the Western press corps. He has earned a reputation as a knowledgeable and influential source; when Israeli Prime Minister Yitzhak Rabin announced a freeze on new settlement activity in July 1992, Ghassan was widely seen being interviewed on network television news reports.

When he is not negotiating with the Israelis, visiting remote Palestinian villages to speak on behalf of the peace process, or working with groups such as Peace Now to end the violence, Ghassan teaches at Birzeit and is the head of the United Agricultural Company, a nonprofit organization. This last receives aid from the European Economic Community (EEC), providing loans to small farmers to help them market their produce abroad, including potatoes, tomatoes, cucumbers, fruit, and green peppers "mainly from the Jordan Valley," he says. Although the company is only four years old, Ghassan says, it already has working capital of $1.5 million. "It was only recently that we were allowed to export directly to the EEC countries. Geographically we go through Israel; it is direct in the sense that we used to go through Israeli companies, but for the first time we are now allowed to export directly without going through an Israeli agent," he says.

Though hardly a front-page news story, it was nonetheless a breakthrough of sizeable proportions for the Palestinians. For the first time an official agreement was signed by an organization of Palestinian exporters from the territories and a group of recognized states, the European Economic Community. The next problem was how to get the produce to market. Israel had always insisted that all produce from the occupied territories be exported through AGREXCO, the official Israeli governmental organization for exporting agricultural goods. "We already have the infrastructure, the trucks and planes and ships. Use our facilities and export under our name," the Israelis said. "We will protect you from a failure." They added this warning: "If you refuse to work with us, you will fall flat on your face!" The Palestinians replied, "Let us try." The ensuing months saw extensive negotiations over how the crates of West Bank goods would be marked. Would they say "Produce of the State of Palestine," or "Produce of the West Bank—Israel," or "Produce of the West Bank—Palestine"? Eventually a compromise was reached: the crates were labeled "Produce of the West Bank." Says *Ha'aretz* correspondent Ori Nir, "It was an important victory for the Palestinians. It gave them a kind of independent status."

But it was also a breakthrough for Ghassan Khatib, for his model of future economic independence, the kind of step that will help prove that a Palestinian state on the West Bank and Gaza Strip can be a viable economic entity and perhaps even usher in a new era of Israeli-Palestinian-Jordanian cooperation. After all, the produce marketed through loans from the United Agricultural Company is grown on land that once belonged to Jordan; the company is Palestinian owned; and the Israelis permit the produce to be shipped to Europe through their ports in the Mediterranean. To Ghassan, it is precisely this kind of pragmatism, this reaching across a seemingly impossible divide, that will eventually enable the Palestinians to become self-sufficient. "In the modern age, natural resources and all the other traditional aspects of wealth are no longer the things one should rely on," he says. "Today economies depend on human resources and capital. I believe we have the human resources, and there is potential capital." He cautions against expecting miracles overnight from the negotiating process. "It will be difficult and it will take time," he says. "But I think it is possible now. We are not suggesting a peace that should take place immediately. We are suggesting transitional phases that aim first at creating confidence and second at testing each other. We will take one step at a time. And whenever we are convinced that the other side is really serious, we will take another step. That is the kind of education and understanding that is worth building on."

Radwan Abu Ayash

███████████

If Hollywood were casting a homegrown Yasser Arafat, forty-two-year-old Radwan Abu Ayash would come close to fitting the part. Like the small-framed Arafat, Radwan is short (though slighter) and bearded (though his beard is neater and trimmer than the guerrilla chieftain's three-day stubble); the dark-skinned Radwan also has a mustache, albeit a bushier one, and similarly piercing eyes. Radwan's eyes, however, are never menacing. They give off a glint of mischief. Both men are scrappy and street smart, zealous in their passion for the plight of their people, and both derive their influence from the ordinary Palestinian, who was forced to flee his home when the state of Israel was created.

Radwan, too, is the archetypical refugee, born in a tent in the Askar refugee camp in Nablus in 1950. But his is the first generation of the Ayash family born poor. His grandparents fled from their home in Jammassin, a well-to-do village that has become a wealthy suburb, Ramat Aviv, north of Tel Aviv. Real estate there today sells for nearly a million dollars a *dunam* (one-quarter of an acre). Abdullah and Naif, his grandfather and grandmother, owned fifty dunams, "almost one-third of the village," says Radwan. They also owned hundreds of orange orchards, pastures where their livestock (horses and cows) used to graze, and—the most valuable natural resource of all—underground natural springs.

When his mother, Aisha, along with her husband, Ibrahim, fled the fighting of the 1948 war, she must have known they would never return. Aisha camouflaged hundreds of pieces of gold in her clothing, says Radwan. She used them sparingly after that, only when her husband or one of her nine children needed medical attention or there was not enough food to feed the family. Radwan says his mother wanted him to know his ancestors had been prosperous. "My mother was very rich. She used to tell me she would hold many pieces of gold in both her hands. When I was fourteen years old she spent the last piece."

Like Arafat, Radwan also is an activist, a street fighter whose troops are the teenagers that make up the bulk of the pro-*Fatah* squadrons of stone-throwing youngsters, the *shabiba*. He regularly visits the refugee camps and the wounded in the West Bank hospitals and has used his considerable power as a journalist to arouse—the Israelis would say enflame—Palestinian emotions. Like so many others, he has served time in prison—a month in 1982, six months in 1987 when he was arrested on the eve of the *intifada*, and five more months during the 1991 Gulf War. But, says an Israeli official, he is far too clever to carry out any acts of violence himself.

Radwan does not deny having covertly channeled PLO money into the territories. Nor does he deny having met secretly with Arafat while abroad. He even acknowledges that he has his own clandestine, underground squadrons in the West Bank, and he is obviously proud of his access to Arafat. When the PLO leader's plane went down in the Libyan desert, he says, he was the one who got the telephone call at 3:30 in the morning informing the *Fatah* leadership on the West Bank of the emergency. "I was the one who told Faisal [Husseini]," boasts Radwan. "I can get directly to him [Arafat] without referring to other 'consultants,' " he adds of his unusual access. "His closeness to me is because of my power in the street. He knows I can do a lot in the street. I can make an army of youngsters."

But, like Arafat, Radwan Abu Ayash also has enemies. They charge that he shares one trait in particular with the PLO leader: corruption. They contend he has diverted thousands of dollars to his personal use and point to his frequent trips to Rome and Paris and London. They say he drives an expensive General Motors car, a white Opel, and that he is a heavy drinker, an odious taboo in these days of heady Muslim fundamentalism. They also charge he is too close to the Israelis. But the most recent and devastating charge of all is that Radwan Abu Ayash is building a new house, not an ordinary house but a luxurious villa in the foothills above Ramallah—with a pool. Not long ago, he relates, a woman even approached his wife Salma and said, "We hear you have a pool in your house." Taken aback, Salma asked, "In what house? Is my husband building a house without my knowledge? Would you show it to me? We can go and move there instead of being squeezed into our tiny apartment!"

Their two-bedroom flat, one of seventy-seven apartments in a complex on Radio Road in Ramallah, is so small and cramped that their fourteen-year-old son, Shadi, must sleep on a sofa in the living room. "There is no space for a dining room," he says. The family eats at a small table squeezed into a narrow hallway. He and his wife share one bedroom, while their three daughters, eighteen-year-old Suna, twelve-year-old Samoud, and six-year-old Sheda, all sleep in the other bedroom. Shadi was hurt recently, says Radwan, when a shelf of books fell on him in the middle of the night. "Tomorrow, if I die, my children will be in big trouble," because for two years, he says, he has not paid the monthly rent of 100 Jordanian dinars (about $150). He notes that other Palestinian leaders have villas. They can relax at home. "I have no home," says Radwan. He adds: "I do not have anything that belongs to me except my children and my faith and my belief in what I am doing."

The constant rumors, Radwan says, of the charges of corruption, spending sprees, and high living, "are part of the war to discredit me." His opponents, he says, could not find "any door in politics through which to attack me, because I am a reasonable and pragmatic person. So they began to spread rumors. If I go to a restaurant and I eat food and I have any kind of drink—'He's a drunkard!' They are intending to take from me the most important value which I have: [the reputation] that this man is the friend of the poor, of this social class."

Ever since he was a young boy, Radwan Abu Ayash has eked out a living. "I started to work when I was nine years old," he says. During school breaks he sold watermelons and hauled rationed food from the U.N. Relief and Works Agency (UNRWA) trucks to the mud and concrete huts of the Askar camp. "I was hoping for a tip of half a piaster to have some money for a shirt or a pair of trousers or to prepare my books for the next year," he recalls. But "even these little pennies my father was not able to save for me." He remembers wading barefoot through pools of mud in melted snow; walking five miles to school and watching, hungry, while others munched a sandwich. His parents sent him to Jahez High School in Nablus, which seemed a world away from the impoverished refugee camp. Even though it was only a few miles from home, every day he passed lush palm trees lining the streets and saw fresh produce in the stores. At school he had an intellectual feast reading all the new books.

Had it not been for the Six-Day War, Radwan would have been able to enroll in one of the West Bank universities. But they were closed after the war, and traveling abroad was too expensive. So after completing secondary school in Nablus, eighteen-year-old Radwan enrolled in the Men's Teacher Training College in Ramallah, an UNRWA institution that the Israelis claim is a "training ground for agitators." In 1969 he was elected the student leader of his school, and a year later he graduated with a diploma that enabled him to begin teaching English at the Silwad Secondary School for boys. His students, he says with a laugh, were almost as old as he was. That taught him the importance of education. But it also opened his eyes, he says, to the propaganda potions that Arab leaders had been using to drug the Palestinian people.

Radwan remembers the hot summer day in June 1967 when foreign tanks rolled through Nablus. He was seventeen, yet he could barely catch his breath as he raced from the refugee camp to the main road. He stopped at the fence of the Jordanian army's stables to watch the troops moving from the mountains of the Jordan Valley toward the old Arab town of 50,000. All around him people were running and rejoicing, and he joined in the celebration, singing and dancing for the soldiers, who he thought had come to liberate Palestine.

No one knew which Arab country the army was from—was it Iraq? Algeria? Morocco? What did it matter. Radwan was puzzled, too, when he caught a glimpse of a blue-and-white flag painted on the cannons. No Arab country he knew of had such a flag, but he would check his atlas just to make sure. He ran home to Askar and took down the reference book, but nothing in its colorful pages resembled what he had seen. Then suddenly he knew: this was not the army of an Arab nation that had come to free them;

this was the army of their enemy, Israel. In the background he could hear voices blaring through loudspeakers, enemy voices telling the people to raise up white flags on their houses; within minutes Askar would become a sea of white. For the first few days of the Israeli occupation Radwan moved only infear, terrified as Isaeli air force planes buzzed Nablus, dropping pamphlets from the sky. On one afternoon, the planes flew so low that the noise of the engines cracked the walls of the concrete huts. Radwan yelled at his younger brother, Adnan, to come with him and hide under a tree; better to die outdoors, he thought, than to be inside.

As the week progressed, Radwan became angry, first at the Israelis for their conquest, then at the Arabs for his lack of education. Why should I be so ignorant? he thought. Why have I not learned about this powerful country, Israel? In his school, Israel was not to be mentioned. In his Arab books, the Israelis were a small bunch of gangsters whom a few Palestinian youths could put in a boat and push out to sea. Every day he heard the platitudes of Jordan's King Hussein. He watched the Israeli army and compared it with the Jordanians. How different these working Israeli soldiers were from the showy Jordanian horsemen with their shiny shoes and their circus acrobatics! "The Israeli generals did not care about twinkling boots. They cared about how to get things done. They didn't care about appearances; they had their shirtsleeves rolled up and they were working," says Radwan. He was disillusioned with Arab rulers. "I began to discover they had built walls in my mind, and every wall was falling. We should get rid of all these bloody slogans, which were like morphine given to us by the Arab leaders. We had to have an open mind."

For the next several years, Radwan taught the youngsters of Ramallah, becoming exposed for the first time to families who had somehow been able to maintain their wealth. He learned Hebrew and developed a following among the teenagers, who would come to him for advice and moral support.

In 1970 Radwan met a girl; after courting her for more than two years he decided, at age twenty-two, that he wanted to marry her. She was the daughter of a well-to-do physician, the scion of an illustrious family, a family of Palestinian notables. Even though Radwan had proposed to her and she had accepted, Arab tradition called for his father and mother to formally ask her parents for her hand in marriage. Until they accepted his proposal, Radwan could not be seen with her in public. "Even after you are engaged, you are not allowed to be alone," he explains.

When he summoned up the courage, he asked his parents, Aisha and Ibrahim, to go to Ramallah to ask for her hand. Radwan remembers his mother's words as if it were yesterday. "They are from a different social class. You shouldn't do that," she admonished. She reminded Radwan of the Arab proverb "*Min tinat biladak lutt khudadak*," which means, he says, "Only put the mud of your own land on your cheeks!" When he protested, his mother cited a more familiar proverb: "Once you make your bed, you have to sleep in it!" Radwan said: "Mother, I want you to go there." She finally agreed but she told him, "I am afraid you will not be able to invite me to your wedding party. Those people have different rules. They will be ashamed to see a woman from my class. I will not come!" She went to Ramallah and was told by the girl's parents that they would consider the offer. "They did not say no on the spot. They said, 'Okay, we'll give you an answer later.' This meant goodbye," says Radwan, still feeling some pain in recounting the story. "My mother went there and she was rejected," he says. "The reason was because I am a refugee."

His fiancée was equally upset. "She wanted to marry me. She told me I should come for her and we would get engaged anyway. She offered to run away with me. But I said no," recalls Radwan. He has never forgotten the incident. "It was one of the points in my life when I discovered that with a liberation struggle or without a liberation struggle, the classes are there." He points to the selection of delegates for the negotiating teams with Israel. "Regardless of the liberation struggle, regardless of who's who in the territories, even the delegation is composed of a tribal balance." Adds Radwan, "We need a social revolution."

In the years that followed, Radwan mixed teaching and writing and, in the manner of everything Palestinian, interlaced them both with politics. When asked when he became politically active, he replies, "I joined journalism in 1975." That was the year he began to work as a translator for *As-Sha'ab*, a pro-PLO daily and the third-largest newspaper in the West Bank and Gaza; like all Palestinian newspapers, *As-Sha'ab* was censored by the Israelis whenever articles were deemed incitement to violence. In 1976, as the chairman of the General Teachers Committee at Al-Bireh Secondary School, Radwan organized the first teachers' strike in the occupied territories.

It was not only the Israelis who found his work threatening, however. Radwan's outspokenness frequently put him in trouble with the Jordanians. After the PLO split with Jordan in 1976, Radwan openly criticized King Hussein. The Jordanians responded by placing his name on their blacklist, and for the next three years prohibited him from crossing the Allenby Bridge into the Hashemite kingdom. Today, as a sign of his new influence, Radwan shows off his green Jordanian passport with the handwritten inscription from the Jordanian prime minister, noting that the document replaces one stolen with his wallet in New York.

In the late 1970s Radwan took additional courses at Birzeit, the leading university on the West Bank, hoping to obtain his bachelor of arts degree. But he never graduated. He was too busy as an activist. He began organizing groups in the *shabiba*, the pro-*Fatah* youth clubs formed for Palestinian social work and anti-Israeli agitation. By now his Hebrew was good enough that he could earn some extra money as a translator. He translated *The Breakthrough*, a book by Moshe Dayan about the Israeli general's role in helping to negotiate the 1979 Egyptian-Israeli peace treaty, as well as a bitterly anti-Israeli work entitled *Spy Masters in Israel*. Radwan also wrote several books of his own, including *Violin Melodies*, a collection of poems, and began writing a daily column for *As-Sha'ab*.

In 1979, after completing several months of courses at the Arab Beirut University, where he met Yasser Arafat for the first time, Radwan left his teaching career to become a full-time journalist in the West Bank, cofounding a new union, the Arab Journalists Association. His subsequent work with the Palestine Press Service, a pro-PLO wire service founded by Raymonda Tawil and her husband, Ibrahim Kara'in, and his work for *Al-Awdah*, a weekly news magazine published by the press service, allowed him to strengthen his leadership role among the *shabiba*. In 1982 Radwan was imprisoned for the first time, for publishing a booklet protesting the censorship practices of the Israeli civil administration. He spent less than a month in jail, but the incident came to the attention of Yasser Arafat, who sent him a note congratulating his

Beirut compatriot for taking such a courageous stand against the occupation.

In August 1982 Radwan ran as a candidate for the governing board of the Arab Journalists Association in the first elections ever held by the organization. He received more votes than the Palestinian who was elected president, but agreed to serve as the head of the public relations committee.

The press club was by far the most powerful organization of its kind in the occupied territories. Among other things, it served as a liaison with the foreign press, to whom Radwan would regularly feed stories. In one instance in 1985, when a Palestinian was found dead in the fields of Beit Horon, Radwan created a smooth news campaign that found its way into major publications in several countries. The story, he told the foreign journalists, was that the man had been inspecting some land that an Arab "collaborator" had sold to the Jews and that the Palestinian had been killed in the field by Jewish settlers. But Israeli agents later learned the story hardly conformed to reality. The Palestinian, it turns out, had been part of a complex network smuggling weapons into the West Bank. The explosives had been carried into the country by one man, then hidden in the field by someone else; when a third man had gone to find them at the drop point, he had been blown to bits: a Russian F-1 hand grenade had exploded in his hand.

For the next three years, Radwan used *Al-Awdah* to promote the *shabiba*. "I used to have a kind of secret organization," he admits, which recruited supporters among eighteen- to twenty-two-year-olds. "I was perceived as their instructor, as the one who can give them advice and get into the schools, get into the universities, get into the camps, and get into the villages and solve their problems morally and financially." Radwan does not disguise the fact that his activities were supported by generous grants from his Palestinian friend Yasser Arafat, who had been forced to relocate his headquarters to Tunis. "Of course, I used to receive money from the PLO for my work," he says. "This meant that I was strong."

Radwan was so successful in managing the news, and was building such a loyal following among the *shabiba*, that he decided in 1985 to run against Akram Hanieh, the editor of *As-Sha'ab* and also the chairman of the Arab Journalists Association.

Radwan was unanimously elected on the first ballot and immediately set out to turn the association into a counterpart of the National Press Club in Washington, D.C. He aimed to give Palestinian correspondents the same rights and privileges that journalists enjoyed in the U.S.A., where freedom of the press was protected by the constitution. It was an ambitious goal, particularly since the Israeli Interior Ministry initially refused to even grant the association a license to accredit foreign correspondents.

But Radwan was determined. In 1986, in his new role as head of the press club, he traveled to America, where he spent a month as the guest of the United States Information Agency, an arm of the U.S. government. He visited New York City, Washington, D.C., Miami, several cities in Nebraska, and San Francisco, learning about the American media, particularly the power of television. He loved the country. But what struck him most was how little people knew or cared about the problems of his people. "They care about the latest song of Madonna, they care about their football games and their wheat. But, except for a few people, nobody cares about the Middle East."

As his second year as chairman began, Radwan was becoming more and more powerful. He became chairman of the Palestinian Coordinating Committee to the Non-Governmental Organizations (NGOs) at the United Nations, representing all the local institutions in the West Bank and Gaza at the world body. "We don't have a government, so I'm responsible for them. This is tremendous power," he says. He became active in raising funds to support the welfare of prisoners convicted of being terrorists; he organized a Teachers Association strike against the civil administration; he even helped to create a theatre group that, according to the Israelis, put on propaganda plays promulgating the use of violence.

Later in 1987 his mentor, Akram Hanieh, was charged with being the chief link to the PLO in Tunis and was deported. The quintessential pro-*Fatah* insider, Faisal Husseini, also was imprisoned. That left a gap in the PLO leadership in the West Bank and Gaza. The Israelis say that Radwan, considered at the time to be high in the hierarchy, stepped into fill the void. His alleged assignments included the channeling of money from Tunis and Europe into the territories and encouraging the *shabiba* to protest the occupation with any and all means at their disposal.

On Tuesday, December 7, 1987, on the eve of the *intifada*, Radwan Abu Ayash was arrested at his Ramallah home. He was held under administrative detention for the next six months. Israeli Housing Minister Ariel Sharon demanded his deportation. The *Jerusalem Post* quoted Israeli military sources as saying the thirty-seven-year-old Palestinian was "a senior *Fatah* activist in the West Bank and Jerusalem" who had extensive contacts with PLO activists in the region and abroad. The sources told the newspaper that his activities included "receiving instructions and funds to promote the organization's aim and to disrupt public order."

Radwan was imprisoned at Jneid, the central jail of the West Bank, in Nablus, and, he says, "a five star Intercontinental compared to the prisons [Ansar III] in the Negev." With the jail being only a mile or two from the refugee camp where he had spent his childhood, the next six months turned out to be a spiritual homecoming for the young Palestinian activist. "We had a very well-organized society; and if you compared it with the outside, you found you were in a real school of thought. It was aschool of uprising, a school of spirit, a school of hope." Adds Radwan, "We read a lot and had lessons; people who wanted to learn English or Hebrew or physics would find one of the prisoners to teach them. And we would have political discussions at night. The communications were superb. If you wanted something to be known, you hid it in a cigarette box—God, the cigarettes were awful—and passed it from cell to cell, then from ward to ward, and then it was transported by laborers from yard to yard. Within five minutes the whole prison can know anything you want. I wrote a long song about the guards watching us and our living in the sun. In a few days everybody in the prison knew the words, and they would sing it all the time."

Radwan tells of his treatment by the prison authorities: "At one point they brought me to the military judge. They accused me of being a senior activist in the PLO. They had evidence in what they call the 'secret file'—clippings from papers, writings, records of my meetings with people, public statements I had made about things like the Iran-Iraq war—but they wouldn't let me or my lawyer see it. I told the judge, 'Listen, man, for God's sake, tell me what's the charge. If you tell what's the charge, I'll accept the punishment, and when I come out I will be very dovish. Just let me know.' But he said, 'I can't tell you. This is secret.' They didn't convict me. Then after six months they came for me one night, and I thought I was going to be deported. They took me out of the cell and everybody was singing. I didn't know where I was going or what would happen. And then they told me I was free."

By May 1988, when Radwan was released, the *intifada* had gathered steam and was taking a toll on the lives of Palestinians. Foreign television networks, newspapers, and magazines had discovered the story and were flooding the West Bank and Gaza with correspondents, particularly from the United States and Europe. Israel's strict military censors were handicapped; with the invention of the satellite dish and portable video camera, a "real-time" revolution had occurred at about the same time as the uprising. The story of the daily stonings, and escalating numbers of dead and wounded in their wake, was now being beamed, virtually live, throughout the world—and the Israeli government was powerless to stop it.

Resuming his post at the press club, Radwan now sought to turn it into an instrument of the *intifada*. He obtained press cards from the International Federation of Journalists in Prague for the entire membership, which had tripled to more than 300, and began to require that foreign correspondents become accredited by the Arab Journalists Association before they could begin working in the territories. This was a direct affront to the Israelis governing the West Bank and Gaza. Israeli police minister Chaim Bar Lev filed suit against the association. "He thought we were creating our own Ministry of Information just like the Israelis, like Beit Agron," says Radwan, which, of course, he was. "They threatened to take me to court. But I challenged them. I told them I had a license from the Interior Ministry and nobody can tell me what to do or not to do." Bar Lev eventually dropped the suit.

Emboldened by his successful standoff with the Israelis, Radwan turned the club into what he concedes was "a real political body." He invited foreign dignitaries to address the club, dramatically raising its public profile and his own importance as chairman. One diplomat who came was Dutch foreign minister Hans Van Den Broek. He negotiated exchange programs with countries in Eastern Europe and scheduled regular press conferences for the foreign media. He even persuaded the Italian government to sponsor a three-month course to train twelve Palestinians in television production; a Norwegian TV station to host three camerapeople for internships; and the German Green Party and International Federation of Journalists to donate expensive photo laboratories, one of them at a cost of $80,000. "I was imitating the National Press Club in Washington," he boasts.

But the most important activity on the club's new agenda was one that Radwan orchestrated himself: making sure that foreign television crews were in place at remote towns and villages *before* the next stoning of Israeli soldiers would take place. This required careful coordination with the Unified National Command (UNC), which was running the uprising, and clockwork precision in alerting the camera crews and making sure they were in the right place at the right time. It all had to be done behind the backs of the Israelis, or Radwan would wind up back behind bars. "I discovered the Zionist movement worked a lot on the media and felt that, within my capabilities, I could do something. Deep in my consciousness I wanted to imitate them," he says, "because I believe in the word, I believe in the picture, I believe in the image, and I believe in the stereotype."

High among his priorities was uncovering Israeli human rights abuses that were taking place beyond the range of the camera lens. Radwan was aware that what he was organizing resembled more of a political action committee than a press club. But he says getting the footage of well-armed Israeli troops in their riot gear, with their helmets and plastic visors pulled over their heads, shooting at rock-throwing Palestinian youngsters, was just what the networks wanted. When the foreign camera crews could not reach the latest stoning, it was the club's responsibility to videotape the incident and provide it to them. "This was the key," says Radwan. "In order to do that, I needed courageous journalists. If the foreign press cannot reach the village, why not the village itself reach the TV through a Palestinian cameraman?"

Radwan admits that the Arab Journalists Association became so powerful it evolved into a kind of pro-*Fatah* political party, with him at its helm. "It was not perceived by the bulk of Palestinians as a labor union but as a political body. It was the most important umbrella group for political work in the territories. Therefore I said the head of this association should be a politician," he explains. In August 1987, when the bylaws called for a new leader of the press club to be elected, the governing board decided the *intifada* had made it too dangerous to convene the entire membership and asked Radwan to serve for another two-year term. He gladly accepted.

Similarly, at the end of his second two-year term, in 1989, "we couldn't convene all the journalists together" and Radwan again was asked to serve for another year. By then, however, some people were beginning to gripe that he was becoming too powerful. They would buttonhole him and remind him it was against the rules for anyone to serve more than one term, much less two terms. "Okay, because of the *intifada*, we've got you for five years," they would tell him, but now is the time to step down. That, of course, was the last thing on Radwan's mind. "I told them there are two kinds of men: some people who build up institutions and some institutions who can build men. I am from the first kind! Besides, no one has the right to tell me that it was the institution that made me an activist," he says.

Radwan says that with the *intifada* having quieted, he planned to assemble the membership for a general election in the fall of 1990—and swears that he had no intention of running—but something else intervened: war in the Persian Gulf. From the August day when Iraq invaded Kuwait, the Palestinians in the West Bank and Gaza cheered for Saddam Hussein. At first Israel tolerated their partisanship. But when Palestinians began to stand on their rooftops cheering for the Iraqi leader, the authorities began to crack down.

High on their list of alleged troublemakers was Radwan Abu Ayash. He was arrested in November 1990 and held for five months under administrative detention, sharing a cell with Palestinian journalist Ziad Abu Zayyad. The Israelis said he was "endangering the public safety and security of the state." But privately the Shin Bet warned him that if he did not stop encouraging an international letter-writing campaign on his behalf, they would throw the book at him. The Israelis, says Radwan rather proudly, warned: "We are ready to go to court, where we will give you proof that you are the head of the *intifada* leadership and gave money to the activists and are part of the Unified National Command." The threat was not an empty one. Harsh punishment would have been certain.

Radwan received another rude awakening while he was in prison. The mumblings of discontent about his continuing reluctance to schedule Arab Journalists Association elections had turned into a clamor for his resignation. Although only a tiny handful of the association's leadership was involved, the campaign was obviously organized by much more powerful figures in *Fatah* who were acting behind the scenes to dethrone him. Three or four people, says Radwan, "representing someone with real power," organized a meeting of about twenty journalists, who decided they would schedule the elections while Radwan was in Jneid. "They sent me a letter through a lawyer asking me for my opinion," he says. The final decision, they wrote, would be up to him. "That hurt me," admits Radwan. "I was angry," he adds. He instructed his lawyer to respond by telling them to go ahead and hold the elections whenever they wanted, noting with obvious sarcasm that "somebody is in jail and all you can think of is rearranging the chairs!" That shamed them and the group backed down.

Radwan was released on May 12, 1991. Israeli Prime Minister Yitzhak Shamir had deliberately refrained from freeing him until U.S. Secretary of State James A. Baker, on his third trip to Jerusalem, had completed his talks with Palestinian leaders and left the region. Nonetheless, "it was a big event when I came out," recalls Radwan, because the press corps wanted to get his reaction to the Baker talks with the Husseini-led delegation. "I said I support Faisal," recalls Radwan, even though he might have had every incentive to do otherwise.

In fact, Radwan held a joint press conference with Husseini at his home in Ramallah. He knew that if he came out against the talks, "many people would support me. I would gain more popularity in the street. But that was not reasonable," explains Radwan. "I said 'Let them go ahead and meet, because it is the only way to solve the problem.'" He even went a step beyond that. "I said we should deal with the transitional period, any transitional period that will take us to an independent Palestinian state." The French wire service, Agence France Presse, sent a bulletin to its clients, and soon his telephone was ringing off the hook.

Among the calls were several from the PLO leadership in Tunis wanting to know why he had made such a conciliatory statement. "It was as if I had started an earthquake!" recalls Radwan. "But I believe in David Ben Gurion's attitude," he explains. "Inch by inch, immigrant by immigrant, gradually things might be set up. It's important to be at the table to talk about the contents that are brought to the table. It is not important to talk about big slogans while outside the table. It's important to get engaged in something and talk about the details. The Israelis call it autonomy. We call it a transitional period. I don't care about the terms. I care about the conditions in which these things are going to be implemented."

As soon as he was released from prison, the rumor mill again began spewing out stories about Radwan's lavish lifestyle, accusing him of running the association as if it were his personal fiefdom. "They were saying 'Radwan is an individualist, he is doing whatever he wants, he is only known because of the association, he is politicizing us, he is not giving us any time for our profession'—all these excuses," says Radwan. He believes those orchestrating the campaign against him calculated that he had simply become too powerful and therefore threatened their dominance in *Fatah*. "They said to themselves, 'Let's search. The Journalists Association is one of his powerful tools.' I can appear in front of everyone, having this umbrella, and talk the way I like. 'We cannot give him so much power because he will uncover our way of work. And besides, why should we?' They know I have very strong roots. This is my strength. I'm talking about the street, the people in the street. So they said, 'Let's organize a competition.'"

Three candidates were proposed as successors to Radwan: Hatim Abdul Kader, the deputy editor at *al-Fajr*; Radi Jira'i, another editor at *al-Fajr*; and Naim Tobassi, a former reporter at *As-Sha'ab*. "Naim is not really a journalist. He used to sell newspapers in the street and to make coffee for Akram Hanieh," scoffs Radwan. Each of the three had their backers at home and abroad: Faisal Husseini supported Hatim Abdul Kader; Akram Hanieh supported Naim Tobassi; another well-known deportee and Arafat aide, Jibril Rejoub, backed Radi Jira'i. Even Ibrahim Kara'in, Radwan's former boss at the Palestine Press Service, and his wife, Raymonda Tawil, took sides. "I saw five people fighting for something," says Radwan. "Everybody wanted to control the association by pushing his man. I said, 'Okay, it is a cake. *Sahaten*! To your health! Take it! Enjoy it! I quit!'"

His supporters organized a petition drive to persuade him to change his mind. They collected enough signatures for him to run and be reelected by a sizeable majority. But Radwan wanted to be chosen unanimously or not to run at all. "I didn't accept it because I wanted everyone from my own constituency to say yes," he explains. "I would have battled against other factions. But not within my group [*Fatah*], because that means within my tribe there are some dissidents. I'm not talking about the kitchen cabinet," he adds bitterly. "I'm talking about the bathroom."

The elections for a new chairman of the Arab Journalists Association were held on August 1, 1991. Naim Tobassi was elected by acclamation. After the results were announced, Radwan was given an opportunity to speak. He read the financial report. Then he pulled two pieces of paper out of his pocket. One was the petition that had been signed by a majority of the members asking that he remain in his post. The other was a message from Yasser Arafat. Radwan had contacted the PLO leader shortly after being released from prison. When he received the response, he had concealed it. Now he produced the handwritten message. "I showed it to the group, to the 'Gang of 100!' The Arafat paper said, 'You should be elected again.' Everyone was silent," says Radwan. Why had he not revealed the existence of the message earlier? "I wanted to prove something: that if I had wanted the presidency, I could have had it. If I had run, I would have won. But I am a democratic person. I wanted to prove we could build an institution."

However, Radwan, too, had a surprise in store for him. Despite his vocal support for the peace process, he was not asked to be a member of either the Palestinian negotiating team headed by Haidar Abdul Shafi or the guidance committee headed by Faisal Husseini. The slight was particularly irritating because, unlike other Palestinians, who were from Jerusalem, Radwan was from Nablus. So he was eligible, under the ground rules the United States had worked out with Israel, to be a member of the delegation sitting across the table from the Israelis. The three Palestinians who made the recommendations to Arafat "of the people they would like to work with," says Radwan, are Akram Hanieh, Faisal

Husseini, and Nabil Shaath.

Radwan was also passed over when a Palestinian delegation was chosen for the multilateral talks with Israel. He feels he would have been well suited for the discussions on the diaspora Palestinians' "right of return," which were held in Ottawa in the late spring of 1992. After all, he is a refugee who has broad support among the poor. "When they talk of the camps, I'm the person who fits," he insists. "I worked a lot in the public sector. I worked in the *shabiba*. I built up these groups. I keep open doors to solve their problems. I have very tight contacts with the leadership, and I do not take sides."

Perhaps because of his close ties to the PLO or because the "insiders" wanted to distance themselves somewhat from the Tunis-based leaders, Radwan was named to head a third circle, a group of people closely identified with the PLO. The fourteen people on this "advisory committee" were given this title, says Radwan, to act "as a kind of think tank: they can make a recommendation but they cannot give an instruction." All three groups—the negotiating team, the guidance committee, and the advisory committee—report to Arafat. "There also are joint meetings regularly between the 'inside' and the 'outside' in order to make decisions. In front of Arafat," says Radwan, "everyone is equal."

He refuses to discuss what anyone's motivations might be for acing him out of the action. The implication, however, is that his exclusion from the negotiating team and his ouster from the presidency of the press club have their roots in the class struggle. "There are two classes in our society," says Radwan. Faisal Husseini represents the elite, the link with the past through his father, Abdel Kader, the Arab hero of the 1948 war, and with the roots of Palestinian nationalism through his uncle Haj Amin. Radwan, on the other hand, insists he has never lost touch with the ordinary Palestinian. "I have the links with the people of the camps, the militant people, the poor people, the ones who have big hopes and big expectations. I can go anywhere. I can speak with anyone."

His whole life he has courted the Palestinian constituency. Radwan recalls that when he was nineteen years old, his students at the Ramallah Teachers Training Center were like brothers to him.

"I used to come early in the morning to give extra lessons and to play football with them. I visited them in the camps and used to sleep with them. We would go and talk under the trees. I listened to every young man or woman and tried to solve their problem," he says, adding somewhat immodestly, "I am perceived as a spiritual father, the ideologist trying to further their aims." Like any good politician, he obtained UNWRA projects for them and persuaded the Common Market countries in Europe to donate improvements, including modern sewer systems for the camps.

Today Radwan believes this same group is an untapped resource and that if *Fatah* does not address itself to their needs, the PLO will lose the battle for the hearts and minds of the Palestinians to the Islamic fundamentalists. He says he had sleepless nights asking himself over and over why *Hamas* won such a landslide victory in the elections for the Chamber of Commerce in Ramallah, a Christian city. "A bell rang in my head," he says. He asked himself, "Why should somebody support me just because I am PLO?" Many people think the PLO is a corrupt organization because "we did not prove we have the ability to do anything on the ground" to improve their lives. "The people," says Radwan, "are the servants of their needs. If we can meet their needs properly, they will join us."

After *Hamas*' victory, he says, he recognized that "I have to compete with the group that provides big feasts for the poor and that gives nice speeches in the mosques every Friday, the group which is getting me to God on an express train!" So on June 19, 1992, Radwan called for a public meeting at Ibrahimah College, across from Faisal Husseini's house on the Mount of Olives in Jerusalem. There he announced the creation of a new organization, the Palestinian Consolidation Society. Of course, Radwan named himself chairman. He invited the foreign diplomatic corps and the media to attend and appointed personalities, including Faisal Husseini and Sari Nusseibeh, to the new board of trustees. More than 800 people showed up, so many that the Israeli police had to surround the college and turn away two busloads of Palestinians from Hebron and Nablus.

Radwan explains that the purpose of the new group is to forge links among those across the political spectrum in order to help the poor. He says this was the original goal of the *shabiba* before the Israelis outlawed the youth groups. That, he explains, "was paralyzing for us." He adds: "We thought we could do it in a more civilized, professional way. We thought, 'If we get together, I may not agree with Mr. X in his political attitude, but I would agree in working with him to solve a social problem.'"

Twenty-three people were named to administer as many different fields, including health, education, charity, journalism, engineering, even religion. Doctors were asked to give one day a week to care for those in the camps; teachers to donate their lessons; engineers to help build roads; journalists to write articles about the importance of the peace process; and the wealthy to set up charitable committees to raise money for the less privileged. "I named sheikhs, merchants, religious people, militants, nationalists, and independents," he says, "depending mostly on those who might be *Hamas* supporters tomorrow—before they become *Hamas* supporters."

It is the recognition of class differences that has made this possible. "We are a tribal society, whether we have a revolution or not. We tribalize politics," admits Radwan. "So I said, 'Okay, there is a place for the religious, you can serve the poor; and there is a place for the merchants in social action. If I am cleaning the streets and 10,000 people see it, I am providing an example of the behavior of the real citizen." He says politics was not his main motivation. "I am not asking you to become a political activist; I am asking you to do your job. People are enthusiastic about this because we are not asking for anything that is beyond the capabilities of anyone," he says.

Not even Radwan, however, tries to disguise the fact that this new, broad-based coalition is helping him regain his power in the West Bank. "Somebody wrote Arafat that this is a political party, that it is being supported by Saudi Arabia, and that it is opposed to the peace process," he says. Others have charged this is Radwan's answer to being left off the delegation negotiating with Israel, that it is his alternative to the official Husseini-led group. None of that is true, he declares. "I won't hide that there is a political aim behind this," he admits. It is "to strengthen the position of the PLO in the occupied territories. I am trying to respond to *Hamas*, to challenge them on the ground, and to prevent *Hamas* from getting there before we do and uniting the people."

Radwan admits he is still bitter over being snubbed. "I have no role in the delegation. I have nothing to decide in the delegation. That's fine," he says. "But we have another role to play internally. If tomorrow the delegation brings a state, how can we build this state if we don't have the social infrastructure? To tell you the truth," he adds without mentioning any names, "those who are getting their legitimacy from the leadership without getting their legitimacy from the ground will fail. But those who are getting their legitimacy from the ground *and* from the leadership will succeed."

What is unsaid, of course, is that Radwan Abu Ayash has found a way to fight back. He expects membership in the new organization to grow steadily. "Ten thousand people is not a joke! They will become 50,000," he predicts, "if we do it slowly, carefully, cleverly, and methodically. It is the best response to *Hamas*, following their own teachings." Explains *Ha'aretz*' Ori Nir, "it is a system to beat *Hamas* on *Hamas*' playing field with the same tools that *Hamas* is using!"

Radwan put his philosophy into practice himself. After returning from the Madrid conference, where he accompanied the Palestinian delegation but did not participate in the negotiations, he traveled to remote villages on the West Bank seeking support for the peace process. "I gave seventeen lectures in very difficult places, places where nobody can go," he says. At each stop he preached about the need to begin making practical progress on the ground, even if that meant it would be years before Palestinians won their own state. "What's the point of demanding an independent state and shouting radical slogans about liberating Palestine if we're not able to settle freely in Jericho?" he asked. "If we are able to settle in Jericho, at least we can set up the offices of an independent state; later we can negotiate about Nablus, about Ramallah, about Jerusalem and other issues."

He told the crowds that the negotiations to begin "a transition period, or full autonomy as accepted by the international community, is an important step towards building up the new realities." He told his audiences that for the first time they will have the opportunity to make a decision that directly affects their lives. If they support the peace process, the occupying army will withdraw from Palestinian towns and villages; the police forces and the school curriculums will be Palestinian; the municipalities will be able to issue deeds for Arab land; and the Jews will stop building settlements. "Both of us, the Israelis and the Palestinians, must test each other practically, not theoretically. We need time, time to pull the rope from both ends. Let's do it on the ground," preached Radwan. He now adds: "I believe it is normal that there should be a transition period. How can we move from liquid to gas without going through some fire?"

He also is optimistic about the future: "If we're talking about the near future, I believe we will have a semi-independent Palestinian state in two to three years." He hopes the autonomous entity will have a legislative council that will function as a parliament. By 1995 there will begin to be "day-to-day cooperation" between Jordan, Israel, and the Palestinians in their new entity. "There also will be a kind of normalization with the Arab countries," predicts Radwan.

And he is not worried about the threat of Islamic fundamentalism. *Hamas'* strength is in the mosques, notes Radwan. "There are 362 of them on the West Bank. Most are in the hands of *Hamas.*" But he contends that "most of their strength comes from the internal lack of unity within *Fatah.*" The fundamentalists, says Radwan, do not have deep roots in the struggle against Israeli rule. "*Hamas* doesn't have history. They only started during the *intifada. Fatah* started in the 1960s." The Palestinian people also are suspicious of any movement that is being financed from abroad. "The Palestinians accept any trend if it is a pure Palestinian trend. If it is imported from someplace else, it won't be accepted. That's why the 'Arabization' of the Palestinian problem did not last forever. *Hamas* is trying to 'Arabize' and 'Muslimize' the Palestinian problem. That means it will be difficult to survive for long."

Radwan concedes that for *Fatah* to compete effectively, the mainstream PLO group has to rid itself of its corrupt image. "We need to reform. Let me be very clear: to behave. But not to 'Arabize' our problem. To have a link with Jordan or Syria or Lebanon is different than being controlled by Syria or Lebanon or Jordan. We have a saying, 'The boss pays the bill.' Who's their boss?," Radwan asks. To his own question, he answers: "*Hamas* is controlled by non-Palestinian authorities. Some believe it is the Saudis. Others

believe some circles in Jordan. Others believe Iran is behind it."
But the power of *Hamas* will diminish if Palestinians obtain
genuine control over their own lives. "Give me some success in
the negotiations, real practical success, and people will follow.
If you are talking about bringing peace to the Middle East and
human rights violations still are increasing in the occupied territories, of course there will be a gap between theory and practice. This gap is going to be filled with radicalism. What created
radicalism?" asks Radwan rhetorically. "People discovered we are
talking about peace but not bringing peace, talking about tomorrow but tomorrow never comes, talking about a transition period
that will ease their suffering but it is not there. How can I support somebody who is talking about something in the abstract?"

The only way to defeat the fundamentalists, he says, is through
improving the conditions of life for the 1.7 million Palestinians
in the West Bank and Gaza. "People realize God through his crea-
tions on the ground. If he had not created something on the
ground, no one would believe in Him! That's why I say, the minute
Palestinians believe the situation is changing on the ground, they
will support the peace process."

Bridging the gap between hope and reality is the biggest
challenge for *Fatah* and other groups that support the talks, he
says. Radwan recalls a meeting in a hotel room in Amman en route
back to the West Bank from the Madrid conference. There, on
November 9, 1991, the three teams of Palestinians, led by Faisal
Husseini and Haidar Abdul Shafi, were gathered to work out their
strategy for the next day. "We were trying to decide what we were
going to tell the people when we got home," recalls Radwan. "The
speech [by Abdul Shafi] was excellent. The conference was nice.
But what were we going to tell them about the future?"

Then something happened that made a deep impression on
Radwan. After crossing the Allenby Bridge from Jordan on
November 10, the three teams of Palestinians were waiting on two
air-conditioned buses to clear the Israeli checkpoint at the
entrance to Jericho, the first Arab city in Israeli-occupied territory.
Thousands of Palestinians lined the streets, standing behind
wooden barriers that had been hastily erected to control the
crowd. Some people held olive branches. Others clutched
bouquets of roses. One elderly Palestinian held a white dove over

his head. As the buses began to slowly move past the checkpoint, the crowd broke through the barricades. The taxis sounded their horns. The olive branches were thrust on the metal grilles of the army jeeps while young Israeli soldiers looked on in astonishment. The crowd shouted out the names of the delegates, and they waved back excitedly. "We were welcomed as if we were heroes coming home from a victory," says Radwan. Meanwhile, a nine-year-old boy jumped up to the window of the bus where Radwan was sitting. Afraid that the lad would fall from the slowly moving bus, Radwan lifted him through the opening and onto his lap. He kissed him, but the youth pulled away. "Oh, Abu Ayash," he asked, "is it true that Palestine is free now? Palestine has been returned to us?" Radwan was at a loss for words. Finally, he replied: "Yes. Palestine will be free! But we are going to wait until you are old enough to enjoy it!" He asked the bus driver to stop and then gently let the boy down from the window. Leaning back in his seat, he thought about the question, oblivious to the tumult around him. It was, says Radwan, like an electric shock, a rude wake-up call from the dreams of Madrid. "I think about this question almost every day now," he says. "I ask myself, 'What are we doing? Are we really going to liberate Palestine through talks?'" The nine-year-old, admits Radwan, "shook my concepts. I began to reevaluate everything."

The youth is typical of the attitude of the next generation, he says. "Wherever you go on the street today, people will ask, 'Do you think this is serious?' It's a mixture of suspicion and optimism, of willingness and hesitation. I can leap over this psychological state if I have something in my hand," he says. It is not the best solution—that clearly would be an independent Palestinian state—but it is the only answer to the boy who jumped on the bus. "If we have a transition period, I can tell the people, 'Look, we have our own health facilities, our own educational institutions, the Israelis are not interfering, they are withdrawing from populated areas, from Gaza and Nablus and Jericho. This is the first step.'" Adds Radwan, sounding as if he is trying to persuade himself as well as his people, "You begin to build your ideology through actions. But if you talk about rosy dreams and the people see that the jails are the same jails, that the shootings in the air are the same shootings and the curfews the same curfews, and we appear on TV with neckties and nice statements, nobody will believe us. We went to Madrid carrying wounds that were seventy years old."

The Palestinians have learned many lessons since the modern Middle East was created at the end of World War I. They have had their hopes crushed repeatedly. Their leaders have encouraged them to harbor impossible dreams that one day they would destroy Israel and return to their homes in Palestine. The dreams will continue, says Radwan, but it is time for a large dose of reality. If anything is to change now, no one should offer more than he or she can deliver. Radwan is confident that life in the West Bank and Gaza will gradually improve. But the challenge for him as a future Palestinian leader is already clear. It is different from the task that has confronted Yasser Arafat for the last forty years. The PLO chairman and the guerilla group he has led have put the Palestinians on the map of the world's consciousness. The next generation has to get them a state. Above all, says Radwan, "we should be credible." The rest, he says, depends on the Israelis. "They are the ones who will decide whether the hopes for peace are going to be real."

Conclusion

███████████

When their infant daughter Sheda was only three months old, Radwan and Salma Ayash discovered something in her left eye. It resembled a small white lump. "We thought something was stuck in her eye. We tried to wash it out," recalls Radwan. When it would not wash away, they took Sheda to a Palestinian pediatrician, who told them not to worry—nature would take care of itself and the problem would disappear. He gave them some eye drops. Even after faithfully using the drops for several weeks, however, Radwan says, "we were still coming and going, coming and going" from one doctor to another. They still did not think it was serious, because as far as they could tell the small lump was not causing the child any pain. "But I felt the doctor was not prescribing the right medicine. I told Salma, 'Let's go and see another doctor.' I went to Hadassah Hospital," says Radwan.

When Professor David Ben Ezra, a noted eye surgeon, examined Sheda, who was by then almost one year old, the Israeli pediatrician asked why they had not taken her to a doctor sooner. "I don't know. I was busy," replied Radwan. "I don't believe you," said the Israeli. "I think you went to other doctors and now you came to me," he told him sternly. Then the Israeli, a Sephardic Jew with dark brown hair and a goatee, told Salma and Radwan that their child had a cataract and needed an urgent operation or she might lose sight in one eye. "This girl should be operated on in the next twenty-four hours," he told them. But it was Friday afternoon. In a few hours, it would be *shabat*, the eve of the sabbath, when all Jews stop work for a full day. The doctor would be going home for dinner with his family, then have Saturday off.

"He forgot all about the *shabat*," recalls Radwan, "and began to make preparations for her operation. He operated for three hours on Saturday morning." The operation was a success.

For the next three months Radwan brought Sheda back for a checkup every week to make sure the eye was healing properly. David Ben Ezra never sent them a bill. Instead he asked for a photo of the Palestinian child to carry in his wallet. "He was a real human being," says Radwan. "I had to pay for the hospital, but I never had to pay him anything." He asked Suleiman Mansour, a noted Palestinian artist, to paint a picture for the physician. A few weeks after the operation, Radwan invited the Israeli to his Ramallah apartment for dinner. The *intifada* was then several months old, and Ben Ezra was worried about making the trip alone. "I told him, don't be afraid," Radwan recalls, and adds militarily, "We 'moved' him from Jerusalem to Ramallah. It was normal." Since then the Palestinian and his family have made return visits to the Israeli physician's home and shared *shabat* dinner with the Ben Ezra family. "He has a smiling face," notes Radwan. "It lightens the impression of the prison guards and of the soldiers in the street. It shows there are always two sides to every story."

This episode is one of a handful that provides a glimmer of hope for the future. Not only are there Israelis who have helped Palestinians, there are Palestinians who have similarly helped Israelis in their hour of need: Said Kanaan, a wealthy Nablus businessman who markets imported cosmetics in the West Bank, once helped an Israeli child obtain a transplant liver from a Palestinian youth who was a victim of the *intifada*; Palestinian shopkeepers in the Old City of Jerusalem recently brought several Israeli soldiers who had been shot to Makassad, an Arab hospital in East Jerusalem; Daoud Mikhail, Hanan Ashrawi's father, even rescued several Israeli soldiers after an Arab ambush and had them driven to a nearby hospital.

But as moving as these stories are, they are exceptions to the rule, a blip on the cardiogram of the *intifada*'s heartbeat, only a promise of what may be possible some day. Reflecting on his experience with David Ben Ezra, Radwan says, "This means, yes, there is room for life between Palestinians and Israelis. But this room is exposed to politics and occupation."

We have tried in these pages to take a closer look at the impact that a quarter century of occupation has had on a generation that reached its political maturity under Israeli rule. We have tried to throw some light on the prejudices and fears, as well as the hopes and dreams, of these Palestinians and their children. To understand exactly what has led to the emergence of a new generation of political leaders, it is worthwhile to recall the historical context of the past twenty-five years, in particular, the setbacks suffered by the Palestinians of the West Bank and Gaza Strip in the era in which they reached their maturity.

By far the most profound setback was the shock of the Six-Day War in June 1967 in which the Palestinans in the Jordanian-administered territories witnessed an almost overnight Israeli victory and Arab defeat; not only was East Jerusalem lost and reunified with the western sector to subsequently become the Israeli capital, but such religiously conservative and traditional Arab cities as Nablus, Tulkarm, and Hebron came under Israeli military occupation. Within three years the Palestinians suffered another setback at the hands of the Jordanians, their former occupier. The PLO-led effort to provoke Jordan into launching a new assault to recover the West Bank, and to topple the regime of King Hussein when he refused, eventually led to tragic results. The king ordered a crackdown on the mounting anti-Israeli guerrilla raids. The resulting confrontation resulted in the deaths of thousands of Palestinians in a bloody battle now known as Black September, and forced thousands more into exile in Lebanon.

The next major setback for the Palestinians came in November 1977, when Egyptian President Anwar Sadat visited Jerusalem and declared his readiness to end the state of war with Israel and sign a separate peace treaty with the Jewish state. The 1978 Camp David Accords seemed to relegate the Palestinians to second-class status: in the eyes of the Palestinians, the Egyptians and Israelis were offering them only autonomy, a form of limited self-rule, without any guarantees this could lead to self-determination or an eventual independent state.

In June 1982, when the Israelis invaded Lebanon and routed the PLO from its headquarters in Beirut, the last contiguous battleground was lost from which guerrilla attacks could be launched against Israel. With Egypt, Jordan, and Lebanon now seemingly neutralized, and the PLO forced to mastermind the armed struggle from faraway Tunis, Palestinians also had to deal with a new threat: a right-wing Israeli government that openly promulgated its claim to Judea and Samaria (the West Bank) by vastly expanding the construction of new Jewish settlements under the leadership of Ariel Sharon.

As the final decade of the twentieth century began, there were two more blows: the wide-scale emigration to Israel by hundreds of thousands of Soviet Jews, threatening to decisively alter the demographic balance of the West Bank, and the influx of thousands of Palestinians who'd been forcibly exiled by Kuwait in the wake of the U.S.-led defeat of Iraq in the Persian Gulf War.

All these events deepened the split between Israelis and Palestinians. It was only with the start of the *intifada* in December 1987 that the Palestinians finally experienced the equivalent of Egypt's "victory" in the October 1973 war: a triumph so stunning in its element of surprise that Israel found itself suddenly on the defensive and the Palestinians began to feel confident enough to bargain from a position of strength. With the start of the *intifada*, an irreversible inching had begun toward Israeli-Palestinian reconciliation. The process was given impetus by the unilteral proclamation of an independent Palestinian state at the Palestine National Council meeting in Algiers in November 1988. When, a month later, PLO leader Yasser Arafat publicly recognized Israel's existence within its pre-1967 borders and renounced the use of terror, the shift toward empowering the insiders that had begun with the *intifada* received another major boost. Finally, in October 1991, the West Bank and Gaza leadership emerged convincingly on the world stage, achieving the breakthrough at the Madrid peace conference that the PLO had vainly sought for decades to achieve: recognition of the Palestinians as a separate people entitled to the fulfillment of their historical claims for justice. When a new Labor-led government was elected in Israel in June 1992 and Prime Minister Yitzhak Rabin ordered an immediate cessation of new settlement activity, a more hopeful climate was created; for the first time in a quarter century there was a prospect that Palestinian claims might be realized.

What changed over the course of those twenty-five years to bring the Israeli-Palestinian conflict to the point where both sides appear ready to make compromises? The answer lies to a great extent in the significance of the five-year-old Palestinian uprising: the *intifada* transformed more than two decades of Israeli rule into a costly, painful, and ultimately intolerable burden, making it clear that a solution could no longer be postponed. "For this is what the Palestinians have brought upon us by means of the *intifada*: they have deprived us, in the most unambiguous way, of the possibility of an 'enlightened occupation,'" wrote Israeli author Ari Shavit in *On Gaza Beach*. "They have forced us to choose: territories or decency, occupation or fairness. And, yes, that is indeed the question of the hour. An acute and urgent question, demanding an answer at once. It is not, at this hour, a matter of territories in exchange for peace. It is a matter of territories in exchange for our humanity." Here then are some thoughts on the significance of the *intifada*.

- *The intifada was the first sustained mass opposition to Israeli military occupation and was initiated by adolescents and children.* This is the generation of Palestinians that has grown up entirely under occupation, that has known no other reality but the Israeli occupier, and whose contacts with Israeli Jews, restricted largely to border police and soldiers, are often violent in nature. These young Palestinians are unfamiliar with anyone remotely resembling a progressive Israeli. Their occupier is perceived as a unidimensional figure responsible for economic hardships, political inequality, and social injustice. "The relationship between the Palestinian and the Israeli," says Radwan Abu Ayash, "is the gun or prison or the keys [to the prison], being in line for permits, licenses, and taxes. They see him as somebody who is depriving them of their rights, everything from raising their flag to freely playing football in the playgrounds."

- *The intifada has assumed a place in Palestinian lore similar to the historical significance to Americans of the Declaration of Independence and the Bill of Rights.* The *intifada* was the first genuine nationalist expression of a people who, prior to 1987, depended on the rest of the Arab world, the two superpowers, and the outside Palestinian leadership in Beirut and later Tunis to deliver them from Israeli occupation. When the revolt of the insiders succeeded, it assumed almost mythological proportions, particularly in view of the abject failure of Arab nations such as Syria, Jordan, and Egypt, with their enormous military might, to liberate the Palestinians. The *intifada* could not have begun without this generation's having acknowledged its own sense of control, rejecting capitulation or self-exile, but also choosing an alternative form of resistance to armed struggle: *sumud* (steadfastness) transposed from the mind into the streets. The *intifada* was not merely an assertion of self-control but choosing a middle ground between armed rebellion and passive resistance; by going into the streets independent of any directive from *Fatah*, *Hamas*, or other political factions, the Palestinians living inside the territories were acknowledging their own power to effect change. "The *intifada*," wrote Sari Nusseibeh in October 1990, "is an idea, it is a frame of mind, it is a way of collective self-consciousness, it is a form of internal liberation and emancipation, and as such the *intifada* is a source of life, not death; and it will continue to give birth to new forms for the Palestinian's existential resistance, until freedom has been achieved."

- *The intifada reduced the image of the Israeli to manageable size.* The June 1967 war created the perception of the invincible Israeli. The scope of that defeat emasculated the Arabs, and on a psychological level produced a sense of inferiority. The Jews became, as Riad Maliki says, "a monster." The *intifada* showed Palestinians that the monster was only a myth. "In the past, when we saw a soldier we were terrified. We accepted him. We thought he was *the* power," explains Radwan. The *intifada* showed that the Israeli is not "the gorilla that can swallow people or that big mountain that nobody can climb," he adds. One of the most unforgettable images for us is the seven-year-old Palestinian boy scavenging for rocks at the feet of Israeli soldiers outside the Askar refugee camp. The fearless youth was collecting the stones, and carefully putting them in a plastic bag, for the next assault against the same Israelis who were patrolling nearby completely oblivious to his activity.

- *The intifada has weakened the traditional source of authority.* In the past, the internal authority was religious or tribal, while the ultimate authority was usually a foreign power. Palestinians were taught to get along with the occupier regardless of whether it was Turkish or British or Jordanian. Even under the first two decades of Israeli rule, the Palestinian made a virtue of *sumud*. In the *intifada*, passive resistance turned to active resistance and the consequences are still being felt. Rebellion has become a normal way of life. Palestinian youths have transferred their anger against the Israeli to more traditional symbols of authority, the family and the school. Parents and teachers, the *mukhtar* and the *sheikh*, are no longer automatically respected. Even the symbol of national unity, the Palestine Liberation Organization, is consistently criticized. The families of notables, those with roots that stretch back to the Prophet Mohammed, such as the Husseinis and Nusseibehs, also can no longer count on automatic allegiance; they must seek support from the grass roots.

The Palestinian delegation to the peace talks reflects the need for this new mix, with representatives from more modest backgrounds, such as Ghassan Khatib, Sameh Kilani, and Zahira Kamal, required to balance the traditional elites. In the post-*intifada* climate, nothing is approved anymore without hours and hours of debate. Palestinians have never lived under a system where authority derives from the consent of the governed and therefore is respected by the majority of the people; thus they have no reason to trust authority and probably will be skeptical of any future leadership, even one of their own choosing. Says Radwan, "People who have spent twenty-five years resisting authoritarian rule and dictatorship will not accept anyone practicing the same thing in the future, particularly if they are from their own flesh and blood."

• *Prisons and refugee camps have replaced bloodlines and universities as the breeding ground for leadership.* This is a consequence of the shutdown of schools for much of the last five years. There is a sense that there is no alternative to the battle for liberation, that it is a political inheritance that cannot be abandoned. When mothers know their children will be throwing stones at the soldiers at the entrance to Nuseirat refugee camp, there is a natural maternal protectiveness; but they know they cannot stop them. Everything must be subordinated to the national struggle. All of the figures in this book willingly told of their imprisonment, aware that their experience helps qualify them for leadership. Sameh Kanaan might not even have been chosen to represent the Palestinians had it not been for the twelve years, almost a third of his life, that he spent in jail. For Sameh, his most important motive now is to give meaning to those years by proving the peace process can produce tangible gains for the Palestinians. "Nobody can say to me, you sold out Palestine," says Sameh proudly. "Nobody can say that," he explains, "because I gave my blood for Palestine and all my youth for

Palestine. So I think to be in the delegation is very important because it helps convince the prisoners especially that they have a representative in the peace process." The prison experience also has been a school of occupation, for it teaches prisoners to look after each other: they meet hundreds of other activists and form strong bonds of friendship; they develop a leadership within the prison society and elect representatives from among their compatriots to negotiate with the Israeli authorities.

- *The PLO is a Palestinian's identity.* "The PLO was the product of Palestinian nationalism and not vice versa," explains Najah University lecturer Saeb Erakat. "So it is in that context that you should view what Arafat and other leaders of the PLO mean to the Palestinians: as a burst of consciousness, a vehicle of identity. It is their vehicle to statehood. Without the PLO, you are merely a refugee." And all holidays help preserve their identity; past sacrifices are not simply historical fact; they extend to the present. The general strike is called for the ninth of every month, which is recognized as the first day of the *intifada*; the fifteen of every month is marked as the anniversary of the end of the British mandate in Palestine; April 9, 1948, is remembered for the Deir Yassin massacre, when members of the Irgun, the Jewish underground army, killed 250 Palestinians in an Arab village less than two miles from West Jerusalem; Land Day commemorates the day in March 1976 when six Israeli-Arabs were killed by Israeli security forces during protests over land expropriations.

- *The intifada has removed much of the joy of life, particularly for children, who are growing up in a somber climate in which death has become routine.* Modesty is dictated in the economic and

social lives of all Palestinians. For example, it is
seen as immoral, even unethical, to openly celebrate; weddings and other normally joyous occasions are more solemn affairs. Death still is
enshrined in the ethos of the *shahid*, the martyr
who sacrifices his life for the sake of his country,
but death has become almost as common as life.
"We used to worship the one who died," says one
Palestinian: the *shahid*'s funeral became a mass
demonstration, with hundreds of people coming
from remote villages; special songs were written to
mark the martyr's ascension to heaven. Today,
funerals are far more common; more than 1100
Palestinians have lost their lives in the *intifada*,
with almost one Palestinian dying every day since
December 1987. Consequently, the ceremonies,
even for the *shahid*, have become smaller; they are
attended only by the immediate family, relatives,
and a few village leaders. "It's like switching the
light on and off or going for a walk," he says.
"That scares me, because when death becomes normal, what is the meaning of life?"

The *intifada* has caused the devolution of
authority, forcing children to become adults. Every
man, says *Ha'aretz* correspondent Ori Nir, knows
that the more you shave, the harsher the stubble
becomes on your face. In the *intifada*, he says, the
Israelis shaved the layers of leadership from the
face of Palestinian society. First they arrested the
primary level of leadership—the professors, university graduates, and highly educated Palestinians
who helped organize the rebellion. Then they
arrested the next level of younger, less educated
nationalists and local leaders. Finally they arrested
the high school students who took over the Unified
National Command. With so many Palestinians in
jail, says Nir, "you started to see little nine- and
ten-year-old children leading demonstrations and
demanding to see reporters' credentials. I will never

forget arriving at a refugee camp and being stopped by someone who was half my height, with a squeaky little voice, who says, 'Before you can enter, I must see your press pass.' I showed him my press pass, which has the symbol of the state of Israel on it, and this," says the Israeli newsman incredulously, "is what he accepted as evidence of my being a legitimate journalist. It is surreal."

- *Despite Israel's pride in being a democracy, the Palestinian sees the Israeli as someone who is depriving him of his rights.* The prevailing Palestinian view is of a society that is harsh and repressive towards Palestinians. For example, Israelis are repeatedly asked, "You aspire to be a democratic society. How can a democratic society do such things?" The question reflects the fact that it is very difficult for most Palestinians to internalize the concept of Israeli democracy; they cannot make the cognitive distinction between the democratic system that exists inside the Green Line and what they experience in their own life: the undemocratic practices aimed at subjugating them, or worse, designed, they believe, to drive them from their homeland. Opportunities for experiencing anything positive with Israelis are limited. There are only two areas, for example, where Palestinians have intense contact with Israelis: in the physical labor of their jobs inside Israel, and in their familiarity with the military aspects of occupation. In a survey Nir personally conducted for *Ha'aretz*, he discovered that the only Hebrew words that Palestinians use in their own vernacular are connected either to their jobs helping to build settlements or to the restrictions imposed on their daily lives. For example, the Hebrew slang term *baal habait*, which means "boss," has been absorbed as *balabait* in Arabic; the Hebrew words *mivreshet* ("paint brush") and *mavreg* ("screwdriver") also

have infiltrated their language. The Hebrew term
for "wireless radio," *makhshir kesher*, has been
shortened in Arabic to simply *makhshir*; the word
for "roadblock," *makhsom*, has been similarly
Arabized into the word *makhszoom*.

There are, of course, Palestinians who
acknowledge that they can learn from Israeli
society, particularly in building their state. But few
Palestinians will publicly acknowledge any admiration for what Israel has achieved. An exception is
Sameh Kanaan. "I'm fond of the Israeli democracy,"
he says. "I would like to have something similar [in
a Palestinian state]. When I see the Knesset, and I
know Hebrew, the Knesset debates, I understand
what they say. They insult each other, they attack
each other, but at the same time they sit beside
each other. In times of danger, all of them are
united. That means something to me. That speaks
well for democracy. Also, the Israeli elections take
place peacefully, without attacks, physical attacks."

• *The Palestinian sees himself as much a victim of
hatred and discrimination as the Israeli*. Even if
the Palestinian understands the fears borne of the
extermination of 6 million Jews, he resents the
implicit transferral of guilt. "We're not Nazis! We're
not the ones who did that to the Jews," we heard
repeatedly. In this environment of rage, the Palestinian, in turn, equates the Israeli with the Nazi.
Comparisons between Israeli treatment of the
Palestinians and the Nazi extermination of the Jews
are specious and farfetched. But the Palestinian
sense of victimization is not. And yet, there are
Palestinians, such as Ziad Abu Zayyad, who have
sought to comprehend the insecurities of the
Israelis by visiting Yad Vashem, the Jerusalem
memorial to the Jews killed in the Holocaust. Ziad
says he also has read several books about the concentration camps. "We're not taught about what

happened to the Jews in Europe in the Nazi era,"
he admits. "Perhaps we can learn something from
the Israelis about their suffering." And perhaps, he
says, Israelis can learn something from the Palestinians. "They have to understand," says Ziad, "that
now we are playing the same role they played during the '30s and '40s, before they had their own
state. We are the Jews of today."

Ironically, it is the same legal system used by the
British against the Jews during the mandate period
that the Israelis now apply against the Palestinians.
The code cited as the legal basis for everything
from demolishing houses to deportation, administrative detention, and even town arrest is the 1945
emergency regulations that the British used to outlaw the *Lehi*, *Irgun*, and *Haganah*, the underground
Jewish armies that fought against the British occupier.
During the 1950s Menachem Begin, who helped
form the *Irgun*, delivered a speech to the Knesset
declaring that Israel had to abolish these regulations
from its legal code because the British had so
flagrantly abused them. But after 1967 they became
the basis on which Israel extended its authority
over the Palestinians in the occupied territories.

- *A genuinely representative leadership has emerged
  out of the intifada that is in a legitimate position
  to negotiate on behalf of the 1.7 million Palestinians in the West Bank and Gaza Strip.* This is
  the first group of Palestinians from inside the territories who have not merely aspired to represent
  their people but also emerged as political figures
  and diplomats able to make a persuasive case for
  their constituency in the rest of the world. This is
  an important breakthrough. It must be remembered,
  however, that this group must constantly strive for
  legitimacy. It is vital for them to maintain an
  explicit link to the outside leadership in Tunis to
  retain credibility inside the territories. They are, in

the final analysis, functioning in an environment
that is deeply fragmented. Traditional forms of
authority have broken down; there have never been
national elections or the establishment of democratic institutions; their society is still divided along
religious, family, and tribal lines; and there is
constant jockeying for power between the inside
and outside leadership. Until truly representative
elections are held inside the territories, these Palestinians will be locked in a never-ending struggle to
be seen as authentic leaders. This is one reason
many of them are compelled to stress their prison
experience or connection to a family of a *shahid*;
"*intifada* suffering" has become the yardstick for
legitimacy.

The last twenty-five years have bred so much anger and hatred
that even those Palestinians who eagerly condone a policy of coexistence insist this must be prefaced by a quiet period of separation. The divorce is required to heal both the symbolic and the
psychological wounds of a quarter century of occupation. If
lasting peace is to be achieved, Palestinians must be able to choose,
of their own free will, to begin building a new relationship with
Israelis that will bury the past. This will take time. Says Radwan
Abu Ayash, "If we solve the land issue and we solve the sovereignty
issue, what's left? History teaches us there are many countries
which used to fight each other. Now they are very close friends.
Why not the Palestinians and Israelis? But in a conflict like the
Israeli-Palestinian conflict, it is impossible to have an immediate
peace. Peace should be built brick by brick, row upon row, a little
at a time, until I can visualize fifteen years from now, if peace
prevails in the Middle East, real cooperation, real human life between the Israeli and the Palestinian. Everything is possible."

Israeli Prime Minister Yitzhak Rabin seems to understand the
need to satisfy Palestinian aspirations provided the process moves
gradually. "There is no possibility, in my humble opinion, to move
by one act from the present situation to a permanent solution,"
he says. Investing the interim Palestinian authority in the West
Bank and Gaza with all responsibilities of self-government, from

health care to collecting taxes and establishing the curriculum for the school systems, is "the only way to start something," he told us. Rabin believes control over land and water rights as well as security obligations can be shared and he has proposed the creation of a 20,000-member Palestinian police force; in short, he appears willing to turn over to the Palestinians substantial authority except over foreign and defense matters during the interim period. In this three-year transition before the start of negotiations to determine the "permanent" disposition of the territories, both Israelis and Palestinians will have to postpone their ultimate objectives. "We oppose the creation during the interim period of any organ or any organization that declares that this is the ideological beginning of an independent Palestinian state," declares Rabin. Israel, likewise, must defer its claims to Judea and Samaria [the West Bank]. Rabin will have to make good on his pledges to end all new settlement activity if he has any hopes of persuading Palestinians that Israel is prepared to negotiate to eventually relinquish sovereignty over most of the West Bank and Gaza Strip.

That is the one area where we believe Rabin is serious. Almost twenty years ago, in late 1973, Yitzhak Rabin was part of a secret study ordered by Prime Minister Golda Meir to determine Israel's options in the West Bank and Gaza Strip in the wake of the October Yom Kippur war. A few months later, in the spring of 1974, Golda would signal her intention to retire and Rabin himself would take over as leader of a new Labor-led government. The participants in the secret study stretched across the Israeli political spectrum: in addition to Rabin, the Labor Party leader, there was the late Moshe Dayan, Yigal Allon, and Herut Party leader Menachem Begin. There also were representatives from the Mossad, the Israeli CIA; the Shin Bet, the Israeli FBI; a special research and intelligence unit in the Ministry of Foreign Affairs; and senior military commanders. Each was asked to prescibe minimum security requirements in the event of (1) total annexation by Israel, (2) return of the territories, or most of them, to Jordan, and (3) the establishment of a separate Palestinian state in the West Bank and Gaza.

Noteworthy even today are the three prerequisites they decided were required for Israel's security regardless of which option was chosen. The first was that Israel would have to have access to the territories, independent of whatever authority exists there, to apprehend anyone suspected of mounting terrorist activities and to hold them in a place that is not under the control of whatever authority exists in the territories. The second prerequisite was that all parties to a settlement agree there will not be a return to the barriers that physically separated Israelis from the Palestinians and that, in the context of peace, there must be open borders between both Israel and the Palestinian entity and that entity and Jordan. The third and final prerequisite was that for reasons of both security and coexistence, the Jewish State "retain a potential for a continued Israeli presence" in the West Bank and Gaza Strip; in other words, that Jews be able to coexist with the Palestinians in the territories.

These three prerequisites are just as valid for Israel today as they were two decades ago. But unlike earlier Israeli leaders, we believe Yitzak Rabin is prepared to contemplate the inevitable: some form of genuine Palestinian independence and even statehood. He does not, for example, foreclose the possibility that, during the three years of self-government, Palestinians could begin to take steps towards self-determination. "I believe," he told us, "that there should be a transitional period in the real sense, with the purpose [being] to realize that they [the Palestinians] are a different entity than us: religiously, politically, you can even say *nationally*." No previous Israeli leader has offered the Palestinians the prospect of achieving both their *political* and their *national* aspirations.

Adds Rabin: "We are not denying them the right to say this [a Palestinian state] is our goal." He recalls that in April 1989 he fathered the initial Israeli proposal for the Palestinians to elect their own representatives to conduct peace talks with Israel. At that time he told us: "I believe there should be a Palestinian entity, and full autonomy by itself is the beginning of the creation of the Palestinian entity." Today Rabin reasserts: "I'm ready. I proposed it in 1989," and holding the door open to any outcome, including the possibility that the "entity" might one day become independent, he adds, "I believe there is a chance. I believe if we succeed in starting this way, many new ideas can be brought up, once we find ways of more limited peaceful coexistence and then realize we are really ready" to consider more lasting solutions. But he adds, with a note of caution, "The permanent solution and all the elements of a permanent solution should be negotiated in accordance with the timetable laid down in the Camp David Accords and accepted in the letter of invitation to the Madrid conference: not later than the third year after the establishment of the interim self-governing authority. I believe there is a really wide national consensus on this in Israel."

Nevertheless, leaders in both Israel and the West Bank and Gaza are beginning to discuss the need for some form of regional cooperation that might link Israel, Jordan, and Palestine in a common market, with open borders between all three states. Interestingly, the idea of confederation has been suggested by both Faisal Husseini and Yitzhak Rabin. The Israeli leader told us that when the Jordanian-Palestinian delegation returned from the Madrid conference in November 1991, Husseini was asked in a television interview what he thought about the idea of a confederation between Palestine and Jordan. According to Rabin, the Palestinian leader replied, "Why not with Israel?" The Palestinians "understand that economic integration with Israel is preferable from their point of view to integration with Jordan," says Rabin.

Husseini agrees that such an economic union may ultimately be more important for the survival of a Palestinian state than either political or security issues. "We may need an army as a symbol of our national identity, but I don't believe an army will be able to protect our security," he explains. "We can never build an army that can face the Israeli army or even the Jordanian army. They could kill us merely by starving us. I would like to see the whole area with a minimum number of armed forces and weapons. What we need are international guarantees that no one will attack us, so maybe we are better off with no army at all," he adds. For Husseini, however, there can be no compromise on the issue of statehood. "The Palestinian state is needed to solve the problem of the Palestinian nation, which is stateless," Husseini recently told *Ha'aretz*. "A Palestinian state," he later told us, "must be able to issue passports and citizenship." He made clear, however, that he envisages the state existing "as a confederation" with *both* Jordan and Israel, because this is mandated by economic reality. "What is Israel? An economic problem. What is Jordan? An economic problem. The same is true of Lebanon and Syria. What will a Palestinian state be if not another regional economic problem? I am not fighting to create an economic problem," he said.

Adds Faisal Husseini: "In our lives as Palestinians, we have been a part of three experiences: the Israeli experience, the Jordanian experience, and the Lebanese experience. As Lebanese we saw freedom without authority; in Jordan we experienced authority without democracy, and in Israel we experienced democracy without equality. We hope our state will be a state of freedom, democracy, equality, and only the authority that is necessary to protect them."

As we conclude *The New Palestinians*, an Israeli-Palestinian agreement on a framework for interim self-government seems within reach. There are other hopeful signs: West Bank and Gaza Palestinians, as well as ordinary Israelis, are no longer prosecuted for meeting with the PLO; even Knesset members now regularly attend international conferences at which the PLO is present. While still refusing direct talks with the Palestinian Liberation Organization, the Israeli government now accepts the role the PLO is playing in legitimizing its Palestinian interlocutors inside the territories. "There has been a gradual shift," explains Ori Nir, "from the PLO being the sole legitimate representative of the Palestinian people to its being the sole 'legitimator' for the insiders representing the Palestinian people." Led by these insiders, many of whom we have profiled in this book, the possibility of lasting peace seems real for the first time in almost a half century.

Yitzhak Rabin told his nation in September that Israel must give up "the illusions of the Greater Land of Israel religion" fostered by his predecessor, Yitzhak Shamir, who viewed every inch of *Eretz Yisrael* as Israel's biblical birthright. "Remember," said Rabin, "there is a people of Israel, a society, a culture, and an economy, and that the strength of a nation is not measured by land, the lands under its control, but rather by its belief and its ability to foster social, economic, and security systems." This kind of spirit, coupled with Faisal Husseini's vision of regional cooperation, could usher in a new era of Palestinian-Israeli coexistence.

Glossary of Terms and Organizations

Black September, 1970-71   Period of civil war in Jordan when Palestinians were defeated by forces loyal to King Hussein.

Democratic Front for the Liberation of Palestine (DFLP)   Established in February 1969 by Nayef Hawatmeh from a split within the Popular Front for the Liberation of Palestine (PFLP) (see below). It disagreed with the PFLP's strategy of launching attacks from outside Israeli territory. It emphasized building grass-roots support for its left-wing doctrines. First known as the Popular Democratic Front for the Liberation of Palestine, the group abbreviated its name to the Democratic Front for the Liberation of Palestine in mid-1974. Hawatmeh is a Christian Arab born in As Salt Jordan in 1935. One of the basic doctrines during the DFLP's early period was that the British plan to partition the mandate area into two states—Jordan and Palestine—created an unnatural division and that Palestinian and Jordanian movements should unite. In September 1969 the group called for the establishment of a popular democratic Palestinian state for Arabs and Jews alike. Since the late 1960s the DFLP has been in contact with Israeli leftist organizations such as Matzpen. In the 1970s the group splintered into two wings, one led by Hawatmeh, the other by Yasser Abed Rabbo. At present, the Yasser Abed Rabbo wing of the DFLP supports the peace process, while the Hawatmeh wing opposes the negotiations in their current form.

Fatah (Harakat at Tahrir al-Filastiniyya)   Established in the late 1950s and early 1960s as a Palestinian nationalist organization, as opposed to one with an Arab nationalist orientation. Among

311

its founders are Yasser Arafat (Abu Amar), Salah Khalaf (Abu Iyad), Khalil Wazir (Abu Jihad, former PLO deputy military commander allegedly assassinated on April 16, 1988, by an Israeli hit squad at his home near Tunis), and Khaled Hassan. It is the largest of the PLO-affiliated groups.

Fatah Revolutionary Council (FRC)   Established in 1973 as a splinter of the mainstream *Fatah* organization. Since 1987 the FRC has been headquartered in Tripoli, although this is denied by Libyan authorities. The group first focused on targeting Syria, with the bombing of a Damascus hotel and assassination of Syria's foreign minister, but later widened its targets to include the PLO. It is held responsible for the wounding of Israel's Ambassador Shlomo Argov in London in 1982.

Green Line   Boundary separating 1948 Israel from the West Bank and Gaza Strip.

Hamas (Harakat Mukawwamah al Islamiyya)   An Islamic fundamentalist group formed from the ranks of the Muslim Brotherhood at the beginning of the *intifada* as a means of demonstrating the brotherhood's participation in the uprising.

Islamic Jihad (al Jihad al Islami)   Established in the 1970s from an ideological split within the Muslim Brotherhood. Some members of the Brotherhood, such as Sheikh 'Odeh and Fathi Shqaqi, inspired by the Iranian revolutionary model and Egyptian Islamic radicalism, criticized the brotherhood's concentration on the re-Islamization of society, with the national struggle taking a secondary role. Islamic Jihad calls for the overthrow of Arab leaders by popular revolution in order to restore *nizam al Islamiyya*, an Islamic order. The group's central focus is the Palestinian cause and, unlike the brotherhood, considers dialogue with nonreligious nationalists, such as the PLO, essential if Israel is to be defeated.

Palestine Liberation Organization (PLO)   Founded in May 1964 in East Jerusalem. It was headed first by Ahmed Shukeiry and later by Yasser Arafat. At the Arab summit meeting in June 1974 in Rabat, the PLO was declared the "sole legitimate representative of the Palestinian people."

Palestine National Council (PNC), al-Mailis at-Watani al-Filastini The main policy-making body in the PLO and accepted as a parliament-in-exile. At its meeting in March 1977 it adopted the goal of an independent Palestinian state. During its session in November 1988 it proclaimed a Palestinian state to coexist alongside pre-1967 Israel.

Palestine National Front (PNF) An organization created during the 1973 PNC meeting for the purpose of coordinating and spearheading nationalist resistance in the occupied territories. It began operations in August 1973, but was declared illegal by the Israeli government in October 1979. The group stressed a pragmatic approach to Palestinian independence and an end to Israeli military occupation. The West Bank wing of the Jordanian Communist Party was among its principal contributors.

Palestine People's Party (Hizb al-Shaab, formerly the Communist Party) Established in the 1920s, originally including both Jewish and Arab members. It has supported recognizing the state of Israel. Since major changes in international communism, the Communist Party changed its name to the People's Party and revised its platform, diminishing its emphasis on Marxist-Leninist principles.

Popular Front for the Liberation of Palestine (PFLP) Founded in 1967 by George Habash, a Greek Orthodox Palestinian physician from Lydda. The group adopted a Marxist-Leninst orientation, with an Arab nationalist ideology, and supported hijacking and international terrorist operations.

Popular Front for the Liberation of Palestine–General Command (PFLP–GC) Established in 1968 from a split within the PFLP (see above). Led by Ahmed Jibril, a former Palestinian officer in the Syrian army, the PFLP–GC rejects both the PLO's recognition of Israel's right to exist and the abandonment of the armed struggle.

Sumud The concept of "steadfastness." There are two forms of *sumud*: (1) Economic *sumud* is codified in the Arab summit meeting in Baghdad in late 1978, where Arab states pledged to contribute aid to the Palestinian resistance inside the territories. This form of *sumud* has been largely discredited. (2) *Sumud* as referring to staying on the land and resisting occupation remains a critical component of Palestinian political life.

UN Security Council Resolutions 242 and 338   242 (November 22, 1967) calls for the recognition of the state of Israel along pre-1967 borders. Resolution 338 (October 22, 1973) calls on all parties participating in the fighting to cease all military activity and to begin implementation of Resolution 242.

*The Palestinian Side of the Joint
Jordanian-Palestinian Delegation*

Expanded Outline

Palestinian Interim Self-Government Arrangements: Concepts, Preliminary Measures and Elections Modalities

List of Contents
Part One: Concepts and Expanded Outline of the PISGA
Part Two: Preliminaries for the Interim Phase
Part Three: Elections Modalities

Part One: Concepts and Expanded Outline of the PISGA

List of Topics
  I. Introduction
 II. The Transitional Nature of the Interim Phase
III. Authority in the Interim Phase
 IV. Powers and Responsibilities of the PISGA

I INTRODUCTION

The immediate objective of the Palestinian-Israeli bilateral talks, as laid out in the co-sponsors' letter of invitation of October 18, 1991, is to negotiate interim self-government arrangements. These talks are conducted within the context of international legitimacy, which recognizes the right of the Palestinian people to self-determination.

The interim self-government arrangements are also intended to provide the basis for the second stage of negotiations on the permanent status of the West Bank including Jerusalem, the Gaza Strip and al-Himmah. According to United Nations Security Council resolutions 242 and 338, the Fourth Geneva Convention and the Hague Regulations, these areas are occupied territories, and Israel is a belligerent occupant. (These territories are hereafter referred to as the Occupied Palestinian Territory—OPT).

The Palestinian people have accepted to negotiate interim self-government arrangements, in a phased approach that would allow them, in the second and final phase, the free exercise of their legitimate right to self-determination. Moreover, the Palestinians in the OPT and in exile are one people, and the interim self-government arrangements should facilitate the exercise of the legitimate rights of those in exile, who will participate in the second phase of the negotiations to determine the final status of the OPT and achieve a comprehensive settlement of the Palestine question in all its aspects.

II The Transitional Nature of the Interim Phase

According to the co-sponsors' letter of invitation, the entire negotiating process we have embarked upon, including the "negotiations along two tracks," are "based on United Nations

Security Council resolutions 242 and 338." These resolutions stipulate that Israel's acquisition of the territories it occupied in the 1967 war is inadmissible, and are the basis of the principle of the exchange of territory for peace. It should be clear that Resolutions 242 and 338 must guide all phases of the negotiations. They must be fully implemented by the final stage.

The interim phase, therefore, does not constitute a regime which would be stabilized short of self-determination. It represents, on the contrary, a framework whereby Resolutions 242, 338, and international legality shall be implemented.

III Authority in the Interim Phase

The term "interim self-government arrangements" can only mean arrangements for an interim self-government: a central, political entity that allows the Palestinian people in the OPT to govern themselves by themselves. The Palestinians in the OPT have the right and have expressed the wish to govern themselves according to democratic principles, i.e. through free elections without external interference.

The success of the transitional process is only possible if the PISGA is vested with all the powers of a true self-governing authority. All the powers presently exercised by the military government and civil administration of the occupier should be transferred to the PISGA upon its election and inauguration.

IV Powers and Responsibilities of the PISGA

1. Being the representative of the Palestinian people in the OPT, the PISGA's authority is vested in it by them. Its powers and responsibilities cannot be delegated by a foreign authority. Israel was never entitled to sovereignty over the OPT, but rather has exercised certain powers as a belligerent occupant since the entry of its armed forces into the areas occupied in 1967. With the start of the interim phase, and the abolition of the Israeli military government and civil administration, Israel shall cease to enjoy all these powers, which shall be assumed by the PISGA.

2. There should be no limitations on the powers and responsibilities of the PISGA, except those which derive from its

character as an interim arrangement and from the mutually agreed outcome of the peace process.

3. In order for the PISGA to exercise freely its powers and responsibilities, and be assured a peaceful and orderly transfer of all powers to it, the Israeli armed forces shall complete their withdrawal in phases to mutually-agreed specific redeployment points along the borders of the OPT by the time the PISGA is inaugurated.

4. The jurisdiction of the PISGA should extend to all of the OPT, including its land, natural resources, water, sub-soil, territorial sea, exclusive economic zone and air space. The PISGA shall exercise its jurisdiction throughout the Occupied Palestinian Territory.

5. The PISGA should have legislative powers. The transition from the state of occupation to the final status necessitates the assumption of such powers. No self-governing authority can function without having the power to enact, amend and abrogate laws.

6. The PISGA should wield executive power. It should formulate and implement its policy without any foreign control.

7. The PISGA shall determine the spheres, objectives and means of cooperation with any states, groups of states or international bodies, and shall be empowered to conclude binding cooperation agreements free of any foreign control.

8. The PISGA should administer justice through an independent judiciary, exercising sole and exclusive jurisdiction throughout the OPT.

9. The PISGA should establish a strong police force responsible for security and public order in the OPT.

10. The PISGA can request the assistance of a U.N. peace-keeping force.

11. A standing committee should be established from representatives of the five permanent members of the U.N. Security Council, the Secretary General of the United Nations, the PISGA, Jordan, Egypt, Syria and Israel, to supervise the implementation of the self-government arrangements during the interim phase and settle disputes arising therefrom.

Part Two: Preliminaries for the Interim Phase

1. The conclusion of the negotiations on the interim phase and the establishment of the PISGA require implementation of a number of necessary preliminary measures and the provision of appropriate conditions for the conduct of elections.

2. The period between the commencement of the peace process on October 29, 1991 and the elections for PISGA and its subsequent inauguration on a date no later than October 29, 1992, during which these preliminary measures are to be implemented, constitutes a *preliminary phase*.

3. The Fourth Geneva Convention and Hague Regulations, and United Nations Security Council Resolutions 242, 338 and 726, provide the basis and principles for the implementation of the above.

4. During its prolonged occupation of the Palestinian Territory, the Israeli military government and the Israeli government have diverged increasingly since 1967 from the principles laid down in the Hague Regulations of 1907, the Fourth Geneva Convention of 1949, United Nations Security Council 242 and 338, and other international conventions and standards.

5. The Israeli authorities have introduced illegally a large number of substantial changes into the body of law applicable in the OPT, which have made possible the establishment and expansion of illegal Israeli settlements. These changes have resulted in the creation of a system approaching apartheid. The consolidation of the system undermines the short- and long-term objectives of the ongoing peace process.

6. Discriminatory and extra-territorial legislation must therefore be rescinded and the issue of new military orders, whether in the guise of primary or secondary legislation, must cease.

7. Dismantling the legal basis of this discriminatory system in the OPT is necessary for the successful transition into the interim phase and for the ultimate success of the peace process as a whole.

8. In order to establish the proper conditions for the conclusion of the interim negotiations, the exercise of the powers and responsibilities of the PISGA, and the conclusion of the second stage of negotiations on the final status of the OPT, the Israeli

authorities should immediately implement the following measures with regard to land and natural resources:

a. Cease all settlement activity, including construction of new settlements or expansion of existing ones, road construction and other infrastructural activity.

b. Cease acquisition, by any means, of land, water and other natural resources.

c. Refrain from any and all unilateral actions affecting the legal, demographic or geographic status quo in the OPT.

d. Revoke military order 291 which suspended the land registration process, thus allowing land registration to continue according to law.

e. Return all land and immovable properties seized under military order 58 on the basis of being absentee property.

9. In order to provide the proper atmosphere and conditions for the conduct of the elections and the establishment of the PISGA, the Israeli authorities should:

a. Release all Palestinian political prisoners, including administrative detainees.

b. End the practice of administrative detention.

c. Allow the return of all deportees.

d. Revoke military order no. 224 that revived the 1945 Emergency Regulations.

e. Refrain from closing educational and other public institutions, blocking economic activity, imposing curfews, or otherwise impeding the normal conduct of the daily lives of the Palestinian people in the OPT.

f. Refrain from all forms of collective punishment.

g. Lift all restrictions on Palestinian social, cultural, political and economic activity, and formally revoke all military orders that affect those areas of daily life in the OPT.

h. Provide full protection of, and free access to, religious sites.

i. Approve all pending family reunification applications.

j. Make available all public records regarding all aspects of the resources and inhabitants of the OPT.

Part Three: Elections Modalities

1. The elections are intended to produce the legislative assembly of the PISGA, comprising 180 members.
2. Basic principles:
   a. The provisions of the Charter of the United Nations and the Universal Declaration of Human Rights provide the universally accepted basis for the conduct of free elections.
   b. The elections for the establishment of the PISGA constitute a significant step towards realizing the national and political rights of the Palestinian people in the OPT.
   c. The PISGA should be the self-governing authority which represents the Palestinian people in the OPT. It should be freely elected on the basis of the universal democratic principle of "by the people, of the people, for the people."
   d. All guarantees should be provided for free elections. It is necessary that elections be conducted and supervised by an international body. All measures must be taken to guarantee that Israel should not interfere in the elections in any way.
2. Purpose of the elections:
   a. To enable the Palestinian people in the OPT to elect democratically accountable representatives.
   b. To provide a democratic basis for the establishment of the institutions of the PISGA.
   c. To give democratic legitimacy to the assumption of its powers and responsibilities by the PISGA in the OPT during the interim phase.
3. Proper conditions. The preliminary measures mentioned in Part Two of this document, including in particular an immediate halt to all settlement activities, should be implemented before the elections. Further steps must also be undertaken in order to provide the proper conditions for the conduct of the elections, as follows:
   a. Withdrawal of Israeli Army units, Border Police and other military and para-military forces outside all populated areas and main communication routes.
   b. Disarming of Israeli settlers, disbanding of their paramilitary formations, and guaranteeing their non-interference

in the elections process.

   c. The provision of international supervision (see below).

4. Full participation. In order to ensure full participation by the Palestinian people in the OPT in the elections, the Israeli authorities should guarantee full freedom of:

   a. Political expression, including the end of military censorship.

   b. Access to, and establishment of, all forms of audio-visual or print media.

   c. Assembly.

   d. Public election campaigning.

   e. Political activity, including the formation of political parties.

   f. Movement throughout the Occupied Palestinian Territory.

5. The various preliminary measures described above should be implemented at least three months before the elections, and by a date not later than 31 July 1992.

6. International supervision. International supervision is to be provided by the United Nations, or any other appropriate and mutually agreed international body. This international body shall provide the following:

   a. Designate a high commissioner to supervise the preparations for, and conduct of, the elections. The commissioner's mandate will continue at least until the inauguration of the Palestinian interim self-governing authority.

   b. Establish an international supervisory committee that, in addition to assisting the high commissioner, will arbitrate disputes arising from implementation and allocate responsibility.

   c. Station UN or other international observers to ensure continued respect of the above-mentioned preliminary measures.

   d. Station UN or other appropriate international or multinational forces to provide for public order during the elections.

   e. There shall be free access throughout the OPT for the international media as well as foreign visitors.

7. The elections:

   a. The elections shall be conducted in accordance with an electoral system endorsed by the international supervisory committee.

b.   The elections shall be based on universal suffrage, and be conducted by secret ballot.

c.   The elections shall take place at least one month prior to the inauguration of the PISGA, which is to take place at a date not later than 29 October 1992.

8.   All Palestinians who, on 4 June 1967, were listed in the relevant official population registers in any part of the West Bank including Jerusalem, the Gaza Strip, and al-Himmah, and their descendants, have the right to vote in the elections or stand as candidates.

9.   In order that all Palestinians eligible to vote can exercise that right, the Israeli military authorities should:

a.   Facilitate the return of all persons displaced and/or deported since 5 June 1967 and their descendants.

b.   Submit all relevant population records for the preparation of electoral registers.

c.   Complete the above measures by a date not later than 31 July 1992, under international supervision.

Washington, D.C., March 3, 1992

Palestinian Document Highlights

Following are excerpts from the document on the 10-point framework for the interim self-governing arrangements presented by the Palestinians to the Israeli delegation in Washington on August 31, 1992:

1. *Interim arrangements:* This section talks about the interim phase and its link with the second stage of negotiations on the permanent status of the occupied territories. The interim phase is seen as a phased approach to the application of UN Security Council Resolution 242 that would allow the Palestinians, in the second and final stage, to exercise their right to self-determination. The document wants the Fourth Geneva Convention and the Hague Regulations to apply in the occupied territories during the interim phase.

2. *Elections:* The interim self-government will be established by means of free, democratic, secret, and direct elections under international supervision and with the participation of all people of the occupied territories, including the deportees and displaced persons, who should be returned to their homeland. Prisoners are also to be released to participate in the elections. The interim authority has to get its legitimacy directly from the people and have full legislative, executive, and judicial authority.

3. *Jurisdiction:* The jurisdiction of the interim government should extend to all the territories that were occupied in 1967, including their land, water, natural resources, economy, and points of entry.

4. *Withdrawal:* The Israeli military forces will be redeployed into mutually-agreed areas. International supervision during the interim period will be guaranteed.
5. *Jerusalem:* The interim arrangements will apply to [East] Jerusalem, which is part of the areas occupied in 1967 according to UN Security Council Resolution 242.
6. *Settlements:* Israeli settlement activity will need to cease immediately and completely. Settlers will abide by the Palestinian rules and regulations.
7. *Security:* This includes the security needs of Israelis and Palestinians as well as internal security, which will be the responsibility of the Palestinians without any Israeli interference.
8. *Return of deportees and displaced persons:* Palestinians who have been displaced or deported since 1967, along with their children, will be allowed to return and participate in the elections both as candidates and as voters.
9. *Supervision and conflict resolution:* In order to avoid recurrence of problems and to ensure an orderly transition of authority, a committee of the five permanent members of the UN Security Council and the secretary-general of the UN, as well as representatives of the Palestinian authority, Jordan, Syria, Egypt, and Israel will supervise the interim agreement and guarantee its execution and solve any conflict that might arise during this period.
10. *Time-frame:* Both sides will agree to reach an agreement for the interim period in no more than three months. Negotiations for the final status will begin no later than October 30, 1994, thus abiding by the time-frame specified in the letter of invitation to the Madrid conference.

Remarks by: Haidar Abdul Shafi, Palestinian Chief Negotiator
Madrid, Spain
Thursday, October 31, 1991

For this historical conference we thank the Palestinian people who are still struggling for freedom and independence. I will now speak on their behalf to you and to all democratic countries and forces in the world in the English language.

Ladies and gentlemen, on behalf of the Palestinian delegation, we meet in Madrid, a city with a rich texture of history to weave together the fabric which joins our past with the future, to reaffirm a wholeness of vision which once brought about a rebirth of civilization and a world order based on harmony and diversity. Once again, Christian, Muslim and Jew face the challenge of heralding a new era enshrined in global values of democracy, human rights, justice and security. From Madrid, we launch this quest for peace, a quest to place the sanctity of human life at the center of our world and to redirect our energies and resources from the pursuit of mutual destruction to the pursuit of long prosperity, progress, and happiness.

We, the people of Palestine, stand before you in the fullness of our pain, our pride, and our anticipation for we have long harbored a yearning for peace and a dream of justice and freedom. For too long, the Palestinian people have gone unheeded, silenced, and denied, our identity negated by political expediency, our rightful struggle against injustice maligned, and our present existence subsumed by the past tragedy of another people. For the greater part of this century, we have been victimized by the myth of a land without the people and described with impunity as the invisible Palestinians.

Before such willful blindness, we refused to disappear or to accept a distorted identity. Our *intifada* is a testimony to our perseverance and the resilience waged in a just struggle to regain our rights.

It is time for us to narrate our own story, to stand witness as advocates of a truth which has long lain buried in the consciousness and conscience of the world. We do not stand before you as supplicants, but, rather, as the torch bearers who knew that in our world of today ignorance can never be an excuse. We seek neither an admission of guilt after the fact nor vengeance for past inequities, but, rather, an act of will that would make a just peace a reality.

We speak out, ladies and gentlemen, from the full conviction of the rightness of our case, the verity of our history, and the depth of our commitment. Therein lies the strength of the Palestinian people today for we have scaled the walls of fear and reticence, and we wish to speak out with the courage and integrity that our narrative and history deserve.

The co-sponsors have invited us here today to present our case and to reach out to the others with whom we have had to face a mutually exclusive reality on the land of Palestine, but even in the invitation to this peace conference, our narrative was distorted and our truth only partially acknowledged.

Palestinian people are one fused by centuries of history in Palestine, bound together by a collective memory of shared sorrows and joys and sharing a unity of purpose and vision. Our songs and ballads, our folktales and children's stories, the dialect of our joys, of our jokes, the image of our poems, that hint of melancholy which colors even our happiest moments, are as important to us as the blood ties which link our families and clans.

Yet an invitation to discuss peace, the peace we all desire and need, comes to only a portion of our people. It ignores our national, historical, and organic unity. We come here wrenched from our sisters and brothers in anxiety to stand before you as the Palestinians under occupation, although we maintain that each of us represents the rights and interests of the whole.

We have been denied the right to publicly acknowledge our loyalty to our leadership and system of government, but allegiance and loyalty cannot be censored or severed. Our acknowledged leadership is more than just the democratically chosen leadership of all the Palestinian people. It is the symbol of our national unity and identity, the guardian of our past, the protector of our present, and the hope of our future. Our people have chosen to entrust it with their history and the preservation of our precious legacy. This leadership has been clearly and unequivocally recognized by the community of nations with only a few exceptions who had chosen for so many years shadow over substance.

The governance of the nation and conditions of our oppression, whether the disposition and dispersion of exile or the brutality and repression of the occupation, the Palestinian people cannot be torn asunder. They remain united, a nation, wherever they are or are forced to be.

In Jerusalem, ladies and gentlemen, the city which is not only the soul of Palestine, but the cradle of three world religions, is tangible, even in its claimed absence from our midst at this stage. Its apparent, though artificial, exclusion from this conference is a denial of its right to seek peace and redemption for it, too, has suffered through more than an occupation. Jerusalem, the city of peace, has been barred from the peace conference and deprived of its calling. Palestinian Jerusalem, the capital of our homeland and future state, defines Palestinian existence past, present, and future, but itself has been denied a voice and an identity.

Jerusalem defies exclusive possessiveness or bondage. Israel's annexation of Arab Jerusalem remains most clearly illegal in the eyes of the world community and an affront to the peace that this city deserves.

We come to you from a tortured land and the proud, though captive, people, having been asked to negotiate with our occupiers, but leaving behind the children of the *intifada* and the people under occupation and under curfew, who enjoined us not to surrender or forget. As we speak, thousands of our brothers and sisters are languishing in Israeli prisons and detention camps, most detained without evidence, charge, or trial, many cruelly mistreated and tortured in interrogation, guilty only of seeking freedom or daring to defy the occupation. We speak in their name, and we say, "Set them free."

As we speak, the tens of thousands who have been wounded or permanently disabled are in pain. Let peace heal their wounds.

As we speak, the eyes of thousands of Palestinian refugees, deportees, and displaced persons since 1967 are haunting us for exile as a cruel fate. Bring them home. They have the right to return. As we speak, the silence of demolished homes echoes through the halls and in our minds. We must rebuild our homes in our free state.

And what do we tell the loved ones of those killed by army bullets? How do we answer the questions and the fear in our children's eyes for one out of three Palestinian children under occupation has been killed, injured, or detained in the past four years? How can we explain to our children that they are denied education or schools so often closed by army fiat or why their life is in danger for raising a flag in the land where even children are killed or jailed? What requiem can be sung for trees uprooted by army bulldozers? And, most of all, who can explain to those whose lands are confiscated and free waters stolen? The message of peace, remove the barbed wire, restore the land and its life-giving water.

The settlements must stop now. Peace cannot be waged while Palestinian land is confiscated in myriad ways and the status of the occupied territories is being decided each day by Israeli bulldozers and barbed wire.

This is not simply a position. It is an irrefutable reality. Territory for peace is a travesty when territory for illegal settlement is official Israeli policy and practice. Settlements must stop now.

In the name of the Palestinian people, we wish to directly address the Israeli people, with whom we have had a prolonged exchange of pain. Let us share hope, instead. We are willing to live side by side on the land and the promise of the future. Sharing, however, requires two partners willing to share as equals.

Mutuality and reciprocity requires—must replace—domination and hostility for genuine reconciliation and co-existence under international legality. Your security and ours are mutually dependent, as entwined as the fears and nightmares of our children.

We have seen some of you at your best and at your worst, for the occupier can hide no secrets from the occupied, and we are witness to the toll that occupation has exacted from you and yours. We have seen you anguish over the transformation of your sons and daughters into instruments of a blind and violent occupation, and we are sure that at no time did you envisage such a role for the children whom you thought would forge your future. We have seen you look back in deepest sorrow at the tragedy of your past and look on in horror at the disfigurement of the victim turned oppressor.

Not for this have you nurtured your hopes, dreams, and your offspring. This is why we have responded with solemn appreciation to those of you who came to offer consolation to our bereaved, to give support to those whose homes were being demolished, and to extend encouragement and counsel to those detained behind barbed wire and iron bars. And we have marched together, often choking together in the nondiscriminatory tear gas, all crying out in pain as the clubs descended on both Palestinian and Israeli alike, for pain knows no national boundaries and no one can claim a monopoly on suffering.

We once formed a human chain around Jerusalem, joining hands and calling for peace. Let us today form a moral chain around Madrid and continue that noble effort for peace and the promise of freedom for our sons and daughters. Break through the veneers of mistrust and manipulated fears. Let's look forward in magnanimity and hope.

To all our Arab brothers and sisters, most of whom are represented here on this historic occasion, we express our loyalty and gratitude for their lifelong support and solidarity. We are here together seeking a just and lasting peace whose cornerstone is freedom for Palestine, justice for the Palestinians, and an end to the occupation of all Palestinian and Arab lands. Only then can we really enjoy together the fruits of peace, prosperity, security, and human dignity and freedom.

In particular, we address our Jordanian colleagues in our joint delegation. Our two peoples have a very special historic and geographic relationship. Together we shall strive to achieve peace. We will continue to strive for our sovereignty while proceeding freely and willingly to prepare the grounds for a confederation between the two states of Palestine and Jordan, which can be a cornerstone for our security and prosperity.

To the community of nations on our fragile planet, to the nations of Africa and Asia, to the Muslim world, and particularly to Europe, on whose southern and neighborly shores we meet today, from the heart of our collective struggle for peace, we greet you and acknowledge your support and recognition. You have recognized our rights and our government and have given us real support and protection. You have penetrated the distorting mists of racism, stereotyping, and ignorance, and committed the act of seeing the invisible and listening to the voice of the silence.

Palestinians under occupation and in exile have become a reality in your eyes and, with courage and determination, you have affirmed the truth of our narrative. You have stated our cause and our case and we have brought you into our hearts. We thank you for caring and daring to know the truth, the truth which must set us all free.

To the co-sponsors and participants in this occasion of awe and challenge, we pledge our commitment to the principle of justice, peace, and reconciliation, based on international legitimacy and uniform standards. We shall persist in our quest for peace to place before you the substance and determination of our people, often victimized but never defeated. We shall pursue our people's right to self-determination, to the exhilaration of freedom, and to the warmth of the sun as a nation among equals.

This is the moment of truth. You must have the courage to recognize it and the will to implement it, for our truth can no longer be hidden away in the dark recesses of inadvertency or neglect. People of Palestine look at you with straightforward, word-for-word, direct gaze, seeking to touch your heart, for you have dared to stir up hopes that cannot be abandoned. You cannot afford to let us down, for we have lived up to the values you espoused and we have remained true to our cause.

We, the Palestinian people, made the imaginative leap in the Palestine National Council of November, 1988, during which the Palestine Liberation Organization launched its peace initiative based on Security Council Resolution 242 and 338 and declared Palestinian independence based on Resolution 181 of the United Nations, which gave birth to two states in 1948, Israel and Palestine.

In December, 1988, a historic speech before the United Nations in Geneva led directly to the launching of the Palestinian-American dialogue. Ever since then, our people have responded positively to every serious peace initiative and has done its utmost to ensure the success of this process.

Instead, Israel, on the other hand, has placed many obstacles and barriers in the path of peace to negate the very validity of the process. Its illegal and frenzied settlement activity is the most glaring evidence of its rejectionism, the latest settlement being erected just two days ago.

These historic decisions of the Palestine National Council wrenched the course of history from inevitable confrontation and conflict towards peace and mutual recognition. With our own hands and in an act of sheer will, we have molded the shape of the future of our people. Our parliament has articulated the message of the people, with the courage to say yes to the challenge of history, just as it provided a reference in its resolutions last month in Algiers and in the Central Council meeting this month in Tunis to go forward to this historic conference.

We cannot be made to bear the brunt of other people's no. We must have reciprocity. We must have peace.

Ladies and gentlemen, in the Middle East, there is no super-fluous people outside time and place, but, rather, a state sorely missed by time and place. The state of Palestine must be born on the land of Palestine to redeem the injustice of the destruction of its historical reality and to free the people of Palestine from the shackles of their victimization.

Our homeland has never ceased to exist in our minds and hearts, but it has to exist as a state on all the territories occupied by Israel in the War of 1967, with Arab Jerusalem as its capital in the context of that city's special status and its nonexclusive character.

This state, in a conditional emergence, has already been a subject of anticipation for too long. It should take place today, rather than tomorrow. However, we are willing to accept the proposal for a transitional state, provided interim arrangements are not transformed into permanent status. The time frame must be condensed to respond to the dispossessed Palestinians' urgent need for sanctuary and to the occupied Palestinians' right to gain relief from oppression and to win recognition of their authentic will.

During this phase, international protection for our people is most urgently needed, and the dual application of the Fourth Geneva Convention is a necessary condition. The phases must not prejudice the outcome. Rather, they require an internal momentum and motivation to lead sequentially to sovereignty.

Bilateral negotiations on the withdrawal of Israeli forces, the dissolution of Israeli administration, and the transfer of authority to the Palestinian people cannot proceed under coercion or threat in the current asymmetry of power. Israel must demonstrate its willingness to negotiate in good faith by immediately halting all settlement activity and land confiscation while implementing meaningful confidence-building measures.

Without genuine progress, tangible, constructive changes, and just agreements during these bilateral talks, multilateral negotiations will be meaningless. Regional stability, security, and development are the logical outcome of an equitable and just solution to the Palestinian question, which remains the key to the resolution of wider conflicts and concerns. Regional stability, security and development are the logical outcome of an equitable and just solution to the Palestinian question, which remains the key to the resolution of wider conflicts and concerns.

In its confrontation of wills between the legitimacy of the people and the illegality of the occupation, the *intifada*'s message has been consistent—to embody the Palestinian state and to build its institutions and infrastructure. We seek recognition for this creative impulse which nurtures within it the potential nation-state. We have paid a heavy price for daring to substantiate our authenticity and to practice popular democracy in spite of the cruelty of occupation. It was a sheer act of will that brought us here, the same will which asserted itself in the essence of the *intifada* as the cry for freedom, an act of civil resistance and people's participation and empowerment. The *intifada* is our drive towards nation-building and social transformation. We are here today with the support of our people who have given itself the right to hope and to make a stand for peace.

We must recognize as well that some of our people harbor serious doubts and skepticism about this process. Within our democratic social and political structures, we have evolved a respect for pluralism and diversity and we shall guard the opposition's right to differ within the parameters of mutual respect and national unity. The process launched here must lead us to the light at the end of the tunnel. And this light is the promise of a new Palestine—free, democratic, and respectful of human rights and the integrity of nature.

Self-determination, ladies and gentlemen, can neither be granted nor withheld at the will of the political self-interests of others. For it is enshrined in all international charters and humanitarian law. We claim this right. We firmly assert it here before you and in the eyes of the rest of the world. For it is a sacred and inviolable right which we shall relentlessly pursue and exercise with dedication and self-confidence and pride. Let's end the Palestinian-Israeli fatal proximity and this unnatural condition of occupation which has already claimed too many lives. No dream of expansion or glory can justify the taking of a single life. Set us free to re-engage as neighbors and as equals on our holy land.

To our people in exile and under occupation who have sent us to this appointment, laden with their trust, love and aspirations, we say that the load is heavy and the task is great, but we shall be true. In the words of our great national poet, Mahmoud Darwish, "My homeland is not a suitcase and I am no traveler." To the exiled and the occupied, we say you shall return and you shall remain and we will prevail, for our cause is just. We will put on our embroidered robes and *kafeeyahs* in the sight of the world and celebrate together on the day of liberation.

Refugee camps are not fit for people who had been reared on the land of Palestine in the warmth of the sun and freedom. The hail of Israeli bombs almost daily pouring down on our defenseless civilian population in the refugee camps of Lebanon is no substitute for the healing rain of the homeland. Yet the international will had ensured their return in United Nations Resolution 194, a fact willfully ignored and unenacted.

Similarly, all other resolutions pertinent to the Palestinian question, beginning with Resolution 181 through Resolutions 242 and 338, and ending with Security Council Resolution 681, have until now been relegated to the domain of public debate rather than real implementation. They form the larger body of legality, including all relevant provisions of international law within which any peaceful settlement must proceed. If international legitimacy and the rule of law are to prevail and govern relations among nations, they must be respected and impartially and uniformly implemented. We as Palestinians require nothing less than justice.

Palestinians everywhere, today we bear in our hands the precious gift of your love and your pain, and we shall sit down gently here before the eyes of the world and say there is a right here which must be acknowledged, the right to self-determination and statehood. There is strength and there is the scent of sacred incense in the air. Jerusalem, the heart of our homeland and the cradle of the soul, is shimmering through the barriers of occupation and deceit. The deliberate violation of its sanctity is also an act of violence against the collective human, cultural and spiritual memory and an aggression against its enduring symbols of tolerance, magnanimity and respect for cultural and religious authenticity. The cobbled streets of the old city must not echo with the discordant beat of Israeli military boots. We must restore to them the chant of the *muezzin*, the call of the ram and the prayers of all the faithful calling for peace in the city of peace.

From Madrid, let's light the candle of peace and let the olive branch blossom. Let us celebrate the rituals of justice and rejoice in the hymns of truth, for the awe of the moment is a promise to the future which we all must redeem. Palestinians will be free and will stand tall among the community of nations in the fullness of the pride and dignity which by right belongs to all people. Today our people under occupation are holding high the olive branch of peace. In the words of Chairman Arafat in 1974 before the UN General Assembly, "Let not the olive branch of peace fall from my hands." Let not the olive branch of peace fall from the hands of the Palestinian people.

Index

Abbas, Mahmoud, 42
ABC-TV
  "Nightline," 1, 5
  "Palestine:A New State of Mind,"
    17
Abed Rabbo, Yasser, 91, 109-110,
    233-234. *See also* Yasser Abed
    Rabbo wing of DFLP
Abu Amar. *See* Arafat, Yasser
Abu Dhab, Nusseibeh, Sari in, 93
Abu Ghosh, 46
Abu Iyad, 19
Abu Jihad, 19, 219
Abul Abed. *See* Husseini, Faisal
Abu Lutuf, 42
Abu Mazzen, 42
AGREXCO, 267
Aker, Khaled, 171-172
Aker, Madhat, 167-168
Aker, Mamdouh, 5, 33, 164-184
  on CNN "Newsmaker Saturday,"
    182-183
  education of, 165
  England, study in, 166
  Gulf War, arrest during, 180-181
  hunger strike, 180-181
  and Husseini, Faisal, 169-170
  intifada and, 176-180
  in Kuwait, 166, 170-171
  at Madrid peace talks, 182-183
  Rabin, Yitzhak, open letter to,
    176-178
  release from prison, 181-182
Aker, Mazzin, 169

Aker, Muhannad, 173, 175-176
Aker, Nidal, 173
Aker, Samir, 169, 184
Aker, Ziad, 165-166, 167-168, 183-184
  in Kuwait, 171-172
  and Masri, Safir, 175
Akkawi, Moustafa, 35
Al-Amari, 136
al-Anbaa, 262
Al-Awdah, 276
al-Azhar, 202-203
al-Farah interrogation center, 142
Algeria, women in, 118
al-Hadaf, 231-232
al-Haq, 232
al-Jabbab al-Falastiniyya. See
  Palestine National Front (PNF)
al Jihad al Islami. See Islamic Jihad
Allenby Bridge, 214
  Ayash, Radwan Abu and, 290-291
All-Palestine Government, 10, 50
  and Nusseibeh, Anwar, 87
Al Mujama 'a al Islami, 212-213
Alon, Menachem, 128-129
Alon, Ruth, 128-129
Alon, Safi, 129, 130
al-Quds, 129
  Aker, Mamdouh, letter from,
    176-177
  Zayyad, Ziad Abu and, 124
al-Watan, 258-259
al Zaatar al-Akdhar, 150
Amashah, Raga, 104
American Colony Hotel, 43

American Friends Service Committee, 181
Americans for Peace Now, 181
American University of Beirut (AUB), 143
Amirav, Moshe, 65-66
  and Arafat, 67-68
  and Nusseibeh, Sari, 86, 94
Amiry, Suad, 102
Amnesty International
  and Aker, Mamdouh, 181
  and Kamal, Zahira, 114
  and Nusseibeh, Sari, 98
an-Najah University, 142-143
  student elections, 229-230
Ansar III, 155-157
  Kilani, Sami at, 155-160
  Rantisi, Abdul Aziz at, 203, 220, 221
Arab Higher Committee
  in Egypt, 55
  Husseini, Haj Amin, influence of, 51, 52
  and Nusseibeh, Anwar, 87
  outlawing of, 53
Arab Journalists Association, 276, 279-281, 282
  successors to Ayash, Radwan Abu, 283-284
Arab Ladies committee, 106
Arab Media Center, 38
Arab Medical Welfare Association, 179
Arab Nationalist Movement (ANM), 210, 232-233
Arab Revolt, 1936, 141
  Husseini, Haj Amin, influence of, 51-52
Arab Studies Society, 70
Arab Workers Congress, 253
Arafat, Yasser, 256, 259, 312. *See also* *Fatah*
  and Aker, Mamdouh, 170
  and Amirav, Moshe, 67-68
  and Ashrawi, Hanan, 18, 29-30
  Ayash, Radwan Abu and, 275-276, 284
  embracing Saddam Hussein, 123, 127
  General Union of Palestinian Students (GUPS), 49-50

  and Hussein, Saddam, 75, 123, 127
  and Husseini, Faisal, 44, 58-59
  identity of, 42-43
  and Jewish immigration, 52
  kaffeyah of, 53
  and Mikhail, Hanah, 21
  myth, ending of, 42
  plane crash, 1992, 38, 41-42, 139, 270
  Sarid, Yossi on, 121-122
  survival of, 79-80
  West Bank, infiltration of, 57
  and Yassin, Sheik Ahmed Ismail, 212
  and Zayyad, Ammar, 136
Arens, Moshe, 97
  and Aker, Mamdouh, 181
Asan, Youssef, 215
Ashrawi, Emile, 26
Ashrawi, Hanan Mikhail, 1-40, 80, 227, 254, 294
  Algiers, rendezvous with Arafat in, 28-29
  and Arafat, Yasser, 18, 29-30
  and Baker, James A., 32
  at Birzeit University, 24-25
  childhood of, 5-6
  on Christianity, 36-37
  and *Fatah*, 16, 19
  and General Union of Palestinian Students (GUPS), 16, 18
  and *Hamas*, 30
  Hussein, King bin-Talal and, 14
  and Husseini, Faisal, 2-3, 5, 32, 38, 39-40
  imprisonment of, 27-28
  and *intifada*, 27
  in Lebanon, 16-18
  and Madrid peace talks, 33
  and Mikhail, Hanah, 19-23
  and other factions, 35-36
  and women, 30-32
Ashrawi, Zeinah, 35
Asifa
  and Kilani, Sami, 143-144
Assad, Hafez, 214
Assad, Naif, 146-147
Assad, Wad'i, 6-7, 13
As-Sha'ab, 66, 73, 274-275
a-Tali'ah, 258
Awad, Mubarak, 175-176, 181

Ayash, Abdullah, 269
Ayash, Aisha, 269-270, 274
Ayash, Ibrahim, 269-270, 274
Ayash, Naif, 269
Ayash, Radwan Abu, 37, 269-292,
    297. *See also* Arab Journalists
    Association
  Allenby Bridge incident, 290-291
  and Arafat, Yasser, 275-276, 284
  arrest in 1987, 278
  Ben Ezra, David and, 293-294
  enemies of, 270-271
  on *Fatah*, 286, 289
  on fundamentalism, 289-290
  Gulf War and, 281
  on *Hamas*, 286, 289-290
  and Hussein, King bin-Talal, 273,
    275
  and Hussein, Saddam, 281
  and Husseini, Faisal, 282
  Ibrahimah College meeting, 286
  imprisonment of, 275-276,
    278-279
  and *intifada*, 279
  on Jews, 298-299
  new relationship with Israelis, 306
  and Palestine Liberation
    Organization (PLO), 285
  rumors about, 271, 283
  Shamir, Yitzhak and, 282
  and Six-Day War, 272-273
  on skepticism, 300
  teachers' strike, organization of,
    275
  and United National Command
    (UNC), 280
  in United States, 277
  writings of, 275
Ayash, Salma, 271
Ayash, Samoud, 271
Ayash, Shadi, 271
Ayash, Sheda, 271, 293-294
Ayash, Suna, 271
Azhar, Muhammed, 190

Baghdad Pact, 10-11
Baker, James A.
  and Aker, Mamdouh, 181
  and Ashrawi, Hanan Mikhail, 3, 32
  and Ayash, Radwan Abu, 282

Maliki, Riad on, 228, 242-243
Balfour Declaration, 107
Banna, Sheikh Hassan, 207, 210
Baramki, Gabi, 265
Barghouti, Bashir, 252, 258-259
Bar Lev, Chaim, 279
Bar-On, Mordechai, 98
Basil, The, 161
Ba'thist faction, 260
Beersheba jail, Kanaan, Sameh in,
    189-190
Begin, Menachem, 55, 305
  and Camp David Accords, 65
Beit Iba, 254
Ben-Dov, Meri, 87
Ben-Elissar, Eliahu, 2
Ben Ezra, David, 293-294
Ben Gurion, David, 283
Ben-Gurion, David, 55
Benvenisti and Zayyad, Ziad Abu, 124
Bethany, 125
Bir Zeit, 45-46
Birzeit University
  Ashrawi, Hanan Mikhail at, 24-25
  Khatib, Ghassan to, 265
  Maliki, Riad at, 240
  Nusseibeh, Sari at, 94
  women at, 104
Black Panthers
  and Dmeiri, Jaber, 78
Black September, 22, 109, 210, 211
  defined, 311
Black Students Alliance, 24
Bourj al-Barahneh, 17
Breakthrough, The (Dayan), 275
British Association of Urological
    Surgeons, 181
British mandate, ending of, 45
Brookings Institution, 214
Bush, George, 226-227
  on Ashrawi, Hanan Mikhail, 20

Camp David Accords, 65, 308-309
  frustrations of Palestinians and, 211
  Kamal, Zahira on, 112
  National Guidance Committee
    opposing, 264
Castro, Fidel, 140
Ceausescu, Nicolae, 68
Censorship of Palestinians, 89

Center for Policy Analysis on
Palestine, 99
Cesno, Frank, 182
CNN "Newsmaker Saturday," Aker,
Mamdouh and, 182-183
Communist Party. *See also* Palestine
National Front (PNF); Palestine
People's Party
and Dakak, Ibrahim, 264
founding of, 250-251
Confederation of Palestine, 309

Dahariyah military camp, 142
Dakak, Ibrahim, 264, 265
Daroushe, Abdul Wahab, 122
Dayan, Moshe, 38, 141
Breakthrough, The, 275
Dayan, Yael, 38
"Death of the Hired Man" (Frost), 164
Deir Yassin massacre, 48, 301
Democratic Front for the Liberation
of Palestine (DFLP), 73-74,
210. *See also* Yasser Abed
Rabbo wing of DFLP
and Ashrawi, Hanan Mikhail, 35
defined, 311
and Federation of Palestinian
Women's Action Committee, 108
Hawatmeh founding, 233-234
and Kamal, Zahira, 102
and Palestine National Front, 257
Democratic Front for the Liberation
of Palestine (DFLP)
and women's issues, 109-110
Dmeiri, Adnan, 77, 78
Dmeiri, Jaber, 78
Duggan, Hoyt N., 24
Dunsmore, Barrie, 17

Egypt. *See also* Nasser, Gamal Abdul
Gaza Strip, administration of, 206
and Suez crisis, 12
Eid, Mahmoud, 207
Eisenhower Doctrine, 12-13
Elad, Moshe, 151-152
Elderly Society, The, 213
Entebbe hostage raid, 4
Erakat, Saeb, 98, 301
Eretz Israel, 65

Erez, General Shayke, 213
European Economic Community
(EEC), 267

Fahd, King, 42
Falasteen al-Thawrah on Nusseibeh,
Sari, 94-95
Falestine al-Thaorah, 131-132
Family planning, 111
Family Reunification Act, 24
Farouk, King of Egypt, 53, 54, 208,
232-233
Fatah
Ansar III, supporters at, 159
Arafat organizing, 57-58
Ashrawi, Hanan Mikhail and, 2-3,
16, 19
and *Asifa*, 143-144
Ayash, Radwan Abu on, 286, 289
on Communist Party, 252
defined, 311
and Dmeiri, Jaher, 78
Husseini, Faisal and, 41
and Islamic Jihad, 217-218
and Islamic University fighting,
216-217
and Kanaan, Sameh, 188-189
at Madrid peace talks, 91
Maliki, Riad and, 228-229, 243-244
and Masri, Safir, 175
meaning of, 16
in 1970s, 210-211
and Nusseibeh, Sari, 83, 86
and Political Committee of
Jerusalem, 137
Popular Front for the Liberation of
Palestine (PFLP) platform on,
228-229
and Tulkarm, 76
Women's Committee for Social
Work, 109
and Zayyad, Khalil abu, 129-131
Fatah Revolutionary Council (FRC),
311-312
Federation of Palestinian Women's
Action Committee (FPWAC),
108, 110-111
accounts of, 115
Fine, Dr. Jonathan, 181
Free Officers, 208

Freij, Elias, 73
Frost, Robert, 164
Fundamentalism
  Ayash, Radwan Abu on, 289-290
  Kamal, Zahira on, 116-117

Gardiner, Antoinette, 13-14
Gavish, Yeshayahu, 144
Gaza Center for Rights and Law, 155
Gaza Medical Association, 221
Gaza Strip
  Israeli policy in, 213
  Muslim Brotherhood in, 214
  Palestinian government in, 50
*Gaza Strip Towards the Year 2000,
  The*, 213
General Strike, 1935-1936, 52
General Union of Palestinian Students
  (GUPS)
  Aker, Mamdouh in, 169, 170
  Arafat heading, 49-50
  and Ashrawi, Hanan Mikhail, 16, 18
General Union of Palestinian Women,
  107
Gesher, 124
  money for, 132
Gissan, Raanan, 97
Glubb, Lt. General, 11
Golon, Galia, 98
Gorbachev, Mikhail, 65
Greenberg, Joel, 74
Green Line, 312
Gulf War
  Ayash, Radwan Abu and, 281
  Hamas after, 196-197
  Kanaan, Sameh and, 193
  Nusseibeh, Sari imprisoned during,
    97-99
  Palestine Liberation Organization
    (PLO) and, 127
  Palestinian attitude about, 172-173
  peace process and, 75
  results of, 296
  and Zayyad, Ziad Abu, 134-135
Gur, Mordecai, 126
Gush Emunim, 126, 129

Ha'aretz, 95-96
Habash, George, 88, 174-175, 210

  in *al-Hadaf*, 231-232
  founding PFLP, 233
  and *Harakat al-Kawmiyyin
    al-Arab*, 143, 232-233
  intifada and, 231
  parliament-in-exile idea, 259
  on Zionism, 231-232
Haganah, 55, 305
  Salameh, Hassan and, 46
Haifa Muslim Society, 141
Haj al-em, 76
Halakha, 185
Hamas, 73-74, 196
  and Ashrawi, Hanan Mikhail, 30
  Ayash, Radwan Abu on, 286,
    289-290
  crackdown on, 219-220
  defined, 312
  and Dmeiri, Jaber, 78
  fundamentalism of, 76-77
  goals of, 222-223
  after Gulf War, 196-197
  Israeli leniency to, 219
  Mithaq, 220
  and Rantisi, Abdul Aziz, 203
  and Tulkarm, 76
  Yassin, Sheikh and, 219
Hamid, Nasser Abu, 247
Hamid, Princess Dina Abdul, 13
Hanieh, Akram, 73, 139, 276-277,
  284-285
  and Arab Journalists Association
    election, 283
  deportation of, 277
  and Tobassi, Naim, 283
Harakat al-Kawmiyyin al-Arab,
  143, 232-233
Harel Brigade, 81
Harrar, Khalida, 36
Harvard University
  Mikhail, Hanah and, 20
  Nusseibeh, Sari at, 93-94
Hashemites, 49
Hashim, Ibrahim, 9
Hawatmeh, Nayef, 109, 110, 233,
  257, 259
  founding DFLP, 233-234
  and Husseini, Faisal, 73-74
Hebrew
  intifada and use of, 303-304
  Kanaan, Sameh learning, 190-191

Heller, Mark, 97-98, 99
  on Hussein and Arafat, 123
Helou, Jihan, 23
Heroes of the Return, 144
Herzog, Chaim, 128
Hezboun, George, 252
Higher Islamic Council, 87
Higher Women's Council, 119
Hillel, 191
Hitler, Adolf, 54
Holy Land Press Service, 95
Horan, Hume, 20, 21-22
Huda, Tawfik Abdul, 9
Hudeibi, Sheikh Hassan Ismail, 208
Huna al-Anbaa, 152-154
Hussein, Abdullah (grandson), 14
Hussein, Faisal, 14
Hussein, King Abdullah, 9-10, 49,
  146, 215
  assassination of, 10, 51
  and Gaza government, 50
Hussein, King bin-Talal, 10, 64, 257,
  295
  Arafat, snubbing of, 65
  and Ashrawi, Hanan Mikhail, 14
  and Ayash, Radwan Abu, 273, 275
  and Baghdad Pact, 10-11
  and Black September, 109, 210
  first elections held by, 11-12
  and Kilani, Sami, 140
  and Kissinger, Henry, 259
  marriages of, 13-14
  and Muslim Brotherhood, 214-215
  renouncing claim to West Bank, 70
  and Samua raid, 144-145
  and Six-Day War, 146
  and Suez crisis, 12
Hussein, Muna, 14
Hussein, Saddam
  and Arafat, 123, 127
  and Ayash, Radwan Abu, 281
  Palestinian reaction to, 122-123
  Palestinian support of, 72
  PLO and, 75
  Sarid, Yossi on, 121-122, 123
Husseini, Abdel Kader, 43, 44-45, 285
  death of, 47-48
  and Harel Brigade, 81
  after partitioning of Palestine,
    45-46
Husseini, Abdel Kader (grandson), 63

Husseini, Faisal, 41-81, 284-285
  and Aker, Mamdouh, 169-170
  Algiers, rendevous with Arafat in,
    28-29
  Amirav, Moshe, meeting with, 66
  in Amman, 1991, 290
  and Arab Journalists Association
    election, 283
  and Arafat, Yasser, 58-59, 79-80
  arrest in 1988, 70-71
  and Ashrawi, Hanan Mikhail, 2-3,
    5, 32, 38, 39-40
  and Ayash, Radwan Abu, 282
  and confederation idea, 309
  in Egypt, 49-50
  experiences of Palestinians, 310
  family court of, 71-72
  and Hawatmeh, Nayef, 73-74
  Husseini, Haj Amin, influence of,
    51-52
  identity card, withholding of,
    62-63
  imprisonment of, 68, 277
  independence of Palestine, 69-70
  interview in 1968, 61-62
  Israeli attitude toward, 80-81
  Jerusalem Post interview, 74-75
  Jordan, linking new state with, 80
  and June, 1967 war, 56-57
  and Khatib, Ghassan, 251-252
  and Likud coalition, 65
  on Madrid peace talks, 34
  and Maliki, Riad, 227-228, 230
  in Moscobiya Jail, 59-60
  and Nusseibeh, Sari, 86
  and Palestine Liberation
    Organization (PLO), 56
  and Palestinian Consolidation
    Society, 286
  personality of, 42-43
  Prophet Mohammed, descent
    from, 44
  as teenager, 55
  at Tulkarm rally, 76-78
  West Bank, infiltration of, 57
  and Zayyad, Ziad Abu, 121, 125-126
Husseini, Haifa, 53
Husseini, Haj Amin, 9-10, 44, 49, 50,
  87, 285
  flight of, 53
  influence on Husseini, Faisal, 51-52

and Jewish immigration, 54
Husseini, Moussa, 48-49, 53
Husseini, Reza, 48, 53
Husseini, Wajiha, 48
   death of, 63-64
Husseini document, 69-70

Ibn Saud, King of Saudi, 53
Ibrahimah College meeting, 286
In'ash al Usra Society, 107-108
*In Search of Leadership: West Bank
   Politics Since 1967* (Sahliyeh),
   214
International Committee for the
   Release of Mamdouh Aker, 181
International Federation of
   Journalists, 279
Intifada, 296. *See also* Unified
   National Command (UNC)
Aker, Mamdouh and, 176-180,
   177-178
Ashrawi, Hanan Mikhail and, 27
Ayash, Radwan Abu and, 279
and death, 301-303
first day of, 203
Habash, George on, 231
and *Hamas*, 203
Husseini, Haj Amin, influence of,
   52
and Islamic Jihad, 218
Jabalya riots, 200-202
Kanaan, Sameh and, 192-193
Khatib, Ghassan on, 248
leadership arising from, 305-306
and Maliki, Riad, 241-242
and *Monday Report,* 95
as national expression of Palestine,
   297-298
in 1991, 75
Intifada
Nusseibeh, Sari on, 89-90
prisons and, 300-301
significance of, 296-306
weakening traditional Palestinian
   leadership, 299-300
women during, 118
Zayyad, Ziad Abu and, 121
*Intifada: The Inside Story of the
   Palestinian Uprising* (Schiff &
   Ya'ari), 212, 219

Iraq. *See* Gulf War; Hussein, Saddam
Irgun, 55, 305
   Deir Yassin massacre, 301
Iron fist policy, 130
Ish-Shalom, David, 65, 80
Islamic Assembly, 213, 216-217
Islamic Jihad, 201, 202-203, 213-214
   defined, 312
   escalation of terrorist activities by,
   218
   by mid-1980s, 217
Islamic Resistance Movement. *See
   Hamas*
Islamic Societies, The, 213
Israeli Defense Forces (IDF), 213
Israeli-Palestinian Physicians for
   Human Rights, 179

Jabal Ashrafiyeh, attack on, 19
Jabal Hussein, attack on, 19
Jabalya riots, 200-202
Jabril, Ahmed, 72, 233
Jaffa Gate, 85
Jalabiyyas, 126
Jarrar, Ghassan, 36
Jawwad, Islah Abdul, 108
Jenin Prison, Kilani, Sami in, 148
Jennings, Peter, 17, 25-26
Jerusalem
   Aker, Mamdouh in, 173-174
   Nusseibeh, Sari in, 84-85
   after partition, 46
Jerusalem Media and Communication
   Center (JMCC), 266-267
Jerusalem Post
   Aker, Mamdouh, letters from,
   177-179
   Husseini, Faisal, interview with,
   74-75
Jewish Agency and Peel Commission,
   52
Jewish-Arab Council for Peace
   Education, 179
Jewish Peace Fellowship, 181
Jibril, Ahmed, 260
Jihad, Kassam, Izz Din and, 141
Jira'i, Radi, 283
Jneid Prison
   Ayash, Radwan Abu in, 278
   Kilani, Sami in, 142, 148, 155

Jordan. *See also* Hussein, King
    Abdullah; Hussein, King
    bin-Talal
  Baghdad Pact, 10-11
  elections, 1956, 11-12
  guerrilla attacks in 1966, 144-145
  Husseini, Faisal and linking new
    state with, 81
  Jabal Ashrafiyeh, attack on, 19
  and National Liberation League,
    253
Jordanian Communist Party, 253

Kach people, 29, 126
Kaddoumi, Farouk, 42
Kader, Hatim Abdul, 283
Kaffeyah, 53
Kahane, Meir, 64, 126
Kamal, Ahmed, 103, 104
Kamal, Fakhrieh, 103, 104
Kamal, Zahira, 5, 101-120, 299
  administrative detention of, 112-113
  and Amnesty International, 114
  education of, 104-105
  and family planning, 111
  and Federation of Palestinian
    Women's Action Committee
    (FPWAC), 108
  as feminist, 105-106
  on fundamentalism, 116-117
  and In'ash al Usra Society, 107-108
  nieces of, 114-115
  as threat to Israelis, 112
  and Women's Work Committee
    (WWC), 108
Kanaan, Hind, 194
Kanaan, Imad, 197
Kanaan, Mazal Maiman, 186-187, 194
Kanaan, Rueda, 194
Kanaan, Said, 294
Kanaan, Samah, 194
Kanaan, Sameh, 185-199
  in Beersheba jail, 189-190
  as cultural hybrid, 185-186
  Fatah and, 188-189
  on Gulf War, 193
  Hamas, wariness of, 196-197
  Hebrew, learning of, 190-191
  jail, experience of, 300-301
  in Nablus jail, 189

and Nusseibeh, Sari, 194-195
  on Palestine Liberation
    Organization (PLO), 194-195
  religious beliefs of, 191-193
  after Six-Day War, 187-188
  at Washington peace talks, 198-199
Kanaan, Taleb, 186
Kanaan, Zein, 194
Kara'in, Ibrahim, 275, 283
Karameh battle, 18
Kassam, Izz Din, 140-141, 143
Kastel, 46-48
Kawasme, Fahd, 265
Ketziot Detention Center. *See*
    Ansar III
Khalaf, Karim, 265
Khalaf, Salah, 19
Khalap. *See* Palestine Liberation
    Organization (PLO)
Khalapniks, 258
Khalidi, Rashid, 33
Khalid ibn al-Walid High School,
    200-201
Khalil, Samihah, 108
Khatib, Abdelheb, 253
Khatib, Fatima, 254
Khatib, Ghassan, 5, 227, 246-268,
    299
  arrest in 1974, 259-260
  beatings of, 249
  to Birzeit University, 265
  childhood of, 253-254
  and Husseini, Faisal, 251-252
  imprisonment of, 249-251,
    260-262
  on *intifada*, 248
  and Jerusalem Media and
    Communication Center (JMCC),
    266-267
  at Manchester University, 265-266
  in Ramallah Prison, 249-250
  torture of, 259-260
Khatib, Hafez, 253-254
Khatib, Omar, 57
Khomeini, Ayatollah, 201
Khreisheh, Amal, 118
Khufrah, al-, 41
Kilani, Adnan, 142
Kilani, Ahmed, 150, 160-161
Kilani, Aisha, 140, 145-146, 148
Kilani, Khalid, 142, 160

Kilani, Mohammed, 147, 148-149
Kilani, Mohammed (grandson), 155
Kilani, Mohammed Zigil, 140
Kilani, Nuha, 152
Kilani, Salim, 142
Kilani, Sameh, 299
Kilani, Sami, 140-163
    at an-Najah University, 142-143
    at Ansar III, 155-160
    arrest in 1987, 154-155
    and *Asifa*, 143-144
    education of, 147
    imprisonment of, 142, 148-149,
        155
    in Jenin Prison, 148-149
    in Jneid, 155
    poetry of, 158
    Sadat, Anwar and, 147-148
    and Six-Day war, 145-146
    student demonstrations, 147
    town arrest of, 151-152
    writings of, 150-152
Kilani, Zoya, 152, 155, 157
King, Martin, 24
Kiryat Shmonah, 226
Kissinger, Henry, 259
Kollek, Mayor Teddy, 251
Koppel, Ted, 38
Kufr-'Ein, 246-247
Kuttab, Jonathan, 181
Kuwait. *See also* Gulf War
    Aker, Mamdouh in, 166, 170-171
    Aker, Ziad in, 171-172
    Civil Service law of 1960, 171
    Palestinian attitude about,
        172-173

Labor Party, 256
Lahat, Shlomo, 126
Langer, Felicia, 112
Lasser passer, 170
League of Nations and Arab Higher
    Committee, 55
Lehakat Hanakhal, 141
Lehi, 305
Levinger, Miriam, 265
Levinger, Moshe, 265
Levy, Gideon, 95
Levy, Rafi, 63-64
Lewis, Anthony, 98

Likud coalition, 65
Litani, Yehuda, 130

Ma'alim fi'il Tariq (Qutb), 209
Madrid peace talks, 308-309
    Aker, Mamdouh and, 182-183
    and Ashrawi, Hanan Mikhail, 33
    Ayash, Radwan Abu and, 288
    Husseini, Faisal and, 72
    Kamal, Zahira on, 117
    Nusseibeh, Sari and, 82-83, 90-91
    Shafi, Haidar Abdul at, 33-34, 252,
        323-333
    Shamir, Yitzhak at, 74
Maiman, Mazal (Kanaan), 186-187,
    194
Maimonides, 191
Maliki, Riad, 5, 83, 225-245
    in Austria, 238
    in Bethlehem, 235-236
    at Birzeit University, 240
    childhood of, 234-235
    Fatah and, 228-229, 243-244
    and Husseini, Faisal, 227-228, 230
    intifada and, 241-242
    on Jews, 298-299
    and Nasser, Gamal Abdul, 236
    in New York, 240, 241
    and October 1973 War, 238
    on Palestine Liberation
        Organization (PLO), 243
    religion, aversion to, 235-236
    and Six-Day War, 236-238
    in South America, 238-239
Mansour, Suleiman, 294
Mao Tse-tung, 140
MAQDEA, 83
Marcuse, Herbert, 28
Marquez, Gabriel García, 28
Martyrdom, 160-161
Marxism, demise of, 210
Masri, Hikmat, 263, 264
Masri, Munrib, 22
Masri, Safir, 174-175, 226
Mecca *Haj al-em*, 76
Meir, Golda, 47, 49, 307
    and Hussein, Abdullah, 9-10
Meridor, Dan, 67
Middle East Watch, 181
Miflaga Kommunistit Isra'elit, 251

Mikhail, Ablah, 5
Mikhail, Daoud, 5-6, 7-9, 8, 254, 294
  and elections in Jordan, 1946, 11-12
  imprisonment of, 13-14
  Jennings, Peter on, 25-26
  and National Socialist Party, 10
  and Palestine Liberation
    Organization (PLO), 15
  Ramallah, house in, 14-15
  and Shukeiry, Ahmed, 15-16
Mikhail, Hanah, 19-23
Mikhail, Hanan. *See* Ashrawi, Hanan
  Mikhail
Mikhail, Huda, 5, 6, 7, 8, 13, 14, 24,
  37
  on Mikhail, Hanah, 21
Mikhail, Muna, 5, 13
Mikhail, Nadia, 5, 14, 26
Mikhail, Wad'ia, 8, 31
Milhem, Muhammed, 265
Mithaq, 220
Moledet, Rehavam Zeevi, 28-29, 126
Monday Report, 95
Mordechai, General Yitzhak, 218
Mossad, 213
Movement for the Revolutionary Left
  (MIR), Chile, 239
Mujahedu Falastin, 220
Mukhabarat, 14, 214
Munich Olympics massacre, 256
Muslim Brotherhood, 203. *See also*
  Hamas
  Arafat and, 50
  and Hussein, King bin-Talal,
    214-215
  Husseini, Faisal and, 55
  and Islamic Jihad, 217
  and Islamic University fighting,
    216-217
  Israeli government and, 213
  Nasser, Gamal Abdul and, 208
  in 1988, 218-219
  and Palestine Liberation
    Organization (PLO), 214
  prison for leadership of, 215
  Rantisi, Abdul Aziz and,
    207-208
  and Sadat, Anwar, 211
Muslim Youth Societies, The, 213
Mussolini, Benito and Husseini, Jah
  Amin, 53-54

Nabhani, Taqi al-din, 76
Nablus
  Aker, Mamdouh in, 164-165
  and Ayash, Radwan Abu,
    272-273
  Hamas and, 197
  Tadammun, 212-213
Nablus Prison
  Kanaan, Sameh in, 189
  Khatib, Ghassan in, 261-262
Nabulsi, Suleiman, 10, 11, 253
  Hussein, King bin-Talal and, 12-13
  and Suez crisis, 12
Nagib, Mohammad, 208
Naqib al-Ashraf, 43
Nashashibi, Raghib, 50
Nasser, Gamal Abdul, 11, 22, 55, 146,
    207, 208, 233
  and Maliki, Riad, 236
  and Palestine Liberation
    Organization (PLO), 15
  Rantisi, Abdul Aziz on, 209, 222
Nathan, Abie, 80
National Council on U.S.-Arab
  Relations, 181
National Guidance Committee,
    264-265
Nationalist Muslim Coalition, 197
National Liberation League, 253
National Socialist Party, 10,
    253-254
  outlawing of, 13
Nazis, 54, 304
Nelson Mandela Institute, 181
Netanyahu, Binyamin "Bebe," 4
New Orient House, 43-44
Nir, Ori, 97, 117, 127, 152, 213, 214,
    267-268
  Hebrew use of, 303-304
  on *intifada*, 302
  and Palestinian Consolidation
    Society, 288
  Popular Front for the Liberation of
    Palestine (PFLP) and, 231
Non-Governmental Organizations
  (NGOs) on United Nations, 277
No Trumpets, No Drums (Nusseibeh
  & Heller), 97
Nowar, General Ali Abu, 12
Nur-Shams, 76
Nusseibeh, Absal, 85, 97

Nusseibeh, Anwar, 84, 87-88
Nusseibeh, Buraq, 85, 97
Nusseibeh, Jamal, 85, 97
Nusseibeh, Lucy, 92
Nusseibeh, Nuzha, 92
Nusseibeh, Sari, 5, 65-66, 67, 73,
    82-100
  in Abu Dhabi, 93
  and Amirav, Moshe, 94
  arrest in 1991, 96-99
  on autonomy, 90
  beating in 1987, 86-87
  at Birzeit University, 94
  childhood of, 84-85
  family of, 83-84
  Ha'aretz interview with, 95-96
  at Harvard University, 93-94
  and Husseini, Faisal, 86
  on *intifada*, 89-90, 298
  at Israeli excavation, 88
  and Kanaan, Sameh, 194-195
  and Madrid peace talks, 90-91
  and Palestinian Consolidation
    Society, 286
  in Ramle Prison, 97-98

October 1973 War
  and Ashrawi, Hanan Mikhail, 25
  Maliki, Riad and, 238
  Meir, Golda and, 307
  and Palestine National Front,
    257-258
Odeh, Sheikh Abdul Aziz, 203, 217,
    219
Olmert, Ehud, 67, 80
Olmert, Yossi, 35
On Gaza Beach (Shavit, Ari), 297
Operation Nachshon, 46
Ottawa peace discussions, 185

"Palestine: A New State of Mind,"
    for ABC, 17
Palestine Democratic Assembly, 252
Palestine Liberation Movement, 56
Palestine Liberation Organization
    (PLO), 210. *See also*
    Arafat, Yasser; *Fatah*
  Aker, Mamdouh and, 169
  Ayash, Radwan Abu and, 285

  creation of, 56
  criticism of, 299
  defined, 312
  elections, April 1976, 263
  founding of, 107
  and Gulf War, 127
  and Hussein, King bin-Talal, 256
  and Hussein, Saddam, 75
  Husseini, Faisal, frustration of,
    64-65
  as identity of Palestine, 301
  and Islamic Jihad, 217-218
  and Islamic University fighting,
    216-217
  Kanaan, Sameh on, 194-195
  Lebanon invasion, 1982, 295-296
  Maliki, Riad and, 243
  and Mikhail, Daoud, 15
  Muslim Brotherhood and, 214
  Nablus election of 1992, 197
  in 1970s, 210-211
  Palestine National Front (PNC) and,
    257
  and Popular Front for the
    Liberation of Palestine (PFLP),
    226
  and Rabat conference, 88
  Rantisi, Abdul Aziz and, 222
  and Samua raid, 145
  Sarid, Yossi on, 122
  and Shukeiry, Ahmed, 143
  and United States, 138-139
  and Yassin, Sheikh Ahmed Ismail,
    212
  and Zayyad, Ziad Abu, 131-132
Palestine National Charter, 60-61
Palestine National Council (PNC)
  Algiers, 1988 meeting, 296
  defined, 312
  parliament-in-exile and, 259
  and Popular Front for the
    Liberation of Palestine (PFLP),
    226
  Sayeh, Abdul Hameed and, 186
  women and, 119-120
Palestine National Front
  elections involving, 263
Palestine National Front (PNF)
  Barghouti, Bashir and, 258
  defined, 312-313
  formation of, 257

Khatib, Ghassan and, 249
October 1973 War and, 257-258
Palestine People's Party, 251-252
defined, 313
Union of Palestinian Working
Women's Committees, 108
Palestinian Center for the Study of
Nonviolence, 175-176, 181
Palestinian Consolidation Society,
286-287
membership in, 288
Palestinian Declaration of
Independence, 119
Palestinian Interim Self-Government
Arrangements (PISGA), 196
contents of, 314-322
Palestinian Writers Union, 154
Palmach, 47-48
Panorama, 225
Partitioning of Palestine, 45-46
Peace Now, 98, 251
Khatib, Ghassan and, 267
Peel Commission, 52
Peres, Shimon, 64-65, 176, 263
Persian Gulf War. See Gulf War
Petah Tikvah, 28-29
PFLP-General Command, 73, 233,
260
defined, 313
Physicians for Human Rights, 181
Political Committee of Jerusalem and
Zayyad, Ziad Abu, 137
Pollack, David, 93-94
Popper, Ami, 3
Popular Front for the Liberation of
Palestine General Command
(PFLP-GC). See PFLP-General
Command
Popular Front for the Liberation of
Palestine (PFLP), 72-74,
143, 210
and Ashrawi, Hanan Mikhail, 35
defined, 313
Fatah, platform on, 228-229
Habash, George, founding,
88, 233
Jabal Ashrafiyeh, attack on, 19
Jabal Hussein, attack on, 19
Maliki, Riad and, 225-245
and Masri, Safir, 174-175
Nir, Ori on, 231

platform of, 228-229
Rejection Front, 226, 259
terrorist activities of, 226
and Union of Palestinian Women
Committee, 109
Popular Palestinian Army and
Nusseibeh, Sari, 94
Purim, 191

Qaddafi, Muammar, 42
Qutb, Sayyid, 207, 208, 209, 210

Rabin, Yitzhak, 80, 230, 296
Aker, Mamdouh, open letter by,
176-178
and confederation idea, 309
freeze on settlement, 267
Husseini, Faisal and, 81
understanding Palestinian
aspirations, 306-308
Washington peace talks, 39
Rajoub, Jabril, 73
Ramadan, 191
Ramallah Prison
Khatib, Ghassan in, 249-250
Ramallah Teachers Training Center,
285-286
Rantisi, Abdul Aziz, 200-224
at Ansar III, 203, 220, 221
education of, 206
in Gaza, 203-206
Hamas and, 203
high school education, 200-201
at Islamic University, 216
and Muslim Brotherhood, 207-208
on Nasser, Gamal Abdul, 209, 222
on pan-Islamic state, 223-224
and Six-Day War, 207
Ratz, 121
Reagan, Ronald, 65
Red Eagle assassination squads, 226
Rejection Front, 226, 259
Rejoub, Jibril, 283
Revolutionary Armed Forces of
Colombia (FARC), 239
Reza Shah of Iran and Husseini, Haj
Amin, 53
Rifai, Samir, 9
Robert F. Kennedy Prize, 232

Royal College of Surgeons at
    Edinburgh, 181
Rubinstein, Amnon, 60-62
Rubinstein, Danny, 73
    and Zayyad, Khalil Abu, 130
    and Zayyad, Ziad Abu, 124
Rubinstein, Elyakim, 34

Sadat, Anwar, 147-148, 211
    and Gaza border shutdown, 1978,
    214
Sahliyeh, Emile, 214
Saiqa, 260
Sakal, Shlomo, 201
Salah al Din, 84
Salameh, Hassan, 45-46
Samua raid, 144-145
Sandstrum, Emil, 45
Sarid, Yossi, 121
    on Hussein, Saddam, 123
    and Husseini, Faisal, 121
    and Zayyad, Abu Ziad, 125
Sayeh, Abdul Hameed, 186
Schiff, Ze'ev, 212, 219, 220-221, 258
Shaath, Nabil, 16, 17, 20, 21, 23, 33,
    37, 139, 285
Shabiba, 275, 276
Shafi, Haidar Abdul, 252, 259, 284
    in Amman, 1991, 290
    Madrid peace talks, remarks at,
    33-34, 323-333
Shahid, 160-161, 208
Shahid, Leila, 2
Shak'a, Basam, 265
Shamir, Yitzhak, 55, 64, 176
    and Ashrawi, Hanan Mikhail, 20
    and Ayash, Radwan Abu, 282
    and Geneva talks, 66-69
    Husseini, Faisal and, 67
    at Madrid peace talks, 34, 74
    Nusseibeh, Sari, arrest of, 98
Sharon, Ariel, 251
Shavit, Ari, 297
Shavuot, 191
Sheikh al-Haramayn, 43
Shin Bet, 155, 213
    and Ayash, Radwan Abu, 281
    and Husseini, Faisal, 68
    mujahedu Falastin, 220
    and Nusseibeh, Sari, 94-95

Shining Path, Peru, 239
Shoval, Zalman, 182-183
Shqaqi, Fathi Abdul Aziz, 217
Shrawi, Hana, 102
Shukeiry, Ahmed, 312
    Husseini, Faisal and, 56
    and Mikhail, Daoud, 15-16
    and Palestine Liberation
        Organization (PLO), 143
Siam, Mahmoud, 216
Signpost on the Road (Qutb), 209
Six-Day War
    and Ayash, Radwan Abu,
        272-273
    Dayan, Moshe and, 141
    Kanaan, Sameh after, 187-188
    Kilani, Sami and, 145-146
    Maliki, Riad and, 236-238
    Rantisi, Abdul Aziz and, 207
    as setback for Palestinians, 295
Sneh, Ephraim, 98
Sourani, Raji, 155, 232
Spiegel, Shimon, 128
Spy Masters in Israel, 275
Stern Gang, 49
Suez Canal, attack on, 12
Suleiman the Magnificent, 84
Sumud, 313
Supreme Muslim Council
    disbanding of, 53
    Husseini, Haj Amin, influence of,
        51

Tadammun, 212-213
Taggart compound, 27
Tahr, Hamad Fadal, 147
Tamir, Shmuel, 60
Tawil, Ibrahim, 265
Tawil, Raymonda, 30, 275
    and Arab Journalists Association
        election, 283
Tawil, Suha, 30
Teachers Training College, Ramallah,
    105
Tel, Wasfi, 22
Tel Aviv University, 126-127
Tel Zatar, 17
Terra Santa College, 235
Thuwwar, 6
Tibbi, Dr. Ahmed, 125

Tobassi, Naim, 283
Tsemel, Leah, 31, 112
Tsomet, 29
Tulkarm rally, 76-78
Tupamaros, Uruguay, 239
Turkish rule over Palestine, 51
Tutwiler, Margaret, 98
21st Year, 179

Ulpan, 124, 128
Unified National Command (UNC)
    Aker, Mamdouh and, 180
    and Ayash, Radwan Abu, 280
    and Islamic Jihad, 218
    Maliki, Riad and, 225
Unified National Leadership of the
    Uprising, 94
Union of Palestinian Women
    Committee, 108-109
Union of Palestinian Working
    Women's Committees, 108
United Agricultural Company, 267
United Arab Kingdom, 256
United Nations Conference on Trade
    and Development (UNCTAD),
    225
United Nations Relief and Works
    Agency (UNRWA), 205
    and Ayash, Radwan Abu, 271-272
    Teachers Training College,
    Ramallah, 105
United Nations Security Council
    Resolution 181, 310
United Nations Security Council
    Resolutions 242 and 338, 313
United States
    Ayash, Radwan Abu in, 277
    Hussein, King bin-Talal and, 12-13
    and Palestine Liberation
    Organization (PLO), 138-139

Van Den Brok, 279-280
Vietnam War, 24
Violin Melodies, 275

Wadi Joz, 43, 58
Wa'd Jedid L'Azidin Al Kassam, 151
Wafd party, 245

Walesa, Lech, 154
Washington peace talks
    Kanaan, Sameh at, 198-199
    Rabin, Yitzhak at, 39
Wazir, Khalil, 19
*West Bank Handbook: A Political
    Lexicon, The*, 124
Women
    intifada affecting, 118
    and Muslim Brotherhood, 214
    in prison, 107
    role of, 101-102
    veiling of, 116
Women's Committee for Social Work,
    109
Women's Work Committee (WWC),
    108

Ya'abad, 141
Ya'ari, Ehud, 64, 212, 219, 220-221,
    258
Yad Vashem, 304
Yasser Abed Rabbo wing of DFLP
    and Kamal, Zahira, 109-110
    Kilani, Sami and, 142
    and Maliki, Riad, 228
Yassin, Sheikh Ahmed Ismail, 203,
    212
    and *Hamas*, 219
    imprisonment of, 215-216
Yediot Acharonot, 190-191
Yemen, Imam of, 45
Yom Kippur War. *See* October 1973
    War

Zahaar, Mahmoud, 216, 222, 223
Zakazik University, 217
Zayyad, Ali, 135
Zayyad, Aminah, 130
Zayyad, Ammar, 135, 136
Zayyad, Hibah, 135
Zayyad, Joumaneh, 135
Zayyad, Khalil Abu (father), 127-128
Zayyad, Khalil Abu (son), 129-130
Zayyad, Lamyah, 135
Zayyad, Nissren, 135
Zayyad, Sari, 135-136
Zayyad, Tariq, 135
Zayyad, Ziad Abu, 83, 91-92, 121-139

arrests of, 132-134
and Ayash, Radwan Abu, 281-282
and Gulf War, 134-135
Hebrew, learning of, 124, 127-128
and Husseini, Faisal, 125-126
and Palestine Liberation
    Organization (PLO), 131-132
Sarid, Yossi and, 125

at Tel Aviv University panel, 126-127
Yad Vashem, visit to, 304
Zionism
    Ashrawi, Hanan Mikhail on, 36
    Habash, George on, 231-232
    and Peel Commission, 52
Ziv, Haggith Gor, 179
Zuhaika, Salah, 65